MW01596056

# INSTRUCTOR'S RESOURCE MANUAL

*for*

## BARON AND BYRNE

# SOCIAL PSYCHOLOGY

*EIGHTH EDITION*

---

*prepared by*

## Jeanine R. Bloyd
*Spoon River College*

Allyn and Bacon
Boston · London · Toronto · Sydney · Tokyo · Singapore

Copyright © 1997, 1994, 1991, 1987, 1984, 1981, 1977, 1974 by
Allyn & Bacon
A Viacom Company
160 Gould Street
Needham Heights, Massachusetts 02194

Internet: www.abacon.com
America Online: keyword: College Online

All rights reserved. No part of the material protected by this copyright notice,
except the Reproduction Pages contained within, may be reproduced or utilized in
any form or by any means, electronic or mechanical, including photocopying,
recording, or by any information storage and retrieval system, without written
permission from the copyright owner.

The Reproduction Pages may be reproduced for use with *Social Psychology,*
Eighth Edition, by Robert A. Baron and Donn Byrne, provided such reproductions
bear copyright notice, but may not be reproduced in any form for any other
purpose without written permission from the copyright owner.

ISBN 0-205-26347-X

Printed in the United States of America

10 9 8 7 6 5 4 3 2 1    01 00 99 98 97 96

# TABLE OF CONTENTS

# PART I

# SUGGESTIONS FOR COURSE STRUCTURE

My first goal in Part I of the *Instructor's Resource Manual* is to share some ideas about how to organize and conduct the course. I'll discuss organization of the course, provide a sample course syllabus, address the assessment of learning styles, and expound upon classroom activities promoting active learning and emphasizing the social psychology of teaching. Suggestions for critical thinking guidelines, multicultural considerations, and methods of evaluation will also be provided.

My second goal is to address the increasing breadth of resources available for improving teaching and learning in psychology. I will include information on psychology teaching conferences, organizations, and publications that contribute to the excellence of teaching and learning. Finally, I will provide a section on classroom assessment, complete with techniques for discovering what students are actually learning.

## INTRODUCTION

It would be presumptuous of me to tell any professional educator how to teach. There are many effective ways to teach a particular course and such diversity contributes to the experience of excellence in higher education. The approach that works best for one person may not work well for another. In order to enhance the academic experience, consideration must be given to the strengths and limitations of the educator, the needs of the student, as well as the literature on learning and teaching effectiveness. I believe three essential ingredients for a successful college course include (1) a genuinely enthusiastic instructor, (2) delivery of meaningful information, and (3) a reasonably organized framework.

I plan to provide materials in this *Instructor's Resource Manual* that will contribute substantively and theoretically to all three of the above categories. Ultimately the instructor can choose the components that fit best with his or her personal style, meet the needs of the student, and remain pedagogically sound. I hope to provide materials that can make the art of teaching easier and more enjoyable for both instructor and student. My goal is to save the instructor time when planning and executing an effective learning environment. Therefore, identification of supplementary sources will be consolidated into a ready-to-use format. With these goals in mind, the following information will be provided in this manual:

In **Part I**, I will offer basic ideas about how to structure the course considering the impact of the social psychological discipline on teaching methods and strategies.

In **Part II**, I will organize a chapter-by-chapter overview providing specific suggestions for stimulating discussion questions, pedagogically sound learning activities, critical thinking essay questions, annotated audiovisual suggestions, and a professional update from current sources.

In **Part III**, transparency masters of key concepts for each chapter will be provided.

In *Plato's Meno*, Socrates responds to Meno's question if virtue can be taught with many more questions than answers. The Socratic dialogue promotes inquiry, eliminating the kind of ignorance that believes it knows. Plato disliked the rhetoric of superficial teaching, aimed at worldly success with little regard for truth. It is my belief that the virtues of social psychology began and continue in honest inquiry. Yet, social psychology moves us beyond merely asking questions, to understanding how the process of questioning makes an impact on our relations with others. I cannot imagine teaching a course in social psychology without applying the vast wealth of discovery this field offers back to the classroom environment. The social psychology of teaching college students considers the influence and use of Social Learning Theory in the classroom; pursues understanding of attitude formation and attitude change in the classroom; and focuses on the use of group process and group dynamics in college teaching. It is my hope that the materials found in this manual might kindle the virtues of social psychological discovery for both instructors and students.

My sincere thanks go to Gene Smith and Bem Allen, who authored the previous editions of this Instructor's Manual. As my professors, each took seriously the virtue of teaching, and as my colleagues, their encouragement has been a tremendous resource. I am also grateful to Bonita Stine, for her tireless computer assistance.

Jeanine R. Bloyd

## A. ORGANIZING THE COURSE

Thoughtful planning and organizing is essential for a successful learning experience. Students deserve to be clearly informed about the organization and format of the course. This is not only an ethical courtesy it also enhances the students' ability to structure their learning experience. This means the instructor needs to decide in advance what the course will involve, how the course will be run, and the obligations of the student. An explicit and detailed course syllabus should anticipate and clearly answer most routine and/or recurrent questions students might have about a course. Upon reading this introductory handout, students have the opportunity to make an informed decision about their commitment to the course. The syllabus also provides the instructor with "official" documentation of class policies and procedures, in case the student protests later. The following suggestions should probably be considered when creating a thorough course syllabus (Appleby, 1990; Nuwer & Jenkins, 1991):

1. Instructor information: Name, office location, hours, phone, pedagogical philosophy, and professional background
2. Text information: Title, authors, whether required or optional, where available
3. Course description: Nature and content of the course, level of course, prerequisites--if required, type(s) or requirement(s) satisfied by completion of course
4. Objectives and goals for the course: Content and/or skills student can expect to learn
5. Organization of course: Outline of the material, number and format of exams and assignments, what the student will be expected to do in the course, calendar of events or approximate time table, how classroom time will be used, significance of lectures (relation to reading assignments, whether students will be tested on lecture material), reading assignments
6. Grading policy: purpose and nature of assignments and extra credit, if any
7. Academic honesty policy: Cheating, plagiarism, fabrication
8. Attendance policy: How attendance will be kept, the impact of absence or tardiness, possibility for make-up work

## References

Appleby, D. (October, 1990). The compleat syllabus. Paper presented at the Mid-America Conference for Teachers of Psychology, Evansville, IN.

Nuwer, P. & Jenkins, V. (October, 1991). What do students really do with your syllabus? Paper presented at the Mid-America Conference for Teachers of Psychology, Evansville, IN.

***See information on *Project Syllabus*, Office of Teaching Resources for Psychology, (found under: H. CONFERENCES & RESOURCES).

## B. SAMPLE SYLLABUS

On the following pages you will find a sample syllabus designed for this course using the current edition of this textbook and providing an example how to structure the course.

SPOON RIVER COLLEGE
Social Psychology - Psy 240 A-1
Spring Semester, 1997

Jeanine R. Bloyd, Instructor
Office: T101
Phone: (309)647-4645 ext.234

Office Hours: MWF 10:00-11:00
TH 12:00-2:00
FAX: (309)647-6498
E-Mail: Jeanine.R.Bloyd@humanomics.sprint.com

## Course Description and Objectives

The college catalog describes this course in the following way: "An introduction to the theory and method of social psychology and the influence of social factors on human behavior. Emphasis is placed on understanding behavior as the individual interacts with others in the social environment."

Prerequisite for this course is Psy. 130 or Soc. 100.

This course is designed for anyone interested in understanding the effects of the social environment upon the human organism. The course will help us understand ourselves and our behavior as we interact with one another in the social environment.

## Master Course Objectives:

By the end of this course the student should be able to:

1.  Discuss the definition, the focus, and the goals of social psychology

2.  Analyze the use of common research methodology employed by social psychology

3.  Identify and relate how social psychologists apply what they know about social psychological concepts and group structure to benefit humankind (i.e. attitudinal, interpersonal, social influence, altruistic, legal, environmental, and industrial/organizational applications of social psychological knowledge)

4.  Propose how knowledge of social psychology can lead to a better understanding of self and others, a more satisfying and productive life, and sharper insights into an ever-changing and increasingly complex world

5.  Identify and appraise the theoretical, methodological and ethical controversies of social psychology that have stimulated intellectual debate and empirical research

6.  Relate the material presented to problems and issues in everyday life

## Instructional Materials

Baron, R. A. & Byrne, D. (1997). *Social Psychology* (8th ed.). Boston, MA: Allyn and Bacon.

Allen, B. P. & Smith, G. F. (1997). *Study Guide for Social Psychology* (8th ed.). Boston, MA: Allyn and Bacon.

Lesko, W. A. (1997). *Readings in Social Psychology: General, Classic, and Contemporary Selections* (3rd ed.). Boston, MA: Allyn and Bacon.

## Handouts

A series of handouts will be distributed periodically.

## Methods of Presentation

### A. Lectures

About half of our classroom time will be used to present lecture material. The lectures will serve two functions:

1. To elaborate upon and explain some of the more significant and/or difficult topics from the textbook.
2. To supplement the text by covering additional topics and by providing more in-depth extensions of topics from the text.

Please note: The lectures *will* contain information that is not found in the text, and you *will* be tested on lecture material.

### B. Discussion

In a class like this, meaningful discussion ought to take place. Students should not be passive "academic garbage cans" into which concepts and facts are dumped. You are encouraged not only to ask questions, but to add your own experience and views to the class. Feel free to challenge an idea at any time. Your class participation *will* affect your grade. I expect a great deal of discussion, both planned and spontaneous.

### C. Audio-Visuals

Audio-visual materials have been selected to have a definite instructional value and are expected to generate class discussion.

### D. Other Activities

Throughout the course you will be expected to engage in various small group simulation activities which are designed to enhance active experiential learning.

## Attendance

Regular attendance will be necessary for you to fully understand the material in this class. Since class participation is an important segment of your grade, it is imperative that you attend class each day and complete reading assignments in preparation for discussion and class activities. Of course I recognize that occasionally there may be circumstances that require you to miss class. Things like illness, or death or illness in your family are understandable reasons for missing a class. In any event, the following procedures will apply:

1. The <u>student</u> is responsible for material covered in class if absent from a lecture session.
2. It will be the responsibility of the student to notify the instructor in writing the day he/she returns to class after an absence.
3. Absence from a scheduled examination: the instructor should be notified <u>before</u> the exam to discuss the possibility of make-up arrangements. Make-ups will be permitted only when the absence is judged to be justifiable. Out of fairness to students who took the exam as scheduled, 5 points will be deducted from make-up exams, and the make-up exams may contain more essays and short-answer questions.
4. The instructor reserves the right to drop a student for excessive unexcused absences or for violation of academic or behavioral standards as described in the student handbook or Policies and Procedures Manual. The student needs to take the responsibility of withdrawing from class prior to the last day to withdraw, if unable to attend regularly.

## Course Requirements and Grading

Your final grade will be based on your performance in four grading categories. The following table shows how much each category counts toward your grade. Following that is a description of each category.

| Category | % of Grade | Points |
|---|---|---|
| Unit Exams (6 at 10% each) | 60.00 | 600 |
| Cumulative portion of Final Exam | 10.00 | 100 |
| Attendance, discussion, homework, & class activities | 10.00 | 100 |
| 2 Application papers | 20.00 | 200 |
| | 100.00 | 1000 |

| Grading Scale | Points |
|---|---|
| A = 92 - 100 | 915 - 1000 |
| B = 84 - 91 | 835 - 914 |
| C = 76 - 83 | 755 - 834 |
| D = 70 - 75 | 695 - 754 |
| F = Below 70 | below 694 |

## Exams

There will be an exam over each of the six major sections of the textbook. Each Unit exam will cover material from one section only, accept for the cumulative portion of the Final Exam, which will address material from the entire course. Your 6th exam will be the final exam and it will be worth 20% of your grade--10% over the last Unit of the course, and 10% cumulative (material from the entire course). Exams will contain multiple choice questions from the primary textbook and lectures. Essay questions will be based on reading assignments, lectures, audiovisuals, discussions, and other class-related activities.

<u>Daily grade</u>

Feedback will be obtained from the students' daily work in a variety of ways. Reading the assigned materials will prepare the student for discussion. Thoughtful questions are encouraged. Active learning projects require students to participate rather than be passive in the classroom and create an atmosphere of challenge and support that fosters curiosity and cognitive development. Participation does not always need to be verbal, thoughtful listening and process notes can also help students actively engage in the discussion. Active learning is not busy work, instead, active learning should stimulate students to think critically about issues. The following two frameworks of thinking and development will be considered when giving feedback to active learning opportunities:

### 1) Bloom's Taxonomy (1956)

| | | |
|---|---|---|
| **KNOWLEDGE** - | use basic recall in order to name, list, match or define | **Lowest Level** |
| **COMPREHENSION** - | basic understanding-but does not see full implications | |
| **APPLICATION** - | use learned materials in new and concrete situations | |
| **ANALYSIS** - | breaking down a information into component parts | |
| **SYNTHESIS** - | constructing a new whole from previously learned information, e.g. proposing, designing, or inventing | |
| **EVALUATION** - | ability to make critical judgments about the value of materials or methods | **Highest Level** |

### 2) Ways of Knowing: (Belenky, Clinchy, Goldberger, & Tarule, 1986)

**SILENCE:** People who know through silence see authorities as being all-powerful, obeying words that are not meaningful to them. They feel dependent, reactive, and passive about learning.

**RECEIVED KNOWLEDGE**: Knowing comes through listening. Ideas appear dualistic, either right or wrong, black or white. Received knowers can take in what others offer, but they have little confidence in their own ability to speak.

**SUBJECTIVE KNOWLEDGE**: Truth is felt rather than thought out. Subjective knowers do not see themselves as part of the process, as constructors of truth, but as conduits through which truth emerges.

**PROCEDURAL KNOWLEDGE**: Emphasis is placed upon objective observation and procedures to know the world. Truth lies beneath the surface and must be dug out. Knowing demands careful observation and analysis. For procedural knowers form takes precedent over content.

**CONSTRUCTED KNOWLEDGE**: Ability to experience oneself as creator of knowledge, valuing both subjective and objective strategies for knowing. Truth is grounded in real-life and seen as a process of construction in which the knower participates developing a passion for learning.

Application Papers

Two papers with rough drafts or outlines will be due in this course:

1. First paper: Rough draft/outline          Due: Thurs., Feb. 27, 1997
         Paper Due: Thurs., March 6, 1997

2. Second paper: Rough draft/outline        Due: Tues., April 15, 1997
         Paper Due: Tues., April 22, 1997

The topic of these papers should relate to issues studied in the field of social psychology. (A handout will be given in class addressing possible topics and references). Each paper will consist of a minimum of two double spaced typed pages or four neatly written pages, plus two references. These papers are designed to be an application of insights gained from the course. They should attempt to interpret and broaden understanding of everyday experiences using social psychological concepts. There are to be two distinct components to each paper:

1. Observation -- the student objectively describes some social behavior from his/her experience or from reading in current news media.

2. Principle -- a written application of a social-psychological concept or principle will be made of the observation. Be sure to analyze how and why your observation relates to research and theory in the field of social psychology. (Refer to the handouts on how to write psychology papers and to the elements of critical thinking).

A basic outline or rough draft will be due prior to handing in your paper (see dates above).

## Course Calendar - (Approximate dates)

UNIT I - Chapters 1 & 2 (pp. 1-73)

Thursday, Jan. 9 - Thursday, Jan. 16 - Chapter 1
    The Field of Social Psychology:  How We Think About and Interact With Others.

**\*Wednesday, Jan. 14, Last day to Add/Drop**

Tuesday, Jan. 21 - Tuesday, Jan. 28 - Chapter 2
    Social Perception:  Understanding Others

**\*THURSDAY, JAN. 30 - UNIT ONE EXAM**

---

UNIT II - Chapters 3 & 4 (pp. 74-149)

Thursday, Jan. 30 - Thursday, Feb. 6 - Chapter 3
    Social Cognition: Thinking About Others and The Social World

Tuesday, Feb. 11- Tuesday, Feb. 18 - Chapter 4
    Attitudes:  Evaluating the Social World

**\*THURSDAY, FEB. 20 - UNIT TWO EXAM**

---

UNIT III - Chapters 5 & 6 (pp. 150-231)

Tuesday, Feb. 25 - Tuesday, March 4 - Chapter 5
    Aspects of Social Identity: Establishing One's Self and Gender

**\*Thursday, Feb. 27 - Rough draft or outline for paper due**

Thursday, March 6 - Thursday, March 13 - Chapter 6
    Prejudice and Discrimination: Understanding Their Nature, Countering Their Effects

**\*Thursday, March 6 - First Application Paper due**

**\*THURSDAY, MARCH 6 - UNIT THREE EXAM - (Mid-term)**

---

**SPRING BREAK -- MARCH 10-14**

---

UNIT IV - Chapters 7 & 8 (pp. 232-315)

Tuesday, March 18 - Thursday, March 20 - Chapter 7

Interpersonal Attraction:  Initial Contact, Feelings of Attraction, Becoming Acquainted

Tuesday, March 25 - Thursday, March 27 - Chapter 8
   The Joys and Sorrows of Close Relationships: Family, Friends, Lovers, and Spouses

**\*TUESDAY, APRIL 1 - UNIT FOUR EXAM**

---

**\*April 4 - Last day to Withdraw**

UNIT V - Chapters 9 & 10 (pp. 316-389)

Thursday, April 3 - Tuesday, April 8 - Chapter 9
   Social Influence:  How We Change Others' Behavior--and How They Change Ours

Thursday, April 10 - Tuesday April 15 - Chapter 10
   Prosocial Behavior:  Helping Other People

**\*Tuesday, April 15 - Rough draft or outline due**

**\*THURSDAY, APRIL 17 - UNIT FIVE EXAM**

---

UNIT VI - Chapters 11 & 12 (13 & 14 Special Topics) (pp. 390-???)

Tuesday, April 22 - Thursday, April 24 - Chapter 11
   Aggression: It's Nature, Causes, & Control

**\*Tuesday, April 22 - Second Application Paper Due**

Tuesday, April 29 - Thursday, May 1 - Chapter 12
   Groups and Individuals: The Consequences of Belonging

Tuesday, May 6 - Chapters 13 & 14 (selected topics)
   Legal and Organizational Applications
   Social Psychology in Action: Applications to Health and Environment

**<u>FINAL EXAM - SEE FINAL EXAM SCHEDULE</u>**

## C. LEARNING STYLES

I have discovered both as a student and as a classroom instructor, that people seem to learn best in various different ways. Several approaches to the identification and measurement of student learning styles have become popular in recent years (Eison, 1984, 1987; Grasha, 1972; McGovern, 1993). Dixon (1985) suggests five ways that instructors' knowledge of student's learning styles can enhance the learning experience:

1.  helps individuals understand themselves as learners (metacognition and metamemory)
2.  encourages individuals to expand their learning styles
3.  broadens the variety of instructional approaches
4.  creates an environment where diversity thrives
5.  creates a climate open to collaborative exchange

In addition, learning styles information can help faculty to better understand their own learning, and teaching styles (Butler, 1987; Eison, 1987; Gano-Phillips & Lease, 1992). Any given individual's approach to learning is not one style but many (Dixon, 1985; Eison, 1987), therefore, learning style information should not be used by faculty to "pigeon hole" students. Instead, classroom teaching techniques and homework assignments can be developed to bridge the differences between learning styles and maximize understanding. According to Gano-Phillips & Lease (1992), "bridges" help students access nondominant learning styles by offering them a way to use their own learning strengths. Instructors may be able to achieve success with a greater proportion of students by using bridging techniques.

Examples of Bridging Techniques
(Adapted from Gano-Phillips & Lease, 1992)

**Concrete Sequential Learner**
- provide models, examples, and references
- use organizers such as diagrams, charts, or outlines
- relate new learning objectives to real life interests
- have students draw venn diagrams, concept maps

**Abstract Sequential Learner**
- make additional readings and bibliographies available
- assign both written reports and oral presentations
- collect students notes and comment on conceptual connection of ideas
- assign research-based papers or policy statement papers

**Abstract Random Learner**
- encourage peer learning and cooperative group work
- share personal anecdotes and use humor
- relate learning to film, television, and mass media
- offer assignments that rely on interviewing and other people-related skills
- assign journals or creative writing assignments that relate day-to-day experiences with concepts covered in class

**Concrete Random Learner**
- use frequent brainstorming and seek alternatives
- value and encourage divergent ideas
- invite revisions in writing assignments
- provide case study materials and practice in problem solving

Measurement of Learning Styles

Several approaches have been devised to assess students' learning styles. If used early in the semester, one of the following popular learning style inventories may provide helpful information to students as they consider how they approach learning experiences.

1.  Grasha Reichmann Student Learning Styles Survey
    Learning Styles Assessed:                     Test Format:
    Competitive                                    90 items
    Collaborative                                  (15 per style)
    Avoidant                              Five-point Likert scale
    Participant
    Dependent

For Additional Information Contact:
   Dr. Anthony Grasha
   Department of Psychology
   University of Cincinnati
   Cincinnati, OH  45221

2.  Inventory of Learning Processes (Schmeck et. al.)
    Learning Styles Assessed:                     Test Format:
    True/False--62 items
    Deep Processing                                18 items
    Methodological Study                           23 items
    Fact Retention                                  7 items
    Elaborative Processing                         14 items

For Additional Information Contact:
   Dr. Ronald Schmeck
   Department of Psychology
   Southern Illinois University at Carbondale
   Carbondale, IL  62901

3.  Learning Style Assessment (Quinn, 1992; Gano-Phillips & Lease, 1992)
    Learning Styles Assessed:                     Test Format:
                                                  28 items
    Concrete Sequential                           7 items
    Abstract Sequential                           7 items
    Abstract Random                               7 items
    Concrete Random                               7 items

For Additional Information See:
    Butler, K. (1987).  Learning and teaching style:  In theory and practice.

4.  Learning Style Inventory (Kolb)
    Learning Styles Assessed:                     Test Format:
    Converger                                     12 items
    Diverger                                      Rank ordering
    Assimilator

For Additional Information Contact:
    McBer and Company
    Training Aids Division
    137 Newbury Street
    Boston, MA  02116

5.  LOGO II (Eison et. al.)
    Learning Styles Assessed:                     Test Format:
    Learning-Oriented Attitudes                   32 items
    Learning-Oriented Behaviors                   (8 per scale)
    Grade-Oriented Attitudes
    Grade-Oriented Behaviors

For Additional Information Contact:
    Dr. Jim Eison
    Center for Teaching and Learning
    Southeast Missouri State University
    Cape Girardeau, MO 63701

## References

Butler, K. (1987). *Learning and teaching style: In theory and practice.* Revised second edition. Columbia, CT: The Learner's Dimension.

Dixon, N. M. (1985). The implementation of learning style information. *Lifelong Learning, 9(3),* 16-18, 26-29.

Eison, J. (1987). *Recognizing and Responding To Learning Style Differences.* Paper presented at the Mid-America Conference for the Teachers of Psychology, Evansville, IN.

Eison, J. (1984). Researchers examine learning styles. *APA Monitor, 15(5),* 34.

Gano-Phillips, S. & Lease, A. M. *Addressing Needs of Students with Differing Learning Styles in the Psychology Classroom.* Paper presented at the Ninth Annual Mid-America Conference for Teachers of Psychology, Evansville, IN, October 9-10, 1992.

Grasha, A. F. (1972). Observations on relating teaching goals to student response styles and classroom methods. *American Psychologist, 27(2),* 144-147.

McGovern, T. V. (Ed.). (1993). *Handbook for enhancing undergraduate education in psychology.* Washington, D.C.: American Psychological Association.

Quinn, P. *Learning Style Assessment.* Paper presented at the Teaching Family Science Conference, Woodstock Center, Harvard, IL, June 5-7, 1992.

Schmeck, R. R., Ribich, F., and Ramanaiah, N. (1977). Development of a self-report inventory for assessing individual differences in learning processes. *Applied Psychological Measurement, 2(4),* 551-562.

## D. CRITICAL THINKING TOOLS

Critical thinking actively engages an open minded pursuit following purposeful direction and promoting the conscious involvement of the thinker. Students bring with them a wealth of life experiences that can be directly related to the concepts of social psychology. I believe we can utilize these experiences to help them develop a more "social psychological" way of understanding the world. I believe the primary goal of this course is to enhance a students' critical thinking skills. Hopefully, by providing the tools necessary for critical thinking, students will embrace the process of discovery throughout their lives.

Tools for thinking critically seem to function best in an environment that remains open to ideas and respects the individual. Some scholars view critical thinking as an attitude or disposition (Gray, 1993; McPeck, 1981; and Siegel and Carey, 1989). Others perceive it as an adventure, process, or journey (Neimark, 1987 and Halonen, 1995). I believe that if the instructor models an attitude that enjoys seeking clearer understanding of human behavior, students will respect this pursuit and desire to expand their own critical thinking skills. The following list of "tools" for thinking critically or cognitive skills, can assist students' active learning experience:

1. SIEVE: (used for straining, sifting, or pureeing).
   COGNITIVE SKILL: Differentiating between facts and opinions.

2. BALANCING SCALES: (a weighing device).
   COGNITIVE SKILL: Comparing and contrasting information and points of view.

3. MAGNIFYING GLASS: (a lens that enlarges the image of an object).
   COGNITIVE SKILL: Recognizing logical fallacies and faulty reasoning.

4. CENTRIFUGE: (separates contained materials of different specific gravities).
   COGNITIVE SKILL: Making judgments and drawing accurate conclusions based on available information.

## References

Gray, P. (1993). Engaging students' intellects: The immersion approach to critical thinking and psychological instruction. *Teaching of Psychology, 20*, 68-70.

Halonen, J. (1995). *The critical thinking companion for Introductory Psychology.* New York, NY: Worth Publishers.

McPeck, J. E. (1981). *Critical thinking and education.* Oxford, England: Martin Robinson.

Neimark, E. D. (1987). *Adventures in thinking.* San Diego, CA: Harcourt Brace Jovanovich, Publishers.

Siegel, M. & Carey, R. F. (1989). *Critical thinking: A Semiotic perspective.* Bloomington, IN: ERIC Clearinghouse on Reading Communication Skills.

## E.  ACTIVITIES AND PROJECTS

Classroom activities and out-of-class projects allow students to experience phenomena described in the chapter. If students are going to expand their critical thinking skills through active learning endeavors, the instructor needs to keep in mind basic ground rules.

**1) Preparation:** Active learning is not "do-it-yourself" learning, it needs to be thoroughly planned by the instructor. Careful consideration must be given to the appropriateness of each activity in relation to the particular objectives and level of student need. Time constraints must be weighed in relation to overall learning potential. Although many activities may take up greater segments of time as compared to a traditional lecture format, the opportunity for critical thinking opportunities and depth of processing is heightened through the effective use of well-planned activities. Instructors must plan how and when to use an activity, considering how it will be integrated with the content and flow or pacing of the class. Preplanning must be thoughtfully thorough, however, facilitation of activities remains responsive and flexible.

**2) Student Feedback/Evaluation:**  The amount, type, and timing of feedback given to students should be determined and communicated to students.  If critical thinking processes are highly valued, then criteria such as Bloom's Taxonomy (1956) or Women's Ways of Knowing (1986) could be applied to students' self assessment.

**3) Ethical Considerations:**  Students' privacy and anonymity should always be protected.  Appropriate levels of self-disclosure need to be modeled by the instructor.  Some students may fear taking the risk of active discourse in the classroom, yet these students should not be excused from participation, instead, instructors must remain sensitive to these students' boundaries and structure participation accordingly (Mathie et al., 1993).  Giving students a choice on some activities may increase willingness to participate (Deci & Ryan, 1985).

**4) Overview & Instructions:**  Helping students realize how and why active learning opportunities may be beneficial to their learning experience may also motivate students to participate.  As much as possible, students need to be informed of how and why a particular activity relates to the goals and objectives of the course.  The degree of structure provided by the instructor depends on the level of autonomy of the students.  Many students may avoid making choices and are threatened by ambiguity (Perry, 1970).  Although they may prefer the instructor to provide detailed structure and the "right answers," instructors are more likely to foster cognitive development by providing an atmosphere of challenge.  However, the level of challenge should match the degree of autonomy demonstrated by the students.  "Active learning is best introduced into courses gradually" (Mathie, et al., 1993, p. 189).

**5) Activity Evaluation:**  The following questions will assist verification of each activity's effectiveness.  Did the activity work?  Were there any technical or procedural problems?  What did the students actually experience and learn from this activity?  Was it what you expected them to learn?  How was the activity integrated into the meaning, logic, and content of the course?  Does this activity need to be revised or modified?

## References

Belenky, M., Clinchy, B., Goldberger, N., & Tarule, J., (1986).  *Women's ways of knowing:  The development of self, voice, and mind.*  New York:  Basic Books.

Bloom, B. S. (Ed.). (1956).  *Taxonomy of educational objectives:  The classification of educational goals.  Handbook:  Cognitive domain.*  New York: Longman.

Deci, E. L., & Ryan, R. M. (1985).  *Intrinsic motivation and self-determination in human behavior.*  New York:  Plenum Press.

Mathie, V. A., Beins, B., Benjamin, L. T., Ewing, M. M., Hall, C.C I., Henderson, B., McAdam, D. W. & Smith, R. A. (1993).  Promoting active learning in psychology courses.  In T. V. McGovern (ed.), *Handbook for enhancing undergraduate education in psychology* (pp. 183-214).  Washington, DC:  American Psychological Association.

Perry, W. G., Jr. (1970).  *Forms of intellectual and ethical development in the college years.*  New York: Holt, Rinehart & Winston.

## F.  MULTICULTURAL CONSIDERATIONS

Social Psychology inherently addresses cultural diversity as a matter of content and concern. Understanding current patterns of variance can contribute to greater respect and acceptance of diversity issues.  For this to happen, we must recognize that people who are from nonmajority segments of society are underrepresented and poorly understood relative to majority groups.  For students to grasp the rapid changes occurring in American demographics and their implications on behavior, more emphasis must be placed on within-group differences rather than between-group differences.  Other influences such as social class may be contributing more than we currently understand.  Baron and Byrne's text strives to unravel these considerations through careful analysis and application.  Several of the Activities and Discussion Questions provided in Part II, are designed to explore these issues thoughtfully.  Two helpful resources for consideration of cultural diversity include Bronstein and Quina's (1988) *Teaching a psychology of people:  Resources for gender and sociocultural awareness,* and Puente, et al's chapter, *Toward a psychology of variance:  Increasing the presence and understanding of ethnic minorities in psychology,* from the McGovern Handbook (1993).

### References

Bronstein, P. A., & Quina, K. (Eds.). (1988).  *Teaching a psychology of people:  Resources for gender and sociocultural awareness.*  Washington, DC:  American Psychological Association.

Puente, A. E., Blanch, E., Candland, D. K., Denmark, F. L., Laman, C., Lutsky, N., Reid, P. T., & Schiavo, R. S. (1993).  Toward a Psychology of variance:  Increasing the presence and understanding of ethnic minorities in psychology.  In T. V. McGovern (ed.), *Handbook for enhancing undergraduate education in psychology* (pp. 71-92).  Washington, DC:  American Psychological Association.

## G.  METHODS OF EVALUATION & CLASSROOM ASSESSMENT

What are students learning from this course and what can be done to improve teaching and learning?  A variety of conventional and nontraditional qualitative measures can be employed to improve both teaching and learning effectiveness.  Overall goals for the learning experience must be considered when designing an assessment approach.  Are you interested in students gaining knowledge of content? Do you expect various levels of thinking to be portrayed in students' work, such as those described in Bloom's taxonomy?  Are you concerned about students' use of application, synthesis, analysis, and evaluation?  Although grading may be unpleasant, I believe it is imperative that you keep in mind just how important grades are to most of your students.  When students put a great deal of time and effort into a course, they deserve accurate and fair grading.  I have provided a systematic, diversified and, I hope, fair way of deriving grades in my sample syllabus.  Depending on the instructor's goals, several of the following methods can assist evaluation of the teaching and learning experience.

1) Exams:  Multiple-choice exams appear to be an objective method of measuring student knowledge.  Although they can be scored quickly, they may not fully assess students knowledge.

Various levels of thinking can be designed into the stem of multiple choice questions (i.e. application questions, factual questions, sequencing questions, etc.). Essay exams provide an opportunity to assess accuracy of information, conceptualization of a problem, and ability to communicate an idea. The Center for Teaching and Learning at Southeast Missouri State University, provides many helpful guidelines for improving your multiple choice exams. They provide a Multiple-Choice Item Writing Inventory, and ten factors that need to be considered when judging the quality of a test; their phone number is (314) 651-2298.

2) Papers: Writing and thinking go hand-in-hand. Papers foster students' ability to assimilate information from a variety of sources. Writing is a concrete way for students to express their ideas and for teachers to understand how their students are actively engaging in the learning process. Writing to learn provides an opportunity for students to think on paper. It is a way to make thoughts external and open for consideration and evaluation. Several articles and presentations on the use of writing in psychology classes (Bloyd, 1992; Blevins-Knabe, 1987; McGovern & Hogshead, 1990; Snodgrass, 1985; Willis, 1992; and Nodine, 1990) support the claim that writing promotes adaptive thinking and active learning with course material. Writing assignments can range from simple in-class paragraphs or process notes, to extensive research papers. Although all writing activities may not be suited for formal grading, all writing assignments should receive some feedback from either the instructor or other students (Mathie et al, 1993, [see reference above]). (Suggestions for writing assignments can be found in the Syllabus section). Below are suggestions for *Process Notes* for learning activities:

a) Description of Activity:
What was done?
How was it done?

b) Purpose of Activity:
Why was this done?
What did it have to do with content of the course?

c) Personal Assessment of Activity:
What did I learn from this experience?
Content:
Process:

d) Level of Processing:

Bloom's Taxonomy--
-knowledge
-comprehension
-application
-analysis
-synthesis
-evaluation

Women's Ways of Knowing--
-silence
-received knowledge
-subjective knowledge
-procedural knowledge
-constructed knowledge

e) Recommendations, Feedback, Other Comments:

3) <u>Classroom discussions, activities, and presentations</u>: The development of oral communication skills, and interpersonal skills can be assessed through the use of these activities. Basic logic, organizational skills, and listening abilities all contribute to these processes of learning. The possibilities here are endless, depending on the creativity of the instructor and the willingness to take some risks in the learning experience. For these approaches to be successful, they demand flexibility and thorough planning. The instructor must be willing to THINK on his or her feet. Examples could include formal debates on a controversial issue, acting out an experiment, holding a student poster session, or experiencing decision-making in groups by creating a mock jury.

4) <u>Classroom assessment activities</u>: Various thinking, writing, and doing activities can be used to explore how students are processing information. Feedback from these activities provides insight into the actual teaching-learning environment. Teachers need to be aware of their students' ongoing level of understanding of the content of a course. Have you ever believed your students were learning just fine, only to be surprised by their poor showing on their first exam? Thomas Angelo and Patricia Cross (1993) present many methods for monitoring student learning in an *ongoing* fashion in *Classroom assessment techniques: A handbook for college teachers*. They believe that learning is most effective when teachers are constantly attuned to their students' efforts, attitudes, successes, and failures related to learning course content. Rather than relying on "teacher's intuition," instructors can use specific, deliberate techniques described extensively in their book. Angelo and Cross include a Teaching Goals Inventory in order to identify course goals. The following categories of teaching goals help organize the type of classroom assessment used:

1. Course-related knowledge and skills
    A. Prior knowledge, recall, and understanding
    B. Analysis and critical thinking
    C. Synthesis and creative thinking
    D. Problem solving
    E. Application and performance
2. Attitudes, values, and self-awareness
    A. Students' awareness of their attitudes and values
    B. Students' self-awareness as learners
    C. Course-related learning and study skills, strategies, and behaviors
3. Reactions to instruction
    A. Reactions to teachers and teaching
    B. Reactions to class activities, assignments, and materials

*Classroom Assessment Techniques* provides a great deal of information about each technique, including a general description of the technique and its purpose, suggestions for use, an example, the procedure for using it, guidelines for analyzing the data you collect, ideas for adapting and extending the technique, pros and cons of the technique, an ease-of-use rating, and caveats.

Some of the techniques I have found to quite informative include: **The Minute Paper**, which asks students to answer one or two questions on material covered during a class session. You might ask (a) What was the most useful/meaningful thing you learned during this class? and (b) What questions remain uppermost in your mind as we end this class? Student responses to these questions never fail to enlighten me regarding students' interest, concerns, conceptualization. After looking them over, I often choose a couple of the themes that appear and open the next class by addressing those points. This not only lends continuity to the flow of the class, as a consequence, students seem to be more invested in pursuit of their own learning process as I become more sensitive to the areas they address.

Another helpful technique is **Directed Paraphrasing**. This is used to see how well students understand material that was covered either through reading, lecture, or an activity. Students are directed to summarize what they've learned about a topic (such as cognitive dissonance or the bystander effect) in *no more than three* concise sentences, and they should do it as if they were communicating this information to a friend who has not taken the course.

## References

Angelo, T. A., & Cross, K. P. (1993). *Classroom assessment techniques: A handbook for college teachers* (2nd ed.). SF: Jossey-Bass.

Blevins-Knabe, B. (1987). Writing to learn while learning to write. *Teaching of Psychology, 14,* 239-241.

Bloyd, J. R. (1992, October). *What's right with writing: Writing to learn and learning to write in psychology.* Paper presented at the meeting of the Annual Mid-America Conference for Teachers of Psychology, Evansville, Indiana.

McGovern, G. V., & Hogshead, D. L. (1990). Learning about writing, thinking about teaching. *Teaching of Psychology, 17,* 5-10.

Nodine, B. F. (Ed.). (1990). Special issue: Psychologists teach writing [Special issue]. *Teaching of Psychology, 17.*

Snodgrass, S. E. (1985). Writing as a tool for teaching social psychology. *Teaching of Psychology, 12,* 91-94.

Willis, Sandra, A. (1992, August). *Integrating levels of critical thinking into writing assignments for introductory psychology students.* Paper presented at the meeting of the American Psychological Association, Washington, D.C.

## H. CONFERENCES, ORGANIZATIONS, AND RESOURCES

Resources for improving students' learning are bountiful. We are extremely fortunate in psychology to have available many publications, organizations, conferences, and individual colleagues dedicated to this purpose. I have included below some of the growing number of opportunities dedicated to improving teaching and learning in psychology. Although some of the names change from year to year, I imagine that if you get in touch with any of the people listed below, they'll assist you in getting the help you want, even if it is no longer their job. That is the wonderful thing I have discovered among the professionals who attend these conferences: they seem to have the heart of a teacher, always willing to give away what they have learned!

Psychology Teaching Conferences

**American Psychological Society Institute.** For information, contact Douglas Bernstein, Department of Psychology, University of Illinois at Urbana-Champaign, 603 East Daniel Street, Champaign, IL 61820 (217-333-4731). (Usually held in late June.)

**Annual Conference on Undergraduate Teaching of Psychology.** For information, contact Gene Indenbaum, Department of Psychology, State University of New York at Farmingdale, Farmingdale, NY 11735 (516-420-2725), e-mail: indenbea@snyfarva.cc.farmingdale.edu.

**International Conference.** The International Conference on Improving University Teaching, is sponsored by Nottingham, England Trent University and the University of Maryland University College in 1996. For more information, write to Improving University Teaching, University of Maryland University College, University Boulevard at Adelphi Road, College Park, MD 20742-1659, e-mail: iut@umuc.umd.edu. (Usually held in July.)

**Mid-America Conference.** For information, write to Joseph Palladino, Department of Psychology, University of Southern Indiana, Evansville, IN 47712 (812-464-1952). (Usually held in October.)

**Midwest Institute.** For information, contact David Shavalia (708-942-2187), division of Social and Behavioral Sciences, College of DuPage, Glen Ellyn, IL 60137. (Usually held in March.)

**National Institute on the Teaching of Psychology.** For information, write to Douglas A. Bernstein, Department of Psychology, university of Illinois, 603 East Daniel Street, Champaign, IL 61820; or contact the conference coordinator, Joanne Fetzner, by phone at 217-398-6969 or 217-244-7902 or by e-mail at jfetzner@psych.uiuc.edu. (Usually held in January, at St. Petersburg, FL.)

**Northeastern Conference.** For information, contact Bernard C. Beins, Department of Psychology, Ithaca College, Ithaca, NY 14850-7290, by phone at 607-274-3512 or by e-mail at beins@ithaca.edu. (Usually held in October.)

**Southeastern Conference.** For information, contact William Hill, Department of Psychology, Kennesaw State College, Marietta, GA 30061, by phone at 770-423-6225 or by e-mail at bhill@kscmail.kennesaw.edu.

**Southwest Regional Conference.** For information, write to John Hall, department of Psychology, Texas Wesleyan University, Fort Worth, TX 76105 (817-531-4956 or 817-531-4974).

**Lewis M. Terman Western Regional Teaching Conference.** For more information, write to Mary Allen, California State University--Bakersfield, Bakersfield, CA 93311-1099 (805-644-2366).

Office of Teaching Resources for Psychology

The OTRP was established by APA'a Division Two (Teaching of Psychology) to distribute psychology teaching resources. The Division Two web server is now on-line. The URL is: http://mulerider.saumag.edu/socsci.html. The alternative address is: http://mulerider.saumag.edu/d2homepage. For more information contact Edward P. Kardas, Department of Psychology, Southern Arkansas University, Magnolia, AR 71753-5000, by phone at 501-235-4231 or by e-mail at epkardas@saumag.edu. Another contact person is Patricia Keith-Spiegel, Department of Psychological Science, Ball State University, Muncie, IN 43706-0520, (317) 285-8197.

Services provided include: *Project Syllabus*, *Mentoring Service,* listing of upcoming conferences, and listing of other Internet resources in psychology.


Membership Organizations

Council of Teachers of Undergraduate Psychology (CTUP)
Maureen Hester
Holy Names College
Oakland, CA 94619
(510) 436-0169

Division Two (Teaching of Psychology)
American Psychological Association
Bernard Beins
Department of Psychology
Ithaca College
Ithaca, NY 14850
(607) 274-3512

National Social Science Association
2020 Hills Lake Drive
El Cajon, CA 92090-1018
(619) 448-4709

Publications

*The Psychology Teacher Network*
Education Directorate
American Psychological Association
750 First St., N.E.
Washington, DC 20002-4242

Published five times a year and mailed free to APA members and affiliates. $15.00 per year for others.

*The Teaching Professor*
Magna Publications
2718 Dryden Drive
Madison, WI 53704-3086

$34.00 per year for monthly newsletter containing discussion and ideas for improving teaching.

*College Teaching*
Heldref Publications
1319 18th St., N.W.
Washington, DC 20036-1802

$27.00 per year for quarterly journal of ideas and techniques for improving teaching.

*Teaching of Psychology*
Journal Subscription Department
Lawrence Erlbaum Associates, Inc.
365 Broadway
Hillsdale, NJ 07642

Quarterly journal of APA's Division Two. Cost included in Division Two dues and $25.00 for nonmembers.

# PART II

## CHAPTER-BY-CHAPTER OVERVIEW

This section of the manual will follow a consistent format designed to assist the instructor's approach to each chapter of the eighth edition of Baron and Byrne's textbook. A brief overview of the layout is provided below. It is my desire to enhance the planning process as you design the focus of your course.

### A. CHAPTER-AT-A-GLANCE

This section is designed to assist the instructor with coordination of various resources available with each chapter. Instruction ideas and a list of supplements are arranged section-by-section to help the instructor organize the learning objectives, critical thinking questions, and activities with the appropriate topics of the chapter.

### B. CHAPTER OUTLINE

The outline includes each bold-faced topic section addressed in the textbook.

### C. LEARNING OBJECTIVES

After studying the chapter, the students should be able to accurately address these. It probably would be helpful to the student to know which of these objectives the instructor plans to emphasize.

### D. DISCUSSION TOPICS & QUESTIONS

Topics related to the material covered in the text are provided in this section. These suggested topics are intended to motivate students toward thoughtful discussion.

### E. LEARNING ACTIVITIES AND HANDOUTS

The learning activities are designed to actively engage the students in the learning process. They demand prior preparation and thought on the part of the instructor. Although they may consume more time than a lecture, they may actually deepen the learning experience. Some of the activities require handouts. Those requiring handouts, are provided on a separate page following the description of that activity (for duplication purposes). The handouts are also provided at the end of the student's Study Guide.

### F. OVERHEAD TRANSPARENCIES

A list of coordinated overhead transparencies is provided in each chapter. These transparency masters can be located in the last section of this manual--PART III (for duplication).

### G. AUDIOVISUAL SUGGESTIONS

A variety of audiovisual suggestions have been included for each chapter. A brief description and references for purchase or rental have also been provided.

### H. CRITICAL THINKING/ESSAY QUESTIONS

These questions are designed to provoke critical thinking. They should challenge the student to engage in application, synthesis, analysis, and evaluation thought processes.

### I. SOURCES FOR LECTURE

A variety of related topics are addressed in an easy to read format in these resources.

### J. PROFESSIONAL UPDATE: CURRENT ARTICLES FROM PROFESSIONAL SOURCES AND RELATED READINGS

# Chapter 1

## The Field of Social Psychology: How We Think About Ourselves and Others

### Chapter-at-a-Glance

| CHAPTER OUTLINE | INSTRUCTION IDEAS | SUPPLEMENTS* |
|---|---|---|
| *I. Social Psychology: A Working Definition* <br>• Social Psychology is Scientific in Nature <br><br>• Social Psychology Focuses on the Behavior of Individuals <br><br>• Social Psychology Seeks to Understand the Causes of Social Behavior and Thought <br><br>• Social Psychology: Summing Up | Learning Objectives 1.1 to 1.5 <br><br>Activities 1.1, 1.2 (Handout) <br><br>Critical Thinking Question 1 | Test Bank Questions 1.1 to 1.30 |
| *II. How We Got Here From There: The Origins and Development of Social Psychology* <br>• The Early Years: Social Psychology Emerges <br><br>• **Cornerstones of Social Psychology**   What Style of Leadership is Best?  Some Early Insights <br><br>• Social Psychology's Youth: The 1940s, 1950s, and 1960s <br><br>• The 1970s, 1980s, and 1990s: A Maturing Field <br><br>• Where Do We Go From Here?  The Year 2000... and Beyond | Learning Objectives 1.6 to 1.12 | Test Bank Questions 1.31 to 1.69 <br><br>Reading: Aron & Aron (1989). *The Heart of Social Psychology: A Backstage View of a Passionate Science, 2nd Ed.* <br><br>(See Sources for Lecture) |
| *III. Answering Questions About Social Behavior and Social Thought: Research Methods in Social Psychology* <br>• The Experimental Method: Knowledge through Intervention <br><br>• The Correlational Method: Knowledge through Systematic Observation <br><br>• Social Psychologists as Perennial Skeptics: The Importance of Replication, Meta-Analysis, and Converging Operations <br><br>• The Role of Theory in Social Psychology <br><br>• The Quest for Knowledge and the Rights of Individuals: Seeking an Appropriate Balance | Learning Objectives 1.13 to 1.25 <br><br>Discussion Topics 1 - 5 <br><br>Activities 1.3, 1.4, 1.5 (Handouts) <br><br>Critical Thinking Questions 2 - 5 | Test Bank Questions 1.70 to 1.150 <br><br>Transparencies 1.1 - 1.5 <br><br>Readings: <br>- Lesko 1, The Sample with the Built-In Bias <br>- Lesko 2, Human Use of Human Subjects <br>- Lesko 3, Most of the Subjects Were White and Middle Class |
| *IV. Using This Book: An Overview of Its Special Features* | | |

* See Audiovisual Suggestions

# 1

# The Field of Social Psychology: How We Think

# About and Interact with Others

---

## Chapter Outline: Getting the Overall Picture

---

# Learning Objectives
### After studying this chapter, students should be able to:

**1.1**   Describe everyday experience as a basis of knowledge in social psychology, and indicate why "common sense" notions present a confusing picture of human social behavior.

**1.2**   Define social psychology.

**1.3**   Explain why social psychology is a "scientific field."

**1.4**   Explain why the field of social psychology focuses its study on the behavior of individuals.

**1.5**   Describe the five major causes of social behavior and thought: (a) the actions and characteristics of others; (b) cognitive processes; (c) ecological variables; (d) cultural context; and (e) biological/genetic factors.

**1.6**   Compare the approaches to social psychology in the 1908 McDougal text and the 1924 text by Floyd Allport.

**1.7**   Describe the growth in social psychology through the 1930s, focusing on the contributions by Sherif and Lewin.

**1.8**   describe how the behavior of the boys who participated in Lewin's experiment was affected by whether their leader was autocratic, laissezfaire, or democratic.

**1.9**   Describe contributions of the 1940s, 50s, and 60s, including emphases on groups, the authoritarian personality, and cognitive dissonance theory.

**1.10**   Describe the growing influence of the cognitive perspective and the recent trend toward application in such areas as health, the legal process, and work settings. as health, the legal process, and work settings.

**1.11**   Explain two guesses offered by the authors offer regarding expected trends to the year 2000 and beyond.

**1.12**   Examine historical changes regarding the assumption that the findings of social psychology are generalizable across cultures and across gender.

**1.13**   Describe the basic steps involved when an investigator conducts an experiment.

**1.14**   Understand the nature of independent variables and dependent variables, drawing examples from the mood/willingness to help experiment.

**1.15**   Give an example illustrating how an interaction between independent variables can be demonstrated only when the study includes two or more independent variables.

**1.16**   Explain why it is important that subjects be randomly assigned to groups in an experiment.

**1.17**   Explain the importance of holding factors other than the independent variable constant.

**1.18**   Describe two circumstances under which it is impossible to use the experimental method to investigate a particular question.

**1.19**   Describe the procedures followed when the correlational method is used to examine a hypothesis.

**1.20**   Describe the major drawback that plagues the correlational method, and give examples illustrating how third variables often underlie correlational findings.

**1.21**   Explain how replication, meta-analysis, and converging operations help increase confidence in the validity of social psychological findings.

**1.22**   Trace the steps in an investigation, from formulating a theory, to deriving a hypothesis, to testing the hypotheses, and finally reexamining the theory.

**1.23**   Understand why social psychologists sometimes deceive their research subjects?

**1.24**   Describe ethical issues raised by the use of deception, and indicate how informed consent and debriefing help to decrease the dangers of deception.

# Discussion Topics and Questions

## 1. Ethics, Invasion of Privacy

Middlemist, Knowles, and Matter (1976) conducted a naturalistic field study to determine the degree to which invasion of one's personal space arouses stress. The researchers observed male users of a college restroom through a periscope to determine whether onset of urination and amount of time taken to complete urination would be affected by the presence of a nearby confederate. Is this an invasion of the subjects' privacy? Ask your students whether they believe this is a legitimate psychological study. (The Middlemist, Knowles, and Matter study is in the *Journal of Personality and Social Psychology, 33,* 541-546.) A later issue of *JPSP* (35, 120-124) has a couple of brief articles debating the ethics of the study.

## 2. Experimental Role Play

Have one of the more verbal students in class engage in role playing. Give the student a complete description of an experiment, and have him or her tell the class how he or she would behave in the experiment; or you might have the entire class write down how they'd behave. The ideal experiment to choose is one in which the role player will behave differently from actual subjects. Possibilities include Milgram's obedience paradigm, the bystander studies, or West, Gunn, and Chernicky's "Watergate Study."

Consider, for example, a role-playing replication of the Milgram obedience study. Describe in detail the teacher's situation, and then ask the students to imagine themselves in the learner's position. Ask the students whether they would obey the experimenter's commands and ultimately deliver 450 volts. Also ask them to estimate the proportion of people in the general population that would deliver 450 volts. If you ask the above questions before your students have been exposed to the results of Milgram's research, you will find that very few expect that they would deliver 450 volts. Furthermore, the students will greatly underestimate the proportion of the population that would fully obey.

After demonstrating that students' predictions are inaccurate, discuss reasons why intuition is unable to predict behavior. Among the reasons that role playing underestimates the level of obedience are the following: (a) people don't know where their focus of attention would lie in the actual situation. Although they imagine that the victim would grab their attention, in the actual situation the experimenter may be the focus; (b) People are unable to recreate the physiological components of their reactions; (c) people can't imagine the degree to which the flow of events traps them into obedience.

You might conclude the discussion by emphasizing the necessity for empirical research using involved subjects. The two methods, role playing and involved subjects, exhibit different behavior, and a psychology that relied on subjects' introspective reports of behavior would often be in error.

## 3. Experimenter Bias

To introduce students to the idea of experimenter bias, a discussion of the role played by the examiner giving a lie detector test might be helpful. The polygraph is, of course, a sensitive physiological recording device that measures the emotional arousal of a suspect by recording changes in galvanic skin potential. The basic assumption is that a guilty person will become emotionally aroused whenever he or she tells a lie in response to an incriminating question. However, it is probable that even innocent people become emotionally aroused when being questioned, and their arousal may well be greatest to "incriminating" questions. The person being questioned knows he or she is a suspect; thus, when the examiner asks a question such as "Where were you the night your neighbor died?" an emotional response may well be elicited, irrespective of guilt.

To correct the above problem, the examiner often determines a set of facts about the crime that only a guilty suspect would know. This relevant information is then presented to the suspect embedded in other equally plausible facts. Presumably, a guilty person will respond more strongly than an innocent person to the special meaning of the significant facts.

Even with the procedure described above, however, there is still a potential problem. The polygraph examiner and others present during the test are usually aware of the critical pieces of information. These people have usually formed a hypothesis about the guilt or innocence of the particular suspect, and they are in a position to influence the suspect's responses. Discuss with students ways in which subtle and inadvertent cues given by the examiner may influence the suspect. Is the examiner in a position analogous to that of the psychological experimenter? What might be done to prevent this kind of subtle influence?

### 4. Should Some Research Topics Be Placed Out of Bounds?

Some persons have argued that some aspects of social behavior are best left unstudied. One such topic is the nature of love. Former Senator William Proxmire of Wisconsin has criticized the work of Ellen Berscheid and Elaine Hatfield (formerly Walster), saying, "Americans want to leave some things in life a mystery, and right at the top of things we don't want to know is why a man falls in love with a woman and vice versa." Are the questions of how people fall in love and how long-term relationships develop worthy of psychological study? Do the students agree with Senator Proxmire that some topics should be placed out of bounds?

### 5. Informed Consent and Demand Characteristics

Does the requirements of obtaining informed consent from research subjects have any effect on their behavior in an experiment? A couple of research studies have suggested that the use of informed consent forms can change subjects' behavior in significant ways. Gardner (1978) argued that the forms change behavior in environmental stressor research. Gardner's article is in the *Journal of Personality and Social Psychology* (36, 628-634). Second, Dill and colleagues (1982) have argued that human subjects regulations are a source of methodological artifact. Their study appears in *Personality and Social Psychology Bulletin,* (8, 417-425).

# Learning Activities: Classroom Exercises/Demonstrations

## 1.1 First Day First Impressions

Art Lyons of Moravian College suggests a demonstration to be used on the first day of the term by faculty members teaching two sections of social psychology. Lyons suggests that the faculty member vary his or her style of dress in the two different sections and gather the students' first impressions of their professor. For example, Lyons reports in *Teaching of Psychology* (8(3), 173-174) that he wears a coat and tie in one section and removes them in another section. Lyons has the students rate him on several trait dimensions using a semantic differential format. He reports that discussion of the results provides an excellent opportunity for active class participation and sets the stage for dealing with both methodological and conceptual issues later in the course. A discussion is found in his *Teaching of Psychology* article. Possible dimensions to be used in the ratings are as follows:

$$
\begin{array}{r}
\text{attractive --!--!--!--!-- unattractive} \\
\text{intelligent --!--!--!--!-- unintelligent} \\
\text{open-minded --!--!--!--!-- closed-minded} \\
\text{conservative --!--!--!--!-- liberal} \\
\text{talkative --!--!--!--!-- quiet} \\
\text{emotional --!--!--!--!-- unemotional} \\
\text{self-confident --!--!--!--!-- lacking in self-confidence}
\end{array}
$$

## 1.2 Common Sense Ideas and Scientific Study

Chapter 1 begins by discussing the wisdom contained in everyday, common sense knowledge. The present exercise is designed to show students that, despite the intuitive appeal of common sense ideas, they should be careful in wholeheartedly accepting them. The exercise can be done as either an out-of-class assignment or an in-class activity.

### a. Out-of-Class Assignment

Each student in the class should provide one friend with information stating that research has supported the idea that similar people like each other, and another friend with information that opposites attract. The friends should be asked to indicate in a sentence or two why they think the statement is true, and then they should rate the degree to which the notion is true. A sheet for your students to use in doing this exercise is found in Chapter 1 of your students' Study Guide and also on the following page. Have the students bring their friends' ratings to class so that you can test whether both of these conflicting statements are rated to be true.

### b. In-Class Activity

Half of the students in the class should be given the statement that similar people like each other, and the other half should receive the opposites attract statement. Each student should be asked to work independently in response to the statement he or she received. Once they have rated the statement, divide the class into discussion groups of four or five (making sure that only those receiving similar statements are in the same group). Have the students share their responses. Then, ask a spokesperson from each group to read the statement they were given, and share with the class supportive reasons for their conclusions. A lively discussion should follow since these appear to be opposite common sense ideas. Such ideas as both may be true under certain conditions, or understanding the nature of relationships is quite complex, or even the subtle deception of receiving differing statements might come up.

**HANDOUT FOR ACTIVITY # 1.2**
**Common Sense Ideas and Scientific Study**

Social psychologists have found in their research that separation intensifies romantic attraction. In other words, there seems to be wisdom in the old saying, "Absence makes the heart grow fonder."

In a sentence or two, why do you suppose this is true?

Does this finding seem surprising to you?

____yes

____no

---

Social psychologists have found in their research that separation weakens romantic attraction. There seems to be wisdom in the old saying, "Out of sight, out of mind."

In a sentence or two, why do you suppose this is true?

Does this finding seem surprising to you?

____yes

____no

Copyright © 1997 by Allyn and Bacon

## 1.3 Reports of Research

Have students watch newspapers or magazines for reports of research. They might watch for stories that draw erroneous conclusions about cause and effect. Or they might watch for reports that they understand better because they're taking social psychology. Encourage them to be alert for these materials, and encourage them to bring relevant articles to class.

## 1.4 Ethics in Research

Quiz the students regarding their own reactions to various field studies in social psychology. This exercise repeats the procedure of the Wilson and Donnerstein (1976) study (published in the *American Psychologist, 31*(11), 765-773). Wilson and Donnerstein read brief descriptions of actual experiments and asked subjects to rate each experiment for its ethics, its appropriateness, its legality, and so forth. The handout with descriptions of the experiments from Wilson and Donnerstein are presented in Chapter 1 of the Study Guide and also on the following page. Have your students answer some or all of the following questions about each of the experiments. For each question, the students should answer "yes," "no," or "not sure."

1. If you discovered that you had been a subject in this experiment, would you feel that you had been harassed or annoyed?

2. If you discovered that you had been a subject in this experiment, would you feel that your privacy had been invaded?

3. Do you feel that such an experiment is unethical or immoral?

4. Would you mind being a subject in such an experiment?

5. Do you feel that psychologists should be doing such an experiment?

6. Is doing such an experiment justified by its contribution to our scientific knowledge of behavior?

7. Does such an experiment lower your trust in social scientists and their work?

8. Do you feel that the psychologist's actions in this experiment are against the law?

## HANDOUT FOR ACTIVITY # 1.4
### Ethics in Research

Descriptions of Studies (from Wilson and Donnerstein, 1976)

1.  Experimenters, walking singly or in pairs, ask politely for either 10 cents or 20 cents from passersby, sometimes offering an explanation for why they need the money (Latane, 1970).

2.  The experimenter comes to a home, says that he has misplaced the address of a friend who lives nearby, and asks to use the phone. If the party admits him, he pretends to make the call (Milgram, 1970).

3.  Automobiles, parked on streets, look as if they were abandoned. (License plates are removed and hoods are raised.) Experimenters hide in nearby buildings and film people who have any contact with the cars (Zimbardo, 1969).

4.  Two researchers visit shoe stores at times when there are more customers than sales clerks in the store. One of the researchers is wearing a shoe with a broken heel. She rejects whatever new shoes the sales clerk shows her. The other researcher, posing as a friend of the bogus customer, surreptitiously takes notes on the sales clerk's behavior (Schaps, 1972).

5.  Letters, stamped and addressed to fictitious organizations at the same post office box number, are dropped in various locations, as if they were lost on the way to being mailed. Some are placed under automobile windshield wipers with a penciled note saying "found near car" (Milgram, 1969).

6.  People sitting alone on park benches are asked to be interviewed by an experimenter who gives the name of a fictitious survey research organization that he claims to represent. At the beginning of the interview, the experimenter asks a person sitting nearby, who is actually a confederate, if he would mind answering the questions at the same time. The confederate responds with opinions that are opposite those of the subject and makes demeaning remarks about the subject's answers; for example, "that's ridiculous," "that's just the sort of thing you'd expect to hear in this park" (Abelson and Miller, 1967).

7.  A person walking with a cane pretends to collapse in a subway car. "Stage blood" trickles from his mouth. If someone approaches the bogus victim, he allows the party to help him to his feet. If no one approaches before the train slows to a stop, another experimenter, posing as a passenger, pretends to help and both leave the train (Piliavin and Piliavin, 1972).

8.  Housewives are phoned. The caller names a fictitious consumer's group that he claims to represent and interviews them about the soap products they use for a report in a "public service publication," which is also fictitious. Several days later the experimenter calls again and asks if the housewives would allow five or six men into their homes to enumerate and classify their household products for a report in their publication. If the party agrees, the caller says he is just collecting names of willing people at present and that she will be contacted if it is decided to use her in the survey. No one is contacted again (Freedman and Fraser, 1966).

Copyright © 1997 by Allyn and Bacon

## 1.5  Research Methodology

Have students respond to the scenarios found on the next page or in their Study Guides, in which they are asked to identify the independent and dependent variables.  If you want to carry the exercise one step further, the next thing you can do is to have them consider the following questions as a way to sharpen their methodological sophistication:

**HANDOUT FOR ACTIVITY # 1.5**
**Research Methodology**

1a.    A study was conducted to investigate the hypothesis that watching televised violence increases aggression in children. Fifty 4-year olds were randomly assigned to watch either a violent or a non-violent television program. After watching the program the children were observed while they engaged in 30 minutes of free play. An observer watched for aggressive acts and recorded all such acts that occurred.

Independent variable   _____        Dependent variable   _____

1b.    What if the observer recording the children's aggressive acts becomes fatigued or bored during the course of the thirty-minute sessions? Would it matter that the observer's criterion as to what represents an aggressive act changed over the course of the thirty-minute sessions?

2a.    A pharmaceutical company hired a team of researchers to study the effectiveness of a new drug for relieving depression. The researchers identified a group of psychiatric patients who were experiencing chronic depression and randomly assigned half of them to receive the drug and half to receive a placebo. One month later the drug group had improved much more than the placebo group, and the pharmaceutical company announced it had found a new anti-depressant drug.

Independent variable   _____        Dependent variable   _____

2b.    Assume that "to avoid confusion" the researchers decide to have the actual drug administered by one psychiatric nurse and the placebo by another nurse. Is this a good idea? Why or why not?

3a.    It was hypothesized that people have a desire to be with other people when they are in a fear-arousing situation. To test this hypothesis an experimenter randomly assigned 50 subjects to either a low or a high fear group. The low fear group was told they would be shocked but that it would be only a small tingle and that it definitely would not hurt. The high fear group was told they would be shocked and that the shock would be quite painful. Each group of subjects was then told they could wait in a room by themselves or with others. The number subjects who chose to wait alone and to wait with others was recorded by the experimenter.

Independent variable   _____        Dependent variable   _____

Copyright © 1997 by Allyn and Bacon

3b.     Some subjects in the high fear condition might choose to discontinue their participation in the experiment after hearing about the painful shocks, and ethical guidelines require that the experimenter release them. Would the experimental procedure be compromised if 15 percent of the high-fear subjects dropped out, but none of the low-fear subjects did so?

4a.     **An investigator wanted to determine how massed versus distributed practice affects learning. To accomplish this she developed a list of nonsense syllables and had subjects learn these under two different conditions. Twenty subjects practiced the list for twenty minutes without any break (massed practice), while another twenty subjects practiced for four five-minute periods with a two minute break between each period (distributed practice). The number of nonsense syllables correctly recalled at the end of practice was recorded for each subject.**

        **Independent variable** _____          **Dependent variable** _____

4b.     The experimenter allowed distributed-practice subjects to "do whatever they wanted" during the two-minute rest periods, and many of them mentally rehearsed the nonsense syllables during this time. Is this a problem? If so, what changes are needed to correct for it?

5a.     **An educator was interested in identifying the most successful teaching technique for his school system. He identified three schools that taught in the traditional manner and another three schools that taught in a new experimental manner. At the end of the school year, he administered an achievement test to all the children in these schools.**

        **Independent variable** _____          **Dependent variable** _____

5b.     Obviously, the educator could not randomly assign the children to attend the various schools. Also, he was not allowed to decide which teacher or schools would use each technique. What problems are caused by: (1) not being able to assign children randomly to the schools? (2) having teachers "choose" which teaching technique to use?

Copyright © 1997 by Allyn and Bacon

## Overhead Transparencies
These appear at the back of this manual.

**1.1**   *Correlation versus Causation*
**1.2**   *Testing a Hypothesis with Correlation Method*
**1.3**   *Testing a Hypothesis Experimentally*
**1.4**   *Confounding of Variables*
**1.5**   *Correlation versus Causation*

## Audiovisual Suggestions

*The Case of ESP,* 1985, color videocassette, 57 mins.  Time-Life Video, 100 Eisenhower Drive, P.O. Box 644, Paramus, NJ 07653.  This "NOVA" program explores research into extrasensory perception and claims for and against paranormal phenomena.  Can serve to introduce discussions of research ethics, values, and methodology.

*Inferential Statistics:  Hypothesis Testing--Rats, Robots, and Roller Skates,* 33877, 1975, color, 28 mins. Pennsylvania State University, Audiovisual Services, Special Services Building, University Park, PA 16802 (814-865-6314).  Uses humorous sketches to explain hypothesis testing, one of the most important applications of inferential statistics.  Illustrates the need for a control group and for random assignment of subjects to groups, the necessity of statistics as a way to overcome population variability, the formulation of a statistical hypothesis and possible errors of decision that can be made, and the way in which hypotheses about the mean are tested.  Produced by Robert Johnson.

*Invitation to Social Psychology,* 32074, 1975, color, 25 mins. Pennsylvania State University, Audiovisual Services, Special Services Building, University Park, PA 16802 (814-865-6314).  Introduction to social psychology with emphasis on three questions:  What is the subject matter of social psychology?  What are its methods of investigation?  What are some of its findings?  Examples include interpersonal events in a cafeteria, reactions of bystanders on a city street, Milgram's obedience study, and Zimbardo's prison simulation.  From the *Social Psychology* series, Stanley Milgram.

*Methodology:  The Psychologist and the Experiment,* 32000, 1975, color, 30 mins.  Pennsylvania State University, Audiovisual Services, Special Services Building, University Park, PA 16802 (814-865-6314).  Documents research methodology used in Stanley Schachter's "fear and affiliation" experiment in social psychology and Austin Riesen's physiological experiment on visual motor coordination.  Discusses independent and dependent variables, control groups, random assignment to conditions, and use of statistics in research.  From the *Psychology Today* series.  A CRM production.

*Social Psychology,* videotape, 30 mins.  CRM Films, 2233 Faraday Ave., Carlsbad, CA 92008 (800-421-0833).  This tape introduces the subject matter and methods of social psychology by tracing attempts to desegregate an urban school.

*Social Psychology Laboratory,* 33167, 1975, color, 24 mins.  Pennsylvania State University, Audiovisual Services, Special Services Building, University Park, PA 16802 (814-865-6314).  Social psychology experiments are used to demonstrate some of the standard features of experimental methodology.  Shows such experimental procedures as briefing and debriefing sessions, as well as aspects of establishing the environmental setting such as design of the laboratory, standard seating arrangements, and the type of apparatus commonly used to monitor the progress of the experiment. Experiments explore the stability of three-person groups, nonverbal communication, and interaction in problem solving. Produced for the British Open University, V. Lockwood.

*Understanding Research,* Number 2 in this 1990 videotape series, 30 mins. The Annenborg Project, Holt, Rinehart & Winston, 1990, contact Lee Sutherlin, Marketing Manager (817-334-7632). Covers basic research techniques used in both the laboratory and the field.

## Critical Thinking/Essay Questions

1. Provide a definition of social psychology and describe the essential features of the field of social psychology.
2. Summarize the basic steps that are followed when one conducts an experiment. Include in your answer a discussion of the independent and dependent variables, random assignment of subjects to groups, and the necessity of avoiding confounding.
3. Under what circumstances do social psychologists use deception methodology in their research? Is the use of deception justified?
4. Compare the experimental and correlational techniques for conducting social psychological studies. What are the advantages and disadvantages of each technique?
5. Describe the role of theory in social psychological research. What is the role of theory in explaining behavior and in predicting behavior?

## Sources for Lecture

Aron, A., & Aron, E. N. (1989). *The Heart of Social Psychology: A Backstage View of a Passionate Science* (2nd ed.). Lexington, MA: Lexington Books. Here, the human qualities of the people who were at the cutting edge of social psychology are depicted with compasion and humor. Selections from this book help bring to life the people involved in the history of social psychology.

Berkowitz, L. (1971). Sex and violence--We can't have it both ways. *Psychology Today,* December, pp. 14-23. Is this a case where social scientists' values, as well as the general public's values, interfere with our ability to interpret the information found in research? Research results on both violence and pornography were similar, yet different policy decisions were advocated.

Campbell, D., & Tavris, C. (1975). The experimenting society: To find programs that work, government must measure its failures. *Psychology Today,* September, pp. 46-56. Campbell advocates using experimental methods to determine which social programs work and which ones don't.

Cornell, J. (1984). Science versus the paranormal. *Psychology Today,* March, pp. 28-34. Why do so many people continue to believe in the paranormal despite disconfirmations? The Committee for the Scientific Investigation of the Paranormal is reviewed.

Hogan, R., & Schroeder, D. (1981). Seven biases in psychology. *Psychology Today,* July, pp. 8-10, 12, 14. Biases in psychology textbooks are reviewed. What kinds of values are being presented to students in this way?

Rubenstein, C. (1982). Psychology's fruit flies. *Psychology Today*, July, pp. 83-84. Do the college students used in so many of our experiments behave and think like other adults? This article argues that the answer may be no.

Rubin, Z. (1983). Taking deception for granted. *Psychology Today*, March, pp. 74-75. This critical overview notes that the use of deception remains at a high level among social psychologists, and it argues that the use of deception retards progress.

## Professional Update: Current Articles from Professional Sources

Anderson, C. A., & Sechler, E. S. (1986). Effects of explanation and counterexplanation on the development and use of social theories. *Journal of Personality and Social Psychology, 50,* 24-34. When subjects explained how or why two variables might be related, it increased their use of and belief in the explained relationship. A counterexplanation task eliminated this bias. Might scientists be affected by these same processes?

Hedges, L. V. (1987). How hard is hard science, how soft is soft science? The empirical cumula-tiveness of research. *American Psychologist, 42,* 443-445. Are research results in the behavioral sciences less replicable than results in the physical sciences? Although many say yes, the article questions this assumption. Methods for examining the consistency of research results are presented and examined.

Horvat, J. (1986). Detection of suspiciousness as a function of pleas for honesty. *Journal of Personality and Social Psychology, 50,* 921-924. This experiment reports a way to measure suspiciousness in deception experiments. Truly suspicious subjects will be found out, whereas naive subjects will be kept from falsely reporting suspiciousness.

Related Readings: The following selections from *Readings in Social Psychology: General, Classic, and Contemporary Selections,* 3rd Edition, by Wayne Lesko (Allyn and Bacon, 1997) accompany this chapter.

Goleman, D. (1993). "Pollsters enlist psychologists in quest for unbiased results." The use of public opinion surveys are extremely common. Given their prevalent use, how accurate and trustworthy are their results and what unintended factors influence their outcomes? Applications are made to several current uses and abuses of the survey method. (Article 1)

Kelman, H. C. (1967). "Human use of human subjects: The problem of deception in social psychologi cal experiments." Common use of deception in social psychological research, creates ethical concerns and demands careful review. Alternative experimental techniques minimizing the negative effects of deception are explored. (Article 2)

Graham, S. (1992). "Most of the subjects were white and middle class: Trends in published research on African Americans in selected APA journals." Research dealing with African Americans is examined in two ways. The first question is the frequency of research with African Americans as subjects. The second question is the type of research in which African Americans have been studied and whether any methodological biases may be present in these studies. (Article 3)

# Chapter 2

# Social Perception: Understanding Others

## Chapter-at-a-Glance

| CHAPTER OUTLINE | INSTRUCTION IDEAS | SUPPLEMENTS* |
|---|---|---|
| *I. Nonverbal Communication: The Unspoken Language* <br> •   Nonverbal Communication: The Basic Channels <br><br> •   Individual Differences in the Use of Nonverbal Cues: Emotional Expressiveness <br><br> •   **Social Psychology: On the Applied Side**   How to Tell When Another Person Is Lying: Nonverbal Cues and the Detection of Deception | Learning Objectives 2.1 to 2.11 <br><br> Discussion Topic 5 <br><br> Critical Thinking Questions 1, 2 | Test Bank Questions 2.1 to 2.61 <br><br> Reading: <br> - Lesko 4, Power of Nonverbal Signals |
| *II. Attribution: Understanding the Causes of Others' Behavior* <br> •   Theories of Attribution: Frameworks for Understanding How We Attempt to Make Sense Out of the Social World <br><br> •   Attribution: Some Basic Sources of Error <br><br> •   Applications of Attribution Theory: Insights and Interventions | Learning Objectives 2.12 to 2.22 <br><br> Discussion Topics 1 - 3 <br><br> Critical Thinking Questions 3, 4 <br><br> Activities 2.1 - 2.6 (Handouts) | Test Bank Questions 2.62 to 2.132 <br><br> Readings: Lesko 6, Victims of Rape <br><br> Transparencies 2.1 - 2.6 |
| *III. Impression Formation and Impression Management: The Process of Combining Social Information--and How, Sometimes, We Profit From It* <br> •   **Cornerstones of Social Psychology**   Asch's Research on Central and Peripheral Traits <br><br> •   Impression Formation: A Cognitive Approach <br><br> •   Impression Management: The Fine Art of Looking Good <br><br> •   **Social Diversity: A Critical Analysis**   Reactions to Nonverbal Displays by Political Leaders in the United States and France | Learning Objectives 2.23 to 2.29 <br><br> Discussion Topic 4 <br><br> Critical Thinking Question 5 <br><br> Activity 2.3 | Test Bank Questions 2.133 to 2.160 <br><br> Reading: <br> - Lesko 5, First Impressions |

*See Audiovisual Suggestions

# 2  Social Perception: Understanding Others

## Chapter Outline: Getting the Overall Picture

I. **Nonverbal Communication: The Unspoken Language**
    A.   Nonverbal Communication: The Basic Channels
        1.   Unmasking the Face: Facial Expressions as Clues to Others' Emotions
        2.   Are Facial Expressions Universal?
        3.   Gazes and Stares: Eye-contact as a Nonverbal Cue
        4.   Body Language: Gestures, Posture, and Movements
        5.   Touching: The Most Intimate Nonverbal Cue
            a.   Gender Differences in Touching: Who Touches Whom, and When?
    B.   Individual Differences in the Use of Nonverbal Cues: Emotional Expressiveness
    C.   Social Psychology: On the Applied Side  How to Tell When Another Person is Lying: Nonverbal Cues and the Detection of Deception

II. **Attribution: Understanding the Causes of Others' Behavior**
    A.   Theories of Attribution: Frameworks for Understanding How We Attempt To Make Sense Out of the Social World
        1.   From Acts to Dispositions: Using Others' Behavior as a Guide to Their Lasting Traits
        2.   Attentional Resources and Trait Attribution: What we Learn--and Don't Learn--from Obscure Behavior
        3.   Kelley's Theory and Causal Attributions: How We Answer the Question *Why?*
            a.   When Do We Engage in Causal Attribution? The Path of Least Resistance Strikes Again
            b.   Augmenting and Discounting: How We Handle Multiple Potential Causes
    B.   Attribution: Some Basic Sources of Error
        1.   The Fundamental Attribution Error: Overestimating the Role of Dispositional Causes
            a.   The Actor-Observer Effect. You fell; I was pushed.
            b.   The Self-Serving Bias. "I can do no wrong, but you can do no right."
    C.   Applications of Attribution Theory: Insights and Interventions
        1.   Attribution and Depression
        2.   Attribution and Rape: Blaming Innocent Victims

III. **Impression Formation and Impression Management: The Process of Combining Social Information--And How, Sometimes, We Profit from It**
    A.   Cornerstones of Social Psychology: Asch's Research on Central and Peripheral Traits
    B.   Impression Formation: A Cognitive Approach
    C.   Impression Management: The Fine Art of Looking Good
        1.   Impression Management: Some Basic Tactics
        2.   Impression Management: To What Extent Does It Succeed?
    D.   Social Diversity: A Critical Analysis  Reactions To Nonverbal Displays By Political Leaders In the United States and France

# Learning Objectives
After studying this chapter, students should be able to:

**2.1** Explain the five basic channels through which we communicate nonverbally.

**2.2** Describe the six (or perhaps seven) basic emotions expressed in unique facial expressions.

**2.3** Describe patterns of physiological activity and self-reported emotions that occur when subjects pose particular facial expressions.

**2.4** Explain how the cross-cultural studies by Ekman and Friesen (1975) demonstrate that facial expressions of basic emotions are universal.

**2.5** Understand to what degree the recognition of basic facial expressions is dependent on the research methods used.

**2.6** Explian how we respond when others: a) maintain high levels of gazing; b) avoid eye contact; and c) stare at us.

**2.7** Describe how body language communicates emotion, including examples from ballet, restaurant servers, and various types of gestures.

**2.8** Describe how being touched by a waitress in the Crusco and Wetzel (1984) study affected the size of customers' tips.

**2.9** Examine gender differences and age differences in touching.

**2.10** Describe how emotional expressiveness affects occupational success and psychological adjustment, and examine the role of ambivalence in determining the impact of emotional expressiveness.

**2.11** Describe five nonverbal cues that help us to recognize that someone is lying.

**2.12** Based on Jones and Davis' theory, understand why correspondent inference, understand the three circumstances that lead us to infer that behavior reflects underlying traits.

**2.13** Compare the ability of subjects in the Gilbert et al. (1992) study to categorize verbal behavior, characterize the speaker, and correct their judgments when listening to a degraded versus a normal audiotape.

**2.14** Using Kelly's theory of attribution, distinguish between internal and external causes of behavior, and define the concepts of consensus, distinctiveness, and consistency.

**2.15** Compare attributions made when consensus is low, distinctiveness is low, and consistency is high with attributions made when consensus is high, distinctiveness is high, and consistency is high.

**2.16** Give examples of how past experience may keep us from engaging in careful causal attribution, and note how unexpected events and unpleasant outcomes heighten our attention to causal attribution.

**2.17** Describe the discounting that occurs when two possible supportive causes for a behavior are present, and the augmenting that occurs when both a supportive and an inhibitory factor are present.

**2.18** Describe the fundamental attribution error, and compare attributions made right away with those made after the passage of time.

**2.19** Explain the actor-observer effect, and why it occurs.

**2.20** Describe self-serving bias, and compare the cognitive and motivational explanations for self-serving bias.

**2.21** Describe the self-defeating attributional pattern that often underlies depression.

**2.22** Explain how each of the following factors influences attributions about a rape: a) whether the rapist is a date or a stranger; b) whether the rater is male or female.

**2.23** Explain how Asch's early work on central traits and on the order of traits supports his assertion that forming impressions of others involves more than simply adding together individual traits.

**2.24** Understand the for factors that determine how much weight a piece of information will receive in forming an impression.

**2.25** Describe the role played by exemplars and by abstractions when we make judgments about others.

**2.26** Explain how research by Sherman and Klein (1994) supports the hypothesis that early impressions of others consist mainly of exemplars, while later impressions consist mainly of mental abstractions.

**2.27** List self-enhancement tactics and other-enhancement tactics used in impression management.

**2.28** Summarize research by Wayne and Liden (1995) documenting that impression management can "pay off" for persons using it.

**2.29** Compare French and American reactions to facial expressions and to party affiliation of political candidates.

---

# Discussion Topics and Questions

---

**1. Attributions Based on One's Name**

How does one's name affect interpersonal judgments? You might ask the class to imagine a person named David, then to list five traits that David possesses. Next, ask the class to imagine a person named Winthrop and have them list his traits. Do the two lists differ? Why?

Another way to approach this question is to ask the class whether they have ever felt that the names they were given implied a certain set of attributes. You might particularly seek responses from those with popular names or those with unusual names to see if they ever felt dissatisfied with their first names and why. Do we form impressions of people based on part of their names?

**2. Attributions Based on Choice of Clothing**

How does one's choice of clothing affect the ratings received from others? Assuming that clothing does influence the personality attributed to a person, is this a case of biased judgment? Or is it simply rational processing of available information?

**3. Attributional Strategies in Advertising**

Have students look for applications of attributional principles in advertising. For example, the person trying to get us to buy a product may be presented as a person who doesn't generally like the type of product. A boy may declare that he "doesn't like bran cereals," for instance. But we then see that the particular brand he tries is so extraordinarily good that it wins him over. In attributional terms, the response to the particular brand is high in distinctiveness.

Another example might be the communicator who tries to convince us that the majority of people prefer a certain brand. This time the attributional strategy is one of high consensus. Many examples of attributional strategies exist. Alert your students to be thinking in attributional terms when they see advertisements and have them report relevant examples to the class.

## 4. Social Perception of People in the Media: Politicians and Celebrities

Discuss the basis for judging celebrities, political candidates, and the like. Do the same rules apply to interpersonal perception in a face-to-face encounter and in our judgment of people we know only in the media? Would it be an advantage for a political candidate to be familiar with the social perception research? It might be interesting to design an advertising campaign to determine whether the principles presented in Chapter 2 are being followed.

## 5. Detecting Deceit

Paul Ekman has thoroughly investigated the use of gestures, voice qualities, and facial expressions as clues to whether a person is telling the truth. There is much evidence that some concealment cues are obvious to most people, while other cues that can be detected only by trained observers. For example, there are muscles located mainly in the forehead that momentarily express our sincere emotions, and that can be detected by a keen observer who knows what to look for. In total, Ekman's behavioral checklist contains twenty-two separate clues for detecting deceit.

An interesting question is the degree to which historical figures have fallen victim to deception from others. Ekman has analyzed several historical cases of deception, including the willingness of British Prime Minister Neville Chamberlain to believe Hitler in 1938 when Hitler said Germany's intentions were nonaggressive. Should a U.S. president be given lie detection training before going off to a summit with a foreign power? (Ekman's work is summarized in the book *Telling Lies* (1985), published by W. W. Norton. Included in the book is the list of twenty-two clues for detecting deceit.)

# Learning Activities: Classroom Exercises/Demonstrations

## 2.1 Blaming the Victim

This exercise asks students to read a story in which six characters appear. The story is presented on the following page and in the study guide. The students are instructed to rank the characters in descending order according to how responsible each is perceived to be for the woman's death. (It is possible to read or tell the story to the class, but the exercise may work better if it is made into an overhead or each student is provided his or her own copy.) List the characters on the board, for the student's reference. Once the students have completed the task, ask them to indicate by raising their hand, whom they considered to be most responsible (FIRST CHOICE), and then ask who was their SECOND CHOICE.

The class will tend to split evenly, with about half the class ranking the wife as most responsible and about half ranking the highwayman first. A few people will also choose other characters. A quite lively discussion can develop, in which each group supports its own choice and challenges the others. As course instructor, you should remain neutral in the debate. Rather than telling them what you believe the correct answer is, challenge them to reach their own conclusions.

This exercise can become an extremely emotional tool in experiential learning. Discussion generated from this activity applies extremely well to the fundamental attribution error. The "just-world phenomenon" can also be introduced by using this exercise. (The idea for this exercise came from *Understanding Sound Welfare* by Dolgoff and Feldstein, 1984.)

The story can be retold with the wife as a widow who works nights, and she has to get back to feed her hungry babies before the baby-sitter leaves. Although the Highwayman's behavior does not change, the results typically do change. Or, other story options include a black woman in a southern town of the 1950's who sits in the front of a bus. A white man pulls her off the bus and beats her. Who is responsible?  Or, an old Jewish man walks the street in Nazi Germany wearing a skullcap, although he is aware of the anti-Semitism that abounds.  He is beaten.  Who is responsible?

As found in cases of rape victims, the tendency to "blame the victim" is pervasive.  Essentially it suggests that those who are disadvantaged, victimized, poor, or handicapped somehow have been responsible for their condition; if they were better or more adequate people, they would not be in a dependent position.

## HANDOUT FOR ACTIVITY # 2.1

### A STORY FROM LONG AGO

Once upon a time, a husband and wife lived together in a part of the city separated by a river from the places of employment, shopping, and entertainment. The husband had to work nights. Each evening he left his wife and took the ferry to work, returning in the morning.

The wife soon tired of this arrangement. Restless and lonely, she would take the next ferry into town each evening and develop relationships with a series of lovers. Anxious to preserve her marriage, she always returned home before her husband. In fact, her relationships were always limited. When they threatened to become too intense, she would precipitate a quarrel with her current lover and begin a new relationship.

One night she caused such a quarrel with a man we will call Lover I. He slammed the door in her face, and she started back to the ferry. Suddenly she realized that she had forgotten to bring money for her return fare. She swallowed her pride returned to Lover I's apartment to borrow the fare. After all, she <u>did</u> have to get home. But Lover I was vindictive and angry because of the quarrel. He slammed the door on his former lover, leaving her with no money. She remembered that a previous lover, whom we shall call Lover II, lived just a few doors away. Surely he would give her the ferry fare. However, Lover II was still so hurt from their old quarrel that he, too, refused her the money.

Now the hour was late and the woman was getting desperate. She rushed down to the ferry and pleaded with the ferryboat captain. He knew her as a regular customer. She asked if he could let her ride free and if she could pay the next night. But the captain insisted that rules were rules, and that he could not let her ride without paying the fare.

Dawn would soon be breaking, and her husband would be returning from work. The woman remembered that there was a free bridge about a mile further on. But the road to the bridge was a dangerous one, known to be frequented by highwaymen. Nonetheless, she had to get home, so she took the road. On the way a highwayman stepped out of the bushes and demanded her money. She told him she had none. He seized her. In the ensuing tussle, the highwayman stabbed the woman, and she died.

Thus ends our story. There have been six characters: Husband, Wife, Lover I, Lover II, Ferryboat Captain and Highwayman. Please list, in descending order of responsibility for this woman's death, all the characters. In other words, the one most responsible is listed first; the next most responsible, second; and so forth.

Copyright © 1997 by Allyn and Bacon

## 2.2 The Actor/Observer Effect

It is relatively easy to demonstrate the difference in causal attributions made by actors and observers. Have the students obtain two subjects outside of class. One subject should respond to the list of behaviors in HANDOUT # 2 below that describes actions performed by the self. The other subject should respond to the list of behaviors that describes actions performed by another person (HANDOUT #2A). Have the class members score the responses from the two subjects, finding the average score on the internal/external dimension for each subject and bring the data to class. Combine the data from class members to see if you can find evidence to support the actor/observer difference. (As an alternative, this activity could be done in class. Half of the students in the class could fill out HANDOUT #2 and half could fill out HANDOUT #2A. Then comparisons could be made.)

## HANDOUT FOR ACTIVITY # 2.2

INSTRUCTIONS: Your task is to imagine yourself in the situations below and rate your action is each situation. Use the following 1 to 5 scale to rate each action.

1--Action was exclusively due to my characteristics.

2--Action was mainly due to my characteristics.

3--Action was equally due to my characteristics and to the situation.

4--Action was mainly due to the situation.

5--Action was exclusively due to the situation.

1. I was at a restaurant and received the wrong meal. I sat quietly and ate it without complaining. ___

2. I just received an A on a term paper. ___
3. I had a fight with one of my best friends. ___
4. I lied on a job application. ___
5. I was walking across the street and saw an accident happen, so I went over to see if I could help. ___

6. Someone was visiting me, but I said I had to study, and I asked my visitor to leave. ___
7. Someone asked me for help moving into a new apartment on Saturday, and I lied and said I had other plans. ___
8. My least favorite professor said something stupid in class, and I laughed out loud, although nobody else did. ___
9. I entered a contest, solved a puzzle, and won $500. ___
10. I gave $100 of the contest winnings to a student aid fund on campus. ___
11. I volunteered to coach a children's athletic team in a local elementary school. __
12. I found a wallet with $50 on the street and gave it to the police. ___
13. I was caught speeding on the way home last week and received a ticket and $50 fine. ___
14. My professor singled me out as an excellent student and offered me a job in the department. ___

Copyright © 1997 by Allyn and Bacon

## HANDOUT FOR ACTIVITY #2.2A

INSTRUCTIONS:  Your task is to imagine a particular friend in the situations below and to rate your friend's action in each situation.  Use the following 1 to 5 scale to rate each action.

1--Action was exclusively due to my friend's characteristics.

2--Action was mainly due to my friend's characteristics.

3--Action was equally due to my fiend's characteristics and to the situation.

4--Action was mainly due to the situation.

5--Action was exclusively due to the situation.

1.  My friend was at a restaurant and received the wrong meal.  My friend sat quietly and ate it without complaining.  ____
2.  My friend just received an A on a term paper.  ____
3.  My friend had a fight with one of his/her best friends.  ____
4.  My friend lied on a job application.  ____
5.  My friend was walking across the street and saw an accident happen, so my friend went over to see if he/she could help.  ____
6.  My friend had someone visiting, but my friend said he/she had to study and asked the visitor to leave.  ____
7.  Someone asked my friend for help moving into a new apartment on Saturday, and my friend lied and said he/she had other plans.  ____
8.  My friend's least favorite professor said something stupid in class, and my friend laughed out loud, although nobody else did.  ____
9.  My friend entered a contest, solved a puzzle, and won $500.  ____
10. My friend gave $100 of the contest winnings to a student aid fund on campus.__
11. My friend volunteered to coach a children's athletic team in a local elementary school.  ____
12. My friend found a wallet with $50 on the street and gave it to the police.  ____
13. My friend was caught speeding on the way home last week and received a ticket and $50 fine.  ____
14. My friend's professor singled him/her out as an excellent student and offered him/her a job in the department.  ____

Copyright © 1997 by Allyn and Bacon

## 2.3  The Central Traits Effect

Warm versus cold is a trait dimension that has been shown to affect dramatically the impression formed of a stimulus person.  This classic finding has been labeled the "central traits" effect, and a discussion of why it occurs can be found in many sources.  You should prepare two lists of traits (given below), one said to be characteristic of Person A and other characteristic of Person B.  Each student in the class receives only on list, either the A or the B list.  In fact the two lists have six traits in common, and only the middle trait (warm versus cold) is different.  If you are unable to prepare the list ahead of time, you can simply present them to the class on the chalkboard.  Have half the class copy each list.  When the "other list" is being presented, have those students who aren't suppose to see it cover their eyes.  The trait lists are:

| *Person A* | *Person B* |
|------------|------------|
| intelligent | intelligent |
| skillful | skillful |
| industrious | industrious |
| warm | cold |
| determined | determined |
| practical | practical |
| cautious | cautious |

After the students have copied their respective lists, ask them to rate their stimulus person using the following six traits:  (a) generous, (b) wise, (c) happy, (d) good-natured, (e) reliable, and (f) important.  For each trait ask the students to make a "yes" or "no" response.  You will find that the warm/cold difference will dramatically affect each of the first four traits, but not the last two traits.

## 2.4  Self-Serving Bias Exam Rating Scale

This exercise should be done as soon as possible after students have received their test scores on an exam.  The exercise asks students to explain the score they received.  The prediction is that students who have done well on the exam will explain their performance internally, whereas students who have done relatively poorly will explain their performance more externally.

To find out whether this hypothesis is confirmed, the class should compute attributions to the internal factors (ability and effort) and to the external factors (the test and luck).  According to the self-serving bias successful people should attribute their success to the internal factors, whereas unsuccessful people should attribute their relative failure to the external factors.  A questionnaire for your use is presented below.

## HANDOUT FOR ACTIVITY #2.4

### EXAM RATING SCALE

To what extent do you think your score on this test was due to:

1.     This particular test--how easy or difficult it was:

Not at all  0  1  2  3  4  5  6  7  8  9  To a great extent

2.     My academic ability or lack of ability:

Not at all  0  1  2  3  4  5  6  7  8  9  To a great extent

3.     How much or little I studied:

Not at all  0  1  2  3  4  5  6  7  8  9  To a great extent

4.     Luck--good or bad:

Not at all  0  1  2  3  4  5  6  7  8  9  To a great extent

5.     What score did you receive on the test? _____

6.     How satisfied are you with this score?

Not at all
satisfied  0  1  2  3  4  5  6  7  8  9  Very satisfied

7.     Was this test:

A poor measure                       An excellent measure
of what I knew  0  1  2  3  4  5  6  7  8  9  of what I knew

8.     Are you: \_\_\_ female \_\_\_ male?

Copyright © 1997 by Allyn and Bacon

## 2.5  Transparencies Applying Kelley's Theory of Attribution

The three situations presented in the transparency section of this chapter can be used to illustrate the basic ideas of Kelley's theory of attribution.  (All transparencies appear at the back of this manual, Part III.)  Each example describes a behavior and then provides consensus, consistency, and distinctiveness information.  At the end of each example, the student is asked to choose the best explanation of the behavior.

Corresponding to this activity, transparency 2.4 contains low-consensus, high-consistency, and low-distinctiveness information and should result in students making attributions to the individual (i.e.  Sue is just "that" kind of person).  Transparency 2.5 contains high-consensus, high-consistency, and high-distinctiveness information and should result in students making attributions to the situation (i.e., Professor Ward).  Transparency 2.6 contains low-consensus, high-consistency, and high-distinctiveness information, and no simple attribution is obvious.

## 2.6  Applying Attribution to Everyday Situations (Kelley's Theory)

### a) Handout Activity #2.6

On the handout below (#2.6), students are instructed to describe the consensus, consistency, and distinctiveness information contained in each of two scenarios.  Have the students respond to the scenarios outside of class (homework); or you might provide time during class.  After students have answered the questions, discuss their answers in class.  Students often appreciate an opportunity to determine whether they understand Kelley's theory.

### b) Role-Play of Kelley's Theory

Have students work creatively in small groups, to develop a short scenario exhibiting either internal or external attribution, based upon Kelley's theory.  Remind them that they must demonstrate the appropriate level of consensus, consistency, and distinctiveness.  Time permitting, choose at least two groups to present their role-play to the rest of the class **without** announcing ahead of time which type of attribution will be exhibited.  The rest of the class must decide whether an internal or external attribution should be made, based upon consensus, consistency, and distinctiveness information.  (Prior to each role-play presentation, basic information may need to be expressed to set the scene, i.e. which character is the class expected to make attributions about?)

## HANDOUT FOR ACTIVITY #2.6

## APPLYING ATTRIBUTION TO EVERYDAY SITUATIONS

You need an expert mountain climber to come along on your next expedition, and you are trying to decide whether Scott is qualified for the job.  One day you observe him climbing a difficult cliff.  You learn that Scott has climbed this cliff several other times without experiencing a mishap.  You also learn that he has successfully climbed many cliffs of varying types.

1.   In this example, consensus is **high low** (circle one).

2.   Describe the consensus information:

3.   In this example, consistency is **high low** (circle one).

4.   Describe the consistency information:

5.   In this example, distinctiveness is **high low** (circle one).

6.   Describe the distinctiveness information:

7.   Based on the information provided, should you take Scott on your mountain-climbing expedi-
     tion? **yes no** (circle one)

   Why or why not?

You are trying to decide whether to go to a restaurant that has been recommended by a friend of yours.  Ann says she has been there several times and liked it a lot each time no matter what kind of mood she was in.  She also mentions that there aren't many restaurants that she likes.  You have also heard from several other friends that this is a good restaurant.

1.   In this example, consensus is **high low**  (circle one).

2.   Describe the consensus information:

3.   In this example consistency is **high low**  (circle one).

4.   Describe the consistency information:

5.   In this example distinctiveness is **high low**  (circle one).

6.   Describe the distinctiveness information:

7.   Based on this information, should you go to this restaurant?  **yes no**  (circle one)
     Why or why not?

Copyright © 1997 by Allyn and Bacon

# Audiovisual Suggestions

## *Allyn and Bacon Videos*

*Constructing Social Reality*, Discusses the factors that contribute to our interpretation of
reality and how understanding the psychological factors that govern our behavior may help us to
become more empathic and independent members of society. (Discovering Psychology Series, On
Tape #10.)

*Communication: Social Cognition and Attribution*, videotape, 28.5 mins. To obtain this
tape, consult your Allyn and Bacon sales representative. Dramatization is used to generate an
exchange between Robert A. Baron and Margaret Clark concerning attributional processes and
nonverbal communication.

## *Other Videos and Films*

*Communication: The Nonverbal Agenda*, 32009, 1974, color, 30 mins. Pennsylvania State
University, Audiovisual Services, Special Services Building, University Park, PA 16802 (814-865-
6314). Discusses the importance of being able to recognize the nonverbal messages that one receives
and sends. Examples include interviews between an executive and three department heads, and a
male-female encounter in a bar. Describes how communication problems between administrators, as
well as manager-subordinate relationships, are worked out. From the *Behavior in Business* series. A
CRM production.

*I Guess I Got the Job*, 21745, 1975, color, 13 mins. Pennsylvania State University, Audiovisual
Services, Special Services Building, University Park, PA 16802 (814-865-6314). Two young men
are
interviewed for the same job. One is completely honest but shows a lack of confidence, while the
other adopts interests and attitudes that he thinks will make him look good. From the *Conflict and
Awareness* series.

*Judging Emotional Behavior*, ES-328, 24 mins. Indiana University, Audiovisual Center,
Bloomington, IN 47401. Presents the emotional responses of subjects to emotion-eliciting stories.
Shows the subjects first without sound, allowing the audience to judge the emotions being expressed;
then shows the same sequences with narration to allow the audience to determine the accuracy of
their judgements.

*Kinesics*, 80036, 1964, 73 mins. Pennsylvania State University, Audiovisual Services, Special Services
Building, University Park, PA 16802 (814-865-6314). Filmed lecture by Raymond L. Birdwhistell of
the Eastern Pennsylvania Psychiatric Institute on linguistic kinesics. Describes a system of
categorizing and defining facial expressions, posturing, and gestures in terms of communicative
meaning.

*Nonverbal Communication*, 21888, 1976, color, 22 mins. Pennsylvania State University, Audiovisual
Services, Special Services Building, University Park, PA 16802 (814-865-6314). Overview of
research and theory on communication through gesture, body posture, intonation, eye contact, and
facial expression. Interviews with Hall on interpersonal distance, Argyle on the equilibrium theory
of eye contact, Rosenthal on sex differences in the perception of nonverbal behavior, Akaret on

gestures and expressions in photographs, and Eibl-Eibesfeldt on biological programming.  From the *Social Psychology* series, Stanley Milgram.

---

## Overhead Transparencies
These appear at the back of this manual.

---

**2.1** *Correspondent Inference:  When Do We Infer the Traits of Others?*
**2.2** *Kelley's Theory of Causal Attribution*
**2.3** *Discounting and Augmenting:  Two Basic Principles of Causal Attribution*
**2.4** *Internal Attribution*
**2.5** *External Attribution*
**2.6** *Mixed Attributional Information*

---

## Critical Thinking/Essay Questions

---

1. Cite evidence to support the idea that humans show universal facial expressions and that they universally recognize the meaning of facial expressions.
2. How do we know whether someone is lying to us?
3. Summarize the role played by each of the following factors in determining whether we make a correspondent inference:
    a. The degree to which the person had free choice.
    b. The degree to which noncommon effects were produced by the behavior.
    c. Whether the behavior was high or low in social desirability.
4. Summarize how our attributions about someone's behavior are affected by consensus, consistency, and distinctiveness information.
5. Describe tactics used for impression management and indicate whether the tactics are likely to succeed.

---

## Sources for Lecture

---

Bower, B. (1985).  The face of emotion.  *Science News*, July 6, 128, pp. 12-13.  Explores the idea that facial expressions cause us to experience various feelings,  with particular attention to Robert Zajonc's resurrection of Waynbaum's (1906) theory.  Also discusses other theorists dealing with the facial feedback issue.
Driscoll, R. (1982).  Their own worst enemies, *Psychology Today*, July, pp. 45-49.  Examines the messages sent by severely self-critical people.
Sadalla, E., & Burroughs, J. (1981).  Profiles in eating:  Sexy vegetarians and other diet-based social

stereotypes. *Psychology Today*, October, pp. 51-57. Eating preferences are correlated with how people see themselves and how others see them.

Snyder, C. R. (1985). Excuses, excuses. *Psychology Today*, September, pp. 50-55. Discusses self-handicapping defensive attributions, as well as other ways that people preserve their self-image and reduce stress.

Trotter, R. J. (1983). Baby face. *Psychology Today*, August, pp. 14-20. Presents evidence that infants possess a rich repertoire of inborn emotional expressions.

## Professional Update: Current Articles from Professional Sources

Alicke, M. D., & Klotz, M. L. (1993). Social roles and social judgement: How an impression conveyed influences an impression formed. *Personality and Social Psychology Bulletin, 19,* 185-194. Subjects instructed to enact the role of introvert saw their partner as more extraverted, while those instructed to enact the role of extravert saw the partner as more introverted. Actual behavior of the partner was held constant; thus role enactment itself was the basis for the judgment of the partner.

Ambady, N., & Rosenthal, R. (1993). Half a minute: Predicting teacher evaluations from thin slices of behavior and physical attractiveness. *Journal of Personality and Social Psychology, 64,* 431-441. Very brief (thirty seconds and less) silent video clips of college teachers' nonverbal behavior significantly predicted end-of-the-semester student evaluations of teachers. These results have important implications for research on impression formation.

Bassili, J. N. (1993). Procedural efficiency and the spontaneity of trait inference. *Personality and Social Psychology Bulletin, 19,* 200-205. How subjects encode information about a target has been shown to be important in determination of trait inferences. Practice with various kinds of inferences influences the spontaneity of further trait inferences.

Bond, Jr., C. F., et al. (1992). Fishy-looking liars: Deception judgment from expectancy violation. *Journal of Personality and Social Psychology, 63,* 969-977. How do we determine that others are lying? This study says we perceive deception when others display behavior that violates normative expectations.

Buck, R., Losow, J. Il, Murphy, M. M., & Costanzo, P. (1992). Social facilitation and inhibition of emotional expression and communication. *Journal of Personality and Social Psychology, 63,* 962-968. How accurately can we tell the type of slide viewed by another person on the basis of his/her facial expression? How is accuracy changed if the person displaying the expression is with a partner who is also viewing the slides? How is accuracy changed if the subject rating the expression is alone versus with another rater? Buck, et al. answer these questions.

Fincham, F. D., & Bradbury, T. N. (1993). Marital satisfaction, depression, and attributions: A longitudinal analysis. *Journal of Personality and Social Psychology, 64,* 442-452. Relates attributions made by partners in a marital relationship to satisfaction in the relationship. Attributions made for negative partner behavior seem to be particularly important.

Gonzales, M. H., & Meyers, S. A. (1993). "Your mother would like me": Self-presentation in the personal ads of heterosexual and homosexual men and women. *Personality and Social Psychology Bulletin, 19,* 131-142. Researchers examined self-presentational strategies in personal ads of heterosexual and homosexual men and women and coded the ways in which attractiveness, financial security, expressiveness, sincerity, and sexual activities were mentioned.  Advantages of using personal ads to understand self-presentation are discussed.

Keltner, D., Locke K. D., & Audrain, P. C. (1993).  The influence of attributions on the relevance of negative feelings to personal satisfaction.  *Personality and Social Psychology Bulletin, 19,* 21-29.  Negative feelings caused by specific events may become incorporated into global self-judgements.  We can understand the degree to which this takes place examining attributions made about the feelings.

*Related Readings:*  The following selections from *Readings in Social Psychology:  General, Classic, and Contemporary Selections*, 3rd Edition, by Wayne Lesko (Allyn and Bacon, 1997) accompany this chapter:

Studies point to power of nonverbal signals.  (1986, April 8).  *The New York Times.*  Nonverbal cues provide influential information, often so subtle, they may remain outside of our conscious awareness.  Even when unintended, nonverbal cues can influence peoples' perceptions and their behaviors.  (Article 4)

Kelley, H. (1950).  The warm-cold variable in first impressions of persons.  Students were presented with two different descriptions of a substitute instructor.  Some students were told their instructor was a "rather warm" person, others that he was "rather cold."  Changing this one adjective affected ratings of the instructor and behavior toward him.  (Article 5)

Bell, S. T., Kuriloff, P. J., & Lottes, I. (1994).  Victims of rape often have the double burden of not only being the victim of a terrible crime but also being held at least partially responsible for the crime having been committed in the first place.  Subjects rating vignettes depicting either a date rape or a stranger rape situation.  Male students blamed the victim to a greater extent than did female students and consistently attributed more blame to the victim in date rape situations than they did in stranger rape situations.  Implications for rape prevention efforts are also discussed.  (Article 6)

# Chapter 3

# Social Cognition: Thinking about Others and the Social World

## Chapter-at-a-Glance

| CHAPTER OUTLINE | INSTRUCTION IDEAS | SUPPLEMENTS* |
|---|---|---|
| **I. Schemas and Prototypes: Mental Frameworks for Holding-- and Using--Social Information**<br>• Types of Schemas: Persons, Roles, and Events<br><br>• The Impact of Schemas on Social Cognition: Attention, Encoding, Retrieval<br><br>• **Social Psychology: On the Applied Side**   Prototypes and Safe Sex: Living Up (or Down) to the Images in Our Minds | Learning Objectives 3.1 to 3.4<br><br>Discussion Topic 4<br><br>Activity 3.1 (Handout)<br><br>Critical Thinking Question 1 | Test Bank Questions 3.1 to 3.18<br><br>Transparency 3.1 |
| **II. Heuristics: Mental Shortcuts in Social Cognition**<br>• Representativeness: Judging by Resemblance<br><br>• Availability: What Comes to Mind First? | Learning Objectives 3.5 to 3.8<br><br>Discussion Topics 1 and 3<br><br>Activities 3.2 - 3.4<br><br>Critical Thinking Questions 2, 3 | Test Bank Questions 3.19 to 3.44<br><br>Transparency 3.2 |
| **III. Potential Sources of Error in Social Cognition**<br>• Rational versus Intuitive Processing<br><br>• Dealing with Inconsistent Information<br><br>• The Optimistic Bias for Task Completion<br><br>• Automatic Vigilance: Noticing the Negative<br><br>• The Potential Costs of Thinking Too Much<br><br>• Counterfactual Thinking and the Experience of Regret<br><br>• Magical Thinking<br><br>• Social Cognition: A Word of Optimism | Learning Objectives 3.9 to 3.16<br><br>Discussion Topic 2<br><br>Activity 3.5 (Handout)<br><br>Critical Thinking Question 4 | Test Bank Questions 3.45 to 3.88<br><br>Readings:<br>- Lesko 7, Thinking Too Much<br>- Lesko 9, Magical Thinking |
| **IV. Affect and Cognition: How Thought Shapes Feelings and Feelings Shape Thought**<br>• The Nature of Emotion: Contrasting Views and Recent Advances<br><br>• Connections Between Affect and Cognition<br><br>• The Affect Infusion Model<br><br>• **Social Diversity: A Critical Analysis**   Trust as a Cognitive Bias: A Cross-National Study | Learning Objectives 3.17 to 3.24<br><br>Critical Thinking Questions 5, 6 | Test Bank Questions 3.89 to 3.140<br><br>Reading:<br>- Lesko 8, Determinants of Emotional State<br><br>Transparencies 3.3, 3.4 |

*See Audiovisual Suggestions

# 3

## Social Cognition: Thinking about Others And the Social World

---

### Chapter Outline: Getting the Overall Picture

---

# Learning Objectives
### After studying this chapter, students should be able to:

**3.1** Define the concepts of schema and prototype, and give an example illustrating each concept.

**3.2** Understand person schemas, role schemas, and scripts.

**3.3** Examine how schemas influence attention, encoding, and retrieval of information.

**3.4** Explain how the favorability of one's prototype regarding pregnant teenagers and one's perceived similarity to these persons is related to willingness to engage in risky sexual behavior.

**3.5** Describe the basic nature of heuristics, indicating how they allow us to reduce cognitive effort and to avoid information overload.

**3.6** Describe the representativeness heuristic, and indicate how use of this heuristic sometimes leads us to commit the base-rate fallacy.

**3.7** Summarize how our judgments regarding others are affected by the availability heuristic.

**3.8** Define the false consensus effect, and indicate why it occurs.

**3.9** Describe research that demonstrates priming, automatic priming, and spontaneous trait inferences.

**3.10** Compare rational thinking and intuitive thinking when subjects had to choose one of the bowls of jelly beans in the Denes-Raj and Epstein (1994) study.

**3.11** Examine the degree to which unexpected information grabs our attention and influences later social judgments.

**3.12** Summarize research by Buehler et al. on the planning fallacy, noting subjects' thinking patterns during planning and their attributions concerning past failures.

**3.13** Describe the automatic vigilance effect, including the face-in-the crowd effect.

**3.14** Based on the Wilson and Schooler (1991) study, indicate how "thinking too much" while rating jams or rating courses lowered the accuracy of ratings.

**3.15** Give examples of counterfactual thinking in response to negative outcomes. Secondly, examine the experience of regret over actions performed vs. actions we didn't do.

**3.16** Describe various forms of magical thinking, including the law of contagion, the law of similarity, and the possibility of inviting catastrophes by thinking about them.

**3.17** Summarize and compare the views of emotion expressed by the Cannon-Bard theory, the James-Lange theory, and Schacter's 2-factor theory.

**3.18** Describe the facial feedback hypothesis, along with research findings relevant to the hypothesis.

**3.19** Explain how being in a happy mood affected each of the following: a) social cognition in the Mayer and Hanson (1995) study; b) creativity in the Estrade et al. (1995) study.

**3.20** Summarize research supporting the conclusion that the effects of positive and negative affect are not always simply opposite in nature.

**3.21** Describe the four ways in which our cognition can influence our current feelings and our moods.

**3.22** According to Forgas' (1994) affect infusion model, explain the two mechanisms through which our feelings influence social thought.

**3.23** Describe circumstances in the Forgas (1994) study where affective states influenced cognition through priming and circumstances where affective states influenced cognition through heuristics.

**3.24** Compare Japanese and Americans in terms of levels of trust and levels of assurance shown in personal relationships.

# Discussion Topics and Questions

## 1. Information Overload

Social cognition is greatly influenced by information overload. Because we are bombarded with thousands of stimuli, it is argued, we need to be efficient in screening, sorting, and storing social information. But an alternative view is that humans simply are not very good at remembering the content of information that is presented to them. Jacoby and Hoyer (1982) had subjects view a thirty-second videotape in U.S. shopping malls and then had them answer twelve true/false questions pertaining to the videotape. Despite the facts that the videotape was viewed under ideal conditions, that the tape was of short duration, and that the testing was done immediately after viewing, only 3.5 percent of the respondents answered all twelve questions correctly. Could it be that what we remember is simply not an accurate representation of what we see? (Jacoby and Hoyer's article appears in *Journal of Marketing, 46,* 12-16.)

## 2. Influence of Drastic Cases in the News

Watch the news for reports of extreme acts of behavior. Can you find evidence that news analysts overemphasize drastic cases in reporting the news? Does reporting of acts of terrorism, for instance, lead us to a distorted perception of the views of the average resident of the terrorists' home countries?

## 3. Homosexuality and Illusory Correlations

An interesting, although perhaps controversial, way to introduce the ideas of covariation and illusory correlation is to examine the relationship between homosexuality and other behaviors. A paper presented by Paul Cameron at the Midwestern Psychological Association meeting in May 1983 argued that homosexuality is disproportionately associated with murder. Cameron based his conclusion on an examination of sexually related mass murders in the United States. Another relationship that is "understood to be true" among some fire investigators is that arson is associated with homosexuality. Consider these examples in contrasting the difference between actual covariation and illusory correlation.

## 4. Ageist Schemas

People have fairly detailed conceptions of the characteristics possessed by various groups. For example, we possess a well-developed schema for the elderly. One aspect of this schema is a notion that there are specific occupations appropriate for elderly. There is evidence that some occupations are age typed. Prepare a list of occupations and ask students to rate them for the most appropriate age of a person in that occupation. What are the processes underlying judgments of age appropriateness for individual occupations: Do people use the availability heuristic; that is, do they search their memories for instances of incumbents of various ages: Do people consider the importance of various work skills? What other factors do they consider? Another aspect of this schema is our view of how a grandmother looks and acts. Brewer, Dull, and Lui (1981) published and interesting article in the *Journal of Personality and Social Psychology (41,* 656-670) in which they explored the traits attributed to a grandmother.

# Learning Activities:  Classroom Exercises/Demonstrations

## 3.1  Students' Perceptions of Their Instructor

This classroom exercise devised by Robin L. Lashley (Tuscarawas Campus, Kent State University), elicits students' perceptions of their instructor in order to demonstrate basic cognitive processes and biases that often render such interpretations inaccurate.  This exercise is most effective if conducted fairly early in the semester, before students have too much information on which to base their judgments.

Students fill-out a two-part inventory.  The first part contains a number of multiple-choice questions requiring students to make judgments regarding the instructor's identifying characteristics (specific information will need to be customized on the questionnaire).  The second section contains a list of 20 personality traits that the student must indicate which resemble the instructor's definition of self.

Students make two copies of their ratings; one copy is retained and the other is collected for a tabular summary.  In this way, anonymity is maintained.  The following principles of person perception may be considered when discussing the data with the class.

1.    Agreements between instructor's and students' judgments demonstrate successful person perception.
2.    Stereotyped thinking may be revealed by students' responses to Section 1.
3.    Instructor can point out how students' first impressions may have influenced selective perception of instructor's subsequent behavior.
4.    The actor-observer effect can be demonstrated by the pattern of responses to Section 2. The "it depends" responses usually exceed that of the students.  Also, the fundamental attribution error can be discussed in relation to this section.
5.    When there is a discrepancy between the instructor's judgment and the majority of the students' judgement regarding a particular trait; discussion regarding validity of self-perceptions versus others' perceptions may follow.  Perhaps a self-serving bias may appear.
6.    Finally, implicit beliefs about people and the causes of behavior may become apparent throughout the discussion of this activity.

***NOTE: The following Handout may need to be customized.**

**HANDOUT FOR ACTIVITY #3.1**
**Student's Perceptions**

My Perceptions of My Instructor

Part I. Respond to the following questions based on your personal impressions of your instructor.

1.      My instructor is _____ years old.

        a. 24   b. 29   c. 34   d. 39

2.      My instructor's marital status is _____.

        a. married     b. single      c. divorced    d. widowed

3.      My instructor has _____ children.

        a. 0    b. 1    c. 2    d. 4

4.      My instructor was born and raised in the state of _____.

        a. New York  b. Illinois      c. Georgia      d. California

5.      My instructor has _____ siblings.

        a. 0    b. 1    c. 2    d. 4

6.      My instructor's father was a(n) _____.

        a. landscaper  b. farmer      c. doctor       d. engineer

7.      My instructor's favorite color is _____.

        a. blue        b. pink        c. green       d. yellow       e. red        f. purple

8.      My instructor's favorite kind of music is _____.

        a. classical   b. jazz        c. country     d. rock n' roll

9.      My instructor's favorite hobbies include (circle all that apply):

        sewing         skiing         piano playing        painting        sailing

        antiquing              going to parties      basketball      needlepoint

Copyright © 1997 by Allyn and Bacon

10. My instructor's ideal vacation would be:

   a. skiing in Colorado  b. sunbathing on a Caribbean island

   c. taking a guided tour of Europe  d. gambling in Las Vegas

11. In high school, my instructor was (circle all that apply):

   shy and insecure  a cheerleader  class valedictorian

   president of the student government  a social butterfly

Part II.  For each of the following traits, check either "Yes" (this trait describes my instructor), "No" (this trait does not describe my instructor), or "It depends" (It depends on the situation my instructor is in).

|  | Yes | No | It depends |
|---|---|---|---|
| organized | | | |
| liberal | | | |
| outgoing | | | |
| assertive | | | |
| undependable | | | |
| shy | | | |
| nervous | | | |
| smart | | | |
| talkative | | | |
| stubborn | | | |
| ambitious | | | |
| confident | | | |
| competent | | | |
| cautious | | | |
| adventurous | | | |
| sloppy | | | |
| optimistic | | | |
| moody | | | |
| punctual | | | |
| short-tempered | | | |

Copyright © 1997 by Allyn and Bacon

The chapter summarizes a variety of biases that contaminate our thinking. A useful way to introduce this chapter is to have students experience some of these biases first-hand. The brief exercises that follow introduce some of these biases. You may want to present these to the class early in your consideration of social cognition, as some of the examples are presented in the text.

### 3.2 The Availability Heuristic

We often use ease of recall as a basis for judging the frequency of events. Just because we can more readily recall one category of events, however, does not necessarily mean that the category is more frequent. Pose the following question to the class: Does the letter k appear more often as the first letter of a word or as the third letter? Most people judge that k appears more often at the beginning of a word, but in fact k is three times more likely to appear as the third letter. Why the error? The reason seems to be that our relative ease of recall words beginning with k convinces us that they are also more frequent.

### 3.3 The Representativeness Heuristic.

Tell the students that you have a series of thumbnail descriptions of one hundred individuals, thirty of whom are engineers and seventy of whom are lawyers. From this sample, the following description has been drawn at random:

John is a thirty-nine-year-old man. He is married and has no children. A man of high ability and motivation, he promises to be quite successful in his field. He is well liked by his colleagues. What is the probability that John is a lawyer?

People generally will respond to this question by saying it is fifty-fifty as to whether he is a lawyer or an engineer. What they have done is ignore the base-rate information and instead relied upon useless anecdotal information. (The probability that John is a lawyer is 70%.)

### 3.4 The False Consensus Effect

To illustrate this effect, you need to have students respond to some informational questions. An obvious source is exam questions. Tell the students whether they answered the particular question right or wrong. Then have them indicate the percentage of students in the class whom they believe correctly answered that particular question. For the questions they answered correctly, students should overestimate the percentage of correct responses. For the questions they answered wrong, they should underestimate the percentage.

### 3.5 The Self-Reference Effect

Chapter 3 discusses the self-reference effect, and it is also summarized in a transparency at the end of this manual. You can have the students do an exercise that demonstrates the effect rather convincingly. The exercise can be done either in class with the instructor serving as the experimenter or outside of class with students serving as the experimenters. Half of the subjects are instructed to read a list of trait adjectives and decide whether each of the words describes themselves. The other half of the subjects reads the same list of trait adjectives and indicates whether each of the words contains an e. After the subjects have gone through the entire list of adjectives, they are given a surprise recall test.

You will find that people who have gone through the list deciding whether the word described the self will recall more of the words than people who simply decide whether each word has an e. This is because the words related to self are processed more deeply than the other words. When I do this exercise in class I find the students are impressed by the analogy between the exercise and their own study habits. Oftentimes studying becomes an exercise of "just reading words." To learn material, a student must process it deeply; one way to accomplish this is to be able to relate it to something already well known.  What is better known than the self?

A list of thirteen trait adjectives to use in conducting the exercise is found below or in your students' Study Guide.  Two identical lists are presented on the assumption that your students may want to gather data from friends by having one person do the test under each instructional set.  You can then have the students bring their data to class and combine the data to see whether you have demonstrated the self-reference effect.

## HANDOUT FOR ACTIVITY #3.5
### The Self-Reference Effect

INSTRUCTIONS: Read each of the following words, and indicate whether the word has an "e" in it by circling either "yes" or "no."

| | | |
|---|---|---|
| aggressive | yes | no |
| intelligent | yes | no |
| sociable | yes | no |
| superstitious | yes | no |
| quiet | yes | no |
| sentimental | yes | no |
| bold | yes | no |
| athletic | yes | no |
| persistent | yes | no |
| trusting | yes | no |
| sensitive | yes | no |
| energetic | yes | no |
| shy | yes | no |

## HANDOUT FOR ACTIVITY #3.5A
### The Self-Reference Effect

INSTRUCTIONS: Read each of the following words, and indicate whether the word describes you by circling either "yes" or "no."

| | | |
|---|---|---|
| aggressive | yes | no |
| intelligent | yes | no |
| sociable | yes | no |
| superstitious | yes | no |
| quiet | yes | no |
| sentimental | yes | no |
| bold | yes | no |
| athletic | yes | no |
| persistent | yes | no |
| trusting | yes | no |
| sensitive | yes | no |
| energetic | yes | no |
| shy | yes | no |

Copyright © 1997 by Allyn and Bacon

# Overhead Transpariences
These appear at the back of this manual.

**3.1** *Self-Schemata and Memory*
**3.2** *Mental Simulations and Sympathy for Victims*
**3.3** *Mood and Social Judgments: A Field Study*
**3.4** *How Cognition Sometimes Shapes Affect*

# Audiovisual Suggestions

### Allyn and Bacon Videos

*Cognitive Processes.* Explores the higher mental processes--reasoning, planning, and problem solving-- and why the "cognitive revolution:" is attracting such diverse investigators, from philosophers to computer scientists. (Discovering Psychology Series, On Tape #5)

*Communication: Social Cognition and Attribution*, videotape, 28.5 mins. To obtain this tape, consult your Allyn and Bacon sales representative. Dramatization is used to generate an exchange between Robert A. Baron and Margaret Clark on the principles of social cognition.

*Remembering and Forgetting.* A look at the complex process of memory: how images, ideas, language --even physical actions, sounds, and smells--are translated into codes, represented in memory, and retrieved when needed. (Discovering Psychology Series, On Tape #5)

### Other Videos and Films

*Information Processing*, 31761, 1971, color, 29 mins. Pennsylvania State University, Audiovisual Services, Special Services Building, University Park, PA 16802 (814-865-6314). Psychologist Donald A. Norman and comedian David Steinberg used a cocktail party to reveal basic principles and far-reaching ramifications of human information processing. Includes short- and long-term memory, the Stroop phenomenon, mnemonics, retrieval strategies, and problem solving. From the *Psychology Today* series. A CRM production.

*Judgment and Decision Making*, Number 11 in this 1990 videotape series, 30 mins. The Annenborg Project, Holt, Rinehart & Winston, contact Lee Sutherlin, Marketing Manager (817-334-7632). A look at the process of making judgments and decisions, how and why people make good and bad judgments, and the psychology of risk taking.

# Critical Thinking/Essay Questions

1.  Explain how person schemas, role schemas, and scripts can make an impact on attention, encoding, and retrieval.
2.  What is the representativeness heuristic, and how is it related to the base-rate fallacy?
3.  Describe the false consensus effect, and give a reason why it occurs.

**4.** Summarize how counterfactual thinking occurs when negative outcomes follow unusual actions.
**5.** Describe the facial feedback hypothesis, and summarize evidence that supports the hypothesis.
**6.** How does our current affective state influence how we process social information?

## Sources for Lecture

Allman, W. F. (1985). Staying alive in the 20th century. *Science '85*, October, pp. 34-41. Compares how the experts' assessments of various risks in everyday life are related to the assessment of the general public. Provides excellent examples of the irrationality of human thought.

Langer, E. J. (1982). Automated lives. *Psychology Today*, April, pp. 60-71. Langer discusses the tendency to engage in "mindlessness"--to do things and to make decisions without really thinking.

LeBrecque, M. (1980). On making sounder judgments. *Psychology Today*, June, pp. 32-42. Provides a review of some common errors in human thinking and offers guidelines for minimizing such errors.

Offir, C. W. (1975). Floundering in fallacy: Seven quick ways to kid yourself. *Psychology Today*, April, pp. 66-68. Discusses common fallacies in human thinking.

## Professional Update: Current Articles from Professional Sources

Rubin, D. C. (1975). The subtle deceiver: Recalling your past, *Psychology Today*, September, pp. 38-46. Our ability to remember the past details of our lives is hampered by our present lives and our beliefs about ourselves.

Slovic, P., Fischhoff, B., & Lichtenstein, S. (1980). Risky assumptions. *Psychology Today,* June, pp. 44-48. Presents examples of how errors in human thinking get us into trouble. Focuses especially on the over-confidence and vividness effects.

Bourgeois, M. J., Horowitz, I. A., & Lee, L. F. Effects of technicality and access to trial transcripts on verdicts and information processing in a civil trial. *Personality and Social Psychology Bulletin, 19,* 220-227. How do jurors deal with information that is too complex? By falling back on simplifying, heuristic devices. The study examined jurors' use of a readily available counterfactual heuristic when highly technical evidence was presented. Access to trial transcripts and blocking use of the heuristic led jurors to process information more systematically.

Bugental, D. B., et al. (1993). Social cognitions as organizers of autonomic and affective responses to social challenge. *Journal of Personality and Social Psychology, 64,* 94-103. Researchers presented computer-simulated children who behaved responsively or unresponsively on a computer game. Women raters first filled out a "Parent Attribution Test" to measure where they perceived the locus of control to reside. The researchers studied how these women responded autonomically and affectively to these "children."

MacLeod, C., & Campbell, L. (1992). Memory accessibility and probability judgements: An experimental evaluation of the availability heuristic. *Journal of Personality and Social Psychology, 63,* 890-902. Procedures that reduce the latency of response for past events also are found to increase subjects' estimates of future probability.

Riemann, R., & Angletner, A. (1993). Inferring interpersonal traits from behavior: Act prototypicality vs. conceptual similarity of trait concepts. *Journal of Personality and Social Psychology, 63,*

356-364. Subjects were presented with six fictitious persons about whom they had to make trait ratings. Two models of the process underlying these trait ratings are investigated.

Showers, C. (1992). Evaluatively integrative thinking about characteristics of the self. *Personality and Social Psychology Bulletin, 18,* 719-729. A comparison was made of persons who think of themselves by clustering positive and negative information together. Persons who generated evaluatively integrated information had higher self-esteem.

Slugoski, B. R., Shields, H. A., & Dawson, K. A. (1993). Relation of conditional reasoning to heuristic processing. *Personality and Social Psychology Bulletin, 19,* 158-166. Two main factors that seem to be involved in reasoning were discovered. The factors correspond to an availability and representativeness dimension.

Wegner, D. M., & Erber, R. (1992). The hyperaccessibility of suppressed thoughts. *Journal of Personality and Social Psychology, 63,* 903-912. Subjects who try to suppress thinking about a target word end up having greater access to the word. Thoughts we try to eliminate from attention remain remarkably near the surface and ready to return to consciousness with minimal prompting.

*Related Readings:* The following selections from *Readings in Social Psychology: General, Classic, and Contemporary Selections,* 3rd Edition, by Wayne Lesko (Allyn and Bacon, 1997) accompany this chapter:

Gladwell, M. (March 4, 1991). "Matters of choice muddled by thought". People asked to analyze their decisions tend to act differently, often for the worse. Gladwell considers cases where "thinking too much" interferes with decision making. There are, he asserts, decisions where nonverbal intuition is "correct" and where verbal reasoning hinders the quality of decision. Research-based examples are provided. (Article 7)

Schachter, S., & Singer, J. (1962). "Cognitive, social, and physiological determinants of emotional state". The question of what determines subjective emotional states is addressed. "Emotion" is partly due to physiological arousal, but without a cognitive label to attach to the arousal, the authors argued that no specific emotion will be experienced. (Article 8)

Keinan, G. (1994). When under high-stress conditions, are we more or less likely to engage in magical thinking? According to Giora Keinan's research with Israeli citizens during the Gulf War, magical thinking was more likely to emerge among individuals experiencing high stress levels. Those with low tolerance of ambiguity had a higher likelihood of this characteristic. Finally, personal control coping strategies were also discussed. (Article 9)

# Chapter 4

# Attitudes: Evaluating the Social World

## Chapter-at-a-Glance

| CHAPTER OUTLINE | INSTRUCTION IDEAS | SUPPLEMENTS* |
|---|---|---|
| *I. Forming Attitudes: How We Come to Hold the Views We Do*<br>• Social Learning: Acquiring Attitudes from Others<br>• Social Comparison and Attitude Formation<br>• Genetic Factors: Some Surprising Recent Findings | Learning Objectives 4.1 to 4.5<br>Discussion Topics 2, 4, 5<br>Activity 4.2<br>Critical Thinking Question 1 | Test Bank Questions 4.1 to 4.33 |
| *II. Do Attitudes Influence Behavior? And If So, When and How?*<br>• **Cornerstones of Social Psychology** Attitudes versus Actions: "No, We Don't Admit That Kind of Person-- Unless They Show Up at the Door!"<br>• When Do Attitudes Influence Behavior? Specificity, Strength, Accessibility, and Other Factors<br>• How Do Attitudes Influence Behavior? | Learning Objectives 4.6 to 4.11<br><br>Discussion Topic 5<br><br>Critical Thinking Question 2 | Test Bank Questions 4.34 to 4.72 |
| *III. Persuasion: The Process of Changing Attitudes*<br>• Persuasion: The Traditional Approach<br>• Persuasion: The Cognitive Approach<br>• Other Factors Affecting Persuasion: Attitude Functions, Reciprocity, and Message Framing | Learning Objectives 4.12 to 4.18<br><br>Discussion Topic 3<br><br>Activities 4.1, 4.3, 4.4, 4.5<br><br>Critical Thinking Questions 3, 4 | Test Bank Questions 4.73 to 4.106<br><br>Reading:<br>- Lesko 10, American Values Test |
| *IV. When Attitude Change Fails: Resistance to Persuasion*<br>• Reactance: Protecting Our Personal Freedom<br>• Forewarning: Prior Knowledge of Persuasive Intent<br>• Selective Avoidance | Learning Objectives 4.19 to 4.21 | Test Bank Questions 4.107 to 4.124 |
| *V. Cognitive Dissonance: How We Sometimes Change Our Own Attitudes*<br>• Cognitive Dissonance: What It Is and How It's Reduced<br>• Dissonance and Attitude Change: The Effects of Forced Compliance<br>• **Social Psychology: On the Applied Side** Dissonance, Hypocrisy, and Safe Sex<br>• **Social Diversity: A Critical Analysis** Attitudes and Economic Growth: A Cross-National Study | Learning Objectives 4.22 to 4.28<br><br>Discussion Topic 1<br><br>Critical Thinking Question 5 | Test Bank Questions 4.125 to 4.155<br><br>Readings:<br>- Lesko 11, Cognitive Dissonance<br>- Lesko 12, Cognitive Dissonance and Regret: An Alternative Hypothesis<br><br>Transparencies 4.1-4.4 |

*See Audiovisual Suggestions

# 4 Attitudes: Evaluating the Social World

## Chapter Outline: Getting the Overall Picture

      1.     Dissonance and Less-Leads-to-More Effect
  C.    Social Psychology: On the Applied Side: Dissonance, Hypocrisy, and Safe Sex
  D.    Social Diversity: A Critical Analysis: Attitudes and Economic Growth: A Cross-National Study

---

## Learning Objectives
### After studying this chapter, students should be able to:

---

**4.1**   Examine the textbook's definition of "attitude" and note reasons why attitudes are important.

**4.2**   Describe evidence to support the idea that attitudes can be formed via classical conditioning, including subliminal conditioning and conditioning of arm flexion vs. arm extension movements.

**4.3**   Explain how particular attitudes can be strengthened or weakened via instrumental conditioning and also through modeling.

**4.4**   Explain how the social comparison process accounted for the attitudes Canadians formed toward the fictitious Camarians.

**4.5**   Examine attitude similarity among identical and nonidentical twins, and describe the significance and validity of these results.

**4.6**   Describe the attitude-behavior inconsistency observed in the LaPiere (1934) study.

**4.7**   Consider how the following aspects of the situation are related to whether people will act on their attitudes: a) norms; b) time pressures; c) having chosen to enter attitudinally-relevant situations.

**4.8**   Consider how these aspects of attitudes are related to whether people will act on the attitudes: a) formed by direct experience; b) strong; c) important; d) serves self-interest; e) fosters social identification; f) possesses value relevance; g) accessible; and h) has specificity.

**4.9**   Explain why attitudes held by low self-monitors more accurately predict their behavior than attitudes held by high self-monitors.

**4.10**   According to the theory of planned behavior, describe the three factors that determine whether persons with the opportunity to engage in careful thought will act consistently with their intentions.

**4.11**   In contrast to the reasoned mode mentioned above, consider how attitudes influence behavior when the person must act quickly and spontaneously.

**4.12**   Summarize the traditional approach to persuasion, and know the eight classic research findings reviewed by the textbook.

**4.13**   Contrast persuasion that takes place on the central route vs. the peripheral route, according to the elaboration likelihood model.

**4.14**   Explain how the persuasion process is influenced by the relevance of a message and by the presence of a distraction.

**4.15**   Describe In what three ways attitude change on the central route has been shown to be more lasting than attitude change on the peripheral route.

**4.16**   Examine the idea that attitudes can serve different functions for the person holding them.

**4.17**   Describe how reciprocity produces "public" attitude change.

**4.18**   Explain when a positively-framed message is more influential, and when a negatively-framed message more influential.

**4.19**   Understand how "reactance" explains the fact that we often show negative attitude change when with hard-sell persuasion attempts.

**4.20**   Describe why we are better able to resist persuasive messages when they are preceded by forewarning of persuasive intent.

**4.21** Describe the roles played by selective avoidance and selective exposure in helping us resist persuasion.

**4.22** Define cognitive dissonance, and describe three strategies people can use to get rid of dissonance.

**4.23** Explain how research by Elliot and Devine (1994) supports the view that dissonance is unpleasant and that the discomfort of dissonance often motivates attitude change.

**4.24** Explain when subjects use trivialization as the mode to reduce their dissonance, and when they actually chance their attitudes toward the attitudinal issue.

**4.25** Describe the attitude change that occurs following forced compliance.

**4.26** Indicate why the less-leads-to-more effect occurs, and know the three circumstances that must exist for this effect to happen.

**4.27** Describe how the hypocrisy procedure was used to get subjects to engage in safe sex.

**4.28** Summarize the relationship between economic attitudes held by individuals and the rate of economic growth and gross national product of nations.

---

## Discussion Topics and Questions

---

### 1. Commitment to an Action: An alternative to dissonance theory

As an alternative to dissonance theory, Charles Kiesler has proposed that the reason we change our attitudes in the direction of counterattitudinal behaviors is that we become committed when we perform an action. Whereas dissonance theory is concerned only with the effects created by our counterattitudinal behaviors, Kiesler has proposed that acting in a manner consistent with what we believe can also have important consequences for our attitudes. Dissonance theory considers attitude-consistent actions irrelevant because they do not arouse any dissonance. Kiesler's ideas are presented in a 1971 book, *The Psychology of Commitment,* (Academic Press).

As in dissonance theory, Kiesler has proposed that only some kinds of behavioral acts will result in a person's becoming committed. Some of the factors determining one's degree of commitment are as follows:

1. *The explicitness of the behavior.* Publicly expressing an opinion is a stronger commitment than expressing your views to a stranger.

2. *The importance of the behavior.* Expressing an opinion to someone important is a stronger commitment than expressing your views to a stranger.

3. *The degree of irrevocability.* Expressing an opinion in a written statement is a stronger commitment than expressing your views orally.

4. *Number of actions.* Expressing an opinion over and over again is a stronger commitment than expressing it only once.

5. *Degree of volition.* Expressing an opinion of your own free will is a stronger commitment than expressing it because someone makes you do it.

6. *Effort.* Going to a lot of trouble to express an opinion is a stronger commitment than expressing it easily.

### 2. Attitude Development

Have the students write down their attitudes on some important topic, and also have them list the people and experiences that contributed to the development of this attitude. You may want to direct their thinking toward some important issue, such as homosexuality, abortion, or racial prejudice, so that the entire class will be thinking about the same issue. After the students have made their lists, introduce the factors that social psychologists have concluded to be important in attitude formation. Do the students have examples of classical conditioning, instrumental conditioning, modeling, and direct experience that they can relate to the class discussion?

**3.  Credibility of Political Figures**

Analyze the credibility of current political figures. This is especially relevant in a presidential election year. Analyze the contribution of expertise, attractiveness, similarity, trust-worthiness, and so on. What is the basis for attributing each of these characteristics to a political figure?

**4.  Construct an Attitude Questionnaire**

A time-consuming but potentially valuable exercise is to have the class construct an attitude questionnaire. During one class period have the students write a set of items relevant to a particular topic. A large number of items (perhaps one hundred) is needed. Next, select the best forty or so items and have the students ascertain their friends' attitudes on these items. Determine which items best discriminate between people who are above or below average on the measured attitude. (The topic should be one that is interesting to students. Allow them to choose the topic from among women's rights, fraternities, raising tuition, or any other issue that is important to them.)

**5.    Public vs. Private Attitudes Regarding Sexually Motivated Behavior**

Lewittes and Simmons published an article in 1975 suggesting that we often engage in impression management when performing a sexually motivated behavior. They suggest that one reason people say one thing and do another is that they sometimes must do things public that they consider embarrassing. For example, some people find it embarrassing to buy contraceptives at the pharmacy counter. Likewise, college students buying *Playboy, Penthouse,* and similar magazines at a university bookstore show discomfort. Lewittes and Simmons found that those buying magazines such as *Playboy* purchased more additional items, such as other magazines or candy, and more often asked for a bag for their purchases. Finally, a Dallas cable television franchise conducted a survey to find out what kinds of services people wanted and didn't want. Adult programming was rated very low in the survey, but 60 percent of the subscribers signed up for the adult channel. When asked to make public statements for the survey, most disapproved the sex and nudity of the adult channel; when they could privately sign up for it, most did so. (Lewittes and Simmons's article appears in the *Journal of Social Psychology, 96,* 39-44.)

---

## Learning Activities:  Classroom Exercises/Demonstrations

---

## 4.1  Trustworthiness of Occupations

Ryckman and Sherman (1974) asked college students to rate the trustworthiness of members of a variety of occupations on a scale of 1 to 4; a rating of 1 meant most trustworthy, while a rating of 4 meant least trustworthy. Your students can repeat the procedure conducted by Ryckman and Sherman (published in *Journal of Applied Social Psychology, 4,* 351-364). Having rated these occupations, ask the students to explain the basis of their judgments. What characteristics do they associate with trustworthiness? What is the reason for some occupations being rated low in trustworthiness? The occupations to be rated are found below and in the study guide.

## HANDOUT FOR ACTIVITY #4.1

## RATINGS OF TRUSTWORTHINESS OF OCCUPATIONS

| | | Rating | | |
|---|---|---|---|---|
| Occupation | Most Trustworthy | | | Least Trustworthy |
| U.S. Army generals | 1 | 2 | 3 | 4 |
| College professor | 1 | 2 | 3 | 4 |
| Lawyers | 1 | 2 | 3 | 4 |
| TV repairmen | 1 | 2 | 3 | 4 |
| Plumbers | 1 | 2 | 3 | 4 |
| Used car salesmen | 1 | 2 | 3 | 4 |
| Corporate executives | 1 | 2 | 3 | 4 |
| Clergy | 1 | 2 | 3 | 4 |
| Newspaper columnists | 1 | 2 | 3 | 4 |
| Physicians | 1 | 2 | 3 | 4 |
| Police officers | 1 | 2 | 3 | 4 |
| Dentists | 1 | 2 | 3 | 4 |
| Judges | 1 | 2 | 3 | 4 |
| Auto repairmen | 1 | 2 | 3 | 4 |
| High school teachers | 1 | 2 | 3 | 4 |
| Politicians | 1 | 2 | 3 | 4 |
| Labor union officials | 1 | 2 | 3 | 4 |

Copyright © 1997 by Allyn and Bacon

## 4.2 Building Familiarity

Make a list of buildings on your campus. Have the students rate these buildings on two different dimensions, once for likability and once for familiarity or how often they've been there. Each of these ratings can be done on a five-point scale. Gather up the ratings and determine their degree of correlation. Is there support for the frequency of exposure/liking hypothesis? Do students report liking those buildings with which they are most familiar?

## 4.3 Analyzing Advertisements

Have students bring in advertisements from newspapers and magazines so that you can analyze the techniques of persuasion being used in them. In a 1985 article in *Teaching of Psychology (12[1], 42-43)*, Vivian Makosky suggests there are three major persuasion techniques that can be identified in this way. In addition, she suggests several variations on the exercise. One variation is to compare the appeals make in men's magazines with those in women's magazines. Another variation is to compare the appeals in *Vogue* with those in *Family Circle*. Still another variation is to analyze what it is that turns people off to certain ads. Whatever avenue you choose, it is clear that advertising is a rich source of material for testing hypotheses on attitude change.

## 4.4 Central and Peripheral Route to Persuasion

Chapter 4 presents a detailed discussion of the difference between the central and the peripheral route to persuasion. Have students describe examples of television ads that use the two routes. The ads using the central route are presented directly to the viewer, whereas ads using the peripheral route are embedded in distraction. Can the students come up with examples of these types of ads? Are those using the central route based on better arguments than those using the peripheral route?

## 4.5 The Self-Monitoring Scale and Influence

Chapter 4 looks at differences between high self-monitors and low self-monitors in terms of the type of communicator that appeals to each. The Self-Monitoring Scale, authored by Mark Snyder, is presented in the next chapter of this manual. An interesting extension of the exercise presented in Chapter 5 is to see whether you can replicate the attitudinal effect; that is, to see whether high self-monitors really are more influenced by a source's attractiveness, whereas low self-monitors are more affected by the expertise of the source. Prepare a persuasive appeal and vary the source of the message. Half the time it should come from an attractive communicator, half from a less attractive source. Can you replicate the self-monitoring effect?

---

# Overhead Transparencies
These appear at the back of this manual.

---

4.1   *Cognitive Dissonance Theory in a Nutshell*
4.2   *The Forced Compliance Paradigm for Studying the Effects of Engaging in Attitude-Discrepant Behavior*
4.3   *Dissonance: The Price of Inconsistency*
4.4   *Rewards and Forced-Compliance: Why "Less" Sometimes Leads to "More"*

# Audiovisual Suggestions

*Persuasion Box*, I-306, film, 21 mins. Audiovisual Services, Western Illinois University, Macomb, IL 61455 (309-298-2417). This film shows how attitudes are changed in everyday life; special emphasis is given to the language of persuasions in advertising and in the mass media.

*The Psychology of Mass Persuasion* 727-GK, 35 mm. filmstrip with accompanying audio cassette, 39 mins. Human Relations Media, 175 Tompkins Avenue, Pleasantville, NY 10570. Provides an analysis of mass persuasion in modern society. Looks at who the mass persuaders are and the techniques they use.

*Social Animal*, 3-I56, 1963, 29 mins. Audiovisual Services, Western Illinois University, Macomb, IL 61455 (309-298-2417). One of the topics covered is the classic experiment by Festinger and Carlsmith (1959) showing the consequences of publicly stating something contrary to one's belief. Cognitive dissonance interpretation is presented.

*Social Psychology*, 31762, 1971, color, 33 mins. Pennsylvania State University, Audiovisual Services, Special Building, University Park, PA 16802(814-865-6314). Documentary footage of the busing of black children to previously all-white schools in a middle-class suburb is used to explain the social comparison theory, how attitudes are formed and changed, and nature of racial prejudice. Commentary by psychologists Kenneth B. Clark, Thomas Pettigrew, David Sears, and Thomas Cottle. From the *Psychology Today* series. A CRM production.

# Critical Thinking/Essay Questions

1. Describe evidence in support of the idea that attitudes can be formed via classical conditioning.
2. Describe an attitude-change program that would not only change targets' attitudes but would also cause the target to behave consistently with the newly formed attitudes.
3. Compare the tradition approach to persuasion and the cognitive approach.
4. If your professor reads your term paper "on the central route," how will your grade be determined? If your professor reads your term paper "on the peripheral route," how will your grade be determined?
5. Describe the less-leads-to-more effect, and indicate the three conditions necessary for the effect to occur.

# Sources for Lecture

Ball-Rokeach, S. J., Rokeach, M., and Grube, J. W. (1984). The great American values test. *Psychology Today,* November, pp. 34-41. can television alter basic beliefs? An experimental TV program aired one night in 1979 set out to find an answer.

Benson, P. L. (1981). Religion on capitol hill: How beliefs affect voting behavior in the U.S. Congress. *Psychology Today,* December, pp. 47-57. An interesting examination of the attitude-behavior relationship.

Diamond, E. and Bates, S. (1984). The political pitch. *Psychology Today,* November, pp. 23-32. A discussion of the problems and pitfalls of political advertising and political commercials.

Kipnis, D. and Schmidt, S. (1985). The language of persuasion. *Psychology Today,* April, pp. 40-46. This article examines whether one should use a "hard" or a "soft" persuasion strategy. The answer is that it depends on some other variables.

Poindexter, J. (1983). Voices of authority. *Psychology Today,* August, pp. 53-61. Lee Iacocca and other chief executives of U.S. corporations seem to be succeeding as communicators in advertising. This article examines why.

---

## Professional Update:  Current Articles from Professional Sources

---

Blasovich, J., Ernst, J. M., Tomaka, J., Kelsey, R. M., Salomon, K. L., & Fazio, R. H. (1993). Attitude accessibility as a moderator of autonomic reactivity during decision making. *Journal of Personality and Social Psychology, 64,* 165-176. Researchers explored the hypothesis that accessibility of an attitude from memory determines the power of the attitude. Attitudes toward abstract paintings were made accessible via rehearsal. The study compared decision making for paintings with accessible and less-accessible attitudes and measured autonomic reactivity.

Breckler, S. J., & Fried, H. S. (1993). On knowing what you like and liking what you smell: Attitudes depend on the form in which the object is represented. *Personality and Social Psychology Bulletin, 19,* 228-240. How is one's attitude toward "blue" different when one rates the word "blue" versus rating an actual blue-colored patch. Research suggests that the form in which an attitude object is presented has an impact on responses. This study compares odors presented descriptively versus odors as scratch-and-sniff patches.

Coleman, L. M., Beale, R. & Mills, C. (1993). Identifying targets of communication styles: An exploratory study. *Personality and Social Psychology Bulletin, 19,* 213-219. Do speakers communicate in distinguishably different ways when speaking to a child, a foreign adult, a mentally retarded adult, or a normally intelligent native speaker? Judges were asked to identify listeners on the basis of audiovisual clips of speakers. Child listeners and normal native adults were most readily identified. Implications are discussed.

DeBono, K. G., & Klein, C. (1993). Source expertise and persuasion: The moderating role of recipient dogmatism. *Personality and Social Psychology Bulletin, 19,* 167-173. Individuals high and low in dogmatism read a counterattitudinal message from either an expert or a nonexpert source who supported the position with either strong or weak arguments. Low-dogmatic individuals tended to be persuaded by the strength of the arguments regardless of the source. High dogmatic individuals were persuaded by the strength of the arguments when the source was a nonexpert but were equally persuaded by strong or weak arguments when the source was an expert.

Miller, A. G., McHoskey, J. W., Bane, C. M., & Dowd, T. G. (1993). The attitude polarization-phenomenon: Role of response measure, attitude extremity, and behavioral consequences of reported attitude change. *Journal of Personality and Social Psychology, 64,* 561-574. Subjects holding extreme attitudes assimilated an essay on capital punishment by showing polarization. The hypothesis that polarized persons would subsequently write particularly strong essays on the topic was not supported.

Peterson, B. E., Doty, R. M., & Winter, D. G. (1993). Authoritarianism and attitudes toward contemporary social issues. *Personality and Social Psychology Bulletin, 19,* 174-184. The authors show that authoritarianism is applicable to understanding attitudes on many important issues of the

1990s. Attitudes about AIDS, drug use, the environment, child abuse, the trade deficit, political changes in the former Soviet Union, and so forth are all shown to be related to authoritarianism.

Pyszczynski, T., Greenberg, J., Solomon, S., Sideris, J., & Stubing, M. J. (1993). Emotional expression and the reduction of motivated cognitive bias: Evidence from cognitive dissonance and distancing from victims' paradigms. *Journal of Personality and Social Psychology, 64,* 177-186. Study 1 determined that writing a counterattitudinal essay and then expressing tension produced by doing so reduces the extent of dissonance-reducing attitude change. Study 2 found that expressing fear of cancer reduced defensive distancing from cancer patients. Implications for the role of affect in defense are discussed.

Related Readings: The following selection from *Readings in Social Psychology: General, Classic, and Contemporary Selections,* 3rd Edition, by Wayne Lesko (Allyn and Bacon, 1997) accompany this chapter.

Ball-Rokeach, S., Rokeach, M., & Grube, J. (November, 1984). "The great American values test." These researchers conducted an unusual experiment in which subjects in Washington state watched a television program that prodded viewers to accept basic American values. Evidence showed that two to three months later, viewers' attitudes and behaviors were still influenced by the program. (Article 10).

Festinger, L. & Carlsmith, J. M. (1959). "Cognitive consequences of forced compliance." This article reprinted from *Journal of Abnormal and Social Psychology, 58,* 203-210, is a classic demonstration of a powerful theoretical model in social psychology known as cognitive dissonance. It is an excellent example of how common sense predictions often are exactly the opposite of what actually occurs. (Article 11).

Gilovich, T., Medvec, V. H., & Chen, S. (1995). "Commission, omission, and dissonance reduction: Coping with regret in the "Monty Hall" problem," provides a contemporary test of the cognitive dissonance hypothesis that was first presented over thirty-five years ago and described in the previous article (11). It addresses an interesting question: "When we experience a negative outcome, are we more likely to value that outcome more if it was due to an action that we took, or when the outcome was due to an action that we failed to take?" Implications for the psychology of regret are discussed. (Article 12).

# Chapter 5

# Aspects of Social Identity: Establishing One's Self and Gender

## Chapter-at-a-Glance

| CHAPTER OUTLINE | INSTRUCTION IDEAS | SUPPLEMENTS* |
|---|---|---|
| **I. The Self: Components of One's Identity**<br>• Self-Concept: The Central Schema<br><br>• **Social Psychology: On the Applied Side**   Increasing the Number of Possible Selves<br><br>• Self-Esteem: Evaluating Oneself<br><br>• **Cornerstones of Social Psychology**   Rogers, Self-Theory, Self-Ideal Discrepancy, and Personality Change | Learning Objectives 5.1 to 5.12<br><br>Discussion Topics 1-4<br><br>Activity 5.2 a, b (Handout)<br><br>Critical Thinking Question 1 | Test Bank Questions 5.1 to 5.60<br><br>Readings:<br>- Lesko 13, Many Mes of the Self-Monitor<br>- Lesko 15, negative Self-Concepts and Marital Commitment<br><br>Transparencies 5.1, 5.2, 5.3 |
| **II. Additional Aspects of Self-Functioning: Focusing, Monitoring, and Efficacy**<br>• Self-Focusing: Attending to Oneself or to the Environment<br><br>• Self-Monitoring: Guiding Behavior on the Basis of Internal versus External Factors<br><br>• Self-Efficacy: "I Think I Can, I Think I Can..." | Learning Objectives 5.13 to 5.17<br><br>Activities 5.1, 5.3 (Handouts)<br><br>Critical Thinking Question 2 | Test Bank Questions 5.61 to 5.89<br><br>Transparencies 5.4, 5.6, 5.7 |
| **III. Gender: Maleness or Femaleness as a Crucial Aspect of Identity**<br>• Gender Identity and Stereotypes Based on Gender<br><br>• **Cornerstones of Social Psychology**   Bem's Concept of Psychological Androgyny as an Alternative to Masculinity versus Femininity<br><br>• Gender-Role Behavior and the Reactions of Others to Gender-Role Behavior<br><br>• When Differences Are Found between Males and Females, Are They Based on Sex, Gender, or Both?<br><br>• **Social Diversity: A Critical Analysis**   Cultural Differences in Concern About Weight | Learning Objectives 5.18 to 5.27<br><br>Critical Thinking Questions 3-5 | Test Bank Questions 5.90 to 5.140<br><br>Reading:<br>- Lesko 14, Measurement of Androgyny<br><br>Transparency 5.5 |

*See Audiovisual Suggestions

# 5 Aspects of Social Identity: Establishing One's Self and Gender

## Chapter Outline: Getting the Overall Picture

I.  **The Self: Components of Your Identity**
    A.  Self-Concept: The Central Schema
        1.  The Cognitive Effects of a Person's Self-Schema
        2.  The Affective, Evaluative, and Behavioral Effects of the Sexual Self-Schema
        3.  One Self-Concept or Many
    B.  Social Psychology: On the Applied Side: Increasing the Number of Possible Selves
        1.  Changes in Self-Concept
    C.  Self-Esteem: Evaluating Yourself
        1.  Self-Esteem and Social Comparison
        2.  Why Do We Engage in Self-Evaluation?
        3.  The Consequences of Positive versus Negative Self-Evaluations
    D.  Cornerstone of Social Psychology: Self-Theory, Self-Ideal Discrepancy, and Personality Change: Carl Rogers

II.  **Additional Aspects of Self-Functioning: Focusing, Monitoring, and Efficacy**
    A.  Self-Focusing: Attending to Oneself or to the Environment
        1.  Cognitive and Affective Aspects of Focusing on Self
        2.  Storing Positive and Negative Information about Self in Memory
    B.  Self-Monitoring: Guiding Behavior on the Basis of Internal versus External Factors
        1.  Conceptualizing Differences in Self-Monitoring
        2.  Differences between High and Low Self-Monitors
    C.  Self-Efficacy: "I Think I Can, I Think I Can..."
        1.  Self-Efficacy and Performance
        2.  Self-Efficacy in Social Situations
        3.  Increasing a Person's Feelings of Self-Efficacy

III.  **Gender: Maleness or Femaleness as a Crucial Aspect of Identity**
    A.  Gender Identity and Stereotypes Based on Gender
        1.  The Origin of Gender Identity
    B.  Cornerstones of Social Psychology: Psychological Androgyny as an Alternative to Masculinity versus Femininity: Sandra Bem
    C.  Gender-Role Behavior and the Reaction of Others to Gender-Role Behavior
        1.  Androgynous versus Sex-Typed Behavior
        2.  The Effects of Gender Roles on Behavior at Home and in the Workplace
        3.  Why Do Traditional Gender Roles Remain Powerful?
        4.  Moving Beyond Gender Stereotyping: Signs of Progress
    D.  When Differences Are Found Between Men and Women, Are They Based on Sex, Gender, or Both?

        1.      Interpersonal Behavior
        2.      Self-Perception
   E.   Social Diversity: A Critical Analysis: Concern about Weight:  Asian versus Caucasian Women

---

# Learning Objectives
### After studying this chapter, students should be able to:

---

**5.1**    Describe the self-concept, including specific content as well as overall structure.

**5.2**    Describe the self-reference effect, and understand the two ways in which recall of self-relevant information is facilitated.

**5.3**    Explain the three major components of sexual self-schema, and how they affect self-reported sexual attitudes and sexual behavior.

**5.4**    Compare the concepts of present self and future self, and summarize the advantages of holding varied and complex future-self schemas.

**5.6**    Compare role-specific self-concepts and general self-concepts.

**5.7**    Examine the concept of self-esteem, including high vs. low self-esteem, global self-esteem, discrepancy between self and ideal self, and the impact of common vs. rare components.

**5.8**    Describe circumstances in which social comparisons lead to increases in self-esteem, and also circumstances in which social comparisons lead to decreases in self-esteem.

**5.9**    Define the three motives that underlie self-evaluation, and summarize ways in which people achieve self-enhancement.

**5.10**  Examine consequences of low self-esteem, including the lowering of serotonin levels and the impact on perceptions of task performance.

**5.11**  Understand why the self-ideal discrepancy is important, and how the therapy developed by Carl Rogers deals with self-ideal discrepancy.

**5.12**  Explain which is a better predictor of depression, consistently low self-esteem or variable self-esteem.

**5.13**  Describe the circumstances that increase self-focusing, and what the effects created when we become self-focused.

**5.14**  Describe high and low self-monitors and indicate the various ways in which the behavior of high and low self-monitors is different.

**5.15**  Define self-efficacy related to physical endurance and success on academic tasks among students and professors?

**5.16**  Explain how self-efficacy is related to physical endurance and success on academic tasks among students and professors.

**5.17**  Examine the role of self-efficacy in social situations, and compare the impact of harm-looming vs. self-efficacy in helping participants cope with a fear-inducing stimulus.

**5.18**  Summarize the development of gender identity by examining parents' reactions to newborns, gender awareness among two-year-olds, and gender consistency among older children.

**5.19**  Give examples of sex-typing that occurs as children learn gender-appropriate stereotypes.

**5.20**  Describe the Bem Sex Role Inventory and the assumptions underlying it, and indicate characteristics of persons who are sex-typed, sex-reversed, androgynous, and undifferentiated.

**5.21**  Summarize advantages that accrue to individuals who are androgynous, and problems often associated with strong adherence to traditional sex roles.

**5.22**  Compare gender role behaviors of men and women within the home.

**5.23**   Examine gender-related effects in the workplace, focusing on expectancies and motivation, occupational restrictions, communication styles, leadership styles, and reactions to successful women.

**5.24**   Give examples from children's stories, movies, television and computers where cultural support is provided for traditional gender roles, along with examples demonstrating movement away from traditional gender roles.

**5.25**   Describe and explain sex differences in willingness to deprive self in order to help others and in the tendency to dominate and control others.

**5.26**   Consider ways in which concern with their own appearance impacts women and causes biases in their self-perceptions.

**5.27**   Compare Asian and Caucasian women with regard to concern about weight.

# Discussion Topics and Questions

## 1. Personality Theorists vs. Social Psychologists

Personality theorists and social psychologists often disagree on the relative importance of traits versus situations as determinants of behavior.  Personality theorists examine the impact of individual differences on behavior and expect that different persons will behave differently from each other.  Social psychologists, on the other hand, examine effects created by the situation and expect that most persons in a particular situation will behave the same way.  Who is correct, the personality theorist or the social psychologist?

To examine this question, consider a characteristic such as shyness.  Ask students what it means to be shy.  Is shyness simply a personality trait, with some people being very shy and others being less shy? or is shyness a common response to certain situations, with most people becoming shy if the situation is "right"?

Another characteristic to consider is friendliness. What are the manifestations of "friendly" behavior?  Ask students to describe the behavior of a friendly, outgoing person versus an unfriendly, introverted person.  Next, compare the "friendliness" of persons who are at work, at a party, or in class.  Which is a better basis for predicting the person's behavior, *who* the person is or *where* the person is?  After pondering this question, students will probably be surprised at the degree to which behavior is determined by situations.

## 2. Interactionist Position

The previous discussion question oversimplifies the personality versus situation issue.  The best conclusion is undoubtedly that *both* personality and situation are important.  Who you are typically interacts with where you are to produce behavior.  The interactionist position is implicitly supported in chapter 5 of the text, since several aspects of the self are discussed first as trait features and then as situationally determined features.  Self-esteem, self-efficacy, and self-focusing are all discussed in this way.  In chapter 7, the test also approaches affiliation from both perspectives, discussing "need for affiliation" as a disposition and then discussing it as a "response to external events."

## 3. Measures of Self-Esteem

Measures of self-esteem generally involve asking people to make an evaluation of themselves by responding to statements such as "On the whole, I am satisfied with myself."  Most measures assume that self-esteem is relatively stable; that is, some people feel good about themselves most of the time, whereas others rate themselves quite negatively a good part of the time.  Positive self-esteem is generally considered good, the mark of a psychologically healthy person; low self-esteem, on the other hand, is considered bad, the mark of an unhealthy person.

An interesting question to examine is the degree to which positive self-esteem involves overestimating the positive aspects of our self.  People who claim to have unrealistic positive aspects generally will score higher on self-esteem scales.  Likewise, those who admit to negative aspects will score lower.  A study by Roth, Snyder, and Pace (1986) suggests that one way we enhance self-esteem is, in fact, to overestimate positive aspects of our selves.  When subjects were asked to respond to items that were positive but too good to be true for most people, a surprising number of people endorsed them.  Furthermore, the people who were most likely to endorse the unrealistic positive items were also likely to score high on a test of self-esteem.  (An example of a too-good-to-be-true item is "I am always courteous, even to disagreeable people.")  The question to ponder with your students is the degree to which positive self-esteem rests on a realistic view of oneself, and degree to which self-esteem is enhanced by unrealistic positive which self-esteem is enhance by unrealistic positive views.  The article by Roth et al. is published in the *Journal of Personality and Social Psychology, 51,* pages 867-874.

## 4.  Social Comparison

There are many features of the self that one can evaluate quickly and easily by comparing one's standing on the characteristic to some objective criterion.  Height, weight, and eye color are examples.  On the other hand, many facets of the self cannot be measured by any objective standard and instead can be evaluated only by comparison of oneself with other people.  Leon Festinger (1954) developed his classic social comparison theory to explain the circumstance under which we seek out other people as a means of evaluation ourselves.

Joanne Wood (1989) has done a recent review of research and theory in this area and has identified research and theory in this area and has identified three reasons people use social comparison.  The first reason is *self-evaluation.*  To get an accurate evaluation of our own ability in some area, we generally choose to compare ourselves to people whose abilities are similar to our own.  High school ball players don't try to evaluate themselves by comparison to major leaguers or to Little Leaguers, but instead compare themselves to someone who plays at the same level they do.  Gender is another relevant factor in choosing a comparison, with people preferring a same-sexed comparison partner.

A second reason people engage in social comparison is *self-enhancement.*  When a person needs to improve his/her self-esteem, it is likely that a comparison person who is worse off than the person will be chosen.  If we do not have a relevant comparison in our personal experience, we may fabricate an imaginary comparison or simply generalize about others who are worse off.  When people enter the hospital, for example they generally feel sorry for themselves; but they usually manage to find a comparison other who is worse off and thereby feel better about their own circumstances.    Wood's article on social comparison is in *Psychological Bulletin, 106,* pages 231-248.

# Learning Activities:  Classroom Exercises/Demonstrations

## 5.1  Mark Snyder's Self-Monitoring Scale

Mark Snyder's Self-Monitoring Scale, found below and in the Study Guide, is perhaps the fastest-growing personality test in the United States.  A large number of research articles relating self-monitoring to a variety of social behaviors have been published since the scale first appeared in 1974.  The scale seems to relate to everything, including dating preferences, responses to ads, and attitude-behavior consistency.  Students enjoy finding out whether they are high or low in self-monitoring, both as a way to learn about themselves and as a way to appreciate the text material on self-monitoring.  Most people are "satisfied" with their own score on this test, and thus some students may be willing to share their score with other class members.  The scale is quite easy to score: the score is simply the number of statements for which the respondent made the high-self-monitoring choice.  The high-self-monitoring choice for each item is as follows: 1.f;2.f;3.f;4.f;5.t;6.t;7.t;8.t;9.f;10.t;11.t;12.f;13.t;14.f; 15.t;16.t;17.f;18.t;19.t;20.f;21.f;22.f;23.f;24.t;25.t.

## HANDOUT FOR ACTIVITY # 5.1

### Self-Monitoring Scale

The statements that follow concern your personal reactions to a number of different situations. No two statements are exactly alike, so consider each statement carefully before answering. If a statement is TRUE or MOSTLY TRUE as applied to you, mark "T" to the left of the statements. If a statement is FALSE or NOT USUALLY TRUE as applied to you, mark a "F" to the left of the statement. It is important that you answer as frankly and honestly as you can.

___ 1.  I find it hard to imitate the behavior of other people.

___ 2.  My behavior is usually an expression of my true inner feelings, attitudes and beliefs.

___ 3.  At parties and social gatherings, I do not attempt to do or say things that others will like.

___ 4.  I can only argue for ideas which I already believe.

___ 5.  I can make impromptu speeches even on topics about which I have almost no information.

___ 6.  I guess I put on a show to impress or entertain people.

___ 7.  When I am uncertain how to act in a social situation, I look to the behavior of the others for cues.

___ 8.  I would probably make a good actor.

___ 9.  I rarely seek the advice of my friends to choose movies, books, or music.

___ 10. I sometimes appear to others to be experiencing deeper emotions than I actually am.

___ 11. I laugh more when I watch a comedy with others than when alone.

___ 12. In a group of people I am rarely the center of attention.

___ 13. In different situations and with different people, I often act like very different persons.

___ 14. I am not particularly good at making other people like me.

___ 15. Even if I am not enjoying myself, I often pretend to be having a good time.

___ 16. I'm not always the person I appear to be.

___ 17. I would not change my opinions (or the way I do things) in order to please someone else or win their favor.

___ 18. I have considered being an entertainer.

Copyright © 1997 by Allyn and Bacon

___ 19. In order get along and be liked, I tend to be what people expect me to be rather than anything else.

___ 20. I have never been good at games like charades or improvisational acting.

___ 21. I have trouble changing my behavior to suit different people and different situations.

___ 22. At a party I let others keep the jokes and stories going.

___ 23. I feel a bit awkward in company and do not show up quite so feel as I should.

___ 24. I can look anyone in the eye and tell a lie with a straight face (if for a right end).

___ 25. I may deceive people by being friendly when I really dislike them.

Copyright © 1997 by Allyn and Bacon

### 5.2  Self-reference Effect

The "self-reference effect" is a robust phenomenon that can be demonstrated quite readily in a classroom demonstration.  The exercise can be done either in class with the instructor serving as the experimenter or outside of class with students recruiting friends to serve as the subjects.  Subjects are presented with a list of trait adjectives and are required to respond to each trait word on the list.  (The handout for this Activity can be found in the student's Study Guide).  Half of subjects are instructed to read the trait list and decide if each word describes themselves.  The other half of the subjects are told to read the list and decide whether each word is long.  After the subjects have gone through the entire list of adjectives, they are given a surprise recall test to determine how many of the adjectives they can remember.

Subjects who previously determined whether each work "describe themselves" will recall more of the words than subjects who simply had to decide whether the words were long.  This occurs because subjects who relate the words to themselves process them more deeply than subjects who respond simply to a physical characteristic of the words.  A list of thirteen trait words to use in doing the exercise is as follows:

## HANDOUT FOR ACTIVITY # 5.2a

### Trait Adjectives

Read the following trait list and decide if each word describes yourself.

| | |
|---|---|
| aggressive | intelligent |
| friendly | superstitious |
| quiet | sentimental |
| bold | athletic |
| persistent | trusting |
| sensitive | energetic |
| shy | |

## HANDOUT FOR ACTIVITY # 5.2b

### Trait Adjectives

Read the following trait list and decide whether each word is long.

| | |
|---|---|
| aggressive | intelligent |
| friendly | superstitious |
| quiet | sentimental |
| bold | athletic |
| persistent | trusting |
| sensitive | energetic |
| shy | |

Copyright © 1997 by Allyn and Bacon

### 5.3  Log Sheet

How does what happens to you influence how you view yourself?  have students fill out the log sheet below.  If students do the exercise described there, they will gain insight and self-understanding.  The exercise provides personal information on the interplay between self-view (personality) and situational determinants ("what happens to you").  Students simply follow the straightforward instructions accompanying the sheet.  The easiest way to score the words is to assign a positive or negative valence to each word, depending on how favorable or unfavorable it is, and then an overall valence, according to whether positive or negative valences are more frequent.  Also, positive or negative valence could be assigned to each description of "what happened to you."  The descriptions should be done first for a block of about ten days (have students make copies of the log sheet).  Then they can be scored and the possible correspondence between the two ratings can be observed.  More objective ratings occur if students place code numbers on their log sheets and have fellow students score the word "happenings" blind.  (A 1983 book by Allen and Potkay entitled *Adjective Generative Technique* and published by Irvington Press deals more formally the issues raised in this exercise.)

## HANDOUT FOR ACTIVITY # 5.3

### Log Sheet

Date:_____Sex:_____Code Number:_____

Write down five words to describe yourself.  Please, use only words, no phrases or sentences.

1._____

2._____

3._____

4._____

5._____

Write down the most important thing that happened to you.

_____
_____
_____
_____
_____

Copyright © 1997 by Allyn and Bacon

# Overhead Transparencies
These appear at the back of this manual.

**5.1** *Some Factors That Make a Difference in Subjective Well-Being*
**5.2** *Personality and Social Psychology*
**5.3** *Personality Development and Measurement*
**5.4** *Interaction of "Strength of Situation" and the Personality Factor "Authoritarianism"*
**5.5** *Integrative Research Using Both Social and Personality Variables*
**5.6** *Five Robust Personality Traits*
**5.7** *Nine Components of the Authoritarian Personality*

# Audiovisual Suggestions

*Allyn and Bacon Videos*

*\*The Self.* How psychologists systematically study the origins of self-identity and self-esteem, social determinants of self-conceptions, and the emotional and motivational consequences of beliefs about oneself. (Discovering Psychology series, On Tape #8.)
*\*Self and Gender.* The ways in which males and females are similar and different, and how sex roles reflect social values and psychological knowledge. (Discovering Psychology series, On Tape #9.)

*Other Videos and Films*

*A Day in the Life of Jonathon Mole,* film, 30 mins. CRM/McGraw-Hill Films, 110 Fifteenth Street, Del Mar, CA 92014. Graphically depicts how personal characteristics and social circumstances interplay to produce a bigoted personality.
*Evaluating Personality,* videotape, 30 mins. Insight Media, 121 W. 85th Street, New York, NY 10024-4401 (800-233-9910). This tape investigates various personality evaluation methods.
*Personality,* film, 25 mins. CRM/McGraw-Hill Films, 110 Fifteenth Street, Del Mar, CA 92014. A college student's personality is analyzed according to traditional trait-personality notions.
*Shyness: Reasons and Remedies,* videotape, 30 mins. Insight Media, 121 W. 85th Street, New York, NY 10024-4401 (800-233-9910). This video studies the causes of shyness and how it affects our personal and social well-being.

# Critical Thinking/Essay Questions

1. In what ways is self-esteem influenced by situational events. Give specific examples.
2. Describe a high and a low self-monitor. Indicate two specific ways in which these two personality types are different from each other and explain the difference in terms of self-monitoring processes.

3. Compare biological and social learning explanations for the sex difference that is typically found between men and women in aggressiveness.
4. Describe a masculine, a feminine, an androgynous, and an undifferentiated person.
5. In what ways do children's books and television provide support for traditional gender roles?

## Sources for Lecture

Fischman, J. (1987). Getting Tough. *Psychology Today,* December, pp. 26-28. the personality characteristic of "hardiness" grew out of the 1970's research linking sickness to emotional stress. Perhaps hardiness is a buffer against life's stresses and the illness they cause.

Horn, J. (1986). Measuring a man by the company he keeps. *Psychology Today*, March, P. 12. Mark Snyder, Ellen Berscheid, and Peter Glick asked high and low self-monitors what kind of information they wanted about potential dates. The lows went for personality information and the highs for physical attractiveness profiles.

Roberts, M. (1988). School yard menace. *Psychology Today,* February, pp. 52-56. Is bullying a personality trait? Or does the school yard bring out meanness in children: Bullies are usually boys and usually come from families that neglect, reject, or abuse, or that create a climate of violence.

Trotter, R. J. (1987). Stop blaming yourself. *Psychology Today,* February, pp. 31-39. The title says it! People whose explanatory style reflects learned helplessness blame themselves and suffer health consequences because of it.

## Professional Update:  Current Articles from Professional Sources

Baumeister, R. R., Heatherton, T. F., & Tice, D. M. (1993).  When ego threats lead to self-regulation failure: Negative consequences of high self-esteem. *Journal of Personality and Social Psychology, 64,* 141-156.  People with high self-esteem often make inflated assessments and predictions about themselves, which carries the risk that they'll make commitments that exceed their capabilities. Setting goals beyond their capabilities was found for high self-esteem subjects under conditions of high ego threat.

Brown, J. D., &  Mankowski, T. A. (1993).  Self-esteem, mood, and self-evaluation:  Changes in mood and the way you see you. *Journal of Personality and Social Psychology, 64,* 421-430.  How does a change in mood affect how people evaluate themselves:  Self-evaluations among high-self-esteem people are not much affected by their moods, but self-evaluations of low-self-esteem persons are more prone to fluctuate.

Crocker, J., Cornwell, T. Kl, & Major, B. (1993).  The stigma of overweight:  Affective consequences of attributional ambiguity. *Journal of Personality and Social Psychology, 64,* 60-70.  The low self-esteem of overweight persons is examined.  Overweight women received either positive or negative feedback from a male evaluator.  Overweight women who received negative feedback attributed the feedback to their weight and did not blame the evaluator.  This pattern of attribution produced negative mood in these women.  Implications for weight-loss programs and psychotherapy for the overweight are considered.

Greenberg, J., et al. (1992).  Why do people need self-esteem:  Converging evidence that self-esteem serves and anxiety buffering function. *Journal of Personality and Social Psychology, 63,* 913-922. This study examined how people responded to such events as a video portraying vivid images of death and anticipated painful shock. It was hypothesized that increasing self-esteem would reduce anxiety. Both success and positive personality feedback reduced physiological arousal in the face of a threat.

Jacobs, J. E., & Eccles, J. S. (1993). The impact of mothers' gender-role stereotypic beliefs on mothers' and children's ability perceptions. *Journal of Personality and Social Psychology, 63,* 932-944. The researchers examined the relationships among mothers' gender stereotypic beliefs, their perceptions of their children's abilities, and their children's self perceptions. Abilities in math, sports, and social domains were examined, and mothers' beliefs clearly influenced perceptions.

James, K. (1993). Conceptualizing self with in-group stereotypes: Context and esteem precursors. *Personality and Social Psychology Bulletin, 19,* 117-121. Female subjects had their attention focused either on their own unique characteristics or on their gender-group conception. Masculinity and femininity scores from the BSRI were obtained as dependent measures. How subjects' responses were affected by their focus of attention depended on their self esteem.

Spence, J. T. (1993). Gender-related traits and gender ideology: Evidence for a multifactorial theory. *Journal of Personality and Social Psychology, 64,* 624-635. College students were given two measures of gender-related personality traits, the Bem Sex Role Inventory and Personal Attributes Questionnaire. The study examined relationships between these and other measures to test various conceptualizations of gender.

Stoppard, J. M., & Gruchy, C. D. (1993). Gender, context, and expression of positive emotion. *Personality and Social Psychology Bulletin, 19,* 143-150. Subjects read a scene in which the main character either did or did not express positive emotion toward the self or another person. After imagining themselves as the main character, subjects rated how others would respond if they behaved as depicted. Findings indicate interesting ways in which norms for expression of positive emotion are gender differentiated.

*Related Readings:* The following selections from *Readings in Social Psychology: General, Classic, and Contemporary Selections,* 3rd Edition, by Wayne Lesko (Allyn and Bacon, 1997) accompany this chapter.

Snyder, M. (March, 1980). "The many me's of the self-monitor." Snyder compares the actions of high and low self-monitors on a variety of behavioral dimensions. High self-monitors, for instance, are skilled in managing the impressions they make on others. Several other characteristics are also explored. (Article 13)

Bem, S. (1974). Bem describes the development of her sex-role inventory. The characteristics of masculine, feminine, and androgynous persons are summarized. Especially highlighted are the characteristics of androgyny. (Article 14)

Swann, W. B., Hixon, J. G., & De La Ronde, C. (1992). Embracing the bitter "truth": Negative self-concepts and marital commitment. People often gravitate toward partners who see them as they see themselves. This means preferring a partner who gives them negative evaluation if that is consistent with their own low opinion of themselves. (Article 15)

# Chapter 6

# Prejudice and Discrimination: Understanding Their Nature, Countering Their Effects

## Chapter-at-a-Glance

| CHAPTER OUTLINE | INSTRUCTION IDEAS | SUPPLEMENTS* |
|---|---|---|
| **I. Prejudice and Discrimination: What They Are, How They Differ**<br>• Prejudice: Choosing Whom to Hate<br><br>• Discrimination: Prejudice in Action | Learning Objectives 6.1 to 6.5<br><br>Activity 6.1<br><br>Discussion Topic 3<br><br>Critical Thinking Ques. 1-3 | Test Bank Questions 6.1 to 6.33<br><br>Transparencies 6.1, 6.2, 6.6 |
| **II. The Origins of Prejudice: Contrasting Perspectives**<br>• Direct Intergroup Conflict<br><br>• **Cornerstones of Social Psychology**  The Economics of Racial Violence<br><br>• Early Experience: The Role of Social Learning<br><br>• Social Categorization: The Us-versus-Them Effect and the "Ultimate" Attribution Error<br><br>• Cognitive Sources of Prejudice: The Role of Stereotypes<br><br>• Other Cognitive Mechanisms in Prejudice | Learning Objectives 6.6 to 6.15<br><br>Activity 6.3<br><br>Discussion Topic 2<br><br>Critical Thinking Questions 4-8 | Test Bank Questions 6.34 to 6.97<br><br>Readings:<br>- Lesko 17, Experiments in Group Conflict<br>- Lesko 18, prejudice Against Fat People<br><br>Transparencies 6.3, 6.4 |
| **III. Striking Back against Prejudice: Techniques That Can Help**<br>• Breaking the Cycle of Prejudice: On Learning *Not* to Hate<br><br>• Direct Intergroup Contact<br><br>• Recategorization: Redrawing the Boundary<br><br>• Cognitive Interventions<br><br>• **Social Psychology: On the Applied Side**  The Paradoxical Effects of Stereotype Suppression | Learning Objectives 6.16 to 6.20<br><br>Discussion Topics 1, 4<br><br>Critical Thinking Question 9 | Test Bank Questions 6.98 to 6.127<br><br>Transparency 6.5 |
| **IV. Prejudice Based on Gender: Its Nature and Effects**<br>• Gender Stereotypes: The Cognitive Core of Sexism<br><br>• Discrimination against Females: Subtle but Often Deadly<br><br>• Sexual Harassment<br><br>• **Social Diversity: A Critical Analysis**  Physical Effects of Stereotypes: Evidence That Memory Loss in Our Later Years Is Influenced by Cultural Stereotypes about Aging | Learning Objectives 6.21 to 6.25<br><br>Activities 6.2, 6.4<br><br>Critical Thinking Question 10 | Test Bank Questions 6.128 to 6.155<br><br>Reading:<br>Lesko 16, Chill in the College Classroom<br><br>Transparency 6.6 |

*See Audiovisual Suggestions

# Prejudice and Discrimination: Understanding Their Nature, Countering Their Effects

## Chapter Outline: Getting the Overall Picture

I. **Prejudice and Discrimination: What They Are, How They Differ**
   A. Prejudice: Choosing Whom to Hate
   B. Discrimination: Prejudice in Action
      1. The New Racism: More Subtle, but Just As Deadly
      2. Tokenism: Small Benefits, High Costs
      3. Reverse Discrimination: Giving with One Hand, Taking with the Other
      4. Subtle Forms of Discrimination: A Note of Optimism

II. **The Origins of Prejudice: Contrasting Perspectives**
   A. Direct Intergroup Conflict: Competition As a Source of Prejudice
   B. Cornerstones of Social Psychology: The Economics of Racial Violence: Do Bad Times Fan the Flames of Prejudice?
   C. Early Experience: The Role of Social Learning
   D. Social Categorization: The Us-versus-Them Effect and the "Ultimate" Attribution Error
   E. Cognitive Sources of Prejudice: The Role of Stereotypes
      1. Stereotypes: What They Are and How They Operate
      2. The Role of Affect in Stereotypic Thinking: The Interface between Feelings and Thought Revisited
         a. Do Stereotypes Involve an Affective Component?
         b. Stereotypes and Mood: One Potential Downside to Being in a Good Mood
   F. Other Cognitive Mechanisms in Prejudice: Illusory Correlations and Outgroup Homogeneity
      1. Ingroup Differentiation, Outgroup Homogeneity: "They're All the Same"--or Are They?

III. **Striking Back against Prejudice: Techniques That Can Help**
   A. Breaking the Cycle of Prejudice: On Learning *Not* to Hate
   B. Direct Intergroup Contact: The Potential Benefits of Acquaintance
   C. Recategorization: Redrawing the Boundary between "Us" and "Them"
   D. Cognitive Interventions: When Stereotypes Shatter--or at Least Become Less Compelling
   E. Social Psychology: On the Applied Side: The Paradoxical Effects of Stereotype Suppression: When Thoughts We Don't Want Come Back to Haunt Us

IV. **Prejudice Based on Gender: Its Nature and Effects**
   A. Gender Stereotypes: The Cognitive Core of Sexism
   B. Discrimination against Females: Subtle but Often Deadly
      1. The Role of Expectations
      2. The Role of Self-Confidence
      3. Negative Reactions to Female Leaders
      4. The Glass Ceiling: Why Women Don't Rise to the Top
   C. Sexual Harassment: When Discrimination Hits Rock Bottom

D.   Social Diversity: A Critical Analysis: Physical Effects of Stereotypes:  Evidence That Memory Loss in Our Later Years Is Influenced by Cultural Stereotypes about Aging

---

## Learning Objectives
### After studying this chapter, students should be able to:

**6.1**   Understand the meaning of "prejudice," "discrimination," and "stereotype."  Explain how prejudice functions like other attitudes.

**6.2**   Indicate the link between the cognitive and affective components of prejudice and the labor saving aspect of stereotypes.

**6.3**   Outline the procedures of the Macrae et.al. (1993, 1994) studies in which stereotype labels freed up the cognitive apparatus for another task.

**6.4**   Tell what has happened to overt expressions of prejudice.  Differentiate "old fashioned racism" and "modern racism" and give some belief statements that reflect the latter.

**6.5**   Describe tokenism and its effects on the "tokens" and relate it to reverse discrimination.

**6.6**   Outline the procedure of the famous Sherif and colleagues summer camp study.  Explain how antagonism between groups of boys was created, how it was resolved and the limitations of the study.

**6.7**   Examine the frustration-aggression hypothesis.  Explain how displaced aggression in relation to economic conditions relates to lynching between 1882 and 1930.  Describe the pluses and minuses of the Hovland/Sears study of lynching.

**6.8**   Taking the social learning view, describe how children acquire prejudice.  Tell if the media depiction of minorities has become more positive or remained negative (or something in between).

**6.9**   Indicate how in-group and out-group members are perceived with reference to the "ultimate attribution error" as applied to the Hong Kong study?  Explain why do we identify with groups?.

**6.10**   Explain how stereotypes make it easy to describe a group.  Understand how we deal with information that is consistent and inconsistent with stereotypes we hold.

**6.11**   Describe the procedure of the Jussim and colleagues study using "rock musician" and "child abuser" targets (and gays).  Explain what happens when affect and then cognition is held constant.

**6.12**   Outline the procedure of the Bodenhausen et al. study of cheating and assault suspects and stereotype labels.  Explain what happened to guilt ratings when stereotypes were activated and subjects were in a good mood.

**6.13**   Define "illusory correlation."  Explain how does the concept plays a role in crime rate estimation.  Explain why infrequent events/stimuli stand out in memory.

**6.14**   Indicate the difference between "out-group homogeneity" and "in-group differentiation."  Explain for whom the "they all look alike" effect is stronger?

**6.15**   Describe how experience, actual level of heterogeneity and individuality influence this effect.  Contrast Lee's and Ottati's American and Chinese subjects on these two dimensions.

**6.16**   Indicate why parents communicate prejudice to their children despite the observation that it makes them suffer (how?) and hampers their viability in today's world (why?).

**6.17**   List the advantages of intergroup contact, the conditions that must prevail if it is to have positive effects and research results supporting prejudice reduction via contact.

**6.18**   Explain how Gaertner and colleagues indicate we can "recategorize" and thereby confirm the "common ingroup identity model".

**6.19** Describe how knowledge about the success of a target counters stereotypes about that target. Explain how these mechanisms relate to affirmative action.

**6.20** Examine the "rebound" effect associated with stereotype suppression in the Macrae et al. study with the "skinhead" target.

**6.21** Relate "sexism" to "gender stereotypes" by contrasting the stereotypes of males and females and by discussing the accuracy of perceived differences between males and females, gender differences in expectations, women's self-confidence and reactions to female leaders.

**6.22** Indicate the circumstances under which women leaders are evaluated lower, according to Eagly and colleagues. Relate the "glass ceiling" to male executives' efforts that keep women down.

**6.23** List the kinds of "developmental opportunities" that women are denied. Describe how Van Velsor and Hughes explain women's lack of advancement, despite the observation that they had as many developmental opportunities as men.

**6.24** Define sexual harassment in terms of what happened to Teresa Harris. Explain when "sexual harassment" is not sexual?

**6.25** Outline the stereotypes of the elderly. Describe how these stereotypes can become self-fulfilling prophesies. Indicate how Levy and Langer showed that culture can moderate the effects of stereotypes about the elderly.

---

## Discussion Topics and Questions

---

1. **Humanizing the Object of Prejudice:** *Paths of Glory*

During World War II dehumanization promoted vicious hatred between Japanese and Americans. The Japanese thought that Americans were less than human, and we regarded them in the same way. As a result we unconstitutionally imprisoned and harassed hundreds of thousands of American citizens of Japanese descent, and they starved and tortured to death several thousand American POWs.

The final scene of perhaps the greatest antiwar film, *Paths of Glory* with Kirk Douglas, can help students understand the role of dehumanizing the targets of bias in the promotion of prejudice against them. In that scene, battle-weary World War I French soldiers are gathered at a night club awaiting the entertainment for the evening. Finally the proprietor emerges from backstage with a youthful German woman in tow. The soldiers roar in laughter as she cowers at the sight of them. Derisive comments about her reverberate around the room. Much to their delight, she is terrorized. As the men drink up, the proprietor forces the woman to sing. Her halting whisper of a voice causes the soldiers to jeer even louder. In response, her utterances increase in volume. Slowly the soldiers come to realize that she is singing a sentimental song familiar to them. The noise begins to subside and one or two soldiers start to sing along with the woman. Instantly she is transformed from daughter of German beast to human being. Soon all the men are singing along, and many are crying. When the soldiers and a representative of the enemy join together in song, they are able to appreciate the tragedy of their common circumstances and, in turn, one another's humanity. *Paths of Glory* can be rented from many videotape stores (or they can find it for you; if not, your audiovisual people probably can). Play that last scene for the students and ask them why the soldiers initially reacted so violently to a harmless noncombatant only to join her suddenly in a show of tender emotions. Point out the implications for perceptions of homogeneity of the outgroup and for the effect of a joint enterprise on dissolution of those perceptions of homogeneity of the outgroup and for the effect of a joint enterprise on dissolution of those perceptions. Help them understand why it is so easy to hate people who are regarded as less than human and so difficult to hate those same people once their humanity is appreciated.

## 2. Cultural Diversity

"Cultural diversity" is becoming a catchphrase on many campuses. Why? Sometime during the next century, the many U.S. ethnic groups of non-European heritage will total more people than the current U.S. majority, just as non-Russians outnumbered Russians in the former Soviet Union. As in the former Soviet Union, extraordinary diversity will characterize the United States. We need to understand diversity better than the Soviets did, or we could suffer their fate: fragmentation of the country. You could start on the light side by showing students how common gestures vary in meaning from culture to culture (see Sources for Lecture for a reference). Tapping the head means "I'm thinking" in Argentina and Peru, but elsewhere it means "He's crazy." Have the students imagine using this gesture in the presence of the wrong audience. The forearm jerk, one hand on the hollow of an elbow joint causing the clenched fist of the other hand to thrust upward about eyeball high, means "_____you" in Mediterranean countries and in the United States but is a sign of appreciation equivalent to a wolf whistle in England. Placing the thumb under the index finger and thrusting the thumb upward, palm outward is an obscene gesture in some European and Mediterranean countries, but in Brazil and Venezuela is such a good-luck symbol that it is reproduced in the form of paperweights and golden amulets worn around the neck. Imagine using these gestures in the wrong place! How about the "impudent third finger?" Since the time of the Romans it has meant much the same around the world.

But how about some less-trivial and more-meaningful cultural differences in our own country? If we learned about these differences, we could avoid some conflicts and appreciate the fact that some distasteful behaviors--from the majority American point of view--are not so bad once understood. For example, consider the old African sang "If you throw a rock into a pack of dogs, the one that yelps is the one that was hit." Knowing this proverb helps to understand why a black person who says "Whites are racists"--but doesn't mean all whites--is suspicious of a white person who responds with denial. To many white Americans, two people who are vehemently yelling at each other are getting ready to fight; to many black Americans, the two are just "woofing" (as long as they continue, everything is fine). If you start a discussion on racism in your class, black students, who are usually taught it is good to air emotions, will likely want to argue things out. White students, however, typically learn it is embarrassing to express strong emotions publicly and will probably clam up. Little wonder it may go badly...unless the two opposite tendencies are discussed first.

Other examples include the observation that whereas some Anglos will march up to the boss and ask for a raise, some Hispanics who are equally loyal and hard-working will wait to be given the raise, because they believe the boss is supposed to reward their loyalty spontaneously. A Japanese boss will not chastise an errant employee in front of his or her peers--it would cause the employee to lose face and reflect badly on the peers. An American boss, however, will not hesitate to dress down an employee in front of peers. (Neither will the Japanese boss, if he or she and the employees have had several drinks together after work!) We "ground" naughty children in their rooms; the Japanese put them outside. Use these and other examples provided by yourself or students as a basis for a discussion on cultural diversity. But be cautious: students must learn to approach people from different cultural backgrounds as unique individuals, while bearing cultural differences in mind so that misunderstandings are avoided. Trying to "learn" someone else's culture can be counterproductive: stereotypes are what is likely to be learned.

3.  **"Tell Us What Your People Think"**

If smooth relations between one cultural group and another, as well as between men and women, are to characterize the future, we must learn to monitor the assumptions behind what we say.  The following examples can serve to illustrate unfortunate assumptions.  College and university administrators are sometimes heard to say, "We are looking for *qualified minority* [or women] faculty."  The phrase "qualified minority" implies that most "minority" academics are not qualified and that therefore one must search hard for the few qualified ones.  The word "minority" may also be offensive, because it lumps all the diverse U.S. ethnic groups together as if they were the same.  Different cultural groups are very proud of their unique identities.  Even the word "Hispanic" is problematic, because of the great diversity among the groups that are called under this label.  "Latino" seems better--most Americans who speak Spanish are from South or Central America--but excludes women ("Latina").

Referring to "natural ability" as an explanation of why members of certain groups are disproportionately represented among the most successful in a certain field can be less than flattering (e.g., Blacks in sports and Asians in high-tech areas).  It implies that these successful people didn't have to do anything to succeed except show up, an affront to their perception that they have had to work very hard, probably harder than others.  Referring to women or members of certain ethnic groups as "hired through our affirmative action program" can be insulting.  It implies that these individuals were less qualified than others who were candidates for the same job.  In fact, the spirit of affirmative action is, "All other things being equal, consider ethnic identification or gender when deciding whom to hire."  Businesses would be cutting their own throats if they hired less-qualified people instead of acting according to that spirit.

Calling on women or members of certain ethnic groups to "tell us what your people think" can be upsetting.  For groups as large as "women" or "Blacks," for example, no one member can represent all the others, because great diversity exists *within* any large group.  If you throw out these examples, and/or other similar ones, it is likely that women and members of different cultural groups on your class will provide many more.  The result could be a very enlightening discussion.

4.  **Understanding Discrimination First-Hand**

One of the previous authors of this Instructor's Manual, Bem Allen, teaches a multicultural course in which there tends to be relatively equal representation of European-American and African-American students.  (There are few other "minority" students.)  Many of the European-American students come to the class not believing African-Americans' claims that they are victims of discrimination.  That they are skeptical is not entirely because of their own prejudices.  In part, it is due to the fact that most have never been victimized themselves.  Having little or no personal insight into discrimination, they are unable to see the often subtle kinds of discrimination that African-Americans experience.  By the end of the class, however, the European-Americans' term papers and in-class comments reflect a different point of view.  They have gotten to know the African-American students in the class--almost every class is dominated by a lively discussion--and they have opened their ears and their minds to their Black classmates' personal experiences with discrimination.

During the course of the semester, the White students have learned how some of their African-American classmates have been repeatedly stopped for no apparent reason and body-searched by police who, finding nothing, then release them.  They hear that African-American students are routinely followed by department store detectives, ignored by clerks, and assumed to lack the money to pay for merchandise.  They learn that Black classmates routinely field racial epithets hurled by Whites.  Many European-Americans leave the class believing that discrimination is an everyday part of African-Americans' lives.  If you talk to your African-American, Hispanic, Asian, or other students of color before having a session on discrimination, they may be willing to disclose instances of discrimination that would be edifying to European-American students. After consultation with students of color, one way to approach the discussion is simply to ask all students, "How many of you have been followed by store detectives?" "Been repeatedly body-searched by police?" and so forth. Looking around the room will make it plain who is most likely to be a target of discrimination. Ask some of the students to describe their experiences. Some insight may be gained by all, as students of color may be amazed at the amazement of European-American students.

## Learning Activities: Classroom Exercises/Demonstrations

### 6.1 Is There Racism at This School?

The following is a set of excerpts from a questionnaire on racism that was actually distributed the classrooms of the Ann Arbor, Michigan, high schools. The results, expressed in numbers that represent percentages, are printed with each item. (A duplicate without the percentages is found on the next page and in the Study Guide.) The questionnaire has been altered slightly to be more appropriate to college students. You could give it to your students and compile their answers as percentages (number of students who answered in a certain way divided by total students present). Students will likely be fascinated to find out how their answers differed from those of younger people who attend high schools that have been fraught with racial conflict (taken from *Phi Delta Kappan*; see Sources for Lecture for the complete reference to this work).

*Is There Racism at This School?*

Below are the percentages collected from the Ann Arbor, Michigan, high schools.

1.  Here are some definitions of racism: check those that you agree with and leave blank those you disagree with.

    **88** Racism is when people aren't given or allowed equal opportunities because of their racial or ethnic background (for example, Black, Asian, Jewish, White, Hispanic, Arab etc.).
    **56** Racism is whenever people are discriminated against.
    **79** Racism is when people are segregated according to which racial or ethnic background they are from.
    **82** Racism is when people hate, dislike, or fear other people because of their racial or ethnic background.
    **80** Racism is something that degrades, demoralizes, or hurts people because they are from a certain racial or ethnic group.
    **13** Other: Please write your own definition_____

2. Is there racism at your school?  YES (**85**) No (**6**) Other (**9**)
   If yes...
   a. In your school how is racism shown?  (Check all that apply.)
   **62** Ethnic slurs              **29** Threats against a person
   **64** Offensive remarks       **21** Threats against a group
   **22** Physical assault          **31** Exclusion
   **38** Physical intimidation    **54** Social segregation
   **64** Mocking stereotypes     **7** Other (be specific):_____

   b. How do you know about racist incidents at your school?  (Check all that apply.)
   **31** You've been in the incident  **56** You witnessed an incident
   **57** Someone told you of one    **8** I know of no racist incidents at my school
   **47** Rumors                     **10** Other:_____

3. To what extent do you feel racism to be a serious problem in your school?  (Rate on a scale of 1 to 5 with "1"=very serious, and "5"=not a problem at all.)  Circle your choice.
   1(**6**) 2(**21**) 3(**39**) 4(**24**) 5(**7**)

4. What causes racism?  (Check all that apply.)
   **40** Feelings of inadequacy    **68** Ignorance        **56** Past experiences
   **45** Peer pressure              **75** Upbringing      **28** Media
   **70** Stereotypes                 **51** Fear              **6** Other_____

5. Check the words or symbols you think are racist.
   **54** swastika             **93** "nigger"        **34** "skinhead"
   **75** "Jap" (Japanese)   **64** "JAP" (Jewish)   **74** "white boy"

6. If you think some social groups are racially segregated, is it because (check if you agree; leave blank those you disagree with):
   **63** People come from different backgrounds    **39** People from the same race or ethnic group have
   **45** People stay with friends from their own         more in common
        neighborhoods                         **16** Other (please explain):_____
   **57** People have racist feelings            **8** I don't think social groups are racially segregated

7. Have you ever seen racism in any of these forms?  (Check if yes, leave blank if no.)
   **25** Discrimination in textbooks          **10** Faculty presenting class material in a discriminatory way
   **31** Faculty ignoring or singling out minority
   **22** Faculty being more negative to minority    **21** Not enough minority faculty members
        students                                **11** Other_____

8. Do you think that minority students discriminate against Whites?  (Circle one.)
   Yes (**72**)   No (**5**)       Other (**15**)

9. Do you and your friends discuss racism?
   Yes (**65**)   No (**26**)

10. Do you hold racist feelings?

    Yes (**23**)     No (**49**)     Other (**10**) (Explain "other.")_____

    The following questions are completely optional.  The reason they are asked is not to be personal, but to find out if certain groups of people feel more or less strongly about racism.  (82% answered these questions)

Sex:  Male / Female
Year in school:  1st, 2nd, 3rd, 4th, 5th
What is your racial identity?  (Ex. Black, Caucasian)_____
What is your ethnic identity?  (Ex. Italian, Jewish)_____

Reprinted with the permission of Shael Polakow-Suransky

## HANDOUT FOR ACTIVITY # 6.1

### IS THERE RACISM AT THIS SCHOOL?

This is an anonymous survey written by students.  Circle or mark all relevant responses--remember there is no ONE right answer.  Any comments are encouraged.  This is not a test.  The survey will probably take about 15-20 minutes.

1.  Here are some definitions of racism; check those that you agree with and leave blank those you disagree with.

    ___  Racism is when people aren't given or allowed equal opportunities because of their racial or ethnic background (for example Black, Asian, Jewish, White, Hispanic, Arab, etc.)

    ___  Racism is whenever people are discriminated against.

    ___  Racism is when people are segregated according to which racial or ethnic background they are from.

    ___  Racism is when people hate, dislike or fear other people because of their racial or ethnic background.

    ___  Racism is something that degrades, demoralizes or hurts people because they are from a certain racial or ethnic group.

    ___  Other, please write your own definition _____

2.  Is there racism at your school?  Yes / No / Other

    If yes

    a.  In your school how is racism shown?  (Check all that apply)?

    ___  Ethnic Slurs            ___  Threats against a person

    ___  Offensive remarks       ___  Threats against a group

    ___  Physical assault        ___  Exclusion

    ___  Physical intimidation   ___  Social segregation

    ___  Mocking stereotypes     ___  Other (be specific)_____

Copyright © 1997 by Allyn and Bacon

b. How do you know about racist incidents at your school?  (Check all that apply.)

___ You've been in the incident.

___ Someone told you of one.

___ Rumors

___ You witnessed an incident.

___ Other _____

3. To what extent do you feel racism to be a serious problem in your school?  (Rate on a scale of 1-5 with "1"=very serious, and "5"=not a problem at all.)  Circle your choice 1 2 3 4 5

4. What causes racism?  (Check all that apply)

___ Feelings of inadequacy      ___ Peer pressure

___ Stereotypes                 ___ Ignorance

___ Upbringing                  ___ Fear

___ Past experiences            ___ Media

___ Other_____

5. Check the words or symbols you think are racist.

___ swastika          ___ "Jap" (Japanese)   ___ "chink"

___ "nigger"          ___ "JAP" (Jewish)     ___ "skinhead"

___ "white boy"

6. If you think some social groups are racially segregated, is it because (Check if you agree, leave blank those you disagree with.)

___ People come from different backgrounds.

___ People stay with friends from their own neighborhoods.

___ People have racist feelings.

___ People from the same race or ethnic group have more in common .

___ Other (please explain)_____

Copyright © 1997 by Allyn and Bacon

7. Have you ever seen racism in any of these forms? (Check if yes, leave blank if no.)

    __ Discrimination in textbooks

    __ Faculty ignoring or singling out minority students

    __ Faculty being more negative to minority students

    __ Faculty presenting class material in a discriminatory way

    __ Other_____

8. Do you think that minority students discriminate against Whites? (Circle one)

    Yes / No / I don't know

9. Do you and your friends discuss racism? Yes / No

10. Do you hold racist feelings? Yes / No / Other (explain "other")_____
    _____

The following questions are completely optional. The reason they are asked is not to be personal, but to find out if certain groups of people feel more or less strongly about racism. [82% answered these questions]

    Sex:    Male / Female

    Year in school: 1st, 2nd, 3rd, 4th, 5th

    What is your racial identity? (Ex. Black, Caucasian)_____

Copyright © 1997 by Allyn and Bacon

## 6.2 Gender makes a difference/ Race makes a difference

Have your students complete the simple "gender makes a difference" and "race makes a difference" scales found on the following page (and in the Study Guide). Students' responses tend to pile up in the middle-to-little-difference end of the race scale. Students have trouble seeing that race affects their reactions. Gender, however, is another matter. Students' responses tend to pile up at the "gender makes a difference" end of the scale. If your students react the same way, ask them why it is relatively obvious to them that they act differently to people of different gender. (If they show a very different pattern, write or call us; we'll be curious and will help with the interpretation.) Some of the answers you will get will relate to courtship. Men and women, maybe especially young, single ones, are heavily invested in appearing attractive to the opposite gender. It also may seem important to reaffirm one's own gender identity when confronting the opposite gender. But why the necessity of these reactions? Does it have to be this way? Perhaps you can lead your students to consider the possibility that one's first reactions to a stranger should be founded on appreciation of that person's unique, human characteristics, regardless of gender.

If you have more than one social psychology section, results might be interestingly different for the two classes if these two scales were given to one of your classes before and one after they read the text material and participated in relevant classroom events. Alternatively, one of your classes might complete the scales under the additional instruction "Respond to these scales according to what you think should be the case, rather than what is the case," while the other class got no instruction or were told to "respond to these scales according to what you think should be the case, rather than what is the case," while the other class got no instruction or were told to "respond to these scales according to what really is the case, not what should be." Any of these procedures could lead to fruitful exchanges.

## HANDOUT FOR ACTIVITY # 6.2A

Imagine that you are encountering a person for the first time. Think of your subtle and overt reactions to the stranger: your posture, amount of eye contact, tone of voice, content of what you would say, willingness to talk, etc. Would the gender of the person make any difference in your reactions? Indicate the degree to which gender would make a difference on the scale below.

<---:---:---:---:---:---:--->

| | |
|---|---|
| sex of the person would make no difference | sex of the person would make a great difference |

---

## HANDOUT FOR ACTIVITY # 6.2B

Imagine that you are encountering a person for the first time. Think of your subtle and overt reactions to the stranger: your posture, amount of eye contact, tone of voice, content of what you would say, willingness to talk, etc. Would the race of the person make any difference in your reaction? Indicate the degree to which race would make a difference on the scale below.

<---:---:---:---:---:---:--->

| | |
|---|---|
| race of the person would make no difference | race of the person would make a great difference |

Copyright © 1997 by Allyn and Bacon

## 6.3 Agreements and Disagreements about European-Americans

As your text author points out, prejudice, and particularly stereotypes, have been assessed from the perspective of European-Americans (Whites). Every European-American "knows" the stereotypes of African-Americans, but what are the stereotypes of Whites? On those rare occasions when stereotypes of European-Americans have been assessed, it has usually been from their own perspective. It might be interesting to consider the stereotypes of Whites from African-Americans' perspective. Ask students anonymously to write down five words to describe "Blacks" and five words to describe "Whites." (You may need the cooperation of colleagues who teach other classes if you have few African-Americans in your class.) Compile a list of words used by at least 5 percent of European-American students in their descriptions of African-Americans and a similar list for self-descriptions. Do the same for the words used by African-Americans. Now compare the two lists describing African-Americans and the two describing European-Americans. Do European-Americans agree with African-Americans on the stereotyped words applicable to African-Americans? Ask the same question about words used by the two groups to describe European-Americans. Then compare your lists with the lists, printed after this exercise, that are taken from some actual research. These lists are also reproduced as transparencies 6.7 and 6.8.

You will undoubtedly find that each group's stereotypes of themselves are different from those attributed by the other group. You may also find that African-Americans "know" European-Americans better than the latter know the former: there is more agreement between the two groups on the stereotyped words applicable to European-Americans than on the stereotypes of African-Americans. If such is the case, how do students explain it?

## TABLE 1: Agreements and Disagreements about European-Americans
(European-American % listed first)

| Words used by about the same % of each sample | Words used at different % by the samples | Words in one sample, but in < 5% of the other |
|---|---|---|
| inventive (18,12)* | prejudiced (10,27)* | egotistical (7,0) |
| competitive (19,18) | corrupt (6,27) | free (6,0) |
| independent (12,14) | | happy (6,0) |
| friendly (15,14) | | kind (6,0) |
| arrogant (15,14) | | jealous (<5,14) |
| conceited (7,9) | | powerful (<5,14) |
| smart (32,27) | | wealthy (<5,14) |
| greedy (19,27) | | mean (<5,18) |
| | | humorous (12,<5) |
| | | lazy (12,<5) |
| *Chi Sqr. did not approach significance | *Chi Sqr. significant at least at the .035 | intelligent (10,<5) |
| | | rich (10,<5) |

**TABLE 2: Agreements and disagreements about African-Americans**
(African-American % listed first)

| Words used by about the same % of each sample | Words used at different % by the samples | Words in one sample, but in < 5% of the other |
|---|---|---|
| corrupt (9,11)* | smart (36,9)* | oppressed (18,<5) |
| arrogant (14,10) | independent (27,10) | proud (14,<5) |
| | athletic (14,40) | competitive (14,<5) |
| | friendly (23,11) | beautiful (14,0) |
| | strong (18,6) | determined (9,0) |
| | | educated (9,0) |
| | | religious (9,0) |
| | | intelligent (9,<5) |
| | | inventive (9,<5) |
| | | loud (<5,25) |
| | | humorous (<5,21) |
| | | funny (<5,10) |
| | | mean (<5,9) |
| | | prejudiced (<5,7) |
| | | musical (<5,7) |
| | | poor (<5,6) |
| | | moody (0,6) |
| *Chi Sqrs. did not approach significance | *Chi Sqrs. significant at .001 to .077 level | fast (0,6) |
| | | obnoxious (0,7) |

## 6.4 Women Leaders

How do women fare as leaders? Let's see. Divide your class into approximately equal groups, with each group not to exceed five members. Make sure that the number of females in each group is proportional to their number in the class. Appoint males as leaders for half of the groups and females as leaders for the remaining groups. As a first order of business, have each member complete a "map" of the first name and seating position of each person so that group members' names can be learned (maps are included on the next page or in the Study Guide). Give each group a social psychology topic to discuss from among those found in currently assigned chapters. Have members gain recognition from the leader before they speak, and instruct leaders to make a brief comment about each speaker's contribution. Allow at least fifteen minutes of discussion. If you don't normally have class discussion of this sort, indicate that you are "trying a new learning technique."

After discussions, have each member vote for the "member who made the greatest contribution to the discussion." There is a suggestion in the literature that you will find leaders getting the most votes, but male leaders doing better than female leaders (see Butler, D., & Geis, F. L., (1990). Nonverbal affect responses to male and female leaders: Implications for leadership evaluations. *Journal of Personality and Social Psychology, 58,* 48-59.) Or you may find that female leaders do no better than rank-and-file members, whereas such is not true for male leaders.

## HANDOUT FOR ACTIVITY # 6.4

### DISCUSSION GROUP SEATING CHART

Position Two
name:

Position Three
name:

Position One
leader's name:

Position Four
name:

Position Five:
name:

Copyright © 1997 by Allyn and Bacon

# Overhead Transparencies
These appear at the back of this manual.

**6.1** *A Theory of the Relationship between Racism and Prejudice*
**6.2** *Methods of Measuring Prejudice*
**6.3** *Theories of Prejudice*
**6.4** *The Tendency to View Outgroups As More Homogeneous Than Ingroups: Empirical Evidence*
**6.5** *Intergroup Contact: How It Exerts Its Effects*
**6.6** *Male and Female Executives: The Stereotype That Failed*
**6.7** *Agreements and Disagreements about African-Americans*
**6.8** *Agreements and Disagreements about European-Americans*

# Audiovisual Suggestions

### Allyn and Bacon Videos

* *Sex and Gender.* This video covers the ways in which males and females are similar and different and shows how sex roles reflect social values and psychological knowledge. (On Tape #9.)
* *Prejudice,* video, 28.5 mins. To obtain this videotape, consult your Allyn and Bacon sales representative. Robert A. Baron and Margaret Clark use dramatizations as a point of departure for a discussion on prejudice.

### Other Videos and Films

From Dr. J. Q. Adams's *Dealing with Diversity* one-hour videotapes on multicultural studies (order Classes 6, 20, and 23 from Television Services, Governors State University, University Park, IL 60466):

> *Class 6--Race: The World's Most Dangerous Myth.*
>> Professor Jerry Hirsch, behavioral geneticist at the University of Illinois, comments on notions of "race," and studio guest Professor Bem Allen talks about race and IQ. Different methods of classifying humans by race are also considered, and students respond to a Racial Quotient Questionnaire.

> *Class 20--Sexual Orientation Issues in the U.S.: Part 1.*
>> Stereotypes about homosexuality, difficulties of gays and lesbians in establishing open relationships, homophobia, and violence against gays and lesbians are considered by studio guests Gavotte Babe and Vernon Hauls of the Illinois Gay Lesbian Task Force.

> *Class 23--Hate Group in the U.S.*
>> Studio guest Arthur Jones of the America First Committee, a former American Nazi and continuing white supremacy advocate, generates quite a reaction from African-American students when, among other insults, he refers to Blacks as "retards." Dr. Adams, who is African-American, responds with such equanimity and intellectual sophistication that Jones is at times left speechless.

*What's the Difference being Different?*, 19511 (video) or #1949 (film), 19 mins. Research Press, Box 3177, Dept. K, Champaign, IL 61821 (217-352-3273). This video or film shows what multicultural education is all about as it goes inside an exciting program in the Nashville schools.

*Perceiving and Believing*, P, video. Insight Media. 121 W. the Street, New Your, NY 10024-4401 (800-233-9910). Ed Abner hosts a show that features dramatic and comic vignettes showing the error or referring to others as "them." Simplistic perceptions and unfair prejudgments are also considered.

*Racism in America*, FC-1919, video, 26 mins. Films for the Humanities and Sciences, Inc., P.O. Box 2053. Princeton, NJ 08543 (800-257-5126). Graphic depictions of the resurgence of bigotry and racially motivated acts of violence and vandalism.

*The Asianization of America*, FC-1912, video, 52 mins. Films for the Humanities and Sciences, Inc., P.O. Box 2053, Princeton. NJ 08543 (800-257-5126). Asians are the nation's fastest-growing group. Stereotypes have been changing: love/hate, then condescension, has given way to admiration and jealousy. This tape looks at where it will lead.

*Sex Role Development*, ESC-1303, film, 30 mins. Indiana University, Audiovisual Center, Bloomington, IN 47401. Considers the influence that sex roles and stereotypes have on people's lives, the way people learn those stereotypes, and new models for behavior.

*Fable of He and She*, CSC-2561, film 15 mins. Indiana University, Audiovisual Center, Bloomington, IN 47401. Cartoon characters portray sex stereotypes and in so doing show the absurdities to which we all may be driven by these stereotypes.

---

## Critical Thinking/Essay Questions

---

1. Thoroughly describe the relationship between prejudice and discrimination. Under what real-life circumstances will prejudice be expressed in discrimination? Not expressed?
2. How do prejudiced attitudes "color" most of what a bigoted person says and does? Give examples from your own experience, including at least one that involves a subtle form of prejudice.
3. Discuss tokenism and "reverse discrimination." Give an example of each from your experience. Tell how both can have benefits and drawbacks for "token" individuals and targets of reverse discrimination.
4. List the principles of realistic conflict theory, then illustrate two of them with examples from your experience.
5. Outline the procedure of the Robber's Cave experiment. How were us-versus-them and social competition illustrated by the experiment's results?
6. Use social learning theory as a framework for examining how stereotypes are formed and can become self-fulfilling. Briefly indicate how "illusory correlation" contributes to stereotypes that would bias jurors in a murder trial where the defendant is African-American.
7. Pick some group to which you belong and describe the variety of traits that members possess. Do the same for some group to which you do not belong. Look at the differences between the descriptions. What do they illustrate?
8. Examine and resolve the dilemma that busyness helps to prevent the activation of stereotypes but that once stereotypes are activated, busyness increases their use.
9. Choose some habitually conflicting groups and design a way to get them to work together and think differently about each other. (Hint: think of the Italian city study and the Robber's Cave experiment.)

10. Give some real-life examples of valued traits that are assigned to men and devalued traits that are assigned to women. If you were president of a company, what could you do to redistribute those trait assignments across your female and male employees?

11. Being targets of prejudice and discrimination increases African-Americans' sense of racial identity. Will knowledge of that link help European-Americans reduce their own prejudices? Hint: What kind of insight will European-Americans experience if they become convinced that African-Americans are showing increased racial identity?

---

## Sources for Lecture

---

Axtell, R. G. (Ed.). (1985). *Do's and taboos around the world,* New York: Wiley.
   Actell compiled this fascinating collection of cultural misunderstandings for the Parker Pen Company to help their international staff avoid blunders. It contains many practical examples of the need to appreciate cultural diversity.

*Beyond Hate with Bill Moyers,* PBS, May 13, 1991. (Order by title; $5.00 from Journal Graphics, Inc., 1535 Grant Street, Denver, CO 80203.) Bill Moyers takes a long and chilling look at hate. White Aryan Resistance representatives, Jimmy Carter, David Duke, Tom Metzger, neo-Nazis, Elie Wiesel, Skinheads, Professor Jerome Kagan, Morris Dees, and John Kenneth Galbraith are among those interviewed.

Dreyfous, L. (1991, August 4). "Jungle Fever" focuses attention on interracial families.
   Associated Press, *Peoria Journal Star,* p. D7. Spike Lee's movie gets people talking about interracial marriages, which increased from 50,000 to 200,000 from 1970 to 1990. Is the increase in interracial marriages (still a tiny percent of marriages) a sign that racism is dying a slow death?

Gregor, T. (1979). Short people. *Natural History, 88,* 14. If you have suspected that short people are objects of prejudice, you're right, especially if you live in the tropical forest of central Brazil.

Polakow-Suransky, S. & Ulaby, N. (1990, April). Students take action to combat racism. *Phi Delta Kappan, 71,* 601-606. This paper chronicles the study of high school students' prejudices--the study that used the questionnaire found in Discussion Topic 1 above. It shows that students can do something constructive about racism.

*Primetime Live,* ABC News, September 26, 1991. (Transcript #212; $5.00 from Journal Graphics, Inc., 1535 Grant Street, Denver, CO 80203.) Correspondent Diane Sawyer follows two young professionals, one African-American and the other European-American, as they examine subtle racism by prowling the department-store corridors, apartment rentals, and employment application beat. The differential treatment of the two men shocks the White man and angers the difficult-to-perturb Black man.

Smart-Grosvenor, V. (1983, June). Obsessed with "racial purity." *Ms.* An obscure Louisiana law, probably dating to the days of slavery, still requires that citizens be classified by race. Suzie Guillory Phipps, who thought she was white, discovered she was "colored" when applying for a passport. To make an ugly situation worse, she fought the classification in the courts. Her husband commented, "Hell, she ain't a nigger."

Toch, T. & Davis, J. (1990, April 23). Separate but equal all over again. *U.S. News and World Report,* pp. 37-38. Deja vu. Even in 1990, Louisiana still had not desegregated its colleges and universities. This case shows that segregation is still very much alive and well.

Trouble at the Top (1991, June 17). (*U.S. News and World Report,* pp. 38-48. Vidid depiction of the "glass ceiling" confronting women in the workplace. Women are shown to be behind in salary in almost every profession; this is true for college professors, elementary teachers, nurses, and waiters, among many others.

Webb, J. (1990, December 14). Car dealers cheat Blacks and women. Associated Press, *Peoria Journal Star,* p. A14. Ian Ayres, a Northwestern University law professor, conducted a study that showed women in general and Blacks in particular are considered "suckers" by auto dealers, who charge them more.

## Professional Update: Current Articles from Professional Sources

Brush, S. G. (1991, September/October). Women in science and engineering. *American Scientist, 79,* 404-419. Examines the observation that women are still seriously underrepresented in the sciences and engineering and have made little progress in the preceding five years. The author concludes that women are "leaking out of the science and engineering pipeline" because those who wish to hire them are not providing adequate incentives, working conditions, and opportunities for promotion. Women are embracing other career opportunities and will not reconsider science and engineering until barriers such as rewards, promotion opportunities, and conflicts with family life are removed.

Crocker, J., Cornwell, B., & Major, B. (1993). The stigma of overweight: Affective consequences of attributional ambiguity. *Journal of Personality and Social Psychology, 64,* 60-70. When can bigoted people display their prejudice and get away with it, not even experiencing the scorn of the victim? If the victim is an overweight woman, she blames her weight for the negative feedback provided by insensitive others, rather than the insensitive people.

Duckitt, John. (1992). Psychology and prejudice: A historical analysis and integrative framework. *American Psychologists, 47,* 1182-1193. Duckitt, a South African psychologist, does an excellent job of tracing the history of our (Western, primarily U. S.) orientation to the study of prejudice. He ends with a reasonable suggestion concerning how psychologists might integrate the various historical themes in the study of prejudice.

Levinson, W., Tolle, S. W., Lewis, C. (1989, November 30). Women in academic medicine. *New England Journal of Medicine, 321,* (22), 1511-1561. The authors, all physicians and two of the three women, conclude that it is possible, but difficult, for women to pursue careers in academic medicine. Most women academics interviewed believed that motherhood slowed their progress.

Monteith, M. J., Devine, P. G., & Zuwerink, J. R. (1993). Self-directed versus other-directed affect as a consequence of prejudice-related discrepancies. *Journal of Personality and Social Psychology, 64,* 198-210. Low-prejudiced subjects, regardless of the type of response, experienced negative *self-directed* affect when they transgressed against their nonprejudiced standards regarding gays. High-prejudiced subjects also had negative affect when they transgressed against their nonprejudiced standards for relatively controllable and unacceptable prejudiced responses, but they directed the affect *toward others.*

Ross, S. I., & Jackson, J. M. (1991). Teachers' expectation for black males' and black females' academic achievement. *Personality and Social Psychology Bulletin, 17,* 78-82. Teachers predicted the academic performance of Black male and female fourth-grade students from twelve case histories. Even when students had equivalent qualities, teachers consistently held more negative expectations for Black males. Lowest expectations were for independent, nonsubmissive Black males, who were least preferred as future pupils.

*Related Readings:* The following selections from *Readings in Social Psychology: General, Classic, and Contemporary Selections,* 3rd Edition, by Wayne Lesko (Allyn and Bacon, 1997) accompany this chapter.

Allen, B. P., & Niss, J. E. (1990). "A chill in the college classroom?" The authors placed video cameras in professors' classes to record their interactions with students. Among other results they found that males were more rewarded than females and that professors used a warmer voice tone when addressing white compared to black students. (Article 16)

Sherif, M. (1956). "Experiments in group conflict." Here are the details of Sherif and colleagues' famous camp study, which is featured in the text. (Article 17)

Crandall, C. S. (1994). This article examines whether prejudice towards fat people operates like symbolic racism. According to this approach, racial prejudice is a combination of negative beliefs passed down from one generation to the next and the belief that the target of the prejudice does not live up to traditional, and treasured, cultural values. Parallels were found between "fatism" and symbolic racism. (Article 18)

# Chapter 7

# Interpersonal Attraction: Initial Contact, Feelings of Attraction, Becoming Acquainted

## Chapter-at-a-Glance

| CHAPTER OUTLINE | INSTRUCTION IDEAS | SUPPLEMENTS* |
|---|---|---|
| **I. Meeting Strangers: Proximity and Emotions**<br>• Physical Surroundings: Repeated Interpersonal Contact Leads to Attraction<br><br>• Positive and Negative Affect: The Basis of Liking and Disliking<br><br>• **Social Psychology: On the Applied Side**   Stigma by Association | Learning Objectives 7.1 to 7.7<br><br>Activity 7.1<br><br>Discussion Topic 2<br><br>Critical Thinking Questions 1, 2 | Test Bank Questions 7.1 to 7.34<br><br>Transparency 7.1 |
| **II. Becoming Acquainted: Needing to Affiliate and Responding to Observable Characteristics**<br>• The Need to Affiliate: Dispositional Differences and External Events<br><br>• **Cornerstones of Social Psychology**   Festinger's Social Comparison Theory<br><br>• Responding to Observable Characteristics | Learning Objectives 7.8 to 7.16<br><br>Activity 7.2 (Handout)<br><br>Discussion Topic 1<br><br>Critical Thinking Questions 3, 5 | Test Bank Questions 7.35 to 7.83<br><br>Readings:<br>- Lesko 19, The Eye of the Beholder<br>- Lesko 18, Prejudice Against Fat People |
| **III. Similarity and Reciprocal Positive Evaluations: Becoming Close Acquaintances and Moving toward Friendship**<br>• Similarity: Birds of a Feather Really Do Flock Together<br><br>• **Cornerstones of Social Psychology**   Newcomb's Effect of Similarity on Attraction<br><br>• Reciprocity: Mutual Liking<br><br>• **Social Diversity: A Critical Analysis**   The Similarity-Attraction Relationship as a Cross-Cultural Phenomenon | Learning Objectives 7.17 to 7.24<br><br>Discussion Topics 3, 4, 5<br><br>Activities 7.3, 7.4, 7.5 (Handouts)<br><br>Critical Thinking Question 4 | Test Bank Questions 7.84 to 7.140<br><br>Readings:<br>- Lesko 20, The Prediction of Interpersonal Attraction<br>- Lesko 21, The Transition From Controlled Laboratory Experimentation to Less Controlled Settings<br><br>Transparency 7.2 |

*See Audiovisual Suggestions

# 7

# Interpersonal Attraction:  Getting Acquainted, Becoming Friends

---

## Chapter Outline:  Getting the Overall Picture

---

I. **Meeting Strangers:  Proximity and Emotions**
- A. Physical Surroundings:  Repeated Interpersonal Contact Leads to Attraction
  1. Why Does Repeated Contact Increase Interpersonal Attraction?
  2. Residential Proximity:  Friendships and Marriage
  3. Manipulating Proximity to Determine Its Effects
- B. Positive and Negative Affect:  The Basis of Liking and Disliking
  1. A Person Who Does Something That Arouses Positive or Negative Affect Is Liked or Disliked Accordingly
  2. A Person Who Is Simply Associated with Positive or Negative Affect Is Liked or Disliked Accordingly
  3. The Affect-Centered Model of Attraction
- C. Social Psychology:  On the Applied Side: Stigma by Association

II. **Becoming Acquainted:  Needing to Affiliate and Responding to Observable Characteristics**
- A. The Need to Affiliate:  Dispositional Differences and External Events
  1. Affiliation Need as a Trait
  2. Affiliation Need as a State
- B. Cornerstones of Social Psychology: Festinger's Social Comparison Theory
- C. Responding to Observable Characteristics
  1. Physical Attractiveness:  A Major Determinant of Liking
  2. Searching for the Physical Details that Constitute Attractiveness
  3. Situational Effects on Perceived Attractiveness
  4. Other Overt Characteristics that Influence Attraction

III. **Similarity and Reciprocal Positive Evaluations:  Becoming Close Acquaintances and Moving Toward Friendship**
- A. Similarity:  Birds of a Feather Really Do Flock Together
  1. Attraction and Attitude Similarity
- B. Cornerstones of Social Psychology: Newcomb's Effect of Similarity on Attraction
  1. Why Do Similar and Dissimilar Attitudes Influence Attraction?
  2. The Matching Hypothesis:  Liking Others Who Are Like Yourself
- C. Reciprocity:  Mutual Liking
- D. Social Diversity:  A Critical Analysis--The Similarity-Attraction Relationship as a Cross-Cultural Phenomenon

## Learning Objectives
After studying this chapter, students should be able to:

**7.1** Examine the relationship between repeated exposure and interpersonal attraction, including subliminal repeated exposure.

**7.2** Describe how propinquity affects: a) friendship formation in dormitories and in other residential environments; b) who one marries.

**7.3** Explain the advantage of manipulating proximity to determine its effects on attraction, and describe what studies have found regarding seating patterns and friendship formation in classrooms.

**7.4** Summarize research demonstrating that when a person does something arousing positive or negative affect, he or she is liked or disliked accordingly.

**7.5** Summarize research demonstrating that when a person is simply associated with positive or negative affect, he or she is liked or disliked accordingly.

**7.6** Explain how the affect-centered model of attraction accounts for the central role played by affective responses in determining who is liked and who is disliked.

**7.7** Summarize research that describes our affective reaction to a stigmatized person and also our reaction to someone simply associated with a stigmatized person.

**7.8** Describe the need for affiliation as a trait, comparing explicit and implicit affiliation needs, and be familiar with Hill's four motives underlying affiliation.

**7.9** Give examples of situations that produce an affiliation need in us.

**7.10** Understand the three basic hypotheses derived from Festinger's social comparison theory.

**7.11** Describe how physical attractiveness is related to the following: a) perceived desirability as a date; b) reproductive success; c) stereotyping; d) reactions to and by infants; e) appearance anxiety; and f) attribution of negative attributes.

**7.12** Explain how Cunningham (1986) determined that males like "childlike" and "mature" features. How did Langlois and Roggman (1990) determine that people like "average" faces?

**7.13** Describe the "contrast effect" in physical attractiveness ratings, along with the effects of knowing others' ratings and the effects of closing time.

**7.14** Examine stereotypes that exist for endomorphs, mesomorphs, and ectomorphs.

**7.15** Examine the negative stereotypes that are found for overweight persons, and indicate how people are affected by these stereotypes.

**7.16** Explain how perceptions of people are influenced by the following: a) youthful-appearing adult; b) behavioral cues; c) male dominance vs. sensitivity; d) food habits; e) wearing glasses; f) first names.

**7.17** Describe research findings supporting the hypothesis that similar attitudes lead to attraction. Compare this hypothesis to the alternate notion that initial attraction is followed by later similarity.

**7.18** Understand the fact that the basis of the similarity-attraction effect seems to be the proportion of similar attitudes expressed, regardless of total number of topics.

**7.19** Explain the role of similar vs. dissimilar attitudes in creating the similarity-attraction effect, according to Rosenbaum's repulsion hypothesis. Describe the basis for rejecting the repulsion hypothesis.

**7.20** Examine the false consensus effect, and indicate its relationship to Rosenbaum's repulsion hypothesis.

**7.21** Describe how each of the following explains the similarity-attraction effect: a) balance theory; b) social comparison theory: and c) Rushton's evolution-based genetic explanation.

**7.22** Give examples of various dimensions on which people are attracted to matched partners, and indicate how we respond to obvious mismatches in physical attractiveness.

**7.23** Describe how our behavior toward an individual is affected by the receipt of a positive evaluation from him/her.

**7.24** Describe whether the usual linear relationship between similarity and attraction was found in all five of the cultures studied. Explain how students in Japan and Texas were different from those in Hawaii, India, and Mexico.

# Discussion Topics and Questions

## 1. The Romantic Ideal

The romantic ideal, the notion that people should marry on the basis of their being "in love," is perhaps more firmly established in the United States than in any other country in the world. Parents still have a great deal to say about the choice of a marriage partner in many countries, and in some cultures parents arrange marriages. An interesting question is the degree to which parents and their children would agree as to the appropriateness of a particular potential mate. Who is in a better position to make a rational choice of a marriage partner--parents or their children? In what ways will their choices be different? Before you begin the discussion, have students indicate their agreement or disagreement with the following statement: "One should not marry against the serious advice of one's parents."

## 2. Factors Influencing Your Friendships

Ask students to think of their best friend and to describe how they became friends. Then ask them to describe generally what it is that causes them to choose others as friends. Compare the students' reports to the theories presented in the text. Do they mention propinquity, conditioned emotional responses, similarity, physical attractiveness, reciprocal evaluations, and so on? Are the same factors important early as well as later in a relationship?

## 3. Love and Liking

Researchers disagree about whether love is just an extreme form of liking or whether love and liking are qualitatively different emotions. Zick Rubin distinguishes between liking and loving and has developed separate scales to measure each. Similarly, there is the commonly made distinction between passionate love and companionate love. A good source to read for background information is the book *Liking, Loving and Relating* by Hendrick and Hendrick, published in 1983 by Brooks/Cole. This is the kind of question on which most people have an opinion, so it's important for you to be familiar with conclusions reached by the experts.

## 4. Six Styles of Love

Lee has proposed a typology of love that includes six major styles of loving. The styles of loving proposed by lee (1977) are as follows:

*Eros:* Loving someone primarily because of his or her physical appearance. The Eros lover searches for a person whose physical appearance matches his or her ideal physical type.

*Ludus:* Playful love. The Ludus lover does not commit to a single relationship but prefers to play the field.

*Storage:* Loving someone as a result of a slowly developing attachment to that person. The Storge lover moves slowly, carefully, without great passion, to a lasting commitment.

*Mania:* Intense romantic love. The Mania lover is jealous, thinks intensely and excessively about his or her beloved, and needs repeated reassurance that he or she is loved in return.

*Agape:* Altruistic love. Given without expectation of getting anything in return; gentle, caring, and dutiful.

*Pragma:* Selecting the "right" person. The Pragma lover looks for someone who has the "right" education, religion, job, and so on.

Lee's typology is presented in an article in *Personality and Social Psychology Bulletin (3,* 173-182). A 1986 article on Lee's typology by the Hendricks is presented in the "Update" section below; included in the 1986 article is a scale for measuring each of the six types.

## 5. Equity Theory and Relationship Satisfaction

Does equity theory predict one's level of satisfaction with an intimate relationship? Some theorists have argued that a love relationship in which a partner is concerned about his or her own outcome is flawed. These theorists contend that true love means that the person is concerned only with what they can *get* from the relationship. On the other hand, equity theorists have maintained that in intimate relationships, just as in other human relationships, people are driven by a desire for equity.

Although a "pure reward" theory might argue that the more one gets for oneself from a relationship, the greater the satisfaction, this doesn't seem to be the case. Instead the most satisfied are those who feel equitably treated. Does your class agree with equity theory prediction?

---

## Learning Activities: Classroom Exercises/Demonstrations

---

### 7.1 Friendship Map

An exercise that students can carry out in their everyday environment is to construct a friendship map of their dormitory floor. The map should be a summary of who is friends with whom. If several students construct maps of their own floors, it would be instructive to combine the information to determine the probability of friendship as a function of propinquity. Are the students surprised to learn how much impact propinquity has on their friendship developments?

### 7.2 Hill's Interpersonal Orientation Scale

The text discusses recent work by Craig Hill that proposes that four basic motives underlie the disposition to be affiliative. Hill has developed the Interpersonal Orientation Scale to measure the four motives. The scale is presented on the following page and in the Study Guide. You are encouraged to have your students find out how they stand on each of the four motives.

The items for each of the four subscales on the Interpersonal Orientation Scale are as follows:

Items on the Emotional Support Subscale: 1, 4, 9, 15, 17, 23

Items on the Attention Subscale: 5, 8, 16, 19, 21, 22

Items on the Positive Stimulation Subscale:  3, 6, 10, 11, 13, 20, 24, 25, 26

Items on the Social Comparison Subscale:  2, 7, 12, 14, 18

To compute score for each subscale, first convert the alphabetic letters on the scales to numeric values:  A = 1, B = 2, C = 3, D = 4, E = 5.  Then add the numeric values together for the items listed for each subscale.

**HANDOUT FOR ACTIVITY # 7.2**

INTERPERSONAL ORIENTATION SCALE

If a particular statement describes your typical reaction or feelings about others very well, then it would be "Completely true" and you would write the letter "E." If a particular statement does <u>not</u> describe you well or is opposite of the way you feel, then it is "Not at all true" and you should write the letter "A." The scale to use in responding to each statement is as follows:

| A | B | C | D | E |
|---|---|---|---|---|
| Not at all True | Slightly True | Somewhat True | Mostly True | Completely True |

____ 1. One of my greatest sources of comfort when things get rough is being with other people.

____ 2. I prefer to participate in activities alongside other people rather than by myself because I like to see how I am doing on the activity.

____ 3. The main thing I like about being around other people is the warm glow I get from contact with them.

____ 4. It seems like whenever something bad or disturbing happens to me I often just what to be with a close, reliable friend.

____ 5. I mainly like people who seem strongly drawn to me and who seem infatuated with me.

____ 6. I think I get satisfaction out of contact with others more than most people realize.

____ 7. When I am not certain about how well I am doing at something, I usually like to be around others so I can compare myself to them.

____ 8. I like to be around people when I can be the center of attention.

____ 9. When I have not done very well on something that is very important to me, I can get to feeling better simply by being around other people.

____ 10. Just being around others and finding out about them is one of the most interesting things I can think of doing.

____ 11. I seem to get satisfaction from being with others more than a lot of other people do.

____ 12. If I am uncertain about what is expected of me, such as on a task or in a social situation, I usually like to be able to look to certain others for cues.

____ 13. I feel like I have really accomplished something valuable when I am able to get close to someone.

Copyright © 1997 by Allyn and Bacon

___ 14. I find that I often have the desire to be around other people who are experiencing the same thing I am when I am unsure about what is going on.

___ 15. During times when I have to go through something painful, I usually find that having someone with me makes it less painful.

___ 16. I often have a strong need to be around people who are impressed with what I am like and what I do.

___ 17. If I feel unhappy or kind of depressed, I usually try to be around other people to make me feel better.

___ 18. I find that I often look to certain other people to see how I compare to others.

___ 19. I mainly like to be around others who think I am an important, exciting person.

___ 20. I think it would be satisfying if I could have very close friendships with quite a few people.

___ 21. I often have a very strong desire to get people I am around to notice me and appreciate what I am like.

___ 22. I don't like being with people who may give me less than positive feedback about myself.

___ 23. I usually have the greatest need to have other people around me when I feel upset about something.

___ 24. I think being close to others, listening to them, and relating to them on a one-to-one level is one of my favorite and most satisfying pastimes.

___ 25. I would find it very satisfying to be able to form new friendships with whomever I liked.

___ 26. One of the most enjoyable things I can think of that I like to do is just watching people and seeing what they are like.

Copyright © 1996 by Allyn and Bacon

### 7.3 Determining Degree of Romanticism

Some theorists have discussed a phenomenon they call *romanticism*. Romanticism tends to have two components. One is a belief that "love will conquer all," and the other is that one should marry for love. On the next page and in the Study Guide you will find examples of statements used to assess people's degree of romanticism. For each of the five statements, the respondent should indicate his or her degree of agreement. Determine scores by adding up the responses. Before the responses are added, items 1 and 3 should be reversed (i.e., agreement with items 2, 4, 5 indicates a romantic attitude, whereas disagreement with items 1 and 3 indicates a romantic attitude). What are the consequences of a belief in romanticism?

## HANDOUT FOR ACTIVITY # 7.3

### ROMANTICISM SCALE

Respond to the following five statements by indicating the degree to which you agree or disagree with the statement. Respond using the following scale for each statement:

| Strongly Agree | Moderately Agree | Neither Agree Nor Disagree | Moderately Disagree | Strongly Disagree |
|---|---|---|---|---|
| 1 | 2 | 3 | 4 | 5 |

__1. Economic security should be considered before selecting a marriage partner.

__2. True love leads to almost perfect happiness.

__3. Most of us could sincerely love any one of several people equally well.

__4. If I were in love with someone, I would marry him/her regardless of his/her social class and family background.

__5. A deep love for another can compensate for differences in religious and economic background.

Copyright © 1997 by Allyn and Bacon

**7.4 Similarity-Attraction Hypothesis and the Adjective Checklist**

This exercise is designed to test the hypothesis that similarity and attraction are related. The text devotes much attention to the similarity-attraction hypothesis. This exercise provides very reliable data and generally serves as an interesting introduction to the chapter.

An Adjective Checklist for use in this activity is presented on the next page. Students are instructed to go through the list of adjectives three times. First, they should go through the list and check those adjectives that describe themselves. Second, they should think of their best friends and check the adjectives that apply. Finally, in the third column they should check the adjectives that apply to a person they know, but with whom they could never be friends.

After the students have completed the checklist, have them count the number of traits in common between self and friend. A trait in common occurs whenever a trait is checked for both self and friend, or whenever a trait is unchecked for both. Likewise, have them count the number of traits in common between self and nonfriend. You will find that students have more in common with their friends than with nonfriends. The handout for this activity can be found on the following page or in the Study Guide.

## HANDOUT FOR ACTIVITY # 7.4

| | SELF | FRIEND | NON-FRIEND |
|---|---|---|---|
| 1. active | ___ | ___ | ___ |
| 2. aggressive | ___ | ___ | ___ |
| 3. ambitious | ___ | ___ | ___ |
| 4. belligerent | ___ | ___ | ___ |
| 5. brave | ___ | ___ | ___ |
| 6. dependent | ___ | ___ | ___ |
| 7. dominant | ___ | ___ | ___ |
| 8. gentle | ___ | ___ | ___ |
| 9. helpful | ___ | ___ | ___ |
| 10. independent | ___ | ___ | ___ |
| 11. needs sympathy | ___ | ___ | ___ |
| 12. obliging | ___ | ___ | ___ |
| 13. passive | ___ | ___ | ___ |
| 14. peaceful | ___ | ___ | ___ |
| 15. protective | ___ | ___ | ___ |
| 16. seeks protection | ___ | ___ | ___ |
| 17. self-centered | ___ | ___ | ___ |
| 18. self-confident | ___ | ___ | ___ |
| 19. sociable | ___ | ___ | ___ |
| 20. tactless | ___ | ___ | ___ |
| 21. timid | ___ | ___ | ___ |
| 22. unconventional | ___ | ___ | ___ |

Copyright © 1997 by Allyn and Bacon

## 7.5 The Dating Survey

Jeffrey Simpson of Texas A & M has published a survey in *Teaching of Psychology (15[1]*, 31-33) that assesses past dating behavior and willingness to change partners, both of which are components of commitment to relationships. The dating survey is found on the next page and in the Study Guide. On the basis of their responses to the survey, students are placed into one of three categories. Students who answer "yes" to the first question on the survey (i.e., those who are dating one person exclusively) are referred to as "exclusive daters." Students who answer "no" to the first question but "yes" to the third one (i.e., those who are not dating one person exclusively but who have dated at least two people in the past year) are referred to as "multiple daters." Those who respond "no" to both questions because they are married or because they do not date cannot provide data for classroom analysis. (Simpson found, however, that only 15 to 20 percent of undergraduates enrolled in daytime courses typically fall into this third category. Even though these students cannot provide data for the exercise themselves, they still find the exercise to be interesting and valuable.)

Once students have completed the dating survey, the next step is to find out whether commitment in dating relationships is related to the widely studied individual difference dimension of self-monitoring. Two studies published by Snyder and Simpson (1984) in *Journal of Personality and Social Psychology (47*, 1281-1291) found that high self-monitors typically adopt an uncommitted orientation to dating relationships, whereas low self-monitors tend to adopt a committed one. The Self-Monitoring Scale is found in Chapter 5 of this Instructor's Manual. After students have completed and scored the Self-Monitoring Scale, determine whether you have replicated the self-monitoring results of Snyder and Simpson. Create four columns on the chalkboard, one for each of the following groups: High self-monitors/exclusive daters; high self-monitors/multiple daters; low self-monitors/exclusive daters; and low self-monitors/multiple daters. Two comparisons are especially suggested. First, using only exclusive daters, compare the number of months in the relationship for high and low self-monitors. The expectation is that low self-monitors will remain in relationships longer. Second, using only multiple daters, compare the number of partners for high and low self-monitors. The expectation is that high self-monitors will report a higher number of partners. Detailed suggestion regarding how to analyze and present the data to your class is found in the *Teaching Psychology* article mentioned above.

**HANDOUT FOR ACTIVITY # 7.5**

DATING SURVEY

1.  Are you currently dating someone exclusively (that is, one person and no one else)?  (Check one.)

    yes____        no____

2.  If yes, how many months have you dated this person?  ____

3.  If you are not dating one person exclusively at the present time, have you dated at least two different people in the past year?  (Check one.)

    yes____        no____

4.  If yes, how many different persons have you dated in the past year?  ____

5.  If you are currently dating someone (whether exclusively or not), please write your current (or most steady) dating partner's initials on the first line below.  Then write the initials of 3 opposite-sex friends on the lines that follow.

    Current partner  ____

    Friend No. 1     ____

    Friend No. 2     ____

    Friend No. 3     ____

6.  If you could ideally form a close, intimate dating relationship with either your current dating partner or Friend No. 1, whom would you choose?

7.  If you could ideally form a close, intimate dating relationship with either your current dating partner or Friend No. 2, whom would you choose?

8.  If you could ideally form a close, intimate dating relationship with either your current dating partner or Friend No. 3, whom would you choose?

From Simpson, J. (1988).  Self-monitoring and commitment to dating relationships.  Teaching of Psychology, 15 (1), pp. 31-33.  Copyright 1988 by Lawrence Erlbaum Associates.  Reprinted by permission of the publisher and author.

Copyright © 1997 by Allyn and Bacon

## Overhead Transparencies
These appear at the back of this manual.

**7.1** *The Reinforcement-Affect Model of Attraction*
**7.2** *The Three-Factor Theory of Passionate Love*

## Audiovisual Suggestions

*Are We Still Going to the Movies?* 21730, 1974, color, 14 mins. Pennsylvania State University, Audiovisual Services, Special Services Building, University Park, PA 16802 (814-865-6314). A young couple's relationship is suffering as a result of their disagreement on the amount of sexual involvement to have with each other. Intended to provoke discussion of premarital sexuality and sex roles. From the *Conflict and Awareness* series. Produced by Tom Lazarus.

*Beauty Knows No Pain*, 31910, 1973, color, 25 mins. Pennsylvania State University, Audiovisual Services, Special Services Building, University Park, PA 16802 (814-865-6314). Coeds aspiring to join the Kilgore College majorettes submit to the ordeal of training and testing. Reactions of both winners and losers show the value that the "Rangerette" ideal holds for them. Produced by Elliott Erwitt.

*Divorce: For Better or for Worse*, Parts 1 and 2, 50423, 1976, color, 51 mins. Pennsylvania State University, Audiovisual Services, Special Services Building, University Park, PA 16802 (814-865-6314). Divorce is "a kind of death," according to one of the narrators, a form of saying good-bye that entails grief and restructuring of lives and that touches most of us in some way. Film focuses on actual case histories of the divorced and divorcing to show the emotional and financial toll, the need for legal reform, and the need for stricter regulation of counselors and therapists. From the ABC News "Closeup" series.

*Kinds of Love*, NET 2037, 29 mins. Audiovisual Center, Indiana University, Bloomington, IN 47401. Interviews with Father Thurston David and Erich Fromm address misconceptions about love, the relationship between sexuality and love, and love as a religious virtue.

*Love and Sex* (from Phil Donahue's "The Human Animal" series), EC-1132, VHS or Beta videotape, color, 52 mins. Falling in love, having sex, making babies--these are easy. Understanding human sexuality is much harder. Phil Donahue takes viewers on an odyssey showing women at a male strip club and a gay rights march, a hospital room where an unwed teenage mother is giving birth, and classrooms where teachers and parents are trying to help teenagers come to grips with their sexual selves. Love, monogamy, hetero- and homosexuality are among the topics covered by Donahue, by consultants Dr. William Masters of the Masters & Johnson Institute and Dr. June Reinisch of the Kinsey Institute, and by Donahue's best resource, ordinary people.

*Love Tapes*, MVCS-1034, 1980 videocassette, 30 mins. Pennsylvania State University, Audiovisual Services, Special Services Building, University Park, PA 16802 (814-865-6314). A series of three-minute statements by people from all walks of life who candidly record their feelings about love against background music of their own choosing. Included are Darrell, a black college student, afraid of love; Darlene, unloved as a child, who finds that men treat her callously; Rose, in her eighties, recalling her changing needs; and Frieda, a disabled professor, who struggles for self-worth. The tapes were recorded as part of an experimental video art project that involved the installation of video recording equipment in museums and other public places. Produced by Wendy Clarke.

*Morning After,* 1983, color, 17 mins. Filmmakers Library, Inc., 133 E. 58th Street, New York, NY 10022. Shows the vulnerability of a seemingly cool, sophisticated man to the breakup of a long-term relationship.

## Critical Thinking/Essay Questions

1.   Summarize the effect that propinquity has on interpersonal attraction.
2.   Describe findings that show how interpersonal liking is influenced by mood induced by situational events. How does the reinforcement-affect model account for these results?
3.   Compare relationships in which partners are matched versus mismatched in physical attractiveness.
4.   Explain how the repulsion hypothesis accounts for the fact that we are more attracted to similar than to dissimilar others.
5.   Explain how the dispositional need for affiliation is related to the acquaintance process.

## Sources for Lecture

Cash, T. F., & Janda, L. H. (1984). In the eye of the beholder. *Psychology Today,* December, pp. 46-52. Attractive women are preferred for dates, friendships, and jobs. On the job, however, women are perceived more positively if they do not look too feminine.

Davis, K. E. (1985). Near and dear: Friendship and love compared. *Psychology Today,* February, pp. 22-30. Friendship and love have much in common, but there are two additional clusters of factors that are typical of love: a "passion cluster" and a "caring cluster."

Fischer, C. (1983). The friendship cure-all. *Psychology Today,* January, pp. 74-78. The California State Department of Mental Health conducted an advertising campaign to convince people to develop their social relationships. This article takes a critical look at the campaign.

Hamburger, A. C. (1988). Beauty quest. *Psychology Today,* May, pp. 29-32. The authors note that cosmetic surgery to improve looks and figures is more common than ever before. What can people expect after undergoing such surgery? Oftentimes, people expect too much.

Lynn, M., & Shurgot, B. A. Responses to lonely hearts advertisements: Effects of reported physical attractiveness, physique, and coloration. *Personality and Social Psychology Bulletin, 10(3),* 349-357. Lynn and Shurgot analyzed personal ads, the lonely hearts classifieds, that appeared in a Columbus, Ohio monthly. They tabulated the number of responses to each ad to determine what characteristics were most appealing to potential romantic partners.

Meer, J. (1985). The dating game: Ladies' choice. *Psychology Today,* March, p. 16. How a woman can ask for a date and not be seen as making a sexual advance. Meer summarizes research by Muehlenhard et al. suggesting that what she should do is emphasize her intelligence.

Rubenstein, C. (1983). Love and romance: A *Psychology Today* reader survey. *Psychology Today,* February, pp. 60-64. A questionnaire surveys the current status of love and romance.

Trotter, R. J. (1986). The three phases of love. *Psychology Today,* September, pp. 46-54. Summary of Sternberg's three-sided theory of love. The components? Commitment, intimacy, and passion.

## Professional Update: Current Articles from Professional Sources

Baumeister, R. F., Wotman, S. R., & Stillwell, A. M. Unrequited love: On heartbreak, anger, guilt, scriptlessness, and humiliation. *Journal of Personality and Social Psychology, 64,* 377-394. Unreciprocated romantic attraction is explored through comparison of narrative accounts of would-be lovers and rejectors. Judgments and attributions made by both are examined.

Forgas, J. P. (1993). On making sense of odd couples: Mood effects on the perception of mismatched relationships. *Personality and Social Psychology Bulletin, 19,* 59-70. Subjects made judgments about couples who were either well-matched or ill-matched for physical attractiveness. Mood of the subjects making the judgments was also varied. Mood had a greater influence on judgments of ill-matched couples than it did on judgments of well-matched couples.

Kenrick, D. T., Montello, D. R., Gutierres, S. E., & Trost, M. R. (1993). Effects of physical attractiveness on affect and perceptual judgments: When social comparison overrides social reinforcement. *Personality and Social Psychology bulletin, 19,* 195-199. Researchers recorded subjects' responses to photos of attractive individuals. Sometimes attractive photo sequences were interrupted by an average face, sometimes not. Results were different for same- and opposite-sex sequences, but results suggest that one's cognitive appraisal of physical attractiveness and one's affective reaction to it operate independently.

Kurdek, L. A. (1993). Predicting marital dissolution: A 5-year prospective study of newlywed couples. *Journal of Personality and Social Psychology, 64,* 221-142. Four approaches were examined for their ability to predict which newlywed couples would remain together and which would part. Factors examined include demographics, personality traits, interdependence, discrepancies in traits, and conflict-resolution styles.

Zebrowitz, L. A., Olson, K., & Hoffman, K. (1993). Stability of babyfacedness and attractiveness across the lifespan. *Journal of Personality and Social Psychology, 64,* 453-466. Changes in babyfacedness and attractiveness as a function of age were examined. A distinction was drawn between differential stability, structural stability, and absolute stability in facial appearance, with relatively low levels of stability generally being found.

*Related Readings:* The following selections from *Readings in Social Psychology: General, Classic, and contemporary Selections,* 3rd Edition, by Wayne Lesko (Allyn and Bacon, 1997) accompany this chapter.

Cash, T. F. & Janda, L. H. (1984). "The eye of the beholder." A large body of research suggests that physical attractiveness makes a significant impact on our judgements of other people although most of us would feel somewhat reluctant to admit that such factors play such an important role. This article suggests that a form of discrimination called *beautyism* may operate in the workplace. (Article 19)

Newcomb T. M. (1956). "The prediction of interpersonal attraction." Studies of friendship patterns in housing developments found that how close people lived to one another was the most important determinant of who would become friends. This early research suggested that propinquity, or physical proximity to others, is an important initial determinant of attraction. However, propinquity may only serve as an initial factor. One additional variable important in determining interpersonal attraction that Theodore Newcomb discovered in his research using "real-life" dormitory students, was similarity. (Article 20)

Byrne, E. (1992). "The transition from controlled labortory expeerimentation to less controlled settings: surprise! Additional variables are operative." This article provides an excellent summary of the similarity-attraction research. Since most of the attraction literature has employed laboratory and often paper-and-pencil measures of attraction rather than field studies of the phenomena, Donn Byrne explores the question of how one makes the transition from laboratory experimentation to generalizing the findings to less controlled, "real world," settings. (Article 21)

# Chapter 8

# The Joys and Sorrows of Close Relationships:
# Family, Friends, Lovers, and Spouses

## Chapter-at-a-Glance

| CHAPTER OUTLINE | INSTRUCTION IDEAS | SUPPLEMENTS* |
|---|---|---|
| *I. Initial Interdependent Relationships: Family Interactions and Close Friendships versus Loneliness* <br> • Close Relatives: It All Begins in the Family <br><br> • Close Friendships: Establishing Relationships beyond the Family <br><br> • Loneliness: Life without a Close Relationship | Learning Objectives 8.1 to 8.7 <br><br> Discussion Topics 3, 4 <br><br> Activities 8.1, 8.3 (Handouts) <br><br> Critical Thinking Question 1 | Test Bank Questions 8.1 to 8.55 <br><br> Transparency 8.1 |
| *II. Romantic Relationships, Love, and Physical Intimacy* <br> • Romantic Relationships <br><br> • Do You Love Me? And What Does That Mean? <br><br> • **Social Psychology: On the Applied Side**   What Does Love Mean to You? <br> • Premarital Sexuality | Learning Objectives 8.8 to 8.13 <br><br> Discussion Topic 1 <br><br> Activity 8.2 (Handout) <br><br> Critical Thinking Questions 2-6 | Test Bank Questions 8.56 to 8.112 <br><br> Readings: <br> - Lesko 22, The Lessons of Love <br> - Lesko 23, Playing Hard to Get <br><br> Transparencies 8.2, 8.3, 8.4 |
| *III. Marital Relationships: Interacting with a Spouse and Responding to Problems* <br> • Moving from a Romantic Relationship to a Married Relationship <br><br> • **Cornerstones of Social Psychology**   Terman's Investigation of Husband-Wife Similarity and the Success of the Marriage <br><br> • Troubled Relationships: Problems and the Effects of Failure <br><br> • **Social Diversity: A Critical Analysis**   Love and Intimacy: Individualistic versus Collectivistic Perspectives | Learning Objectives 8.14 to 8.21 <br><br> Discussion Topic 2 <br><br> Critical Thinking Questions 7-11 | Test Bank Questions 8.113 to 8.155 <br><br> Reading: <br> - Lesko 24, Mate Selection Preferences <br><br> Transparencies 8.5, 8.6 |

*See Audiovisual Suggestions

 **8**

# The Joys and Sorrows of Close Relationships: Family, Friends, Lovers, and Spouses

---

## Chapter Outline: Getting the Overall Picture

---

**I.** **Initial Interdependent Relationships: Family Interactions and Close Friendships versus Loneliness**
   A. Close Relatives: It All Begins in the Family
      1. Attachment Style: The Infant's Experience with Its Mother
      2. Additional Aspects of Relationships between Parents and Their Offspring
      3. Relationships between and Among Siblings
   B. Close Friendships: Establishing Relationships beyond the Family
      1. Childhood Friendships
      2. Close Friendships among Adolescents and among Adults
   C. Loneliness: Life without a Close Relationship
      1. What Is It Like to Be Lonely?
      2. Why Are Some People Lonely?
      3. What Can Be Done to Reduce Loneliness?

**II.** **Romantic Relationships, Love, And Physical Intimacy**
   A. Romantic Relationships
      1. Similarities between Romantic Relationships and Close Friendships
      2. Differences between Romantic Relationships and Close Friendships
   B. Do You Love Me? And What Does That Mean?
      1. Passionate Love Is Not Like Friendship
      2. Why and How Do People "Fall in Love"?
      3. Love Can Take Many Forms
   C. Social Psychology: On the Applied Side: What Does Love Mean To You?
   D. Premarital Sexuality
      1. Patterns of Sexual Behavior
      2. Has the Sexual Revolution Stalled--or Even Gone into Reverse?
      3. Premarital Sexual Experiences: Do They Affect Marriage?

**III.** **Marital Relationships: Interacting with a Spouse and Responding to Problems**
   A. Moving from a Romantic Relationship to a Married Relationship
      1. Similarity and Marriage
   B. Cornerstones of Social Psychology: Terman's Investigation of Husband-Wife Similarity and the Success of the Marriage
      1. Relationships among Young Married Couples
      2. Marital Sex, Parenthood, and General Satisfaction
   C. Troubled Relationships: Problems and the Effects of Failure
      1. Problems: General and Specific
      2. Relationship Failure: When Dissatisfaction Leads to Dissolution

D. Social Diversity: A Critical Analysis: Love and Intimacy:  Individualistic versus Collectivistic Perspectives

---

## Learning Objectives
After studying this chapter, students should be able to:

---

**8.1** Understand the difference between secure, avoidant and ambivalent attachment styles and explain how behaviors differ among infants and adults with differing styles.

**8.2** Outline how discipline during childhood affects relationships in adulthood.  Explain what happens to parent-child relationships at puberty.  Define the two factors Jeffries felt lie behind love of parents.  Describe the effects of cohesion among the Chinese.

**8.3** Discuss the life-course of sibling relations.  Explain what the upside of negative sibling relations during childhood.  Consider the two familiar factors that govern childhood relationships.  Explain how attachment styles affect relations at childhood and at adolescence.

**8.4** Indicate how gender and parting (graduation) affect close relations.  Consider the two dimensions and four styles offered by Bartholomew.  Relate the earlier to this newer attachment schema.

**8.5** Contrast "alone" and "lonely."  Describe the "lonely" pattern and relate it to the false consensus effect.  Define the two factors that are associated with teen loneliness.

**8.6** Contrast socially skilled and unskilled.  Outline the college student loneliness pattern.  Describe the self-perception and interaction pattern of the socially unskilled.

**8.7** Describe the cognitive therapy and modeling (social skills training) strategies for "curing" loneliness.  List the varieties of romantic relations and discuss how do experiences and partner selection practices differ for secure and insecure persons.

**8.8** Contrast friendships with dating and restricted with unrestricted sociosexual orientation regarding major goals.  Discuss abuse and termination of relations involving it.

**8.9** Understand unrequited love and passionate romantic love.  Explain the function of gazing. Compare the proportions of secure, ambivalent, and avoidant adult romantic lovers with the proportions of these styles in childhood.

**8.10** Historically, discuss how bonding relates to success at "passing on one's genes?"  Understand the three conditions of passionate love arousal and discuss the supposed role of skin color in mate selection and how do life-time celibates and gay/lesbian people contradict evolutionary rules?

**8.11** State the role of mistaken emotions.  Contrast companionate and passionate love.  List and define the Hendricks' six love styles; provide example behaviors as well.  Discuss how friendship relates to love.  Understand relations among the corners of the love triangle.

**8.12** Describe changes wrought by the sexual revolution.  Describe the role of ethnicity and gender in partner selection and attitudes.

**8.13** Discuss the teen pregnancy legacy of the free love period.  Describe the herpes and AIDS epidemics.  Track behavioral changes accompanying the spread of HIV/AIDS.  Discuss how premarital sex affects marriage and psychological health.

**8.14** Consider people's marriage aspirations as well as the prevailing presence of fathers and blended families.  Discuss the role of similarity during the course of courtship and marriage.

**8.15** Describe the implication of settling for less than the perfect match.  Discuss how similarity relates to happiness in marriage.  Define the four states of early marriage uncovered by Johnson.

**8.16** Contrast Johnson's four states of early marriage on marital satisfaction and parenthood.  Look at intercourse frequency among partners whose relationships vary in length and commitment.  Relate the decline in passionate love to relationship satisfaction and having children.

**8.17** Discuss how the marriage/happiness relationship has changed. Explain the current state of marriage, statistically speaking. Examine clashes of marital partners' personal interests, opinions and coping strategies.

**8.18** Relate self-descriptions to marital satisfaction. Contrast the genders on sources of marital upset. List marital issues upon which conflicts and changes in perceptions of partners' attributes can develop.

**8.19** Explain how relationship satisfaction relates to the expression of affect. Understand the two active and two passive responses to marital conflict and how they relate to self-esteem.

**8.20** Name three factors that relate to reconciliation. Describe the role of attachment styles in satisfaction and abuse. Contrast collectivism and individualism.

**8.21** Contrast individualistic and collectivistic societies on the importance of romance, the role of partner evaluations, and maintenance of intimacy.

---

# Discussion Topics and Questions

---

## 1. Prenuptial Agreements and Marriage Contracts

"Prenuptial agreements" have become familiar to the public since several famous media stars revealed that they sought to avoid large settlements in the event of divorce by drawing up marriage-dissolution papers before their vows were taken. A related phenomenon may be the wave of the future: marriage contracts; see A. K. Shulman, A marriage agreement, in A. Jaggar and D. Rothenberg (Eds.), *Feminist frameworks* (pp. 311-315), New York: McGraw-Hill. One of the components of such a contract might be division of labor: who will do what housework and which child-care duties. Prime the students with this information. Then give each student, say, twenty minutes to write up what would be an ideal contract from his or her point of view. Next, have students indicate the aspects of marriage they have covered in their contracts and put them on the board (e.g., sexual fidelity, allocation of house space, provisions for continuation of hobbies and interests, etc.). After having determined what aspects are included in students' contracts, ask students to provide examples of provisions they have included in their contracts that relate to these aspects. (Tell them they are not obliged to reveal sensitive informa-tion.) A lively discussion should ensue.

## 2. The Role of Chance in Determining Whom One Marries

The fact that chance may play a role in whom one marries may be unsettling to students. They are apt to think that someone is predestined to be their "one and only," or that they will carefully sort through candidate partners to find the one that suits them best. In fact, as Albert Bandura pointed out some time ago (*American Psychologist*, 1982, 37, 747-755), pure chance will in great part determine whom one marries. Ask several students to indicate how their parents came to know each other well enough to end up married. Put the examples up on the board until you have several that involve pure chance (e.g., "My dad was driving home from a business meeting and had a car wreck. He spent several weeks in a hospital outside a small town he had never heard of before. My mother was his nurse, and six months later, they were married"). Now point these examples of chance out to students. Be ready for arguments about the difference between chance and destiny!

### 3.  The Romeo and Juliet Effect:  Parent Interference

How do parents figure into a romantic relationship?  There is a thing called the "Romeo and Juliet effect.  Interference by parents may actually drive lovers closer together (see Driscoll et. as., 1972, *Journal of Personality and Social Psychology, 24,* 1-10).  Ask students to indicate their direct and indirect experience with parental interference in romantic relationships.  Determine whether there is a pattern fitting the Romeo and Juliet effect.  If you refer only to cases of interference that occurred *before* marriage, you will probably find support for the effect.  If you do, identify the effect and inform students that their experience confirms it.  If you do not, students will be interested in the observation that their experience is an exception to the Romeo and Juliet "rule."  In any case, it will be informative to have students speculate concerning why parental interference tore apart, bonded together, or had no effect on the romantic relationships in their experience; (e.g., if increased closeness occurred, did the parties involved misattribute the arousal due to parental meddling to love?)

### 4.  What Is, and Is Not, a Friend?

To get at "what's a friend?", it is helpful to discover what is not a friend.  The students discuss each of the following, indicating the nature of each and telling why each is not "true friendship"; then end the discussion by concluding what is true friendship.  Non-true friendships:  acquaintances (passersby, co-workers, schoolmates); neighbors; confederates (two people engaged in some joint enterprise in which a symbiotic relationship exists, but who have little connection outside of the pursuit--e.g., robbing banks, selling cars, working for the homeless); pals (people with some activity in common, such as beer buddies, horse-lovers, or shopping companions); close kin; convenience friends (people who trade babysitting chores, borrow from one another, share rides to work); and people in a mentor relationship (where a usually older person shows the ropes to an up-and-coming neophyte; e.g., a full professor and a new assistant professor).

---

## Learning Activities:  Classroom Exercises/Demonstrations

---

### 8.1  What Is It Like To Be Lonely?

According to *Psychology Today* surveys, it is young people--adolescents and young adults--not elderly people who are the loneliest.  And loneliness is a personality trait that matters; as indicated in the text, it is related to important issues such as health.  Get your young people to open up about the issue. You could begin by having them indicate "what it is like to be lonely."  An exercise included on the next page (and in the Study Guide) can help.  Students could do the Robert Weiss exercise in class before an exchange of experiences begins.  After the exercise and any student testimonials, ask students why young people are the most lonely.  Relate loneliness to shyness and introversion.  Have students come up with solutions to the problem.

## HANDOUT FOR ACTIVITY # 8.1A

### IMAGING THE LONELINESS OF EMOTIONAL ISOLATION

Read these instructions and then close your eyes and implement them

You live in an apartment. You are there alone. So far as your feelings go, you are entirely alone. You have no one to call, no one to talk to. There is no one sharing your life, no one at all. This is the way it is; this the way it is going to be. If you were to go out, you would still be alone.

Please take note in your mind of the way you feel.

After you have implemented the instructions, open your eyes and write down what your feelings are.

Copyright © 1997 by Allyn and Bacon

**HANDOUT FOR ACTIVITY # 8.1B**

IMAGING THE LONELINESS OF SOCIAL ISOLATION

Read the following instructions, then close your eyes and implement them

You are with someone with whom you are sharing your life, someone you are married to or are living with.

The two of you are in a part of the country that is new and strange to you. You have been there for two months. You have seen all the movies, and you have gone to several of the bars. People are pleasant but distant. The only people you have to talk to are each other. You don't really know anyone else in town. It is evening again and again it is just the two of you.

What are your feelings? Please think of them now.

Write down your feelings as you thought of them.

Copyright © 1997 by Allyn and Bacon

Adapted from Weiss (1987).

## 8.2  Is the Sexual Revolution Over?

As the text indicates, the sexual revolution is probably not over yet. However, it may have changed its character. Have students answer several questions anonymously; better have them do so outside of class and bring results to you in identically sealed envelopes. Questions can be found on next page (or in the Study Guide).

Once you collect the questionnaires, simply tally the numbers; compute averages when the questions call for a number or frequencies for questions that can be scored "yes" or "no." Display this data for the students in class. What do the numbers say? The sexual revolution may be said to be "still on" for students if they start young and currently practice sex at least a few times a month, on average. But has it changed its character? The revolution has taken a turn if students tend to have single rather than multiple partners. Is love the main reason for single partners? Do students take precautions against disease and pregnancy? Discuss the students impressions of how the revolution may have changed. Do you find any gender differences?

## HANDOUT FOR ACTIVITY # 8.2

Please complete the following questions honestly and DO NOT put your name on it to keep findings anonymous, and protect confidentiality.

1.  Are you currently married?

2.  Are you male or female?

3.  At what age did you first become sexually active?

4.  Currently, how many times a month do you have some form of sex with some person (or with different persons)?

5.  If you are sexually active, do you have a single partner to whom you are committed, or do you have sex with several people?

6.  If you have a single partner with whom you exclusively have sex, why is that?  Love for the partner? Fear of sexual disease?  Practicality (for example, convenience of living together)?  Other (indicate)?

7.  Do you currently use protection against pregnancy most of the times you have sex?

8.  Do you currently take precautions against disease--for example, use a condom--most of the times you have sex?

Copyright © 1997 by Allyn and Bacon

## 8.3 Rate Your Friendship

Consider ideal friendship by using the "Rate Your Friendship" scale found on the next page ( in the Study Guide). Have students imagine an ideal friend, then complete the scale with that friend in mind. The goal is to score as high as is possible. The higher the score, the more students have grasped the qualities of true friendship.

The Rate Your Friendship scale is a test of quality of friendship. Have students count the left-most scale as an 8, then number to the right so that the right-most point is 1. Next, for each scale item, have the students write down the value of the scale points that they have checked. Finally, have them add their scale scores over the ten scales. If they score 70-80, their grasp of the qualities of friendship is very good. Those who score 10-20 have a poor grasp. Scores in the range of 60-70 and 30-20 may also be interpreted as high and low, respectively.

**HANDOUT FOR ACTIVITY # 8.3**

RATE YOUR FRIENDSHIP

Select one of your important friendships. By checking some point along each of the scales below each statement, indicate the degree to which each statement applies to you friendship.

1. Each of us accepts the other as he/she is. We don't try to change each other.

$$8 \quad 7 \quad 6 \quad 5 \quad 6 \quad 4 \quad 2 \quad 1$$
<--:--:--:--:--:--:--:-->

clearly applies       clearly does not apply
to our relationship     to our relationship

2. We trust each other and feel we can count on each other.

$$8 \quad 7 \quad 6 \quad 5 \quad 4 \quad 3 \quad 2 \quad 1$$
<--:--:--:--:--:--:--:-->

clearly applies       clearly does not apply
to our relationship     to our relationship

3. We respect each other. We respect each other's advice, competence, and ability to "do the right thing."

$$8 \quad 7 \quad 6 \quad 5 \quad 4 \quad 3 \quad 2 \quad 1$$
<--:--:--:--:--:--:--:-->

clearly applies       clearly does not apply
to our relationship     to our relationship

4. We support each other. Each knows the other is "there for me."

$$8 \quad 7 \quad 6 \quad 5 \quad 4 \quad 3 \quad 2 \quad 1$$
<--:--:--:--:--:--:--:-->

clearly applies       clearly does not apply
to our relationship     to our relationship

5. We confide in each other. There is hardly anything we wouldn't tell one another.

$$8 \quad 7 \quad 6 \quad 5 \quad 4 \quad 3 \quad 2 \quad 1$$
<--:--:--:--:--:--:--:-->

clearly applies       clearly does not apply
to our relationship     to our relationship

Copyright © 1997 by Allyn and Bacon

6. We know what makes one another "tick." Each can decipher why the other is upset or troubled.

8 7 6 5 4 3 2 1
<--:--:--:--:--:--:--:-->

clearly applies                    clearly does not apply
to our relationship                to our relationship

7. Spontaneity characterizes our relationship. We feel we can say or do whatever we want around one another.

8 7 6 5 4 3 2 1
<--:--:--:--:--:--:--:-->

clearly applies                    clearly does not apply
to our relationship                to our relationship

8. We are loyal to one another. We stand in each other's corner no matter what.

8 7 6 5 4 3 2 1
<--:--:--:--:--:--:--:-->

clearly applies                    clearly does not apply
to our relationship                to our relationship

9. We are generous with each other. Each gives to the other and neither keeps scores.

8 7 6 5 4 3 2 1
<--:--:--:--:--:--:--:-->

clearly applies                    clearly does not apply
to our relationship                to our relationship

10. We are honest with each other. We tell each other the truth, even if it hurts.

8 7 6 5 4 3 2 1
<--:--:--:--:--:--:--:-->

clearly applies                    clearly does not apply
to our relationship                to our relationship

From Allen, PERSONALITY ADJUSTMENT, Brooks/Cole, 1990; used with permission.

Copyright © 1997 by Allyn and Bacon

## Overhead Transparencies
These appear at the back of this manual.

**8.1** *Reinforcement-Affect Theory: How Some Relationships May Start*
**8.2** *An Unromantic Explanation of Passionate Love*
**8.3** *Levinger's Theory That Relationships Pass through Five Stages from Beginning to End*
**8.4** *Sternberg's "Triangular Model of Love"*
**8.5** *Relationships among Findings in the Lauers' Study of 351 Married Couples*
**8.6** *Behaviors That Upset Men versus Behaviors That Upset Women*

## Audiovisual Suggestions

### Allyn and Bacon Video

\* *Friendship,* video, 28.5 mins. To obtain this tape, see your Allyn and Bacon representative. A dramatization leads Robert A. Baron and Margaret Clark to an in-depth discussion of friendship, especially as it differs for men and women.

### Other Videos and Films

*Love and Sex,* FC1132, video, 52 mins. Films for the Humanities & Sciences, P.O. Box 2053, Princeton, NJ 08543 (800-257-5126). This is possibly the best of Phil Donohue's excellent "The Human Animal" series. Love and sex and their joys and heartbreaks are covered in poignant fashion.

*The Sexual Brain,* EC1738, video, 28 mins. Films for the Humanities & Sciences, P.O. Box 2053, Princeton, NJ 08543 (800-257-5126). The battle of the sexes that sometimes ends in marriage, sometimes in friendship, and sometimes in mutual rejection starts with the brain. This tape ends with questions about the structural and reproductive roots of the differences between the sexes.

*Are We Still Going to the Movies?,* 21730, film, 14 mins. Pennsylvania State University, Audiovisual Services, Special Services Building, University Park, PA 16802 (814-865-6314). A young couple's relationship is suffering as a result of their disagreement on amount of sexual involvement.

*Love Tapes,* MVCS-1034, video, 30 mins. Pennsylvania State University, Audiovisual Services, Special Services Building, University Park, PA 16802 (814-865-6314). An interesting and varied sample of people talk candidly about their experiences with love.

*Divorce: For Better or Worse, Parts 1 & 2,* 50423, film, 51 mins. Pennsylvania State University, Audiovisual Services, Special Services Building, University Park, PA 16802 (814-865-6314). Focuses on actual case histories of divorced and divorcing couples and on the emotional as well as financial toll that divorce exacts.

*Morning After,* film, 17 mins. Filmmakers Library, Inc. 133 E. 59th Street, New York, NY 10022. Shows the vulnerability of a seemingly cool, sophisticated man to the breakup of a long-term relationship.

*Kinds of Love,* Net 2037, film, 29 mins. Audiovisual center, Indiana University, Bloomington, IN 47401. Misconceptions about love, the relationship between sexuality and love, and love as a religious virtue are discussed in interviews with Father Thurston David and Erich Fromm.

## Critical Thinking/Essay Questions

1. Indicate how the stage is set for loneliness during childhood. What are lonely people like in terms of traits and social behavior, and what can be done to change them in a way that is likely to lessen loneliness?

2. Consider the Berscheid, Snyder, and Omoto (1989) study of close relations among college students. What kind of relationship was closest for these students, and what kind lasted longest? Was there a gender difference in perceived closeness of closest relationships?

3. Contrast friendship and romantic love. What does each have that the other lacks? Also contrast romantic love in general with a more specific variety, passionate love.

4. Contrast Sternberg's triangular model with Hendricks' "basic love styles" approach. Could you collapse them into one model?

5. Are there alternatives to the text explanations of why older men prefer younger women as potential partners? Describe one of them.

6. Some say the sexual revolution has come and gone. What was beneficial about it, and what was detrimental? Contrast the "revolution" period with today's orientation to sexual matters.

7. Describe the way marriage has changed since the early 1970s. How have men and women's views of marriage changed in different directions? What must be shared among spouses in the future if the trend toward marital problems is to be halted?

8. Paint a picture of a jealous person. What will that individual's characteristics be? How does jealousy vary around the world? What aspects of the jealous person will be most in need of change?

9. What happens when boredom sets in during the course of a marriage? What makes it happen, and how can it be corrected?

10. What are the factors that cause dissimilarities to arise during marriage, and can the development of negative attributions be short-circuited?

11. Examine divorce and remarriage. How likely is divorce? Is divorce more or less likely in a second marriage than in a first? Indicate a major effect of divorce on children.

## Sources for Lecture

Bower, B. (1991), October 21). Darwin's minds: Psychologists probe the decent of the human psyche. *Science News, 140,*232-234. Award-winning science writer tracks the progress of evolutionary explanations of human behavior. Considers sexual attractiveness as well as sex differences in mating preferences and in jealousy.

Budiansky, S. (1987, May 4). All by your lonesome. *U.S. News and World Report,* p. 71. Summarizes research on what it is like to be isolated.

Fuhr, J. (1987). Standardization of divorce mediation. *Conciliation-Courts-Review, 25,* 65-68. Mediation between spouses can sometimes stop divorce before it is final. If not, it can lead to more manageable agreements. This article concentrates on the child custody aspect of divorce settlement.

Mainardi, P. (1992, May-June). The politics of housework. *Ms.,* pp. 40-41. Examines men's excuses for not helping out more.

Roberts, M. (1988, March). Be all that you can be. *Psychology Today,* pp. 28-29. This article indicates which, among the several self-improvement methods available, really may help lonely people develop the kinds of skills that allow success in general and social success in particular.

Tan, N. T. (1988, Spring). Developing and testing a family mediation assessment instrument. *Mediation Quarterly,* pp. 53-68. An instrument to assess couples who present themselves for mediation reveals some dimensions that are important to the mediation process.

Tavris, C. (1988, November). coping with jealousy. *Psychology Today,* p. 302. Carol Tavris is well known for her theorizing about anger and has also turned her attention to jealousy. Here she provides useful information about coping with jealousy.

## Professional Update: Current Articles from Professional Sources

Bradbury, T. N., & Fincham, F. D. (1992). Attributions and behavior in marital interaction. *Journal of Personality and Social Psychology, 63,* 613-628. Spouses were asked to report their marital quality, to make attributions for marital difficulties, and to engage in problem solving. Spouses' maladaptive attributions were related to less-effective problem-solving behaviors, particularly among wives, as well as to higher rates of negative behavior and, for wives, to increased tendencies to reciprocate negative partner behavior.

Cantor, N., Acker, M., & Cook-Flannagan, C. (1992). Conflict and preoccupation in the intimacy life task. *Journal of Personality and Social Psychology, 63,* 644-655. A study of sorority women's pursuit of romantic intimacy. For those in a serious relationship, conflict was associated with romantic satisfaction, but also with a narrow focus on communion in the relationship. For those dating casually, conflict was associated with the perceived difficulty and dissatisfaction of the intimacy task.

Gootman, J. M., & Levenson, R. W. (1992). Marital processes predictive of later dissolution: Behavior, physiology, and health, *Journal of Personality and Social Psychology, 63,* 221-233. Based on conversations between spouses at two different times, researchers classified married couples as "regulated" (showing a balance of positive and negative interaction) and "nonregulated." Nonregulated couples had more severe marital problems at time one, poorer health at time two, more negative ratings of interactions, more negative and less positive emotional expression, greater defensiveness, and greater risk of dissolution.

Kurdek, L. A. (1993). Predicting marital dissolution. A 5-year prospective longitudinal study of newlywed couples. *Journal of Personality and Social Psychology, 64,* 221-242. Through five annual assessments, researchers studied 222 couples, 64 of which dissolved their marriages. Husbands and wives who would dissolve their marriages showed a greater decline in interdependence scores and had greater increases in discrepancies on interdependence variables than did husbands and wives in stable marriages.

Sedikides, C., Olsen, N., & Reis, H. T. (1993). Relationships as natural categories. *Journal of Personality and social Psychology, 64,*71-82. To show that people organize social information around relationship categories, investigators informed some subjects about targets grouped as four married couples; other subjects were informed about targets but were not told whom targets were married to. As expected, the first set of subjects did organize information about targets around couple categories more than the second set. We tend to see married couples as a unit.

*Related Readings:* The following selections from *Readings in Social Psychology: General, Classic, and Contemporary Selections,* 3rd Edition, by Wayne Lesko (Allyn and Bacon, 1997) accompany this chapter.

Livermore, B. (1993). "The lessons of love." This *Psychology Today* article examines the evolution of research on love, and summarizes what researchers now know (and don't know) about this seemingly mysterious experience. The role love plays in the decision to get married is explored in the context of our contemporary society. A measure of the "colors of love" is provided. (Article 22).

Walster (Hatfield), E., Walster, G. W., Piliavin, J., & Schmidt, L. (1973). "Playing hard to get: Understanding an elusive phenomenon." Folklore suggests that the woman who plays hard to get is a more desirable catch than the woman who too eager for a relationship. However, there is a catch to such folklore. Research indicates that the selectively hard-to-get woman (one who is hard for all other men to get, but easy for the subject to get) is preferred to either a uniformly hard-to-get woman, a uniformly easy-to-get woman, or a woman about which the subject has no information. (Article 23).

Sprecher, S., Sullivan, Q., & Hatfield, E. (1994). "Mate selection preferences: Gender differences examined in a national sample." This article examines mate selection preferences in the context of both sociobiological (an evolutionary approach arguing that our preferences are due to biological issues, e.g., promoting reproductive success), and sociocultural predictions (suggesting that such preferences are culturally bound through socialization and economic realities). Respondents for this sample were representative, unlike many studies that rely primarily on the responses of college students. (Article 24).

# Chapter 9

# Social Influence:  How We Change Others' Behavior--
and How They Change Ours

## Chapter-at-a-Glance

| CHAPTER OUTLINE | INSTRUCTION IDEAS | SUPPLEMENTS* |
|---|---|---|
| *I. Conformity: Group Influence in Action*<br>• **Cornerstones of Social Psychology**   Asch's Research on Conformity: Social Pressure--the Irresistible Force?<br><br>• Factors Affecting Conformity: Cohesiveness, Group Size, and Type of Social Norm<br><br>• The Bases of Conformity: Why We Often Choose to "Go Along"--and What Happens after We Do<br><br>• The Need for Individuality and the Need for Control: Why, Sometimes, We Choose *Not* to Go Along<br><br>• Minority Influence: Does the Majority Always Rule? | Learning Objectives 9.1 to 9.7<br><br>Discussion Topic 2<br><br>Activity 9.1 (Handout)<br><br>Critical Thinking Questions 1-6 | Test Bank Questions 9.1 to 9.56<br><br>Reading:<br>Lesko 25, The Education of Torturers<br><br>Transparencies 9.1, 9.2, 9.5 |
| *II. Compliance: To Ask--Sometimes--Is to Receive*<br>• Compliance: The Underlying Principles<br><br>• Tactics Based on Friendship or Liking: Ingratiation<br><br>• Tactics Based on Commitment or Consistency: The Foot in the Door, the Lowball, and Others<br><br>• Tactics Based on Reciprocity: The Door in the Face, the Foot in the Mouth, and the "That's -Not-All" Approach<br><br>• Tactics Based on Scarcity: Playing Hard to Get and the Fast-Approaching-Deadline Technique<br><br>• Other Tactics for Gaining Compliance: Complaining and Putting Others in a Good Mood<br><br>• **Social Psychology: On the Applied Side**   The Pique Technique: Preventing Mindless (Automatic) Refusals | Learning Objectives 9.8 to 9.15<br><br>Discussion Topics 3, 4<br><br>Activities 9.2, 9.4<br><br>Critical Thinking Questions 7-9 | Test Bank Questions 9.57 to 9.99<br><br>Reading:<br>- Lesko 27, Hey Buddy, Can You Spare Seventeen Cents? Mindful Persuasion and the Pique Technique<br><br>Transparencies 9.3, 9.4, 9.6 |
| *III. Obedience: Social Influence by Demand*<br>• Destructive Obedience: Some Basic Findings<br><br>• Destructive Obedience: Its Social Psychological Basis<br><br>• Destructive Obedience: Resisting Its Effects<br><br>• **Social Diversity: A Critical Analysis**   Gender Differences in Social Influence: More Apparent Than Real | Learning Objectives 9.16 to 9.22<br><br>Discussion Topic 1<br><br>Activity 9.3 (Handout)<br><br>Critical Thinking Question 10 | Test Bank Questions 9.100 to 9.140<br><br>Reading: Lesko 26, Behavioral Study of Obedience |

*See Audiovisual Suggestions

# Social Influence: How We Change Others' Behavior--
# and How They Change Ours

---

## Chapter Outline: Getting the Overall Picture

---

1. Gender and Status: Additional Evidence Indicating That Gender Differences in Conformity are More Illusory Than Real
2. A Possible Exception to the "No Difference" Rule: Judgments of Physical Attractiveness

## Learning Objectives
After studying this chapter, students should be able to:

**9.1** Define "social influence," "norms," "conformity," "obedience," and "compliance." Contrast written and unwritten norms. Discuss the result of wholesale disregard of norms, and how norms have changed.

**9.2** Detail the classic Asch studies of conformity. Indicate the result of breaking the unanimity among false judges.

**9.3** Understand the difference between public compliance and private acceptance. Discuss cohesiveness and, when it is high, how it will affect one's views that are different from the group. Tell what Crandall found when investigating strength of sorority friendships and binge eating.

**9.4** Explain why people get suspicious when the number of group members agreeing on issues increases beyond 3-4. Contrast descriptive and injunctive norms and explain how the Reno group investigated these norm types in the bag dropping study.

**9.5** Identify what two needs that determine our level of conformity along with certain cognitive processes. Contrast normative with informational social influence. Give the story interpretations of people who did and did not go along with others' risky advice given to a potential music student.

**9.6** Consider how individuation places limits on conformity for the purpose of gaining others' favor. Describe Daubman's research with people high or low on desire for control.

**9.7** Give a contemporary example of a minority inserting influence on the majority. Outline three conditions making minorities successful influence agents.

**9.8** Explain how Cialdini learned from real-life compliance experts. Outline six basic principles for gaining compliance.

**9.9** Explain the Freedman study involving phone requests to homemakers, and their rates of compliance.

**9.10** Explain throwing the "low ball". Discuss "bait and switch".

**9.11** Understand reciprocity and give examples. Explain what the "that's not all" strategy and how reciprocity is involved?

**9.12** Describe what social ploy lies behind the "foot-in-the-mouth" method.

**9.13** Relate "scarce commodity" to "playing hard to get." Indicate how the "deadline techniques" is used in sales.

**9.14** List the six complaint categories uncovered by Alicke and colleagues. Discuss the most and least common reasons for complaining and explain the role of gender.

**9.15** Indicate why "can you spare some change?" is less effective than "can you spare 34 cents?".

**9.16** Define "obedience" and give examples. Explain why it is a matter of extraordinary seriousness. Outline the basic components of Milgram's experiments (teacher-learner).

**9.17** Explain the effects of switching an unprestigious setting, a foreign site, or pleas for release on the part of the shock victim. Discuss participants' reactions to the experiments. Describe the role of responsibility in obedience.

**9.18**   Explain how the symbols of authority affect obedience level.  Indicate why gradual escalation increases obedience.  List the four kinds of knowledge that impart resistance to destructive obedience.

**9.19**   Understand gender differences in proneness to social influence.  Suggest reasons why earlier and later studies of gender differences in submission to social influence yielded different results.

**9.20**   describe how Eagly showed that gender differences in status account for differences in susceptibility to social influence.

**9.21**   Give Graziano's and colleagues' procedures showing that physical attractiveness judgments constitute one area where the genders do differ in proneness to social influence.

**9.22**   Explain the gender difference in physical attractiveness judgments.

---

# Discussion Topics and Questions

---

## 1.  Blind Obedience?

One day in class, arbitrarily begin to reseat class members.  Giving no reason, curtly order some students to sit on the front row and others to sit in the back, some on the aisle and some in the center portion.  Reshuffle again, until someone asks "Why?"  Discuss what was going through subjects' minds as they were arbitrarily pushed and pulled about and why they complied.  Was it thoughtless obedience?  "To save you embarrassment?"  To save themselves embarrassment by avoiding the question "Why?"  Some hypothesis about your (the instructor's) reasons?  Or responses to pressure that seemed to be exerted by students who were obeying quickly and efficiently?  An interesting twist on this discussion might occur if someone other than the instructor conduct this "rearrangement" of the class.  How far will students comply or obey when a "stranger" gives them orders?

More generally, ask students what instructor characteristics and aspects of peer behavior led to initial obedience.  Also, ask students under what circumstances might all or most of them refuse rather immediately or continue to obey without asking why.  (A former colleague of the previous authors of this manual, a behavior modification expert, ordered opposite-sexed students signed up for weight-loss/Behavior-modification class to disrobe in preparation for a weigh-in.  They began to comply so quickly and in such large numbers that the colleague had trouble stopping them with assurances that it was just a joke!)

## 2.  Conforming to Voice Amplitude

Begin a lecture talking in an unusually low voice approaching a whisper.  Tape the session without students' knowledge by placing a tape recorder where you can see it but the students cannot--e.g., in an open attaché case.  Elicit questions and comments from class members.  Subtly record the tape counter points at which given students' voices are recorded; also record the counter number when you terminate the taped session.  As the lecture continues, slowly begin to raise your voice until it goes well above its normal level, again asking for questions and comments.

First, ask students if they were aware of anything unusual.  Play the tape.  Before revealing what is reflected on the tape, ask students if they are, at this point, aware of conforming to subtle pressure applied by you.  Some will say yes; then ask them to indicate the form of their conformity.  If they have trouble, cue them by making reference to your voice amplitude.  Pick out a few students you have on the tape and ask each if he or she showed conformity.  If a given one denies it, play the tape back for her or him. Now you are ready to talk about the sometimes unconscious nature of conformity. Playing the very beginning and the very ending of the tape will make your point and stimulate further discussion.

### 3. Ethical Implications of "Sales Techniques"

A class discussion of the ethical implications associated with the various "sales techniques" should be enlightening. Methods such as "door in the face" and "foot in the door" could be considered legal confidence games. The way to avoid being duped by these methods is to understand at a commonsense level how the methods' users deceive us.

Just what are the deceptions involved with such methods? The answers come from a "real-life" understanding of the theoretical explanations for why these methods work. By probing students for "off-the-top-of-the-head" explanations, you can cause them to arrive at the theories.

For example, in regard to the "foot-in-the-door" technique, if a student says something like "He [the requester] is getting me to grant a small request so I'll look at myself and think 'I must be a pretty good person to help somebody out like this,'" point out the implications for self-perception. If another exclaims, "After I grant the first small request and she [the requester] heaps lavish praise on me, she will expect that I'll get addicted to granting requests; then, zap, the big one comes," point out how this statement fits the "positive view of helping" explanation.

Use a similar strategy for "foot in the door." By probing for everyday explanations that fit the relevant theories, you will allow your students to gain a firsthand appreciation of sales techniques. More important, this level of awareness will allow them to resist these methods.

### 4. Subtle Methods of Ingratiation

Have students discuss subtle methods of ingratiation, such as "encouraging other people to talk about themselves." Salespeople use these methods as well. Cue students concerning the "talk about self" method by asking, "If you wanted to get someone to feel good about themselves in your presence so you would get credit you could use at request time, but wanted to be sure that you didn't look like a flatterer, what could you do to pump up the person's ego?" If students don't come to the "let them talk about themselves" method right away, give a clue: "What would asking them questions about themselves do?"

Pointing out feelings in common with a client is a favorite example: on a hot and humid day, salesperson says to client, "Gee, I feel hot and sticky today. How about you, Mr. Mark?" You might cue this technique by asking students, "What social rule have you learned so far in this course that is a powerful cause of people liking each other?" The answer you are looking for is, of course, similarity. When some student identifies "similarity" one way or another--it's okay to expand on what they say a bit--ask students how they would establish similarity during a conversation with the "mark." Move them in the direction of pointing out trivial similarities--"so you're a Midwesterner too!"--that they can easily establish prior to a request. Have students think of additional methods of ingratiation. Include ones that backfire--for example, pointing out too many of one's negative traits during a self-disclosure session designed to make one look humble, or slavishly conforming to the mark's opinions.

This exercise may cause students to become conscious of their own, probably unconscious attempts to manipulate others, and of their occasional victimization. To make sure they learn to protect themselves and avoid exploitive behavior, be sure to lead them in poking fun at these underhanded methods.

# Learning Activities:  Classroom Exercises/Demonstrations

### 9.1  Symbols For The Study of Aesthetics

Before getting into the conformity material--and also before students read about--tell your students that you would like to replicate an experiment on "aesthetics." You are interested in comparing results obtained from former students enrolled in this class during a previous semester with those produced by your present students. Give to them the handout provided on the next page (or in the Study Guide), where they will find a set of numbered symbols grouped in 10 different sets. For each set, labeled A-J, pick one symbol at random (give the number of the column in which it is found) and tell students that it is the one picked as most interesting and intriguing by at least 80 percent of former students. (Be sure to note which you picked for each set.) Then ask the students to pick the symbol they think is the most interesting and intriguing, and circle it. Do this for all 10 sets. Then ask students to exchange sheets and score each other's sheets. Beginning with set A, call out the "previous students' favorite" that you actually picked at random and tell them to circle the letter for the set (A) if the students whose sheets they are scoring made the same choice as the "previous students." Do the same for sets B-J. Then collect the sheets and count the number of sheets that have at least  6 of the 10 letters circled.

After explaining that actually the symbols were picked at random--you invented the other class's responses, and there is no evidence that any of the symbols are more interesting and intriguing than the others--you can report to the class the percentage of students who "agreed" with the phantom "previous students'" responses (number of students "agreeing" at least 6 out of 10 times divided by the total number of students).

You may expect that at least 33 percent of students will have "gone along" in a majority of the ten cases. Explain to them how the "previous students" were "exerting pressure on them" to make the same choices as they supposedly made. Ask them for reflections, and be ready to entertain the subject of deception in social psychological experiments. (You may have to explain that telling the absolute truth and asking them to "pretend that some other students had made the [actually random] responses" would have generated attempts to appear uninfluenceable, rather than genuine responses on their part.)

**HANDOUT FOR ACTIVITY # 9.1**

## SYMBOLS FOR THE STUDY OF AESTHETICS

1   2   3   4   5

A. Ω  ≈  ç  √  ∫

B. ~  μ  ≤  ≥  ÷

C. å  ̋  δ  ▯  ⊖

D. η  Δ  ψ  ...  æ

E. Σ  ˈ  Φ  †  ¥

F. S  ̈  ˙  ϕ  π

G. β  ʻ  @  |  ™

H. ✚  £  ¢  ∞  ˋ

I. ¶  &  ●  ✱  ♭

J. ♮  +  !  ≠  =

Copyright © 1997 by Allyn and Bacon

## 9.2 Three Basic Appeals Used In Advertising

Dr. Vivian Parker Makosky has identified three basic appeals used in advertising (in *Teaching of Psychology, 12,* February 1985, pp. 42-43). A straightforward and, according to her experience, fascinating demonstration for students involves locating magazine ads that represent examples of each kind of appeal, or combinations of them. The first of these appeals is "the appeal to or creation of needs." It is based on four of the needs in Maslow's hierarchy. Examples include "Aren't you hungry for Burger King now?" (physiological needs); "Get a piece of the rock" (safety and security needs); "Brush your breath with Dentine" (belongingness and love needs); and "When E. F. Hutton speaks..." (self-esteem and status needs). (Appeals to Maslow's cognitive, aesthetic, and self-actualization needs are much less common.)

The second group are "social and prestige suggestion" appeals--buy it because all kinds of people do. Examples include the "Pepsi generation" ad, the Wrigley's Spearmint Gum ad, and other ads "featuring lots of people, in different types of clothes and /or settings, often of different ages and races..." (p. 43). Examples of "prestige suggestion" appeals--buy it because famous people do--are Michael Jordan for Wheaties, Michael J. Fox for Pepsi, and various famous athletes for light beer.

The third kind of appeal is "loaded words and images." "This technique is the most subtle because it is not what is said so much as how it is said, or what you are seeing while it is being said" (p. 43). Examples include ads with attractive, athletic people touting snacks like Snickers candy bars; the use of buzzwords such as "natural" for beauty products or foods, or "light" in order to make all kinds of foods seem dietetic; and the use of "images" associated with products, such as Harvey's Bristol Cream sherry as a symbol of the sophisticated life-style, BMW the emblem of wealth and status, or Ford (or Chevy) trucks the epitome of masculine good times.

Because the three categories of appeals each have subcategories, it is possible, and productive, to divide the class into groups, each to bring to class examples of some subcategory. The groups can then discuss their example ads in class, pick the best illustrative ads for their subcategory, decide why these ads are appropriate examples of their subcategory, and report to the class on their conclusions. Other questions for groups to consider: What kinds of ads appeal to men and what kinds to women? What kinds of ads may be true "turn-ons," and what kinds may actually backfire? What kinds of ads are most effective for what kinds of products? What kinds of ads are most effective for which age groups?

Or let them have some fun while they learn 'a la *Crazy People* with Dudley Moore, a movie about truth in advertising ("buy Metamucil, it will help you go to the toilet;" "your fear of flying may be valid...fly with us...more of our passengers arrive alive than any other airline;" "buy Volvo, it's boxy but it's good"). Have students rewrite some ads to bring their hidden appeals up front. Examples: "Buy a Whopper, it will fill you up, and you won't be hungry for a long time." "Buy Coca Cola, because almost all cola drinkers do (except those who drink Pepsi)." "Buy Imperial 'Light' margarine so you won't be fat." "Buy a BMW so people will think you are rich, sporty, and sexy." "Eat Wheaties so you can be more like Michael Jordan."

## 9.3 Estimates of Level of Obedience

Before getting into Milgram's research, briefly describe his basic study to students. A description like that in the book is adequate. Alternatively, show them one segment from Milgram's film (see the film list below) involving one subject in the standard experiment. In either case, don't reveal the proportion who obeyed. Rather, have students estimate how many out of 100 would obey, and whether they personally would obey. (Let "obey" be defined as "go all the way to the last switch, the 450-volt switch.") The needed response sheet can be found on the following page or in the Study Guide.

Ask students to indicate whether they had previously heard of or read about Milgram's work. Separate the responses into those who have heard of the Milgram research and those who have not. For both groups, determine students' estimates of how many people out of 100 will obey and compare to 65 percent. You will almost certainly find that students think that fewer than 65 percent of others would obey and that an even smaller proportion of themselves would obey, regardless of group. Students with prior information should come closer to estimating correctly the proportion of others who would obey, but such knowledge should not affect their estimates of their own behavior very much. (Predicted results are based on an instructor's use of this demonstration.)

## HANDOUT FOR ACTIVITY # 9.3

### ESTIMATES OF LEVEL OF OBEDIENCE

My sex is____(M or F)        My age is____

How many U. S. citizens out of 100 would obey fully and use all the switches including the one marked "450 volts?" [circle one number]

  10  15  20  25  30  35  40  45  50  55  60  65  70  75  80  85  90  95  100

I myself would ____ would not ____ obey fully and use all the switches including the one marked "450 volts?" [check "would" or "would not"]

____    "Before today, I had never before heard of the Milgram obedience experiment, or I have heard about it but can't remember anything significant about it?"

____    "I have heard about the Milgram obedience experiment and have a least some recollection regarding its results."

Copyright © 1997 by Allyn and Bacon

### 9.4 Two Feet in the Door Technique

Illustrate the "two-feet-in-the-door" technique. In one of your classes, pass out index cards. Ask students to write their phone numbers on the cards and place them in a receptacle by the door as they leave if they are willing to "donate two out-of-class hours of your time to colleague's research project...unfortunately, there is no compensation.") In your social psychology class, ask your students to stay beyond class time, "just a couple of minutes," to help you with your research. After class, simply write a phone number on the board and indicate a time to call that is convenient to you or your assistant. Make sure that this process only takes a couple of minutes.

To those who call, ask whether they are willing to "donate two out-of-class hours of your time to a colleague's research project...unfortunately, there is no compensation." Compare the number of cards you collected with the number of affirmative answers from the social psychology students who called. The number of students who volunteer to participate in the two-hour out-of-class "research" should be greater for the social psychology class "sucked in" by compliance to the prior small requests for "two minutes after class" and the time it takes to make a phone call than for those in the other class who were given only the larger request for two out-of-class hours. Revelation of results and explanation of the "foot-in-the-door" technique should generate lively classroom discussion.

---

## Overhead Transparencies
These appear at the back of this manual.

---

**9.1** *Arch's Line-Judging Task:  Example Lines*
**9.2** *The Sexes and Conformity*
**9.3** *Methods of Gaining Compliance*
**9.4** *The Tendency to Obey:  Some Key Contributing Factors*
**9.5** *The Social Influence Model (SAM)*
**9.6** *Basins and Rule's Complete List of Means for Gaining Compliance*

---

## Audiovisual Suggestions

---

### Allyn and Bacon Videos

*Conformity*, video, 28.5 mins.  To obtain this video, consult your Allyn and Bacon sales representative. Robert A. Baron and Margaret Clark use dramatizations as points of departure for a discussion of conformity and other forms of social influence.

*The Power of the Situation*, 30 mins; On Tape #10 of the series available through your Allyn and Bacon representative.  This video tells how social psychologists attempt to understand human behavior within its broader social context, and how beliefs and behavior can be influenced and manipulated by other people and subtle situational forces.

## Other Videos and Films

*Obedience,* U-60027, film, 50 mins. University of Iowa, Audiovisual, Iowa City, IA 52242. Perhaps the most significant media presentation ever produced about social psychology. Filmed excerpts from Milgram's actual obedience research contain an element of suspense, several surprises, and a profound conclusion.

*Conformity and Independence,* 21885, film, 23 mins. Pennsylvania State University, Audiovisual Services, Special Services Building, University Park, PA 16802 (814-865-6314). Includes much in only twenty-three minutes: Sherif's experiments on norm formation, Asch's conformity research, Milgram's experiment on "action conformity," and some prominent theorists discussing their ideas.

*Group Pressures,* film, 25 mins. University Films of Canada, 7 Hyden Street, Suite 305, Toronto, Ontario, Canada M4Y 2P2. This film on laboratory and field research on conformity includes Asch's work.

---

# Critical Thinking/Essay Questions

---

1. Give some everyday examples of conformity. Include some that are beneficial, some that are not, and at least one that involves conformity by a large majority.
2. Indicate some factors that promote group cohesiveness. When group cohesiveness is high, is the discrepancy between public compliance and private compliance likely to be great or small?
3. Explain why directing influence attempts to several targets instead of just one lowers the impact of those attempts. When one is in the minority, as the number of allies one has increases, what happens to one's impact on others?
4. Discuss the reasons why females have been seen as more conformist and the reasons why that perception is incorrect. As females gain in status within a group, what happens to usual assumptions about their degree of influenceability?
5. Contrast "normative social influence" and "informational social influence" by providing real-life examples of each.
6. Describe some famous people in history--other than those included in the text--who constituted minorities of one regarding some important issue. Be sure that at least one of them was a person who sought to be unique--to separate him- or herself from the majority--and that one exerted influence without creating obvious behavioral change during his or her own time.
7. Come up with a scheme to ingratiate yourself with a "boss"--a scheme different from those discussed in the book.
8. Contrast the foot-in-the-door and door-in-the-face techniques. Also, provide at least one real-life example for each that illustrates when each would likely fail.
9. Indicate how the "That's not all!" (TNA) method overlaps with the "door" techniques and is different from them.
10. Describe how you would alter the basic Milgram obedience procedure in order to lower obedience to near zero. The smaller the change you make and still have a good argument for near-zero obedience, the better your answer.

# Sources for Lecture

Cookson, P., & Rerseel, C. The price of privilege. (1986, March). *Psychology Today,* pp. 31-35. Money may be a rich child's ticket into an elite prep school, but once there, the child must often buy acceptance and success at the price of stifling conformity.

Cooper, M., & Soley, L. C. (1990, February-March). All the right sources. *Mother Jones,* pp. 20-26/45-48. Are the news media evenhanded and unbiased or, as many suspect, subtly designed to infuse the public mind with the points of view that are favored by whoever happens to be in power? A two-year study found that the "experts" typically interviewed by the major networks were more often spokes*men* for the status quo than unbiased analysts.

Nissani, M. (1990). A cognitive reinterpretation of Stanley Milgram's observations of obedience to authority. *American Psychologist, 45,* 1384-1385. This short "cognitive reinterpretation" asserts that Milgram's subjects, to be disobedient, would have had to undergo a "conceptual shift." Supposedly, they obeyed because they "knew" that nothing bad would happen, and they believed in the morality of the experimenter. Only a shift from this position would allow disobedience.

Pines, M. (1981, May). Unlearning blind obedience in German schools. *Psychology Today,* Have the German people learned from the lessons of World War II? According to this 1981 article, the answer seemed to be yes.

Remley, A. (1988, October). From obedience to independence: Parents used to raise their children to be dutiful. *Psychology Today,* p. 54. The times have changed. Now parents are raising their children to be self-reliant, rather than obedient.

Sheridan, C., & King, R. (1974). Obedience to authority with an authentic victim. *Proceedings of the American Psychological Association Convention,* 165-166. What happens when a learner is actually shocked? Who obeys the most, males or females? See this paper for the answers.

# Professional Update: Current Articles from Professional Sources

Bond, C. F., Omar, A., Pitre, U., Lashley, B. R., Skaggs, L. M., & Kirk, C. T. (1992). Fishy-looking liars: Deception judgment from expectancy violation. *Journal of Personality and Social Psychology, 63,* 669-677. One of the ways that people attempt to influence other people is through lying to them. Subjects in the United States and in India viewed people describing acquaintances while performing weird behavior such as arm raising and staring. In both countries subjects inferred lying from weird behavior. That is, if people act weird when telling us something, we are apt to infer that they are lying to us.

Buck, R., Losow, J. I., Murphy, M. M., & Costanzo, P. (1992). Social facilitation and inhibition of emotional expression and communication. *Journal of Personality and Social Psychology, 63,* 962-968. Senders viewed provocative slides (e.g., with sexual content), and their video-recorded reactions constituted messages to receivers. Accuracy of receivers' guesses about slide content was a function of who was present during sending. When senders had a stranger present during recordings, accuracy of guessing slide content was inhibited. Friends, however, had a facilitory effect for some slides and an inhibitory effect for others.

Dillard, J. P. (1991). The current status of research on sequential-request compliance technique.

*Personality and Social Psychology Bulletin, 17,* 283-288. Compares recent meta-analyses of foot-in-the-door research and door-in-the-face research, then tries to build a theoretical perspective that accounts for both.

Petty, R. E., Schumann, D. W., Richman, S. A., & Stathman, A. J. (1993). Positive mood and persuasion: Different roles for affect under high- and low-elaboration conditions. *Journal of Personality and Social Psychology, 64,* 5-20. Yes, positive mood tends to generate positive attitudes in the context of persuasive attempts, but the path through which it works can be Byzantine. If subjects do not have the opportunity to elaborate on thoughts associated with the persuasive attempt, the path is direct: Positive mood generates positive attitudes. If they can elaborate, the path is through positive thoughts created in the process of elaboration.

Prentice, D. A., & Miller, D. T. (1993). Pluralistic ignorance and alcohol use on campus: Some consequences of misperceiving the social norm. *Journal of Personality and Social Psychology, 64,* 243-256. "Pluralistic ignorance" is when everyone believes something or other, but no one really does. In this case, students believed that the average student was relatively comfortable with campus alcohol use in the direction of the position they mistakenly believed that other students held. That is, they were conforming to a norm that didn't exist.

Reno, R. R., Cialdini, R. B., & Kallgren, C. A. (1993). The transituational influence of social norms. *Journal of Personality and Social Psychology, 64,* 104-112. Two kinds of norms were investigated; descriptive norms specifying what is typically done in the setting, and injunctive norms specifying what is typically approved by society. The injunctive norm "It's wrong to litter" had more general impact: It suppressed littering in both clean and littered environments, and it worked in the setting where the norm was evoked as well as in a different setting.

*Related Readings:* The following selections from *Readings in Social Psychology: General, Classic and Contemporary Selections,* 3rd Edition, by Wayne Lesko (Allyn and Bacon, 1997) accompany this chapter.

Gibson, J., & Haritor-Fatouros, M. (1986). "The education of a torturer." This article begins by pondering the age-old question of whether people who torture and kill do so because they are monsters, ordinary people "just following orders," or the products of special training. The authors choose the latter and illustrate by an analysis of Greek torturers. (Article 25).

Milgram, S. (1963). "Behavioral study of obedience." This is the classic paper by Milgram on his research. It is certainly one of the most important research publications in the history of psychology. (Article 26).

Santos, M. D., Leve, C., & Pratkanis, A. R. (1994). "Hey Buddy, can you spare seventeen cents? Mindful Persuasion and the Pique technique." What type of requests are we mindlessly more likely to comply with? Research in this article indicates that subjects are more likely to comply to strange requests. (Article 27).

# Chapter 10

# Prosocial Behavior: Helping Other People

## Chapter-at-a-Glance

| CHAPTER OUTLINE | INSTRUCTION IDEAS | SUPPLEMENTS* |
|---|---|---|
| *I. Responding to an Emergency: Are Bystanders Helpful or Indifferent?*<br><br>• **Cornerstones of Social Psychology**  Darley and Latane: Explaining the Unresponsive Bystander<br><br>• To Help or Not to Help?  Five Choice Points<br><br>• **Social Psychology: On the Applied Side**  Responding to an Abused Child<br><br>• Who Are the Helpers?  Dispositional Influences on Prosocial Behavior | Learning Objectives 10.1 to 10.9<br><br>Discussion Topics 1, 2<br><br>Activities 10.1, 10.2 (Handouts)<br><br>Critical Thinking Questions 1-4, 8 | Test Bank Questions 10.1 to 10.73<br><br>Readings:<br>- Lesko 28, When Will People Help in a Crisis?<br>- Lesko 29, From Jerusalem to Jericho<br>- Lesko 30, Bystander Responses to Public Episodes of Child Abuse<br><br>Transparencies 10.1, 10.2, 10.3 |
| *II. Additional Factors That Influence Prosocial Behavior*<br>• The Role of Social Models<br><br>• Some Victims Are More Likely to Receive Help Than Others<br><br>• **Social Psychology: On the Applied Side**  Does Gender Matter?  Male and Female Police Officers Responding to Male and Female Traffic Offenders<br><br>• Volunteering to Help:  Responding to the AIDS Epidemic<br><br>• Prosocial Acts from the Viewpoint of the Person Who Needs Help | Learning Objectives 10.10 to 10.16<br><br>Activities 10.3, 10.4<br><br>Critical Thinking Question 9 | Test Bank Questions 10.74 to 10.118<br><br>Transparencies 10.4, 10.5 |
| *III. Additional Theoretical Explanations of Prosocial Motivation*<br>• The Effect of a Positive versus a Negative Mood on Helping<br><br>• Possible Alternative Motives Underlying Prosocial Behavior<br><br>• **Social Diversity: A Critical Analysis**  Evaluating Prosocial Motivation Across Age Groups and Across Nations | Learning Objectives 10.17 to 10.21<br><br>Discussion Topics 3, 4<br><br>Critical Thinking Questions 5, 10 | Test Bank Questions 10.119 to 10.150 |

*See Audiovisual Suggestions

# 10

# Prosocial Behavior:  Helping Other People

---

## Chapter Outline:  Getting the Overall Picture

---

I. **Responding to an Emergency:  Are Bystanders Helpful or Indifferent?**
    A.    Cornerstones of Social Psychology: Darley and Latane'--Explaining the Unresponsive Bystander
    B.    To Help or Not to Help?  Five Choice Points
        1.    Step 1.  The Bystander Must Perceive the Emergency
        2.    Step 2.  Correctly Interpreting the Situation As an Emergency
        3.    Step 3.  Assuming Responsibility to Act
        4.    Step 4.  Knowing What to Do
        5.    Step 5.  Making the Final Decision to Help
    C.    Social Psychology: On the Applied Side: Responding to an Abused Child
    D.    Who Are the Helpers?  Dispositional Influences on Prosocial Behavior
        1.    Influence of Specific Dispositions on Prosocial Behavior
        2.    Combining Dispositional Variables to Predict Prosocial Behavior

II. **Additional Factors That Influence Prosocial Behavior**
    A.    The Role of Social Models
    B.    Some Victims Are More Likely to Receive Help Than Others
        1.    Helping a Liked Victim
    C.    Social Psychology: On the Applied Side: Does Gender Matter?  Male and Female Police Officers Responding to Male and Female Traffic Offenders
        1.    Similarity of Victim to Bystander and Attributions of Victim Responsibility
    D.    Volunteering to Help:  Responding to the AIDS Epidemic
    E.    Prosocial Acts from the Viewpoint of the Person Who Needs Help
        1.    Asking for Help
        2.    How Does It Feel to Be Helped?

III. **Additional Theoretical Explanations of Prosocial Motivation**
    A.    The Effect of a Positive versus a Negative Mood on Helping
        1.    Effects of a Positive Mood
        2.    Effects of a Negative Mood
    B.    Possible Alternative Motives Underlying Prosocial Behavior
        1.    Unselfish Motivation:  Empathy Leads to Helpfulness
        2.    Selfish Motivation:  Helping in Order to Feel Better
        3.    Selfish Motivation:  Helping Because It Feels Good to Have an Impact
        4.    Selfish Motivation:  Helping Similar Others to Preserve Your Common Genes
    C.    Social Diversity: A Critical Analysis: Evaluating Prosocial Motivation Across Age Groups and Across Nations

## Learning Objectives
After studying this chapter, students should be able to:

**10.1** Describe cases where someone helped or failed to help in an emergency. Describe the Kitty Genovese case and give the procedure and results of the Darley and Latane' "seizure study."

**10.2** Define the "bystander effect." Understand the first step in the procession to helping. Describe the procedure and results of Batson's "seminary student study."

**10.3** Give the second step leading to eventual help. Explain how possibly "looking silly" inhibits assessing a situation as an emergency. Use "pluralistic ignorance" to explain the "smoke study."

**10.4** Outline the third and fourth steps leading to help and define "diffusion of responsibility." Explain fifth step.

**10.5** List social interactions that are "nobody's business." Explain what the Christy/Voight survey revealed about intervention by witnesses of abuse.

**10.6** Explain the findings on survey respondents and the bystander effect? Outline what did and did not relate to intervention by witnesses of abuse.

**10.7** List dispositions that relate to actual helping. Indicate the difference between "altruism" and "egotism."

**10.8** Indicate three traits of empathic people. Discuss how gender relates to empathy. Say what part of empathy is genetic and give the three characteristics that Knight and colleagues found to jointly affect helping in children.

**10.9** List and define the five traits in the personality cluster of persons who help.

**10.10** Tell how Lassie inspired helping. Outline the "wrong number technique" used to determine whether gays would be helped as much as "straights."

**10.11** Explain whether dependency eclipses similarity as a determinant of helping. Discuss the role that police officers' gender plays in writing citations. Describe the effect of judging the victim responsible for her or his calamity.

**10.12** Explain how the gender of the typical perpetrator and victim of rape explain reactions to such attacks. Discuss cognitive mechanisms that help us avoid fear of victimization.

**10.13** Tell what leads up to helping a distant victim. Indicate the attributions and fears that lessens help to AIDS victims.

**10.14** Indicate who is reluctant to ask for help and explain why any person is reluctant to ask for help, except, possibly, from a stranger. Describe the role of requester's traits and manner of asking for help in receiving help.

**10.15** In U.S. society, describe what negative trait is seen in requesters of help. Discuss some other attributions that may be aimed at requesters of help.

**10.16** Discuss the two most general reasons why we help. Explain what kinds of manipulations researchers have used to study mood and helping. Discuss when a good mood inhibit helping.

**10.17** List conditions under which negative mood inhibits helping or promotes it. Outline how subjects' level of empathy interacted with ease of getting out of the experiment in confirming Batson's theory.

**10.18** Explain when people avoid empathy-producing information. Contrast Batson's position with that of "negative state relief." Explain what Cialdini and colleagues found when they separated sadness from empathy.

**10.19** Describe the "empathic joy" hypothesis. Explain what Smith and colleagues found when subjects got feedback about the effect of their help? Discuss the "helper's high."

**10.20** Describe the genetic hypothesis regarding helping.  Indicate what this theory predicts about who will receive help.

**10.21** Explain three standards that relate to helping (Reykowski).  Indicate how he and colleagues studies these standards in a cross-cultural study.

## Discussion Topics and Questions

### 1.  The Carnegie Hero Fund

In 1904, industrialist Andrew Carnegie founded the Carnegie Hero Fund with an endowment of $5 million.  The purpose of the fund is to reward heroes who risk their own lives in efforts to save the lives of others.  Since 1904, more than 63,000 people have been nominated for heroism awards, but only 7,313 (about 11 percent) have been chosen to receive them.  Of those chosen for awards, 91 percent have been males.  Each recipient is awarded $2,500, accompanied by a bronze medal inscribed with the New Testament verse:  "Greater love hath no man than this, that a man lay down his life for his friends."  More than 1,500 Carnegie heroes, or roughly 21 percent, have died performing their rescues, the most common cause being drownings or fires.  In these cases additional monetary compensation is often provided in the form of pensions for beneficiaries, funeral expenses, and scholarships for surviving dependents.

Candidates are excluded from awards if they are obligated to act because of their occupation, such as fire fighter or lifeguard.  A person who rescues a family member is also excluded, unless the rescuer is severely injured or killed.  A candidate is not excluded for failing to save the person's life; the awards are for those who risk their *own* lives in an effort to save others.

Discuss the issue of heroism with the class.  In conjunction with the discussion, watch the news for actions that are described as "heroic."  Students respond positively to current examples.  Ask the students to define *heroism*, and get them to list the criteria they would use to grant Carnegie awards.  Finally, compare the definition of *hero* with the text's definition of *prosocial behavior*.

### 2.  Urban versus Rural Help

Who is more likely to help others in need, an urban dweller or a person who lives in a small town?  Where is a person more likely to be helped, in the city or in the country?

Most of the social psychological research indicates that small-town residents are more likely than city dwellers to help.  The kinds of help studied have varied considerably, including such actions as helping people who called wrong phone number, giving back over-payments to customers, mailing lost letters, buying greeting cards from the Multiple Sclerosis Society, helping to pick up dropped envelopes, and correcting inaccurate directions.  If you want to read on this topic, studies by Amoto (1983) in the *Journal of Personality and Social Psychology (45,* 571-586) and by Korte and Kerr (1975) in the *Journal of Social Psychology (95,* 183-184) would be helpful.  In any case, you can relate the kinds of help-needed situations that are likely to occur in real life (e.g., car has flat tire, person passes out, auto breaks down, someone needs change) so that students have a knowledge sufficient for discussion.

Having primed students with this information, you can ask them to relate their experiences of helping, being helped, or watching others being helped or not.  Although my college is primarily rural, I still am able to elicit some reports from students who have had experiences of helping in an urban setting.  You will probably also get a variety of interesting and illuminating reports, from both urban and rural students, to compare helping behavior in the country and the city.

### 3. Long-term Helpers

The research conducted by social psychologists has generally dealt with helping that occurs in response to an immediate, short-term need. Researchers create a "victim" and systematically vary aspects of the situation to determine their impact on helping. A logical question is whether the results of these short-term studies adequately explain long-term helping, particularly long-term helping carried out despite great danger and cost to the helper. An example is the behavior of persons who hid Jews from the Nazis in occupied countries during World War II. To have been caught in this humanitarian effort could have resulted in death for the helper. Is this type of long-term, carefully planned altruism caused by different factors than the help that occurs in short-term emergency situations? Have students speculate on how the psychological dynamics may be different for these extraordinary helpers. Here individuals know that helping on one occasion will increase rather than decrease the likelihood of future requests for help from victims. In fact, help on the first occasion commits the helper to supplying aid for an indefinite period of time, exactly the opposite of the usual short-term help circumstance. Also ask students how well these long-term helpers, whose lives are continually at risk, fit the egotistic/self-serving theories of helping.

### 4. Altruism Debate: Why Do People Help?

Focus on those theories that claim people help because there is always something in it for them-- distress reduction, self-esteem enhancement, and so forth. Generate a debate among students: is there any such thing as altruism untainted by self-centered need fulfillment? Start the debate by asking if there is anyone who is willing to argue that the reason people help is to get something out of it. Ask if some other person will take the other side: argue that people can and do help others solely to benefit them, not for personal gain at any level of abstraction. If you can induce these two volunteers to debate, other students will surely break in to support or challenge one debater or the other.

---

## Learning Activities: Classroom Exercises/Demonstrations

---

### 10.1 Is It Prosocial Behavior?

On the next page (or in the Study Guide) you will find descriptions of several situations that may or may not show prosocial behavior. Have the students respond to these items individually and then poll the class to find out how many students considered each item to be prosocial. You will find that there is considerable disagreement whether most of the situations represent prosocial behavior. Go through the items one at a time, asking students who indicated that the situation was not prosocial behavior to explain why. The ensuing discussion should help students to develop a better idea of the meaning of prosocial behavior, and also to appreciate the difficulty of determining underlying motivation for behavior.

## HANDOUT FOR ACTIVITY # 10.1

### IS IT PROSOCIAL BEHAVIOR?

|  | Yes | No |
|---|---|---|

1. John, a college student, spends two hours per week as a "Big Brother" to a nine-year-old boy whose parents are divorced.

   Why or why not?

2. Arnold, a firefighter, rescues an elderly woman trapped in a fire.

   Why or why not?

3. Sandra agrees to donate her organs for transplant in the event of her death.

   Why or why not?

4. Marie makes a $50 contribution to charity and thus gets a chance to attend a banquet with a celebrity.

   Why or why not?

5. Bob attempts to save his six-year-old son from drowning.

   Why or why not?

6. Tom informs the manager of the bookstore about a college students who shoplifted a book.

   Why or why not?

7. Ann makes an anonymous donation of $1,000 to her church's building fund.

   Why or why not?

8. Marty buys a raffle ticket from a charitable organization.

   Why or why not?

Copyright © 1997 by Allyn and Bacon

## 10.2  The Self-Report Altruism Scale

Rushton et al. (1981) devised a scale to measure helpfulness in which subjects provide an estimate of the frequency with which they have performed various concrete helping acts. The Self-Report Altruism Scale, found on the next page (or in the Study Guide), is a twenty-one-item scale requiring respondents to estimate the number of times they have performed such acts as making change for another, donating blood, holding the door open for someone, and so forth. Have the students respond to the scale anonymously, then score it by adding the responses to the twenty-one items. Display the average (or median) reported performance of each prosocial behavior included on the scale. Do the students who show social desirability also tend to show high levels of helpfulness? If so, talk about their sincere perceptions of being helpful and fact of nonhelpfulness in real-life settings when, among other considerations, there are meaningful consequences to helping. To some degree the students will show more of an inclination to help in terms of some items than others. Ask them to explain why helping is more likely in some situations than in others.

## HANDOUT FOR ACTIVITY # 10.2

Indicate the number of times in the past month that you have performed each of the following actions.

___1.  I have assisted someone experiencing car trouble (changing a tire, calling a mechanic, pushing a stalled or stuck car, etc.).

___2.  I have given someone directions.

___3.  I have made change for someone.

___4.  I have given money to charity.

___5.  I have given money to someone who needed it (or asked for it).

___6.  I have done volunteer work for charity.

___7.  I have donated blood.

___8.  I have helped carry another person's belongings (books, parcels, etc.)

___9.  I have delayed an elevator and held the door open for another.

___10. I have allowed someone to go ahead of me in a line (in the supermarket, during registration, etc.).

___11. I have another a ride in my car.

___12. I have pointed out a clerk's error (in a bank, at the supermarket, etc.) in undercharging me for an item.

___13. I have let someone borrow an item of some value to me (clothes, jewelry, stereo, etc.).

___14. I have helped another with a homework assignment when my knowledge was greater than his or hers.

___15. I have voluntarily looked after another's plants, pets, house, or children without being paid for it.

___16. I have offered my seat in a crowded room or on a train or bus to someone who was standing.

___17. I have helped another to move his or her possessions to another room, apartment, or house.

___18. I have retrieved an item dropped by another for him or her (pencil, book, packages, etc.)

___19. I have held the door open to a room or building for another to enter.

Copyright © 1997 by Allyn and Bacon

___20. I have helped another with a personal project (painting, repairing a car, etc.)

___21. I have helped one or more people in an emergency involving the threat or sustenance of bodily injury to the victim(s).

Copyright © 1997 by Allyn and Bacon

## 10.3 Creation of "Help-Needed" Situation(s)

Consider offering students extra points applicable to final grades if they will go out into the real world and create help-needed situations. Be cautious about what they propose to do. Have them run all proposals by you before they are allowed to execute them. There are many simple scenarios that can be enacted. For example, have them volunteer to collect money for some real organization (of course, they would get prior permission from the organization). They could collect while dressed up as they would be to attend church or go to a sales job. Then have them dress very casually and conduct the same collection. Does the amount of money collected differ across the two conditions? Another possibility is to leave an auto's lights on and doors open in a variety of settings. In what kinds of settings do passersby stop, open a door, and turn out the lights, thus preserving the battery? Or students could ask for directions while well dressed or dressed like a "street person." Perhaps some African-American and some European-American students could panhandle at the same sites on alternate days and compare results. How about the tone of the help request? Students could enter some local government office asking for information that should be available, using either a polite voice or a cold and subtly demanding tone. Students might find it interesting to make requests of local offices identifying themselves either as students or as nonstudents. There are a variety of interesting alternatives.

## 10.4 Modeling Prosocial Behavior

Demonstrate that children can learn prosocial behavior by observing a model. If yours is a fairly large, urban college or university class, or a community college, you will have students with children aged two to five. Have one of them bring a child to class. Stage a help-needed situation. Perhaps, in front of the class (or in private, if you can arrange a videotaping session outside of class), have one adult drop something, such as a stack of small paperback books. The child's parent would then help pick up the books. The scene may have to be repeated, even seven times (if an audience is present, warn them in advance not to laugh). Will the child join in the task of picking up the books? Alternatively, for extra credit, have a student go into a local preschool and stage a similar scene. The school may be glad to have the student teach prosocial behavior to its pupils. Results could be reported back to the class.

---

# Overhead Transparencies
These appear at the back of this manual.

---

# Audiovisual Suggestions

*Allyn and Bacon Videos*

* *Helping and Prosocial Behavior,* videotape, 28.5 mins. To obtain this tape, consult your Allyn and Bacon sales representative. Using dramatizations as a stimulus, Robert A. Baron and Margaret Clark discuss the mechanisms behind helping or not helping.

*Other Videos and Films*

*Aspects of Behavior,* color film also available on video, 30 mins. CRM Films, 2233 Faraday Avenue, Carlsbad, CA 92008 (800-421-0833). The social psychology section is about ten minutes. This film includes an excellent portrayal of the smoke-filled room study by Latane and Darley. Interviews with Latane and Darley on the bystander effect and with Milgram on city living are also included.

*Invitation to Social Psychology,* color film, portion on helping approximately 5 mins. Harper & Row Media, 10 E. Rad Street, New York, NY 10022. John Dearly and BBB Laden discuss bystander apathy.

*Social Modification of Organically Motivated Behavior,* silent, 12 mins. Indiana University, Audiovisual Center, Bloomington, IN 47401. Hungry rats display both altruistic and competitive behavior.

*When Will People Help? The Social Psychology of Bystander Intervention,* 25 mins. Harcourt, Brace, & Jovanovich, 757 Third Avenue, New York, NY 10017. Daryl Bem is narrator for reenactments of some of the early Laden and Dearly studies, including the smoke-filled room study and the seizure study.

# Critical Thinking/Essay Questions

1. Discuss why "bystander apathy" was so readily accepted by the press and the public when cases of failure to help began to appear regularly in the media. Why are we so pessimistic?

2. Examine the "five steps to helping." Are these all that are needed? Can you add some? If not, consolidate the five steps into just three.

3. Indicate the essential qualities of the victim that would maximize her/his likelihood of being helped. What are the traits that would greatly lower the probability a person would get help in an emergency?

4. Construct three scenarios where help is needed. Be sure to make them quite different from each other. Outline how successful help requests would have to differ for the three situations.

5. Argue either for the "pure altruism" point of view (people help for selfless reasons) or for one of the theories that asserts that people help because there is "something in it for them."

6. Think up some help-needed situations in which positive mood would be faciliative. Be sure to tell how these situations are different in such a way that one kind of mood or the other is facilitative.

7. Become a sociobiologist and argue that people help in order to "promote their genes." Exactly who will be helped if this theory is sound? In what situations will they be helped? In what ways will they be helped?

8. Paint a picture of the altruistic personality. What would be the essential characteristic of a person who would reliably help others who suffer emergencies?

9. Make some suggestions concerning how to motivate people to volunteer for work with AIDS victims. How would you reassure them? How would you convince them that their help is vitally important?

10. Imagine you have some preschool children in your charge. Map out a strategy to teach them to be helpers. Of course, you will have to show them when help is needed and what help is appropriate and possible for them to carry out. Tell how role models would be useful and how children's natural empathic responses (e.g., if one child cries, others will follow suit) might be called into play.

---

## Sources for Lecture

---

Devore, I., & Morris, S. (1977). The science of genetic self-interest. *Psychology Today,* February, pp. 42-51, 84-88. Describes the selfishness "built into our genes" from a sociobiological point of view.

Fogelman, E., & Weiner, V. L. (1985). The few, the brave, the noble. *Psychology Today,* August, pp. 60-65. During World War II some people risked their lives to save Jews from Nazis. Why? Some were motivated by deep moral values, whereas others were motivated by personal attachments or identification with the victim.

Kohn, A. (1988). Beyond selfishness. *Psychology Today,* October, pp. 34-38. We start helping others early in life, though we're not always consistent. What makes us helpful sometimes and sometimes not?

Luks, A. (1988). Helper's high. *Psychology Today,* October, pp. 39-42. The author asserts that people feel physically and emotionally good when they help others. In the same manner that running promotes inner calm, helping is said to promote good health.

Pines, M. (1979). Good Samaritans at age two? *Psychology Today,* June, pp. 66-77. Examines altruistic behavior in very young children. Some babies as young as one are capable of comforting others who are in pain or are crying. More sophisticated behaviors are demonstrated before age three.

Shotlan, R. L. (1985). When bystanders just stand by. *Psychology Today,* June, pp. 50-55. The author reviews the literature on personal and situational factors that determine whether a bystander will help a crime victim.

---

## Professional Update: Current Articles from Professional Sources

---

Clark, M. S. (Ed.). (1991). *Prosocial behavior* in the series *Review of personality and social psychology.* Newbury Park, CA: Sage Publication. Review of prosocial behavior research. Features chapters by some of the major contributors to the area, including Daniel Batson, Mark Snyder, Arie Nadler, Peter Salovey, Sam Gaertner, John Dovidio, Jane Piliavin, and John M. Dearly.

Collins, W. A., & Kuczaj, S. A. (1991). *Developmental psychology.* New York: MacMillan. Contains an unusually complete and readable section on prosocial behavior in children.

Corey, G., Corey, M. S., & Callanan, P. (1993). *Issues and ethics in the helping professions.* Pacific Grove, CA: Brooks/Cole. Three practicing help professionals relate their experiences with moral and ethical issues endemic to the health professions. People needing help are vulnerable. This book tells how to avoid doing more harm than good.

Eisenberg, N. (1992). *The caring child.* Cambridge, MA: Harvard University Press. Provides as near a complete understanding as is currently available of the motivations behind prosocial behaviors in children and how these motives develop and are elicited in various situations.

Krebs, D. L., Denton, K. L., Vermeulen, S. C., Carpendale, J. I., & Bush, A. (1991). Structural flexibility of moral judgment. *Journal of Personality and Social Psychology, 61,* 1012-1023. Thirty men and thirty women responded to two of the dilemmas in Kohlberg's Moral Judgment Interview and to a prosocial dilemma as well as an impaired-driving dilemma. Half of them responded to the prosocial and impaired-driving dilemmas from the perspective of a hypothetical character, and half responded from their own perspective. No sex or perspective differences in moral maturity were observed. Subjects scored highest on Kohlberg's dilemmas, intermediate on the prosocial dilemma, and lowest on the impaired-driving dilemma.

*Related Readings:* The following selections from *Readings in Social Psychology: General, Classic, and Contemporary Selection,* 3rd Edition, by Wayne Lesko (Allyn and Bacon, 1997) accompany this chapter.

Dearly, J. M., & Laden, B. (1968). "When will people help in a crisis?" The authors describe their classic work on the bystander effect and examine the steps an intervener must go through in order to explain when help will be given. (Article 28)

Dearly, J. M., & Batson, D. (1973). "From Jerusalem to Jericho: A study of situational and dispositional variables in helping behavior." Seminary students, some of them on their way to give a talk on the "good Samaritan," encountered a shabbily dressed person slumped by the wayside. Religious and personality variables, and whether they were to give a talk or not, failed to predict helping. (Article 29).

Christy, C. A., & Voigt, H. (1994). "Bystander responses to public episodes of child abuse." Nearly half of a college-aged population surveyed indicted that they had witnessed public episodes of child abuse. However, only about one in four made some type of intervention. Implications of the findings are discussed. Proposal is made to educate people to intervene on behalf of abused children. (Article 30).

# Chapter 11
## Aggression: Its Nature, Causes and Control

## Chapter-at-a-Glance

| CHAPTER OUTLINE | INSTRUCTION IDEAS | SUPPLEMENTS* |
|---|---|---|
| **I. Theoretical Perspectives on Aggression: In Search of the Roots of Violence**<br>• Instinct Theories: Aggression as an Innate Tendency<br>• Biological Theories<br>• Drive Theories: The Motive to Harm Others<br>• Social learning Theory: Aggression as Learned Social Behavior<br>• Cognitive Theories of Aggression: The Roles of Scripts, Appraisals, and Affect | Learning Objectives 11.1 to 11.5<br><br>Activities 11.1, 11.3 (Handouts)<br><br>Critical Thinking Question 1 | Test Bank Questions 11.1 to 11.38<br><br>Transparency 11.2 |
| **II. Social Determinants of Aggression: How Others' Actions, Or Our Understanding of Them, Influence Aggression**<br>• **Cornerstones of Social Psychology** The Buss Technique for Studying Physical Aggression: "Would You Electrocute a Stranger?" Revisited<br>• Frustration: Why Not Getting What You Want (Or What You Expect) Can Sometimes Lead to Aggression<br>• Direct Provocation: When Aggression Breeds Aggression<br>• Exposure to Media Violence: The Effects of Witnessing Aggression<br>• Heightened Arousal: Emotion, Cognition, and Aggression<br>• Sexual Arousal and Aggression: Are Love and Hate Really Two Sides of the Same Behavioral Coin?<br>• Sexual Jealousy and Aggression: Do We Want to Hurt the Ones We Love If They Have Been Unfaithful?<br>• **Social Psychology: On the Applied Side** Violent Pornography: A Potential Cause of Rape? | Learning Objectives 11.6 to 11.13<br><br>Discussion Topics 1, 4<br><br>Activities 11.2 (Handout) and 11.5<br><br>Critical Thinking Questions 2-7 | Test Bank Questions 11.39 to 11.106<br><br>Readings:<br>- Lesko 31, Why Violent Toys are Good for Kids<br>- Lesko 32, Transmission of Aggression<br>- Lesko 33, Female Aggression as a Response to Sexual Jealousy<br><br>Transparencies 11.1-11.6 |
| **III. Personal Causes of Aggression**<br>• The Type A Behavior Pattern: Why the A in type A Could Well Stand for *Aggression*<br>• Perceiving Evil Intent in Others: Hostile Attributional Bias<br>• Irritability, Rumination, and the "Big Five" Dimensions<br>• Gender Differences in Aggression: Are They Real? | Learning Objectives 11.14 to 11.17<br><br>Activity 11.4<br><br>Critical Thinking Ques. 8, 10 | Test Bank Questions 11.107 to 11.125 |
| **IV. Child Abuse and Workplace Violence: Aggression in Long-Term Relationships**<br>• Child Maltreatment: Harming the Innocent<br>• Workplace Violence: Aggression on the Job | Learning Objectives 11.18 to 11.19 | Test Bank Questions 11.126 to 11.136 |
| **V. The Prevention and Control of Aggression: Some Useful Techniques**<br>• Punishment: An Effective Deterrent to Violence?<br>• Catharsis: Does Getting It Out of Your System Really Help?<br>• Cognitive Interventions: Apologies and Overcoming Cognitive Deficits<br>• Other Techniques for Reducing Aggression: Exposure to Nonaggressive Models, Training in Social Skills, and Incompatible Responses<br>• **Social Diversity: A Critical Analysis** Cultural and Ethnic Differences in Aggression | Learning Objectives 11.20 to 11.24<br><br>Discussion Topic 3<br><br>Critical Thinking Questions 9, 11 | Test Bank Questions 11.137 to 11.160<br><br>Transparency 11.3 |

*See Audiovisual Suggestions

# 11

## Aggression: Its Nature, Causes, and Control

---

### Chapter Outline: Getting the Overall Picture

---

V.  **The Prevention and Control of Aggression: Some Useful Techniques**
    A.  Punishment: An Effective Deterrent to Violence?
    B.  Catharsis: Does Getting It Out of Your System Really Help?
    C.  Cognitive Interventions: Apologies and Overcoming Cognitive Deficits
    D.  Other Techniques for Reducing Aggression: Exposure to Nonaggressive Models, Training in Social Skills, and Incompatible Responses
        1.  Exposure to Nonaggressive Models: The Contagion of Restraint
        2.  Training in Social Skills: Learning to Get Along with Others
        3.  Incompatible Responses: Positive Affect As a Means of Reducing Anger
    E.  Social Diversity: A Critical Analysis: Cultural and Ethnic Differences in Aggression

---

# Learning Objectives
After studying this chapter, students should be aboe to:

---

**11.1**  Discuss the problem of aggression in the world today vs. in the past. Define aggression. Describe Freud's version of "instinct theory" and contrast Freud's view to Lorenz's. Discuss aggression and sociobiology.

**11.2**  Cite the two reasons that aggression is probably not controlled by the genes. Describe the biochemistry that is linked with aggression against self or others.

**11.3**  Discuss how testosterone affects female transsexuals. Discuss the interplay of biological and cultural/environmental factors in producing aggression. Describe the drive theories.

**11.4**  Outline the social learning theory of aggression and explain what we learn that directs our aggressiveness (three categories).

**11.5**  Define a "script" and indicate when we appraise and reappraise. Discuss Berkowitz's "negative affect" and the factors that produce aggression or not, according to cognitive theory.

**11.6**  Outline the Buss technique for studying aggression and describe the critical difference with Milgram's method. Discuss the controversy over whether the Buss method involves real aggression.

**11.7**  Understand the logic behind the frustration-aggression hypothesis, as well as the problems with it.

**11.8**  Describe how we tend to react to provocation (Harris), and indicate an unexpected source of violent portrayals on TV. Characterize the laboratory experiments using media presentations to provoke subjects.

**11.9**  Indicate what is involved in the "static observation" studies. Outline the procedures of the 10 and 20 year follow-up "longitudinal" study by Huesmann and Eron. Discuss the gender difference in the exposure to TV violence-aggression link.

**11.10**  Discuss Zillmann "excitation transfer" theory. Tell how cognition influences the effects of residual arousal.

**11.11**  Consider when sexual arousal decreases aggression and when it increases it. Discuss the factors in Zillmann's "two component" theory of response to erotica. Define sexual jealousy and describe the sex difference in response to a sexual infidelity.

**11.12**  Unravel the web of gender-related emotions relating to infidelity as it once was and as modern contraception has made it. Outline how people tend to react when exposed to violence toward women in a sexual context.

**11.13**  Discuss the effects of "pornography" and whether rape is a sex act or an act of violence.

**11.14** Describe the Type A and Type B personality patterns. Examine Berman and colleagues study about the joint effect on aggression of Type A orientation and testosterone. Contrast Type As and Bs with regard to hostile and instrumental aggression.

**11.15** Discuss hostile attributional bias. Describe how Dodge and colleagues demonstrated that this bias predicts real-life bias. List and define the "Big Five."

**11.16** Discuss our beliefs about gender differences in aggressiveness and the reality of gender differences. Indicate the situations that interact with gender to influence aggressiveness. State Eagly's "social role" explanation of gender differences in aggressiveness.

**11.17** Explain how testosterone relates to aggressiveness. Indicate Gladue's finding when male and female heterosexuals and homosexuals were tested on testosterone levels and aggressiveness.

**11.18** Define child mistreatment and indicate whether mistreatment as a child absolutely predicts mistreatment of children as an adult. Describe the three classes of variables that relate to child abuse.

**11.19** Describe three factors that abuse prevention programs target. State the facts about workplace violence vs. the myths, and discuss some organizational sources of increased aggression at work.

**11.20** Explain the "bone of contention" in the controversy over capital punishment. Outline the conditions under which punishment can be expected to deter aggressiveness.

**11.21** Describe "catharsis" and indicate how it is supposed to reduce aggressiveness. Explain how cognitive processes limit catharsis' effectiveness.

**11.22** Describe how perceived level of control exercised by an attacker influences the effectiveness of his/her excuses. Indicate the way a "cognitive deficit" contributes to aggressiveness.

**11.23** State how models can reduce aggressiveness. List the deficits of the socially unskilled, how they contribute to aggressiveness and how they can be remedied. Describe some responses that are incompatible with aggression (note the Richardson et al study).

**11.24** Describe cross-cultural studies of violence. Describe Osterman et al studies of aggressiveness among children in several societies.

---

## Discussion Topics and Questions

---

### 1. Rape and the "Just World Hypothesis"

A popular movie starring Jody Foster was based on an actual incident involving gang rape. In the actual case, four men raped a twenty-one-year-old mother of two for 120 agonizing minutes while fellow patrons at a New Bedford, Massachusetts, bar cheered the attackers and taunted the victim. No one helped the victim, but two men were accused of assisting the rapists.

At first there was sympathy for the victim. About 2,500 to 4,000 people joined a candlelight procession in protest of the outrage, and a local women's group began organizing a rape crisis center and sensitivity training for police officers. Letters arrived containing expressions of understanding and money for the victim. But then the local mood grew into something different. Although her identity was unknown, callers to a local talk show claimed that the victim was actually a prostitute who "got what she deserved."

There are at least two potentially interesting topics for discussion here. First, the label "prostitute" suggests the victim was looking for sex and, thus, got what she was seeking. That is, rape is a sexual act. If rape is sexual, then some women might be seen as getting what they were looking for. But what if the rape victim is assumed to be humiliated, beaten, and dehumanized?

Second, the attribution of "prostitute" to the victim can be viewed as supporting the "just world hypothesis." In the just world, you get what you deserve and deserve what you get (see the writings of psychologist Melvin J. Lerner). By believing the "just world," New Bedford citizens could reason that "a bad thing happened to the rape victim, because she is a bad and careless person; I'm good and careful and thus need not worry." In this second case, discussion could center on how belief in the 'just world" promotes violence by destroying sympathy for victims of aggression.

## 2. Ways Parents Teach Aggression to Their Children

Discuss the multitude of ways that parents teach aggression to their children. Besides what is implied by information in the text, consider subtle methods such as permitting aggressive acts and thus tacitly approving of aggression. Also, consider the subtle ways parents communicate that aggression is appropriate for male children, but not for female children.

## 3. Methods of Controlling Aggression

Discuss methods of controlling aggression in addition to those included in the text. For example, imagine a parent recoiling with horror at discovering his or her two children mutually masturbating. Would people aggress very often if every time they did, witnesses reacted with similar repugnance? What would happen if people stopped patronizing violent movies and clicked off their TVs when violent programs were scheduled? What if football and hockey game attendance dropped dramatically? What if public figures were as roundly condemned and as thoroughly ruined for acts like punching a photographer as were some members of the British royalty for their sexual escapades?

## 4. Highway Violence

During the late 1980s several appalling incidents occurred on the highways of California. July 30: a teenager motorist was shot dead while driving away from an argument involving his passenger. The death brought fifty California police agencies onto the freeways in a show of force. August 3: between June 18 and August 3 there had been sixteen shooting incidents on the nation's highways. Ninety percent of the shootings had involved handguns. On August 3, in Sun Valley, a tanker truck was hit by gunfire coming from occupants of a green Chevy panelvan. Soon after the tanker incident, a motorist ran afoul of the van and received gunfire. Another van was the source of gunfire in a separate occurrence. Still later, a motorist reported drawing fire from a van with tinted windows.

These actual incidents further illustrate the authors' point that something about being behind the wheel brings out aggression in drivers. Philip Zimbardo's theory of deindividuation suggests that the driver and passengers of one vehicle constitute an antagonistic group in opposition to drivers and passengers of other vehicles. Further, tinted windows, enclosed vans, and sunglasses make occupants of different vehicles anonymous to one another. Add the arousal that comes from driving under congested and competitive conditions, the noise of the crowded freeway, fatigue after a day's work (most shooting incidents have been in the afternoon), and the presence of alcohol in the systems of some drivers, and all the ingredients for aggression on the highway are in the mix. Describe the above incidents to students and ask them if they know of others. Then ask them to come up with conditions, listed above, that contribute to aggression on the highway. Finally, offer them the opportunity to suggest ways to avoid aggression among motorists.

# Learning Activities:  Classroom Exercises/Demonstrations

## 11.1  Provocation Can Lead to Aggression

Under the guise of conducting an "impression formation" demonstration, have each class member stand up in front of the class and present name, home town, major, and favorite hobbies to other students.  For each presentation, have other students write a few lines on scratch paper giving their impression of the speaker.  On each sheet of notes have students identify themselves and the speakers by name.  A few days later, pass back a few "impressions of you" to each student, implying that the choices of impressions were random.  Among the bits of feedback each student receives will be a contrived description with the name of a collaborator from among class members.  For half the students, the bogus "impression" will be very positive, and for the others very negative.  Collect these from at the end of class so they can't compare notes.  Some time later announce that in the interest of studying persuasive communication a student has volunteered to read a paper just completed for a communications class.  Have the collaborator, whose name was on the bogus positive or negative impression received by each student, give his or her name and read the paper as a persuasive attempt.  Students should then "evaluate" the communicator with the favorability scale presented on the next page (or in the Study Guide).  You can just sum over agreement scores for each student and compare mean agreement for the positive and negative groups (just calculate the two means and display them or compare them with simple t-test).  Separating the evaluations of the communicator by students given a positive "impression" by him or her from those by students given a negative "impression' will allow you to demonstrate how provocation can lead to aggression expressed in the form of negative evaluations.

## HANDOUT FOR ACTIVITY # 11.1

### COMMUNICATOR EVALUATION FORM

On the scale below each statement check a point between the words "agree" and "disagree" to indicate the extent to which you agree or disagree with the statement. Use any point you wish.

The communicator was convincing.

agree 1 : 2 : 3 : 4 : 5 : 6 : 7 disagree


The communicator was expert about the topic covered.

agree 1 : 2 : 3 : 4 : 5 : 6 : 7 disagree


The communicator is a trustworthy source of information.

agree 1 : 2 : 3 : 4 : 5 : 6 : 7 disagree


The communicator is a likable person.

agree 1 : 2 : 3 : 4 : 5 : 6 : 7 disagree


I tend to think like the communicator.

agree 1 : 2 : 3 : 4 : 5 : 6 : 7 disagree


The communicator is a generally knowledgeable person.

agree 1 : 2 : 3 : 4 : 5 : 6 : 7 disagree


I would like to learn what the communicator knows about other topics.

agree 1 : 2 : 3 : 4 : 5 : 6 : 7 disagree

Copyright © 1997 by Allyn and Bacon

## 11.2 Mitigating Circumstances and Aggression

Consider the appreciation of "mitigating circumstances" in alleviating the need to respond to others' aggressive acts. After all, aggression is often a response to someone else's hostile acts. For the class in which this exercise is to be done, recruit a student you know reasonably well. On test day, have the student come up during a test to complain about items, using moderate amplitude of voice tone. At the end of the test, have the student slam her or his test down and stomp out of the room, complaining loudly about the "unfair items" and unreasonable professor as he or she departs. Exclaim, "Wonder what's wrong with him (or her)?"

Next class, have students respond to the Understanding Aggression Form. (It might be a good idea to have the student who attacked your test be absent on the day the form is completed, at least until the exercise is over.) The form, found on the next page (or in the Study Guide), is designed to create insights concerning mitigating circumstances. Have the class use the form to analyze the angry student's reactions to the test. Tally the results up on the board under the categories used on the form: (1) reasons for the aggression relating to the target of aggression (you, the instructor, in this case); (2) reasons relating to the aggressor's relationships with people other than the target; (3) reasons relating to the aggressor's feelings about himself or herself and his or her skills and efforts. Use a representative sampling of responses in each category; otherwise there will be too many reactions to write on the board and too much for students to appreciate. When the total picture is displayed on the board, step back and say, "Here are three possible categories of reasons for the student's behavior toward me after the last test. If you knew that I had decided to retaliate against the student in some way--I may scold the student the next time I see him/her--which category would you guess that I had assumed contains the real reasons for the student's behavior?" Students should tend to choose the reasons in category 1. If they don't you may ask questions like, "Why would I retaliate if I knew that the student's aggression had nothing to do with me; it was caused by a quarrel with a lover?" (or "test anxiety" or "lack of self-confidence"). The point is to show students that targets of aggression are unlikely to resort to aggression themselves if they know that the person who has attacked them has done so for reasons unrelated to them.

## HANDOUT FOR ACTIVITY # 11.2

### UNDERSTANDING AGGRESSION

First, fix in mind an aggressive act committed by someone. It can be real or imaginary. Below are three categories of reasons why the person has committed the aggressive act. List reasons for the act that fall into the three categories. First, list reasons that relate to the target of the attack. For example, the target insulted the aggressor. Second, list reasons related to people other than the target of the attack. For example, the aggressor just was humiliated by his or her brother, and the target happened to be handy when the aggression exploded. Third, list reasons related to the aggressor's feelings about him or herself or his or her skills and efforts. For example, the aggressor may feel bad about him or herself, because his or her application for a desirable job has just been turned down.

### Reasons for aggression relating to target of aggression

[List reasons for the aggressive act that relate to the target of the aggression] I think that the student believes the professor has been made an unfair test. Possibly the student just doesn't like the professor...personalities sometimes clash. The professor was unsympathetic when the student came up to complain about the test.

### Reasons for aggression relating to persons other than the target

It looked to me that the student was in a bad mood. Probably his girlfriend jilted him or something like that.
My guess is that this guy has just been pushed around to much. Maybe he came to class with a chip on his shoulder, because his friends have been teasing him.
One possibility is that he has trouble at work. Maybe the boss has been on his back.

### Reasons relating to the aggressor's feelings about self or abilities and efforts

This guy looked like he was down on himself. I think he has low self-esteem. It seems possible to me that this individual has been used to failing. He has lost confidence that he can succeed in school. This student...he is socially inept. He just doesn't know how to register a complaint.

Copyright © 1997 by Allyn and Bacon

## 11.3  What is Aggression?

Psychologist Ludy T. Benjamin of Texas A&M University has devised a method for providing insightful answers to the question, "What is aggression?" (See Benjamin [1985], Defining aggression...*Teaching of Psychology, 12,* 40-42.)  The method allows students to define aggression for themselves through an ingenious exercise.  On a list of twenty-five statements, students simply anonymously check all statements that they believe indicate aggressive acts (form included on next page and in the Study Guide).  Then have them pass in their lists of statements, shuffle them, and redistribute them to the class.  (With this procedure students don't necessarily call out their own responses and can thereby avoid embarrassment.)  For each statement get a show of hands as to how many students thought the statement indicated aggression.  Write on the board only those statements that at least 80 percent saw as indicating aggression or that 20 percent or fewer saw as indicating aggression (number of hands divided by the number of students present).  Now you can take up issues such as "does aggression involve harm to living versus nonliving things?"  (items 9 and 23); "accident versus intention?" (8,11); "actual damage versus no physical damage?"  (10, 13, 18); "self-defense?" (3, 13, 14); "duty or job responsibility?" (3, 4, 19, 20, 22); "predation and instinctual behavior?" (1, 2, 25) "survival?" (1, 6, 16); "acts involving animals other than humans?" (7,16,17,18); "covert acts?" (11, 14); "inaction?" (12, 15); "self-injury?" (24); and "killing for sport?" (17, 25).

## HANDOUT FOR ACTIVITY # 11.3

### AGGRESSION QUESTIONNAIRE

1.  A spider eats a fly.
2.  Two wolves fight for the leadership of the pack.
3.  A soldier shoots an enemy at the front line.
4.  The warden of a prison executes a convicted criminal.
5.  A juvenile gang attacks members of another gang.
6.  Two men fight for a piece of bread.
7.  A man viciously kicks a cat.
8.  A man, while cleaning a window, knocks over a flowerpot, which, in falling, injures a pedestrian.
9.  A girl kicks a wastebasket.
10. Mr. X, a notorious gossip, speaks disparagingly of many people of his acquaintance.
11. A man mentally rehearses a murder he is about to commit.
12. An angry son purposely fails to write to his mother, who is expecting a letter and will be hurt if none arrives.
13. An enraged boy tries with all his might to inflict injury on his antagonist, a bigger boy, but is not successful in doing so. His efforts simply amuse the bigger boy.
14. A man daydreams of harming his antagonist, but has no hope of doing so.
15. A senator does not protest the escalation of bombing to which he is morally opposed.
16. A farmer beheads a chicken and prepares it for supper.
17. A hunter kills an animal and mounts it as a trophy.
18. A dog snarls at a mail carrier, but does not bite.
19. A physician gives a flu shot to a screaming child.
20. A boxer gives his opponent a bloody nose.
21. A Girl Scout tries to assist an elderly woman, but trips her by accident.
22. A bank robber is shot in the back while trying to escape.
23. A tennis player smashes his racket after missing a volley.
24. A person commits suicide.
25. A cat kills a mouse, parades around with it, and then discards it.

Copyright © 1997 by Allyn and Bacon

## 11.4 Hostility Questionnaire and Steps to a More Trusting Heart

The entire constellation of Type A behavior was once thought to put Type A people at risk for health problems. More currently, however, Type A behavior in and of itself is not believed to be the factor that puts its possessors at risk. Rather, the problem is a single trait that is part of the constellation of Type A traits: hostility. Psychiatrist Redford Williams of Duke University has developed a measure of hostility that may predict health problems (included on the next page and in the Study Guide). Have students complete his questionnaire anonymously. Those who answer two out of three questions with "often" or "always" may consider themselves at risk. They may also be people so prone to hostile orientation to others that they are in danger of in some way harming important people in their lives and destroying social relations with them.

You could simply collect the questionnaires and tally the number of students who show destructive levels of hostility. This should provide a benchmark so that other students could evaluate how they stand relative to other students. Then have them respond to William's "Twelve Steps to a More Trusting (and healthy) Heart," also on the following page. Students could check all those statements that represent steps they feel confident they could take. This second part of the exercise will sensitize students concerning how to avoid hostility and reassure those who scored "at risk" for health and social relations problems that they have a way to deal with their hostility.

## HANDOUT FOR ACTIVITY # 11.4A

### HOSTILITY QUESTIONNAIRE

1.  When anybody slows down or stops what I want to do, I think they are selfish, mean and inconsiderate.

    Never          Sometimes          Often          Always

2.  When anybody does something that seems incompetent, messy, selfish, or inconsiderate to me, I quickly feel angry or enraged.  At the same time, my heart races, my breath comes quickly and my palms sweat.

    Never          Sometimes          Often          Always

3.  When I have such thoughts or feelings (No. 2), I let fly with words, gestures, a raised voice and frowns.

    Never          Sometimes          Often          Always

## HANDOUT FOR ACTIVITY # 11.4B

### TWELVE STEPS TO A MORE TRUSTING HEART

1.  Monitor your cynical thoughts by recognizing them.

2.  Confess your hostility and seek support for change.

3.  Stop cynical thoughts.

4.  Reason with yourself.

5.  Put yourself in the other guy's shoes.

6.  Laugh at yourself.

7.  Practice relaxing.

8.  Try trusting others.

9.  Force yourself to listen more.

10. Substitute assertiveness (firmness) for aggression.

11. Pretend today is your last day.

12. Practice forgiveness.

Copyright © 1997 by Allyn and Bacon

## 11.5  Activity on Conflict and Peacemaking

Timothy J. Lawson from College of Mount St. Joseph, describes an exercise that requires students to apply the social psychology of conflict and peacemaking to the analysis of a real-life tragedy involving the death of 94 soccer fans in Sheffield, England in 1989.  After students have read material on conflict and peacemaking, they are asked to read an article (Gammon, 1989) where over 3,000 Liverpool fans massed against an entrance gate and down a tunnel onto a terrace, crushing 94 other soccer fans against barriers in the process.  Gammon stated that the Liverpool fans (a) were angry because they had been given fewer game tickets than the opposing team's fans; and they (b) "tried to reach Nottingham rivals at the other end of the stadium, evidence of the fearsome passions that are at the root of Britain's inability to control its soccer crowds" (pp. 24-25).

After studying conflict and peacemaking, students are asked to consider in groups of five, the following: "Social psychologists have identified many factors that contribute to conflict.  Identify as many of these as you can that may have operated to cause the Hillsborough tragedy" (Lawson, 1996, p. 4); and (b) "identify possible solutions aimed at preventing this from happening in the future" (p. 4).

The following causes of conflict that seem relevant to this tragedy include:  social dilemmas, problems resulting from individuals pursuing their own interests to their common detriment; competition; perceived injustice, or inequity; and misperceptions (e.g., perceiving another group as evil and one's own group as moral).  Finally, the situational forces contributing to this event must not be overlooked.  We often underestimate these powerful determinants of behavior and fall prey to the fundamental attribution error.  Explore recommendations students make to prevent the possibility that such a tragic event will be repeated.

This paper was presented at the Council of Teachers of Undergraduate Psychology (CTUP) conference, May 4, 1996, Chicago, Illinois; and used with the permission of Timothy J. Lawson.  For more information, he can be reached at College of Mount St. Joseph, Cincinnati, OH  45233 (e-mail: Tim_Lawson@mail.msj.edu).  [Note: The Gammon article can be found in the April 24, 1989 issue of *Sports Illustrated, 70* (18), 24-25.]

---

## Overhead Transparencies
These appear at the back of this manual.

---

**11.1**  *What Is Sexual Harassment?*
**11.2**  *Theoretical Conceptions of Aggression*
**11.3**  *Aggression: Causes and Cures*
**11.4**  *Media Violence:  Mechanisms Underlying the Effects*
**11.5**  *Aggression According to the Neoassociationists*
**11.6**  *The Effects of Violent and Nonviolent Pornography on Males' Aggression toward Females*

# Audiovisual Suggestions

## Allyn and Bacon Video

*\* Aggression,* video, 28.5 mins. To obtain this tape, see your Allyn and Bacon sales representative. Robert A. Baron, an expert on the topic, and Margaret Clark use dramatizations as a basis for a discussion on aggression.

## Other Videos and Films

*Black on Black Violence,* FC1932, video, 26 mins. Films for the Humanities & Sciences, Inc., P.O. Box 2053, Princeton, NJ 08543 (800-257-5126). An American black male has a 1 in 29 chance of being murdered; for white men, the odds are 1 in 186. This video explores the reasons for the difference.

*Rape: An Act of Hate,* FC1055, video, 30 mins. Films for the Humanities & Sciences, Inc. P.O. Box 2053, Princeton, NJ 08543, (800-257-5126). Veronica Hamel of "Hill Street Blues" seeks to determine why people rape and to help potential victims protect themselves.

*Sexual Harassment: From 9 to 5,* FC1711, video, 26 mins. Films for the Humanities & Sciences, Inc., P.O. Box 2053, Princeton, NJ 08543 (800-257-5126). The motivations for sexual harassment and rape have much in common. In this video, some men of the business world couldn't understand that "no!" meant "no!" until they were sued. How employees are taught the difference between romance, harassment, and sexual extortion is a major feature.

*Violence in the Family,* PB81, video, 55 mins. Insight Media, 121 W. 85th Street, New York, NY 10024-4401 (800-233-9910). Those who don't believe that violence starts at home (literally) will be convinced by this video.

*Human Aggression,* film 22 mins. Associated Films, Inc. 512 Burlington Avenue, La Grange, IL 60525 (312-352-3377). This film features several well-known aggression researchers and some other public figures. Activities of an actual youth gang provide the opener.

*The Question of Violence,* CS-1942, film, 59 mins. (two reels). Indiana University, Audiovisual Center, Bloomington, IN 47401. The social, historical, and psychological factors that seem to underlie violence in modern life are the subject of this film.

*Aggression or Love?* ESC-1055, film, 24 mins. Indiana University, Audiovisual Center, Bloomington, IN 47401. Examines the possible biological and evolutionary roots of aggressive behavior. Raises the question, "Can love cure aggression?"

*Sexual Assault,* three videos, 30 mins. each. NETCHE Videotape Library, P.O. Box 83111, Lincoln Nebraska 68501. Three tapes explore rape from the point of view of the victim, the assailant, and the police officer, respectively.

# Critical Thinking/Essay Questions

1. Contrast Freud's view of aggression, the notion of "fighting instinct," sociobiological theory, the drive notion, aggression as a response to aversive events, and aggression as a learned social behavior. Which view do you anticipate will be most supported in the remainder of the chapter?

2. Discuss the teacher-learner method of studying aggression, indicating the controversies that surround it. Can you devise a better way to study aggression?

3. What is wrong with the idea that "frustration" is a major "cause" of aggression? Indicate why the "direct provocation" notion provides a better account of why aggression occurs.

4. List the kinds of studies that have been used to investigate the possible effects of media presentations on aggression, and provide an example of each. Given that the media do affect aggressiveness, why does this happen?

5. Consider Zillmann's ideas about "excitation transfer" and how they may explain the process by which a chain of events involving "heighten arousal" may or may not end up increased aggressiveness.

6. Use Zillmann's "two-factor" theory to explain how sexual arousal influences aggressiveness. How does violent pornography compare with nonviolent pornography in its effects on males' aggressiveness toward females?

7. Explore how alcohol affects aggressiveness. How does alcohol affect the brain in ways that will produce heightened aggression? How does social pressure to increase aggressiveness influence the difference between alcohol and no-alcohol conditions in an aggression experiment? Does alcohol always increase aggression?

8. Explain how Type A's and Type B's differ in general and in terms of the level and kinds of aggression they show. How do Type A drivers differ from Type B drivers?

9. Discuss the reasons why punishment and catharsis are quite limited as means of lessening aggression. How could each be made less limited?

10. Explore the question of gender differences in aggressiveness. Try to decide whether more biological or more cultural explanations provide better accounts of the differences.

11. Indicate the merits of apologies, nonaggressive models, social training, mitigating circumstances, and incompatible responses as means of reducing or controlling aggression.

# Sources for Lecture

Bower, B. (1991, November 30). Females show strong capacity for aggression. *Science News*, p. 359. Anthropological work in the Israeli kibbutz, ethnographic work among female gangs in Mexico, and psychological investigations in Finland support the assertion that females are more aggressive than we assume, and may be not such second-class aggressors compared to males as we have thought.

Horn, J. (1985). Fighting migraines with the Force. *Psychology Today*, November, p. 74. Type A-like boys who are described as "brightest," "head of the class," and "most athletic" have numerous problems. They are likely to be highly aggressive and some report migraine headaches. But, alas, biofeedback doesn't work with these high-strung kids. However, conjuring up the Jedi ritual allows them to relax. May the Force be with them.

Steele, C. (1986). What happens when you drink too much? *Psychology Today,* January 1986, pp. 48-52. Drinking makes people's responses more extreme. Compared to sober people, drinkers were more aggressive, looked at sexual slides longer, gambled more, disclosed more about themselves, and took greater risks.

Stone, R. (1992, October 9). HHS "violence initiative" caught in a crossfire. *Science, 258,* 212-213. If there were a link between genes and violent crime, shouldn't scientists be free to investigate it, even if a particular race? Would the discovery of such genes lead to "rounding up" people with the genes, even if they weren't violent? Such questions haunt the new violence initiative of Health and Human Services.

Taubes, G. (1992, October 9). Violence epidemiologists test the hazards of gun ownership. *Science, 258,* 213-215. Arthur Kellerman, among others, is arguing that, in effect, the trigger does pull the finger. His work and that of others is showing that the presence of guns, especially in the home, contributes to violent behavior.

"20/20" (ABC News Transcript for 9/17/1991 show "Battered women" and "Women and violence" (order for $5 from Journal Graphics, Inc., 1535 Grant Street, Denver, CO 80230). This transcript graphically portrays the plight of battered women, whose pleas for help are too often ignored until it is too late. It also examines the lives of women imprisoned for killing their abusive male partners and asks, "Should they be set free?"

## Professional Update: Current Articles from Professional Sources

Buss, A. R., & Perry, M. (1992). The aggression questionnaire. *Journal of Personality and Social Psychology, 63,* 452-459. Buss, one of the early investigators of aggression, and Perry have developed a new aggression questionnaire that they show to be both valid and reliable.

Gentry, J., & Eron, L. D. (1993). American Psychological Association Commission on violence and youth. *American Psychologist, 48,* 89. These authors introduce a series of articles on youth violence and how it might be controlled.

Hutton, H. E., Milner, M. H., Blades, J. R., & Langfeldt, V. C. (1992). Ethnic differences on the MMPI Overcontrolled-Hostility Scale. *Journal of Personality Assessment, 58,* 260-268. Although race, with African-Americans scoring higher than European-Americans, was the only predictor of scale scores, an examination of clinical histories and criminal records indicated that actual descriptors of overcontrolled aggressors were unrelated to scale scores. Thus, African-American patients are more likely to be incorrectly labeled as overcontrolled-hostile personalities.

Lore, R. K., & Schultz, L. A. (1993). Control of human aggression. *American Psychologist, 48,* 16-25. Lore and Schultz argue that both humans and other animals have aggression-inhibitory mechanisms that are equally as potent as any tendency to aggress. Aggression, therefore, is not inevitable; it can be suppressed when it is in our best interest to do so.

Malamuth, N. M., Sockloskie, R. J., Koss, M. P., & Tanaka, J. S. (1991). Characteristics of aggressors against women:  Testing a model using a national sample of college students.  *Journal of Consulting and Clinical Psychology, 59,* 670-681.  These researchers found that high sexual promiscuity coupled with high-hostile masculinity yielded aggression against women.

McFarland, S. G., Ageyev, V. S., & Abalkina-Paap, M. A. (1992).  Authoritarianism in the former Soviet Union.  *Journal of Personality and Social Psychology, 63,* 1004-1010.  Studies in the former Soviet Union show that authoritarianism is associated with support of military aggression among the populace.

Reifman, A. S., Larrick, R. P., & Fein, S. (1991).  Temper and temperature on the diamond:  The heat-aggression relationship in major league baseball.  *Personality and Social Psychology Bulletin, 17,* 580-585.  Major league pitchers follow the linear heat-aggression curve closely:  The hotter it is, the more likely they are to aggress against batters by hitting them.

*Related Readings:*  The following selections from *Readings in Social Psychology:  General, classic, and Contemporary Selections,* 3rd Edition, by Wayne Lesko (Allyn and Bacon, 1997) accompany this chapter.

Skoler, G. (1989).  "Why violent toys are good for kids."  Yes, you read it correctly.  This journalist believes in contradiction to the "aggressive cues" notion, that violent toys are good for kids.  Parents inhibit their use for reasons of parental hangups, not for the benefit of the kids.  (Article 31).

Bandura, A., Ross, D. & Ross, S. (1961).  "Transmission of aggression through imitation of aggressive models."  This classic study shows how it is all too easy for children to learn aggression from models.  (Article 32).

De Weerth, C. & Kalma, A. P. (1993).  "Female aggression as a response to sexual jealousy:  A sex role reversal?"  The authors examine the conditions under which both males and females might feel sexual jealousy, and how they would respond to such feelings.  The results of this study challenge the commonly held belief that males are more jealous of a partner's infidelity than vice versa, and likewise that males would be more likely to resort to an aggressive response.  (Article 33).

# Chapter 12

# Groups and Individuals:  The Consequences of Belonging

## Chapter-at-a-Glance

| CHAPTER OUTLINE | INSTRUCTION IDEAS | SUPPLEMENTS* |
|---|---|---|
| **I. Groups: Their Nature and Function**<br>• Group Formation: Why Do People Join Groups?<br><br>• How Groups Function: Roles, Status, Norms, and Cohesiveness | Learning Objectives 12.1 to 12.5<br><br>Discussion Topic 1<br><br>Activity 12.1 (Handout) | Test Bank Questions 12.1 to 12.28 |
| **II. Groups and Task Performance: The Benefits--and Costs--of Working With Others**<br>• Social Facilitation: Performance in the Presence of others<br><br>• **Cornerstones of Social Psychology**  Performance in the Presence of Others: The Simplest Group Effect?<br><br>• Social Loafing: letting Others Do the Work in Group Tasks | Learning Objectives 12.6 to 12.12<br><br>Discussion Topics 2, 4<br><br>Critical Thinking Questions 1, 2 | Test Bank Questions 12.29 to 12.70<br><br>Reading:<br>- Lesko 35, Many Hands Make Light the Work<br><br>Transparencies 12.1, 12.2 |
| **III. Perceived Fairness in Groups: Getting What We Deserve-- or Else!**<br>• Judgments of Fairness: Outcomes, Procedures, and Courtesy<br><br>• Reactions to Perceived Unfairness<br><br>• **Social Psychology: On the Applied Side**  When Employees Bite the Hand that Feeds Them | Learning Objectives 12.13 to 12.16 | Test Bank Questions 12.71 to 12.90 |
| **IV. Decision Making By Groups: How It Occurs and the Pitfalls It Faces**<br>• The Decision-Making Process: How Groups Attain Consensus<br><br>• The Nature of Group Decisions: Moderation--or a Tendency to Go Straight off the Deep End?<br><br>• Potential Dangers of Group Decision Making: Groupthink and the Tendency of Group Members to Tell Each Other What They Already Know | Learning Objectives 12.17 to 12.23<br><br>Discussion Topics 3, 5<br><br>Activities 12.2 (Handout), 12.3<br><br>Critical Thinking Questions 3, 4 | Test Bank Questions 12.91 to 12.131<br><br>Readings:<br>- Lesko 34, Groupthink<br>- Lesko 36, Space Shuttle Challenger and Groupthink |
| **V. Leadership: Patterns of Influence within Groups**<br>• Who Becomes a Leader? Traits, Situations, or Both?<br><br>• How Leaders Operate: Contrasting Styles and Approaches<br><br>• Gender Differences in Leadership<br><br>• Transformational Leadership<br><br>• **Social Diversity: A Critical Analysis**  Social Loafing: An International Perspective | Learning Objectives 12.24 to 12.28<br><br>Activity 12.4 (Handout)<br><br>Critical Thinking Question 5 | Test Bank Questions 12.132 to 12.150<br><br>Transparency 12.3 |

*See Audiovisual Suggestions

# 12 Groups and Individuals: The Consequences of Belonging

---

## Chapter Outline: Getting the Overall Picture

---

2. Why Groups Often Fail to Pool Their Resources: Information Sampling and the Common Knowledge Effect

V. **Leadership: Patterns of Influence within Groups**
  A. Who Becomes a Leader: Traits, Situations, or Both?
  B. How Leaders Operate: Contrasting Styles and Approaches
  C. Gender Differences in Leadership
  D. Transformational Leadership: Leadership through Vision and Charisma
    1. The Basic Nature of Charisma: Traits or Relationships?
    2. The Behavior of Transformational Leaders
    3. The Effects of Transformational Leaders: A Very Mixed Bag
  E. Social Diversity: A Critical Analysis: Social Loafing: An International Perspective

---

# Learning Objectives
### After studying this chapter, students should be able to:

---

**12.1** Examine the text's definition of a group, and know the six key aspects of the definition.

**12.2** List the five reasons people join groups.

**12.3** Describe how the group benefits by having different members fulfill different roles, and indicate how role conflict and constraints imposed by roles can sometimes be detrimental to group functioning.

**12.4** Describe how the prestige of various roles is reflected in status differences, and also indicate how prescriptive and proscriptive norms affect group members' behavior.

**12.5** Define cohesiveness and list factors that contribute to group cohesiveness.

**12.6** Explain how the presence of others affected subjects' ability to produce word associations and to counterargue in Allport's classic research.

**12.7** Explain how Zajonc's drive theory resolves the "puzzle" created by the fact that performance is sometimes improved by an audience and sometimes impaired.

**12.8** Describe research findings regarding the evaluation apprehension hypothesis, indicating which are consistent and which are inconsistent with the hypothesis.

**12.9** Describe research findings that support the distraction-conflict theory.

**12.10** Give examples that illustrate the concept of social loafing.

**12.11** According to the collective effort model, describe the conditions that produce the social loafing effect.

**12.12** Understand the five techniques that can be used to reduce social loafing.

**12.13** Describe how outcomes must be distributed among members of a group in order for a member to perceive that equity exists.

**12.14** Describe the conditions that lead a person to conclude that procedural justice existed as well as the conditions that lead to the perception of interpersonal justice.

**12.15** Summarize strategies to restore fairness used by persons who feel they've been treated unfairly.

**12.16** Explain how apologies and explanations influence employees' willingness to steal from employer who cuts their wages.

**12.17** Summarize the four social decision schemes used by groups to make decisions, and indicate when "majority-wins" and "truth-wins" are used.

**12.18** Explain how decision-making groups are affected by straw polls.

**12.19** Describe group polarization and explain this phenomenon in terms of social comparison and the arguments presented during discussion.

**12.20** Define groupthink, and explain how it is related to group cohesiveness, emergent group norms, and collective entrapment.

**12.21** Describe three steps that can be taken to reduce the likelihood of groupthink.

**12.22** Explain why the hoped-for advantage of pooling resources often fails to occur in group discussions.

**12.23** Describe under what two circumstances might groups manage to counter their tendency to ignore unshared information.

**12.24** List key traits that are characteristic of leaders, and how the social situation affects leadership.

**12.25** Describe how leadership style is influenced by each of the following: a) autocratic vs. democratic style; b) directive vs. permissive style; c) talk orientation; and d) person orientation.

**12.26** Explain how female and male leaders differ in their leadership styles. Describe circumstances in which female leaders tend to be down-rated compared to male leaders.

**12.27** Describe the relationship between charismatic leaders and their followers, and indicate tactics used by transformational leaders to generate this special kind of relationship.

**12.28** Examine the occurrence of social loafing in individualistic cultures such as the United States in comparison to collectivistic cultures such as Israel and China.

---

# Discussion Topics and Questions

---

## 1. Home Court Advantage

Students who are sports fans are well aware of the home court advantage in competitive sports. Playing at home is generally correlated with winning. Greer (1983) studied the performance of basketball players at Illinois and at Kansas State to determine the impact of noisy fan demonstrations on performance. Greer found that turnovers and scoring favored the home team regardless of crowd noise. The factor most affected by crowd noise was the number of fouls called against the visiting team. For fifteen seconds following noisy crowd demonstrations, the number of fouls called against the visiting team increased. Perhaps some of your students would like to replicate Greer's phenomenon. (Greer's research is found in *Social Psychology Quarterly, 46,* 252-261.)

## 2. Social Loafing by the Beatles

Research by Jackson and Padgett (1982) has suggested evidence for a social loafing effect in songs written by John Lennon and Paul McCartney of the Beatles. The social loafing effect hypothesis was that the songs cowritten by Lennon and McCartney would be of lower quality than the songs written by either of them alone. Jackson and Padgett concluded that there is evidence of a social loafing effect, but only for those songs written after 1967. (For a full explanation, consult the research reported in the *Personality and Social Psychology Bulletin, 88,* 672-677.)

## 3. Additive, Compensatory, Disjunctive, and Conjunctive Tasks

Challenge students to come up with examples of tasks that are additive, compensatory, disjunctive, and conjunctive. A way to help them understand the nature of these types of tasks is to have them produce illustrative examples.

### 4. Impression of Group Functioning

Ask the students to report on their experience in extracurricular activity groups. The students might comment on such things as the emergence of leadership in the group, polarization effects, social loafing, and social facilitation. Also, you might encourage the students to attend a meeting of a group of which they are not currently members so that they can observe the group's functioning. By observing a group of which they are not a member, students may be better able to gain insight into the group. Encourage the students to write down their impressions of the group and to share them with the other class members.

### 5. Structural Factors Defining Roles in a Group

Before peace talks for ending the Vietnam War could get under way in earnest, negotiators had to settle the issue of what shape the negotiating table would be. Negotiators for the United States and South Vietnam wanted to present the appearance of a two-sided negotiation, whereas the North Vietnameses wanted the appearance that four equal parties were negotiating--the Americans, the South Vietnamese, the North Vietnamese, and the National Liberation Front. The United States considered the National Liberation Front to be sponsored by North Vietnam and thus not an independent party. The final compromise, reached after eight months of negotiating, involved a round table without dividing lines. Sometimes the roles people play in a group are determined by structural factors, such as seating pattern.

---

## Learning Activities: Classroom Exercises/Demonstrations

---

### 12.1 What Constitutes a Group?

One topic discussed in Chapter 12 is the notion of what constitutes a group. One way to get students thinking about this question is to present them with several situations and have them determine whether the people described there are a group or simply a collection of individuals. Several situations of this type are presented on the next page and in the Study Guide. In addition to their yes/no responses, have students write down the reasons for their decisions. Afterward, you can determine the number of students who thought each situation described a group and ask them to discuss their judgments. The text's definition of a group is as follows: "two or more interacting persons who share common goals, have a stable relationship, are somehow interdependent, and perceive that they are in fact part of a group." Do the students' judgments support the text's definition?

## HANDOUT FOR ACTIVITY # 12.1

### IS IT A GROUP?

For each of the following, indicate whether the situation describes a group.  Indicate the reason(s) for your decision in the space beneath each example.

|  | <u>yes</u> | <u>no</u> |
|---|---|---|
| 1.  The people riding together on an airliner | — | — |
| 2.  The 22,000 people attending a rock concert | — | — |
| 3.  The students taking this course | — | — |
| 4.  The members of a particular labor union | — | — |
| 5.  People riding together on an elevator | — | — |
| 6.  The members of a particular fraternity on campus | — | — |
| 7.  The employees of General Motors | — | — |
| 8.  The members of the school debating team | — | — |
| 9.  The employees of your school's Financial Aid Office | — | — |
| 10.  The "starting five" on a basketball team | — | — |
| 11.  All the students enrolled at your university | — | — |

Copyright © 1997 by Allyn and Bacon

### 12.2 Choice Dilemmas Questionnaire (CDQ)

This activity not only demonstrates the nature of polarization effects but gives students a chance to interact with fellow students in a small-group setting. Students respond twice to each of six items from the Choice Dilemmas Questionnaire (CDQ), one time on their own and the second time after a three-minute discussion. Before the class period, the instructor should prepare enough copies of the CDQ for each student in the class to have one copy. (The six CDQ items are presented on the next few pages of this manual as well as in the Study Guide.) Read the following instructions to the class before the exercise is begun:

On the page(s) that I going to give to you, you will find descriptions of situations that might occur in everyday life. In each situation a person is faced with a choice between two courses of action. The person can continue his or her present course of action, or the person can embark on a new, more adventurous course. Your task is to decide how certain you would want to be before you would advise the person to try the new course of action.

For each situation, your task is to indicate the **minimum** probability of success that you would demand before recommending that the person attempt the new course of action. Note that you are not asked to indicate what the chances of success would actually *be*, rather, you are asked to indicate the smallest chance of success that you would accept and still advise the person to go ahead and try the new course of action. If you say one in ten, you are telling the person to try the new course of action even if there is only one chance in ten of succeeding. On the other hand, if you say nine in ten, you are telling the person to try the new course of action only if very sure of succeeding. (At this point, I usually write on the board 1/10 = "Go for it," even though the chances are slim. 9/10 = Only "go for it" if it appears to be a sure thing. Students often get the direction of these odds backwards, so you may need to check their responses as they work in small groups.) [Pass out the CDQ's.]

Read each situation carefully before giving your judgment. Try to place yourself in the position of the person in each situation and then indicate the smallest chance of success that you would accept and still advise the person to try the new course of action.

After everyone in the class has finished responding, the students should divide up into discussion groups of four or five persons. Groups are instructed that their task is to spend three minutes discussion the Alan situation (i.e., the first CDQ situation). Tell them that at the end of three minutes you will interrupt to ask them to write down their response to the Alan situation. You should emphasize to them the importance of keeping an open mind and of considering all points of view during the discussion. After the three-minute discussion, ask each person again to write down on his or her questionnaire the minimum probability of success that he or she would demand, considering the points made by the group.

After completing the first situation, the groups should discuss the next situation for three minutes. At the end of the three minutes, again ask people to respond to the item. After the groups have completed their six discussions, ask each group to prepare a summary of their data. For each situation, have them obtain a prediscussion and a postdiscussion sum. They should add together the responses of each group member so that it can be determined whether their group changed in a "risky" direction (the postdiscussion sum is smaller than the prediscussion sum); changed in a cautious direction ( the postdiscussion sum is larger than the prediscussion sum); or stayed the same. It is expected that groups will show a risky shift on the Peter, Henry, and George situations. It is expected that groups will show a cautious shift on the Betty and Mark/Susan situations. The Alan situation produces somewhat ambivalent results, although risky shifts are more prevalent than cautious shifts. These predictions are based on the assumption that groups cause shifts in the direction of the initial response tendencies of the group members. (Be prepared to take approximately 45 minutes for this activity.)

## HANDOUT FOR ACTIVITY # 12.2

### CHOICE DILEMMAS QUESTIONNAIRE

Alan, an electrical engineer, who is married and has one child, has been working for a large electronics corporation since graduation from college five years ago. He is assured of a lifetime job with a modest, though adequate, salary, and liberal pension benefits upon retirement. On the other hand, it is very unlikely that his salary will increase much before he retires. While attending a convention, Alan is offered a job with a small, newly founded company which has a highly uncertain future. The new job would pay more to start and would offer the possibility of a share in the ownership if the company survived the competition of the larger firms.

Imagine that you are advising Alan. What is the <u>lowest</u> probability or odds of the new company's proving financially sound that you would consider acceptable for Alan to take the new job?

The chances should be _____ in 10 that the company will prove financially sound.

Betty, a newlywed, has been informed by her physician that a heart ailment makes it inadvisable for her to have children. Having been an only child, Betty had always hoped to raise a large family herself. The physician suggests that a delicate medical operation could be attempted which, if successful, would completely relieve the heart condition. But its success could not be assured, and, in fact, the operation might prove fatal.

Imagine that you are advising Betty. What is the <u>lowest</u> probability or odds that the operation will prove successful that you would consider acceptable for the operation to be performed?

The chances should be _____ in 10 that the operation will be a success.

Peter is an earnest young state representative who would like to run for governor of his state. Since he has a reputation as an able and conscientious legislator, several influential persons have pledged their support to him should he decide to run. But his opponent would be the incumbent governor who has a well-organized political machine behind him, so it would not be an easy campaign.

Imagine that you are advising Peter. What is the <u>lowest</u> probability or odds of Peter's winning the election that would make it worthwhile for Peter to run for this office?

The chances should be _____ in 10 that would win the election.

Copyright © 1997 by Allyn and Bacon

ACTIVITY # 12.2 (Continued)

Henry is a writer who is said to have considerable creative talent but who so far has been earning a comfortable living by writing cheap Westerns. Recently, he has come up with an idea for a potentially significant novel. If it would be written and accepted, it might have considerable literary impact and be a big boost to his career. On the other hand, if he was not able to work out his idea or if the novel was a flop, he would have expended considerable time and energy without remuneration.

Imagine that you are advising Henry. What is the <u>lowest</u> probability or odds of the novel's being a success that you would consider acceptable for Henry to attempt to write the novel?

The chances should be _____ in 10 that the novel will be a success.

Mark is contemplating marriage to Susan, a girl who he has known for a little more than a year. Recently, however, a number of arguments have occurred between them, suggesting some sharp differences of opinion in way each views certain matters. Indeed, they decided to seek professional advice from a marriage counselor as to whether it would be wise for them to marry. On the basis of these meetings with a marriage counselor, they realize that a happy marriage, while possible, would not be assured.

Imagine that you are advising Mark and Susan. What is the <u>lowest</u> probability or odds that their marriage would prove to be a happy and successful one that you would consider acceptable for Mark and Susan to get married.

The chances should be _____ in 10 that the marriage would be happy and successful.

George, a competent chess player, is participating in a national chess tournament. In an early match he draws the top-favored player in the tournament as his opponent. George has been given a relatively low ranking in view of his performance in previous tournaments. During the course of his play with the top-favored man, George notes the possibility of a deceptive, though risky, maneuver which might bring him a quick victory. At the same time, if the attempted maneuver should fail, George would be left in an exposed position and defeat would almost certainly follow.

Imagine that you are advising George. What is the <u>lowest</u> probability or odds that the deceptive play would succeed that you would consider acceptable for George to attempt the play?

The chances should be _____ in 10 that the play would succeed.

Copyright © 1997 by Allyn and Bacon

## 12.3  Collective Information Exchange

Gary Stasser of Miami (Ohio) University has provided a task for illustrating the vagaries of collective information exchange en route to a collective judgement. The task uses standard playing cards and requires that a group decide whether there are more black or red cards in an oversized deck constructed from two or more standard decks. Of course, the experimenter or instructor can control which color is more frequent in the deck as well as the degree to which the more prevalent color dominates.

The procedure involves dealing a set number of cards (eleven works well, but this can be varied to simulate high- versus low-information conditions) to each member of a group. Then, as an analog of obtaining prediscussion preferences in typical group decision-making exercises, each member privately chooses either red or black as their judgment (guess) based on the information in their own hands. Ratings of certainty of judgment and a record of the actual contents of their hands are also obtained for later purposes. After these private responses are obtained, the group "discusses" by members playing, in turn, cards face up on the table. Play is continued in round-robin fashion until about fifteen cards are displayed on the table. (The number of cards played can be varied to simulate short or long discussions.) After the predetermined number of cards is played, "discussion" is stopped and the group, without further revelation of the contents of their individual hands, reaches a collective judgment based on their pooled information (i.e., the cards on the table). Of course, the cards that individuals retain in their hands can still influence their individual judgments and, thus, their votes or stated preferences in reaching the group's decision.

Even though the task is simple and the "discussion" mechanical, it does capture some of the dynamics of information exchange. First, members must actively decide what kind of information they are going to share. Second, as in most group discussions, not all of the information available to members is shared. Third, the task is cooperative, in that the collective goal is to reach the correct or best decision.

There are many kinds of data that one can quickly summarize from this task. For example, one can compare members' certainty of judgment before and after "discussion;" rated certainty is typically higher afterward, suggesting that individual feel that they have benefited from the information exchange and are able to make a better judgment as a result. One can also compare the groups' decisions with reality. It is educational to point out in this context that whereas this task allows one to judge the correctness of the decisions, many real-life contexts do not.

The outcome that generates the most class discussion is usually the comparison of what cards are played with the cards in members' hands. Almost without exception, the color that is dominant in the hands before discussion is overrepresented on the table. For example, suppose there are five members who are dealt the following hands:

|  | *Member* | | | | |
|---|---|---|---|---|---|
|  | A | B | C | D | E |
| Number of red cards | 6 | 4 | 6 | 3 | 5 |
| Number of black cards | 5 | 7 | 5 | 8 | 6 |

Three of the five members' hands favor black; and, summing across members' hands, we see that thirty-one (56 percent) or the fifty-five cards dealt are black. A typical outcome is that 70 to 80 percent of cards played on the table will be black in the above case, and the group (as well as individual members) will end up confidently concluding black (which may or may not be right).

Such a result illustrates the tendency for shared information to overrepresent the biases that may exist in members' information before discussion. Moreover, it is instructive to ask members how they decided what to play. They often say, "I played the color that I had the most of," or, "I played the color that I thought was most likely to be correct." Members who find themselves in the "minority" (e.g., members

A and C in the above example) often say, "I played red at first because I had more of those, but when others seemed to be favoring black, I decided that they could be right and didn't want to mislead the group--so I started playing black." There are many manipulations one can implement using this task. Thus, it lends itself to illustrating research methods in addition to examining some of the dynamics of information exchange. It requires few materials and is easily explained to participants. Moreover, groups can be run through several trials by using different decks. (Thanks to Gary Stasser for providing this exercise.)

### 12.4 Skills Needed in Today's Leaders
What attributes do people perceive to be important in today's political leaders? A way to begin a discussion of the topic is to have students rate the list of characteristics found on the next page (or in the Study Guide). The rating students should make is how much they believe these attributes are needed in today's leaders.

## HANDOUT FOR ACTIVITY # 12.4

## SKILLS NEEDED IN TODAY'S LEADERS

For each of the following skills or traits, indicate the degree to which you think the characteristic is important for a political leader in today's world. Use the following scale in making your ratings: 1 = extremely important; 2 = very important; 3 = important; 4 = somewhat important; 5 = not important.

| | | | | | |
|---|---|---|---|---|---|
| Political ability | 1 | 2 | 3 | 4 | 5 |
| Common sense | 1 | 2 | 3 | 4 | 5 |
| Intellectual excellence | 1 | 2 | 3 | 4 | 5 |
| Courage | 1 | 2 | 3 | 4 | 5 |
| Social concern | 1 | 2 | 3 | 4 | 5 |
| Moral integrity | 1 | 2 | 3 | 4 | 5 |
| Charisma | 1 | 2 | 3 | 4 | 5 |
| Grasp of economics | 1 | 2 | 3 | 4 | 5 |
| Foreign-affairs expertise | 1 | 2 | 3 | 4 | 5 |

Copyright © 1997 by Allyn and Bacon

# Overhead Transparencies
These appear at the back of this manual.

**12.1** *The Drive Theory of Social Facilitation*
**12.2** *The Distraction-Conflict Theory of Social Facilitation*
**12.3** *Contingency Model of Leadership Effectiveness*

# Audiovisual Suggestions

### Allyn and Bacon Video

*Group Decision Making and Leadership,* videotape, 28.5 mins. To obtain this tape, consult your Allyn and Bacon sales representative. After examining a business group's discussion concerning whom to hire, Robert A. Baron and Margaret Clark get inside the workings of group decision making.

### Other Videos and Films

*Diagnosing Group Operations,* 1961, 30 mins. Audiovisual Services, Kent State University, Kent, OH 44242. An analysis of group functions using Bale's categories.

*Dynamics of Leadership,* 5 films from 1961, 30 mins. each. Audiovisual Services, Kent State University, Kent, OH 44242. The five films analyze group structure, operations, communication, and leadership.

*Experimental Studies in Social Climates of Groups,* 32519, 1953, 30 mins. Pennsylvania State University. Audiovisual Services, Special Services Building, University Park, PA 16802 (814-865-6314). Classic study by Kurt Lewin in which a hidden camera observes three boys' clubs operated under autocratic, democratic, and laissez-faire principles. Shows how boys react when conditions of leadership are changed to another method. K. Lewin, R. Lippitt, and R. White.

*Four More Days,* color, 32 mins. New York University Film Library, 26 Washington Place, New York University Film Library, 26 Washington Place, New York, NY 10003. The film presents the prisoner-guard experiment by Philip Zimbardo.

*Group Dynamics: Groupthink,* 21762, 1973, color, 22 mins. Pennsylvania State University, Audiovisual Services, Special Services Building, University Park, PA 16802 (814-865-6314). Presents the eight symptoms of groupthink as proposed by Dr. Irving L. Janis in his book *Victims of Groupthink.* Offers examples of group decision making processes that influenced historical events such as Pearl Harbor, the Korean War, and the Bay of Pigs, and describes how effective leadership can prevent a decision-making group from falling into groupthink. From the *Behavior in Business* series. A CRM production.

*Individual Motivation and Behavior,* 30531, 1963, 30 mins. Pennsylvania State University, Audiovisual Services, Special Services Building, University Park, PA 16802 (814-865-6314). Why do people join groups, and why do some members block or dominate group action? Professor Knowles offers comments before and after practical demonstration and discusses the motivation of each person who participates in the demonstration. One person wants to go home, another hates arguments, another wants everyone to like him, and one believes that others are trying to dominate him. From the *Dynamics of Leadership* series. Produced by NET.

*Leadership: Style or Circumstance?*, 32006, 1974, color, 30 mins. Pennsylvania State University, Audiovisual Services, Special Services Building, University Park, PA 16802 (814-865-6314). Considers the difference between Fiedler's relation-oriented and task-oriented leadership styles. Interviews with presidents of Baskin-Robbins and Deluxe General, Inc., show that each style can be effective and that it is important to gear leadership training programs to the specific group to be led or to the task to be accomplished. From the *Behavior in Business* series. A CRM production.

*Problem Solving Strategies: The Synthetics Approach*, 1980, color film, 27 mins. Also available on videotape. CRM Films, 2233 Faraday Avenue, Carlsbad, CA 92008. Shows several strategies for improving the quality of group problem solving.

*Social Group*, videotape, 30 mins. Western Illinois University Television Services, Macomb, IL 61455 (309-298-1880). From the *Understanding Human Behavior* series, this entry explores how social group form and function.

## Critical Thinking/Essay Questions

1. Summarize the assumptions underlying Zajonc's drive theory of social facilitation, the predictions the theory makes about behavior, and the conclusions drawn from research findings.
2. Compare the performances of individuals and groups on additive, compensatory, disjunctive, and conjunctive tasks.
3. Compare the exchange of shared versus unshared information in a group.
4. Describe the group polarization effect. Compare the explanations for group polarization put forth by the social comparison theory and by the persuasive arguments theory.
5. Describe one of the text's theories of leadership, and summarize evidence supporting and contradicting this view.

## Sources for Lecture

Burrows, W. E. (1982). Cockpit encounters. *Psychology Today*, November, pp. 43-47. What makes for efficient task performance by the small group working in the cockpit to fly an airplane?

Ciulla, J. B., (1986). Corporate leadership: Try a little tenderness. *Psychology Today*, March, pp. 70, 75. Reviews of five recent books, all of which essentially take the view that the feared, powerful, Machiavellian leader has been replaced by a problem solver who empowers his or her followers.

Fiedler, F. A. (1969). Style or circumstance: The leadership enigma. *Psychology Today*, March, pp. 38-43. Fiedler's leadership theory states that both personal style and the situation are important in determining the leader's success. He examines task-oriented and relationship-oriented styles and discusses the conditions under which each is effective.

Fiedler, F. A. (1987). When to lead, when to stand back. *Psychology Today*, September, pp. 26-27. Here Fiedler probes directive and nondirective leadership styles and also looks at the role played by leader intelligence.

Goleman, D. (1985). Following the leader: Sometimes it's folly to go along with boss. *Science, 85,* October, pp. 18-20. How could E. F. Hutton continue its practice of illegally overdrawing its bank accounts without someone blowing the whistle? Goleman explains in terms of groupthink.

Hall, J. (1971). Decisions, decisions, decisions. *Psychology Today,* November, pp. 51-54, 86-88. Group decisions *can* be superior to those of individuals. The achievement of satisfactory group solutions is explored.

Latane, B., Williams, K., & Harkins, S. (1979). *Psychology Today,* October, pp. 104-106, 110. Again, the people who did the work tell us about it! These authors review their research on social loafing and question the value of working as a team in a group.

Markes, M. L. (1986). The question of quality circles. *Psychology Today,* March, pp. 36-46. The basic feature of "quality circle" programs is that small groups of people who perform similar work meet on a regular basis to analyze work problems and propose solutions to then. The article analyzes their success.

McCall, W. M., & Lombardao, M. M. (1983). What makes a top executive? *Psychology Today,* February, pp. 26-31. Two behavioral scientists from a leading think tank map the pitfalls along the corridor to the executive suite.

McCullough, D. (1983). Mama's boys. *Psychology Today,* March, pp. 32-38. Many famous historic leaders adored their mothers and were adored in return. Is the mother-son relationship crucial to leaders?

## Professional Update: Current Articles from Professional Sources

Baron, J., & Jurney, J. (1993). Norms against voting for coerced reform. *Journal of Personality and Social Psychology, 64,* 347-355. Some reforms, such as the passing of a prohibitive law or a binding agreement to solve a social dilemma, involve coercion. This study found that subjects responded to hypothetical coerced reforms with a lack of support, even though they acknowledged the reforms would improve matters. Ways in which subjects justify their resistance are examined.

Malloy, T. E., & Janowski, C. L. (1993). Perceptions and metaperceptions of leadership: Components, accuracy, and dispositional correlates. *Personality and Social Psychology Bulletin, 18,* 700-708. Mixed-sex problem-solving groups showed considerable agreement as to who their leaders were. Most of the variance (91 percent) in judgments of leadership was explained by quantity of speaking, quality of ideas, and friendliness. Leaders generally held accurate perceptions of how they were viewed. The study also explored the impact of gender and stereotypic masculine and feminine traits.

Paulus, P. B., Dzindolet, M. T., Poletes, G., & Camacho, L. M. (1993). Perception of performance in group brainstorming: The illusion of group productivity. *Personality and Social Psychology Bulletin, 19,* 78-89. When brainstorming in groups, people produce fewer ideas than when brainstorming alone. People continue to believe they are more productive in groups, however. The basis for this illusion of group productivity is explored.

Prentice, D. A., & Miller, D. T. (1993). Pluralistic ignorance and alcohol use on campus. *Journal of Personality and Social Psychology, 64,* 243-256. Students were found to be generally uncomfortable with campus alcohol practices but believed others did not share their discomfort. Over the course of a semester, male students increasingly shifted toward the perceived norm, with students who perceived themselves deviant from the norm feeling alienated from campus culture.

Reno, R. R., Cialdini, R. B., & Kallgren, C. A. (1993). The transsituational influence of social norms.

*Journal of Personality and Social Psychology, 64,* 104-112. Explores ways to increase compliance to social norms against littering. Considers the effectiveness of two types of norms: descriptive norms specify what is typically done in a given situation, whereas injunctive norms specify what is typically approved. Focusing on injunctive norms produced stronger behavioral effects.

*Related Readings:* The following selections from *Readings in Social Psychology: General, Classic, and Contemporary Selections,* 3rd Edition, by Wayne Lesko (Allyn and Bacon, 1997) accompany this chapter.

Janis, I. (1973). "Groupthink." Janis himself discusses his well-known work on groupthink. The symptoms of groupthink are highlighted, with excellent examples of each symptom. (Article 34).

Latane, B., Williams, K., & Harkins, S. (1979). "Many hands make light the work: The causes and consequences of social loafing." This article suggests that when people perform in groups, the members are each more likely to give less than if they were doing the same thing by themselves. Some conditions that can minimize social loafing are also explored. (Article 35).

Moorhead, G., Ference, R., & Neck, C. (1991). "Group decision fiascoes continue: Space shuttle Challenger and a revised groupthink framework." Analysis of the situation surrounding the decision to launch the space shuttle Challenger in 1986 is analyzed in terms of groupthink. Presents a revised framework proposing that time and leadership style moderate the manner in which group characteristics produce groupthink. (Article 36).

# Chapter 13

# Social Psychology and Society:
## Legal and Organizational Applications

## Chapter-at-a-Glance

| CHAPTER OUTLINE | INSTRUCTION IDEAS | SUPPLEMENTS* |
|---|---|---|
| *I. The Application of Social Psychology to the Interpersonal Aspects of the Legal System*<br><br>• The Initial Steps: Police Interrogation and Pretrial Publicity<br><br>• **Social Psychology: On the Applied Side** Pretrial Decisions about O.J. Simpson: Prejudice and Pretrial Publicity<br><br>• Eyewitness Testimony: How Accurate Is It?<br><br>• **Cornerstones of Social Psychology** Hugo Munsterberg on the Inaccuracy of Eyewitnesses<br><br>• How Attorneys and Judges Can Affect the Jury's Verdict<br><br>• How Decisions Are Influenced by Characteristics of the Defendants and the Jurors | Learning Objectives 13.1 to 13.16<br><br>Discussion Topics 1, 2, 3,<br><br>Critical Thinking Questions 8-10<br><br>Activities 13.1 (Handout), 13.2, 13.3, 13.4 (Handout) | Test Bank Questions 13.1 to 13.93<br><br>Readings:<br>- Lesko 37, Women of the Jury<br>- Lesko 38, Beautiful But Dangerous<br><br>Transparency 13.3 |
| *II. Social Psychology and Business: Work-Related Attitudes, Impression Management in Job Interviews, and Conflict*<br><br>• Work-Related Attitudes: Job Satisfaction and organizational Commitment<br><br>• Job Interviews: Impression Management Revisited<br><br>• Organizational Politics: Tactics for Getting Ahead-- Whatever the Cost to Others<br><br>• Conflict in Work Settings: A Social Psychological Perspective<br><br>• **Social Diversity: A Critical Analysis** The Effects of Working in Another Culture: What Happens When Expatriates Come Home? | Learning Objectives 13.17 to 13.22<br><br>Discussion Topic 4<br><br>Critical Thinking Questions 8-10 | Test Bank Questions 13.94 to 13.140<br><br>Reading:<br>- Lesko 39, Stealing in the Name of Justice |

*See Audiovisual Suggestions

# 13 Social Psychology and Society: Legal and Organizational Applications

---

## Chapter Outline: Getting the Overall Picture

---

I. **The Application of Social Psychology to the Interpersonal Aspects of the Legal System**
   A. The Initial Steps: Police Interrogation and Pretrial Publicity
      1. Interrogation: Seeking the Truth or Seeking a Confession?
      2. Less Obvious Techniques to Elicit Confessions
      3. Effects of the Media: General Perceptions about Crime
      4. Effects of the Media: Pretrial Publicity and Perceptions of a Specific Crime and a Specific Suspect
   B. Social Psychology: On the Applied Side: Pretrial Decisions about O.J. Simpson: Prejudice and Pretrial Publicity
   C. Eyewitness Testimony: How Accurate Is It?
   D. Cornerstones of Social Psychology: Hugo Munsterberg on the Inaccuracy of Eyewitnesses
      1. Eyewitness Accuracy and Inaccuracy
      2. Attempts to Increase Eyewitness Accuracy
   E. How Attorneys and Judges Can Affect the Jury's Verdict
      1. Attorneys: Adversaries with Opposite Goals
      2. The Judge: Bias from the Bench
   F. How Decisions Are Influenced by Characteristics of the Defendants and the Jurors
      1. Are All Defendants Equal under the Law?
      2. Who Is Sitting in the Jury Box?
II. **Social Psychology and Business: Work-Related Attitudes, Impression Management in Job Interviews, and Conflict**
   A. Work-Related Attitudes: Job Satisfaction and Organizational Commitment
      1. Factors Affecting Job Satisfaction
      2. The Effects of Job Satisfaction: Weaker Than You Might Guess
      3. Organizational Commitment: Attitudes toward One's Company
      4. Effects of Organizational Commitment
   B. Job Interviews: Impression Management Revisited
      1. Applicants' Appearance
      2. How Interviewers Sometimes Get the Results They Want: Expectancy Confirmation in Job Interviews
   C. Organizational Politics: Tactics for Getting Ahead--Whatever the Cost to Others
      1. Controlling access to information
      2. Cultivating a good image
      3. Developing a base of support
      4. Dirty tricks
      5. Protecting Yourself and Others against Organizational Politics

        a.      Clarify job expectations
        b.      Insist on (or at least encourage) open communication
        c.      Be on the lookout for, and do not tolerate, political game players
  D.    Conflict in Work Settings:  A Social Psychological Perspective
        1.      The Causes of Conflict at Work:  Organizational and Interpersonal
        2.      Strategies for Dealing with Conflict:  Contrasting Patterns, Underlying Dimensions
        3.      Techniques for Reducing the Harmful Effects of Conflict
  E.    Social Diversity: A Critical Analysis: The Effects of Working in Another Culture:  What Happens When Expatriates Come Home?

---

# Learning Objectives
### After studying this chapter, students should be able to:

---

**13.1**    Define "forensic psychology," and describe the dimensions of interrogation and accompanying styles.

**13.2**    Describe how minimization vs. maximization induces a suspect to confess.  Discuss the Kassin and McNall findings regarding the effectiveness of the two techniques with jurors.

**13.3**    Give an example of a leading question.  Indicate the role of the interrogation setting.

**13.4**    List the three typical feelings of the witness during leading questions, and say what happens when the typical target of leading questions answers definitely and confidently.

**13.5**    Contrast the `90s and `80s crime rates and youth gun death across the two decades.  Discuss our belief in "presumed innocence," and whether exposure to media "facts" about a crime affects jurors' dispositions regarding guilt.

**13.6**    Indicate the implications of "automatic vigilance" and that the U.S. public is not "sequestered."  Give examples of how stereotypes shape our perceptions about who committed heinous crimes.

**13.7**    Describe the racial rift in the O.J. trial, and the findings of Page and Gropp in their investigation of pre-trial publicity in the O. J. case.  Explain how emotions eclipse thinking in such cases.

**13.8**    Discuss our perceptions of the reality about the reliability of eyewitness testimony.

**13.9**    Describe Munsterberg's personal experience as an eyewitness.  Discuss the accuracy level of "experts" witnessing a staged assault, and the effect of "misleading postevent information" on memory of an event.

**13.10**  Describe conditions in which eyewitness' memory remains intact.  List the circumstances under which confidence in memory increases and decreases.

**13.11**  Discuss the use of hypnosis in court.  Explain why a line-up is like an experiment.

**13.12**  Tell how to identify an accurate witness based on her/his experience during an identification.  Explain how the goal of attorneys in selecting jurors is different from our perception of the ideal?.

**13.13**  Discuss leading questions and list some sources of bias on the part of judges.  Describe Hart's study of judges non-verbal video-communications conveying their own private opinion concerning guilt.

**13.14**  Describe the profile of the likely successful defendant, and when the traits can backfire.  Indicate the value of a smile (LaFrance and Hecht), and for whom attractiveness an asset?  Tell how attractiveness affects judges and attorneys.

**13.15**  Discuss the interplay of defendant's and victim's attractiveness level (Castellow and colleagues).  Examine the observation that African-Americans commit more violent crimes, with special attention to the death penalty.

**13.16** Discuss when a suspect is most suspect, and whether language is a barrier to acquittal. List Adler's suggestions for a better juror system. Contrast competent and incompetent, experienced and inexperienced, authoritarian and lenient, pro- and anti- death penalty and pro or anti- expert attitudes of jurors.

**13.17** Describe "industrial-organizational psychologists." Contrast attitudes toward jobs and attitudes toward companies. Describe when people tend to report high job satisfaction (JS). List and describe organization factors in JS. Describe the Melamed et al findings on monotony and JS, and personal factors that relate to JS.

**13.18** Give the reasons why JS relates poorly to work behaviors. Describe the three components of organizational commitment uncovered by Allen and Meyer.

**13.19** Describe what effects of organizational commitment are reflected in "organizational citizenship behavior." Explain "workaholicism." Detail "impression management" during job interviews. List the interview factors Pengitore et al studied.

**13.20** Discuss how interviewer-expectations become self-fulfilling prophesies. Discuss tactics that slant "office politics" in one's favor (attend to "office chameleons," "when push comes to shove," "dirty tricks," "hidden agendas" and "human resources").

**13.21** List the anti-office-politics" countermeasures. Contrast workplace "conflict" and "aggression." Describe the organizational and interpersonal sources of workplace conflict and modes of reacting to conflict. Contrast concern for own vs. others outcomes.

**13.22** Describe three "negotiation" tactics. Explain "incompatibility error" and "superordinate goals." Describe the questions asked of "expatriate managers" by Guzzo et al and the answers provided.

---

## Discussion Topics and Questions

---

### 1. Our Love/Hate Relationship With Lawyers

"Why could shipwrecked lawyers safely swim past sharks, while others were eaten alive?" Answer: "Professional courtesy." "How can you tell the difference between road-killed lawyers and equally unfortunate animals?" answer: "Tire skid-marks in front of the animals." "How many lawyers could you cram into a typical underground nuclear test site?" Answer: "Not nearly enough."

These are just a few examples of popular "lawyer" jokes. You and your students probably know many more (you could ask them). Despite this apparent malice toward legal counselors, TV is full of "lawyer shows" promoting positive images of the law profession, and they are well watched. Why this ambivalence? Have the students talk about it. Maybe we "hate" lawyers because they control so much of our lives. On the other hand, perhaps we "love" them because of the power they possess as manifested in the megabucks they make and their ability to shape what happens in our society.

### 2. Analyzing Leadership

Tapes or films of the famous John F. Kennedy--Richard M. Nixon TV debate of 1960 are readily available. (If your college doesn't have a copy, your audiovisual people can probably borrow it from another college.) Play as much of the debate as you think is necessary to give students the flavor of each candidate's strategy, appearance, manner, and orientation to the facts. In the eye of the viewing public, Kennedy was the clear winner. In terms of getting facts straight and speaking to the issues, some experts on debate saw Nixon as the winner. Get the students to indicate who they thought won and why. Most will likely say that Kennedy won. Their reasons will be various, but call attention to those reasons that relate to JFK's handsome looks and cool demeanor. Perhaps you can also get them to notice that he spoke in generalities more than did Nixon, who was often quite factual. In contrast, Nixon's upper lip was, as usual, sweating, and he looked pale, unhealthy and nervous. being substantive didn't pay off, but looking good and in charge did. Note the implications of this debate for the importance of optimism, attractiveness, apparent leadership ability, charisma, and saying "what people want to hear" rather than speaking about substantive issues.

### 3. The Death Penalty

The death penalty is supported by a majority of Americans but remains controversial. Whatever you feel about it personally, you can preside over a productive discussion of it. Nobel Prize winning organization Amnesty International is conducting an international campaign to abolish the death penalty. They argue the death penalty does not deter murder (often a crime of passion that is not preceded by any thoughts of future consequences); that it is more costly than keeping murderers in prison for life (special housing inflates costs, but the legal costs of appeals balloon the costs of capital punishment the most); and--among other concerns--that it is discriminatory. Even beyond the fact that all-White juries have sent many Blacks to death row, the U.S. Supreme Court has acknowledged the observation that people who kill White persons are significantly more likely to get the death penalty; that is, Blacks killing Whites and Whites killing Whites get the ultimate penalty, not those who kill Blacks.

The counterarguments include the view that only legally sanctioned execution will ensure murderers don't end up on the streets again (too many murderers are released after only short stays in prison); that consideration of victims and their families dictates that murderers should be executed (family anguish ends only with execution); and that the deterrence value of execution has not been properly tested, because the death penalty has been too rarely meted out (few convicted murderers end up on death row, and few of those on death row are executed).

Let students hash out these arguments in class; prompt them if they forget some of the points made above. Then raise the critical question: What can social psychologists do to help resolve these issues? For example, can it be shown in the lab that all-White juries are "more likely to hang" a Black person accused of murder, especially if the victim is White? Can studies be designed to show that penalties for resorting to violence deter the use of violence? (For example, during an aggression experiment in which subjects can shock someone who has offended them, will a relatively severe penalty for using shock deter its use?)

### 4. On the Job

What primarily occupies people's time and thoughts on the job--concern and involvement in job-related tasks, or interpersonal events? We know of many cases where most energy is expended on interpersonal conflict and/or socializing (positive interpersonal events). Most of your students will have held jobs at one time or another; many will be currently employed. Have them talk about where the balance of interpersonal versus job related cognitive and emotional energies lies. Many of them may be surprised to discover, upon reflection, that they and others are spending an inordinate amount of time on non-job-related matters. Have them speculate about how to reduce interpersonal conflict on the job so that more time and energy can be devoted to efficient job performance, an outcome that will increase job satisfaction.

# Learning Activities:  Classroom Exercises/Demonstrations

### 13.1  Attractive versus Unattractive Candidates

Hold an election to convince students that attractive candidates are most likely to win when other factors are held constant.  Find a copy of a yearbook that is old enough so your students won't recognize the photos, but recent enough so that photos won't reflect out-of-style clothes and hair.  Look through it until you find a block of photos that are all posed the same (seniors will probably work).  Next, pick out the most attractive three males and three females you can find.  Then pick out the most unattractive three males and three females.  Copy the pages containing these twelve photos on transparency plastic and cut the twelve photos from their surrounds.  Now check with colleagues to be sure that the final product reflects the appropriate attractiveness differences.  These are your twelve "candidates" for a hypothetical student government presidential election.  Next list a half dozen innocuous campus issues. (Example:  The student fee for parking should not be further increased; faculty should be required to return tests within five class days of the test administration; faculty should be required to provide example essay questions at the beginning of each semester; students should be allowed two unpenalized absences per class per semester; the administration should notify students about discussions of tuition increases before they begin deliberation; 10 percent of faculty raises should be based on student ratings of faculty effectiveness.)

Select three of the issue positions (pro or con) and assign them to one of the attractive "candidates." Assign the same positions on the same issues to a candidate of the same gender from among the unattractive photos.  Repeat this process until you have six matched pairs, each consisting of one attractive and one unattractive photo, both of the same gender, and each espousing the same positions on the same issues.  Now you are ready for the "election."  Randomly assign the names on the ballot included below to the photos--with the restriction that gender-appropriate names be assigned.  Then present the transparencies of the photos in random order, mentioning the name and positions on the issues associated with each photo.  Have the students take notes on each candidate and then "vote" by marking the ballot on the next page.  The simplest method is to have them vote for one candidate, collect the ballots, and see who received  the most votes (very likely one of the attractive candidate).  To be more sure of obtaining the expected result--attractive candidates receive more votes--have the students rank-order the candidates, giving a rank of 1 to the most favored candidate, a 2 to the next most favored, etc.  Then take the mean of ranks (or take median ranks if the distribution dictates) for "attractive" and "unattractive" candidates separately.  Viewing these and average ranks may be enough, but you may also want to perform a test of differences in average ranks, with "attractive" and "unattractive" being the conditions.

STUDENT GOVERNMENT PRESIDENTIAL ELECTION BALLOT (ACTIVITY #13.1)

| CANDIDATE | VOTE |
|---|---|
| Sarah Smithers | — |
| Ralph McLeRoy | — |
| Josh Monroe | — |
| Karen Foster | — |
| Suzanne Albert | — |
| Preston Sims | — |
| Anne Harvey | — |
| Kate Sampson | — |
| Shane Jackson | — |
| Marvin Allen | — |
| Rudy Anderson | — |
| Jennie Harper | — |

## 13.2 Judges' Impact on Jury Decisions

Judges's instructions to members of the jury may have great impact on jury decisions, as noted in the text. To illustrate this point, divide the class into "jury panels" of about six people (four, if the class is small; eight to twelve if the class is large). Then read the following case to all students: "Robert Edward Farness stands accused of killing a fellow patron at a local bar. Eyewitness testimony indicates that Farness was talking to a woman, for whom he had provided a drink, when the victim approached and began attempting to convince the woman that she should leave Farness and accompany him. Farness and the victim began to shout at one another; it was clear from what they were yelling that they knew one another and had had conflicts before. At the height of the argument, Farness was heard to shout, "I told you I'd kill you if you bullied me again!" At that point the victim broke off the neck of a beer bottle and began to thrust the jagged edge at Farness. Farness grabbed a chair, swung it at the victim, and dislodged the broken bottle from the victim's grasp. Witnesses testified that Farness then continued to bludgeon the victim with the chair, even after it was clear that he was no longer in danger. By the time Farness was restrained, the victim was so badly injured he died on the way to the hospital."

Next, give half the groups (juries) a written copy of the following "judge's instruction to the jury:" "You are instructed that, should you find the accused guilty, you must provide a sentence of life in prison without parole." Give this instruction to the remaining groups: "You are instructed that should you find the accused guilty, you may provide a sentence ranging from a minimum of ten years in prison --parole considered after five years--to a maximum of life in prison without parole." Now have the "juries" deliberate for twenty minutes or so and return a "guilty" or "not guilty" decision. Ask them to reach a unanimous decision, if they can, but to record the outcome of each vote they take before the final vote (require at least three votes). You should find that, at the minimum, "juries" given the first instruction have more difficulty reaching a decision, as reflected in more and closer votes. Chances are you will also find that "guilty" decisions are less frequent with the first instruction than with the second. Ballots are provided on the next page and in the Study Guide.

## HANDOUT FOR ACTIVITY # 13.2

FIRST BALLOT

FIRST NAME OF JUROR          "GUILTY" OR "NOT GUILTY" VOTE

SECOND BALLOT

FIRST NAME OF JUROR          "GUILTY" OR "NOT GUILTY" VOTE

THIRD BALLOT

FIRST NAME OF JUROR          "GUILTY" OR "NOT GUILTY" VOTE

FOURTH BALLOT

FIRST NAME OF JUROR          "GUILTY" OR "NOT GUILTY" VOTE

FIFTH BALLOT

FIRST NAME OF JUROR          "GUILTY" OR "NOT GUILTY" VOTE

SIXTH BALLOT

FIRST NAME OF JUROR          "GUILTY" OR "NOT GUILTY" VOTE

Copyright © 1997 by Allyn and Bacon

## 13.3  Selecting a Jury

Have the class select a jury.  Some volunteers can act as potential jurors and others as attorneys (half for the prosecution and half for the defense) who pose screening questions.  Allow each attorney to address ten questions to the potential jurors.  Record the questions.  After each attorney has posed her or his questions, have all indicate up to ten traits they considered critically important in jurors and were therefore trying to assess through their questions.

Next make a copy of Transparency 13.3 (Table 13.2) and, on it, tally the frequency with which attorneys used each of the traits listed in the table.  (You could do separate tallies for prosecutors and defense attorneys.)  Also tally the number of times questions similar to each of those in the table were asked by attorneys.  Finally, make a transparency of your tallies so that you can present it to the class.  Did students follow the practices of real attorneys?  Have your "attorneys" indicate why they did or did not endorse the traits or questions contained in Transparency 13.3.  Maybe they can conclude that some of their questions and traits make more sense than those more typically endorsed by real attorneys.

## 13.4  Job Satisfaction

Do different job satisfaction questionnaires yield similar results?  The question may be answered for students if you have them complete the questionnaires in Transparency 13.5.  Make copies from the transparency master (13.5) and distribute to students.  To put scores on the same scale, score the JDI answers as follows:  Routine 1, Satisfactory 3, Good 5; Dead-end job 1, Few promotions 3, Good opportunity for promotion 5.  Average the scores for each student for each scale separately.  These average scores can then be fed into a T-test for paired observations.  Discuss why scores on the two tests turned out differently or not as a function of whether the tests measure different factors.

## 13.5  Voting Record

Why don't people in Western democracies vote?  Because it is a touchy subject, ask students to indicate anonymously whether or not they voted in the most recent presidential election and, if not, why not.  Present the voting record (percentage of students who voted) to the class and ask whether some students would like to indicate why they did not vote.  In addition to (or instead of ) this process, you could indicate categories of reasons why students did not vote; for example, "one vote doesn't matter," "one person can't change the system," " politicians are disgusting," and so on.  In this way students' anonymity could be preserved.  Ask class members to rebut these arguments against voting.  A lively interchange should result.

---

# Overhead Transparencies
These appear at the back of this manual.

---

# Audiovisual Suggestions

*Allyn and Bacon Video*

*\*Group Decision Making and Leadership,* video, 28.5 mins. See your Allyn and Bacon representative to learn how you may obtain this tape. Robert A. Baron and Margaret Clark discuss issues of leadership that are relevant to politics and business.

*Other Videos and Films*

*Political Marketing: The Selling of America's Candidates,* videotape, 34 mins. Television Services, Western Illinois University, Macomb, IL 61455 (309-298-1880). Illustrates the principles of marketing that have been used to sell political candidates in past presidential elections. This one does double duty--politics and business.

*Sexual Harassment on the Job,* videotape, 28 mins. Films for the Humanities & Sciences, Inc., P.O. Box 2053, Princeton, NJ 08543-2053 (800-257-5126). Over 70 percent of working women experience pressure to exchange favors for advancement or continued employment. Susan Meyers defines the problem and how to solve it.

*The Death Penalty,* FC-1938, video, 26 mins. Films for the Humanities & Sciences, Inc., P.O. box 2053, Princeton, NJ 08543-2053 (800-257-5126). Argues that new evidence suggests that death sentences are imposed arbitrarily and that little evidence exists to support the contention that the death penalty is a deterrent to murder.

*Crime & Human Nature,* FC-1327, video, 26 mins. Films for the Humanities & Sciences, Inc., P.O. Box 2053, Princeton, NJ 08543-2053 (800-257-5126). Anthropologist Ashley Montague and other experts join Phil Donahue in addressing issues that relate to the structure of our current laws.

*Twelve Angry Men,* commercial video (1957, United Artists) available for rental at many video stores, 95 mins. This film is perhaps the most respected attempt by Hollywood to look behind the dynamics of jury deliberation. It is outstanding.

# Critical Thinking/Essay Questions

1. Discuss aspects of the judicial process where lawyers think they have a solid understanding of underlying dynamics but where the evidence says otherwise.
2. Indicate the implications of the finding that individuals who kill Whites are more likely to end up on death row.
3. If judges can be divided up into "hanging" and "soft on crime" categories, what does that say about their objectivity?
4. Why did Bill Clinton win in 1992? Discuss those of his characteristics that fit the typical mold of the desirable president and those that do not. Do our perceptions of what makes a desirable candidate and admired president, as described in the text, fit Clinton well?
5. Argue that you are different than other people: you vote on the issues, not on the appearance of the candidate, her or his ability to dodge controversial issues, or his or her ability to *look* like a leader.

Be sure to eliminate the latter three considerations from those matters that you weigh in selecting who to vote for.

6. Can you defend not voting? Build as convincing an argument as you can.

7. Write a brief description of an optimal strategy for an unknown politician to use to get elected to the U.S. Senate. Be sure to include factors such as possible name change, optimism/pessimism, appearance similarity to voters, charisma, and leadership style.

8. Construct your own job satisfaction test. Come up with ten items that you think would adequately assess job satisfaction. Be sure to include the factors involved in job satisfaction that are included in the text.

9. Pretend that you are the boss. How would you go about motivating employees? Set up a ten-point program that would translate into high worker morale and high productivity.

10. What are the kinds of interpersonal conflicts that you would expect to develop in a typical job context? Choose from department store clerks, assembly line workers, or auto sales personnel--or some other, if you have intimate knowledge of it. Be sure to include relevant conflicts that are covered in the text.

---

## Sources for Lecture

---

Ellsworth, P. (1985, July). Juries on trial. *Psychology Today,* pp. 44-46. A 1968 case is used to introduce the issue of "death-qualified" juries. The relationship between social psychological research and court cases since then is discussed.

Kaplan, S. M. (1985, July). Death, so say we all. *Psychology Today,* pp. 48-53. The author describes the emotional turmoil experienced by jurors who sat through a lengthy and traumatic trial that resulted in a death-sentence recommendation.

Mahoney, H. (1987, September). When the law is not enough. *Ms,* p. 85. Judges can make some horrible mistakes, beyond misinstructing or otherwise biasing a jury. In this case a young woman's plea for protection from her husband was ignored by a judge who told her to "act as an adult." She was subsequently murdered by the husband.

---

## Professional Update: Current Articles from Professional Sources

---

Allen, B. P. (1994). *Personality Theories.* Needham Heights, MA: Allyn and Bacon. Sections on Albert Bandura summarize his work on self-efficacy and work efficiency. Material on George Kelly provides an overview of personal construct principles applicable to personnel and product evaluation.

Azzi, A. E. (1992). Procedural justice and the allocation of power in intergroup relations: Studies in the United States and South Africa. *Personality and Social Psychology Bulletin, 18,* 736-747. This study examined proportionality versus equality principles in the allocation of political power and other resources between majorities and minorities. Subjects from the United States and South Africa were more likely to divide a procedural resource (political power) equally between two simulated ethnic groups differing in size when led to identify with a minority rather than a majority. Equality was also more salient to members of real ethnic minorities than to members of ethnic majorities.

Brockner, J., Wiensenfeld, B. M., Reed, T., Grover, S., & Martin, C. (1993). Interactive effect of job content and context on the reactions of layoff survivors. *Journal of Personality and Social Psychology, 64,* 187-197. Field and lab studies examined the determinants of survivors' (people who survive their companies' layoffs) reactions to job layoffs. Change in perceived job quality was strongly and positively related to survivors' organizational and task commitment when the layoffs were seen as fair.

Hafer, C., & Olson, J. M. (1993). Beliefs in a Just World, discontent, and assertive actions by working women. *Personality and Social Psychology bulletin, 19,* 30-38. Researchers assessed working women's Belief in the Just World (BJW: what you get is what you got coming) along with personal discontent, group discontent, self-directed behavior, and group-directed behavior. Those high on BJW reported less group discontent than those low. High BJWs showed fewer self- and group-directed behaviors.

*Related Readings:* The following selections from *Readings in Social Psychology: General, Classic, and Contemporary Selections,* 3rd Edition, by Wayne Lesko (Allyn and Bacon, 1997) accompany this chapter.

Ruben, D. (1995). "Women of the jury." The author examines the impact gender may have on the judicial process. Although lawyers often consider the gender of potential jurors to be important in certain types of trails, the impact of gender in a trail may not be as great as some might think. In fact, the impact may not be in the direction that was anticipated. (Article 37).

Sigal, H. & Ostrove, N. (1975). "Beautiful but dangerous: Effects of offender attractiveness and nature of the crime on juridic judgment." In this classic piece of research, the authors investigated the impact of the defendant's physical attractiveness on the severity of sentences given to her. This study not only examined the role of physical attractiveness in a trial-like setting, but also how the nature of the crime and attractiveness interact to influence judgments about the defendant. (Article 38).

Greenberg, J. (1993). "Stealing in the name of justice: Informational and interpersonal moderators of theft reactions to underpayment inequity." This article examines what produces a sense of monetary inequity at work, what may mediate the feeling of inequity, and how feelings of inequity may lead to behaviors like stealing as a means of reducing the perceived injustice. Some practical ideas are presented that may be of interest to people in managerial positions who are concerned with the productivity (and honesty) of their employees. (Article 39).

# Chapter 14

# Social Psychology in Action:
# Applications to Health and Environment

## Chapter-at-a-Glance

| CHAPTER OUTLINE | INSTRUCTION IDEAS | SUPPLEMENTS* |
|---|---|---|
| ***I. Health Psychology: Maintaining a Healthy State and Coping with Illness*** <br>•   Dealing with Health-Related Information <br><br>•   **Social Psychology: On the Applied Side**   Success in Encouraging People Not to Smoke Cigarettes and the Reasons that Many Teenagers Do So Anyway <br><br>•   Stress and Illness <br><br>•   Taking Active Steps to Cope with Stress <br><br>•   Responding to Health Problems <br><br>•   Coping with Medical Care | Learning Objectives 14.1 to 14.14 <br><br>Discussion Topic 1 <br><br>Critical Thinking Questions 1-3 <br><br>Activities 14.1, 14.2, 14.3 (Handouts) | Test Bank Questions 14.1 to 14.87 <br><br>Reading: <br>- Lesko 40, AIDS <br><br>Transparencies 14.1, 14.2, 14.3, 14.4 |
| ***II. Environmental Psychology: How Environmental Factors Affect Human Behavior and How Human Behavior Affects the Environment*** <br>•   Environmental Effects on Human Behavior <br><br>•   The Effects of Human Behavior on the Environment <br><br>•   **Social Diversity: A Critical Analysis**   Differences between Asians and Americans in Responding to Illness | Learning Objectives 14.15 to 14.22 <br><br>Discussion Topics 2-5 <br><br>Critical Thinking Questions 4-9 <br><br>Activities 14.4, 14.5 (Handout) | Test Bank Questions 14.88 to 14.140 <br><br>Readings: <br>- Lesko 41, Territorial Defense and the Good Neighbor <br>- Lesko 42, A Whiff of Reality <br><br>Transparencies 14.5, 14.6 |

*See Audiovisual Suggestions

# 14

## Social Psychology In Action: Applications to Health and Environment

---

### Chapter Outline: Getting the Overall Picture

---

I.   **Health Psychology:  Maintaining a Healthy State and Coping with Illness**
   A.    Dealing with Health-Related Information
       1.    What Information Is Most Available?
       2.    What Information do We Accept?
   B.    Social Psychology: On the Applied Side: Success in Encouraging People Not to Smoke Cigarettes and the Reasons That Many Teenagers Do So Anyway
   C.    Stress and Illness
       1.    Illness As a Consequence of Stress
       2.    Individual Differences in Vulnerability to Stress
   D.    Taking Active Steps to Cope with Stress
       1.    Increasing Physical Fitness
       2.    Creating Positive Affect
       3.    Seeking Social Support
   E.    Responding to Health Problems
       1.    Attending to Symptoms--Noticing That Something Is Wrong
       2.    Deciding What the Symptom Means
       3.    If You Decide It's a Medical Problem, Do You Contact a Physician?
   F.    Coping with Medical Care
       1.    Patient--Physician Interactions
       2.    Dealing with Diagnosis and Treatment
       3.    The Role of Perceived Control in Coping with Treatment

II.  **Environmental Psychology: How Environmental Factors Affect Human Behavior and How Human Behavior Affects the Environment**
   A.    Environmental Effects on Human Behavior
       1.    Noisy Environments:  Unpleasant and Unpredictable Sounds
       2.    High Temperatures:  Negative Affect and Negative Interpersonal Behavior
       3.    The Negative Effects of Breathing Polluted Air
       4.    Electrical Ions in the Atmosphere
   B.    The Effects of Human Behavior on the Environment
       1.    The More People, the More Effect They Have on the Environment
       2.    Some of the Effects of Our Actions:  Producing Waste, Altering the climate, and Causing the Spread of New Diseases
   C.    Social Diversity: A Critical Analysis: Differences Between Asians and Americans in Responding to Illness

# Learning Objectives
After studying this chapter, students should be able to:

**14.1** Define "health psychology." Consider what and how much to drink, and whether we misperceive health dangers. Indicate when inducing fear is best and when a positive message is best.

**14.2** Outline the procedures and results of the Liberman and Chaiken caffeine and breast cancer study. Explain how sensitizers and repressors react differently to messages about breast cancer (Millnar and Millnar).

**14.3** Consider the smoking rate worldwide, government preventive efforts, attempts to start teens smoking and positive effects of smoking. List five strategies emerging from the DeVries et al study using the "bogus pipeline" that may lessen smoking among teens.

**14.4** Define stress and name the major work stressors, college student stressors, and commuter stressors. Discuss reasons why stress generates physical illness. Describe "Psychoneuroimmunology" and the causal chain linking stress with secretory immunoglobulin A and illnesses.

**14.5** Contrast reactions to stress and traits of disease-prone persons vs. the self-healing personalities. Indicate the health-importance of perceived control. Give real-life examples of attempts to obtain or maintain control.

**14.6** Describe how Bandura immunized subjects against stress-produced health-related physiological reactions. Outline the Compas and colleagues two-level stress management program.

**14.7** Describe how Emmons interpreted his findings when he studied high level and low level goals of undergraduates along with their negative emotions and illnesses. Contrast Type As and Bs on physical health indexes.

**14.8** Describe "fitness" and Brown's findings with regard to its health benefits. Indicate why "counterfactual thinking" is harmful. Discuss which is worse, an increase in negative events or a decrease in positive events.

**14.9** Discuss the effect of good smells. Tell why social support helps. List some real-life areas where social support lessen stress. Describe the plight of the support provider and those with a support deficit.

**14.10** Discuss over- and under-attention to physical symptoms. Outline the effects of pre-existing anxiety on complaints during illness, Type As' control need and illnesses, as well as the problem of perceived pain in relation to illness.

**14.11** Describe the dangers of self-diagnosis and medication discontinuation. Indicate how self-efficacy plays a role in "being your own physician." Explain when people call the physician and when they self-medicate.

**14.12** Indicate the kinds of people who consult a physician and those who do not. Show how dependency relates to seeking medical advice.

**14.13** Discuss private physician talk, and "doctor interpersonal skills" as related to doctor-patient relations and "framing." Examine sources of distraction as alleviators of threat.

**14.14** Give real-life examples of how increased perceived control boosts coping. Discuss Freudenheim's laser-disk source of control.

**14.15** Define "environmental psychology." Link "technophobia" to environmental fears. Consider ineffective coping with environmental threat. Describe "noise" and when it is most noxious.

**14.16** Consider the devices for eliminating noise. Give real examples of heat, hot tempers, and aggression.

**14.17** Indicate whether heat and aggression are related in straight line fashion or aggression drops off with very hot temperatures.

**14.18** Indicate an appropriate index of pollution's harmful effects. Describe how good smells affect performance.

**14.19** Discuss positive and negative ions and their effects. List real-life ways that we affect our environments.

**14.20** Characterize the "population explosion," and outline the three philosophies of world population growth.

**14.21** Give some sources of greenhouse gases, and explain what are CFCs. Indicate how we can reduce these gases. Discuss the two major consequences of reducing the rain forests. Relate the ebola threat to rainforest destruction.

**14.22** Describe the "bone of contention" for an Asian and a European-American doctor debating about treatment of a Korean woman. Indicate the dimensions of cultural difference they considered. Discuss the relevance of collectivism vs. individualism as related to medical care.

---

# Discussion Topics and Questions

---

## 1. Sources of Stress and How We Deal With It

Some degree of stress is a fact of life for everyone (well, almost everyone). The first step in dealing with stress is to identify its sources. Have students talk about what aspects of college life "stress them out" the most. You may even want to tally these sources on the board, keeping a count of which ones are experienced by how many students. Knowing that others have the same kinds of problems helps students feel less odd and unusual. That knowledge alone lowers anxiety, a first step toward dealing successfully with stress.

Next, have students suggest how they deal with the various sources of stress, or the stress itself. When the problems are personal, it is surprising how the simplest solutions fail to occur to even the brightest of people. (An example of an easy solution; "When my roommate bugs me, I leave the room for a couple of hours. It works every time.") You may even want to have the students vote on which coping method mentioned in conjunction with a given source of stress is the most effective. Consensus can be a powerful determinant of beliefs, and when people believe strongly enough in a method, they will often make it work.

## 2. Pro-life...and...Pro-choice

Abortion is becoming an option for population control worldwide. It is an explosive issue that you may well wish to avoid. Nevertheless, you are guaranteed a lively discussion if you bring up the topic. The problem is avoiding offense. If there was just some way to satisfy people on both sides of the issue...Maybe there is.

Carl Sagan and Ann Druyan have attempted to develop a strategy that allows choice and at the same time is "pro-life" (see Sources for Lecture). You will need to read their article; but, to get a glimpse of it, consider a world in which contraception was widely and conscientiously used. In such a world, people would be exercising their choice to decide when or whether they would have children. At the same time, because conception would be avoided, the issue of killing the embryo or fetus would not arise. To start this discussion, begin with the question posed in the title of the Sagan-Druyan article: "Is it possible to be pro-life and pro-choice?" To avoid problems, you may want to work very hard to keep your point of view out of the discussion. Consider acting as a facilitator and moderator. You probably should guide students in the direction of considering birth control; as you know, however, even endorsement of contraception can be offensive.  Rather than endorsing it, considering raising it as an issue and refer to the text authors' point that the world's population could conceivably become so great that human life itself could not be sustained.  This is tricky business, but you could do some real good if you tackle this issue.

### 3.  How We Contribute to Pollution

People seem rather unaware that they themselves contribute to pollution.  Have students list all of the cases they can think of where a typical person contributes to pollution (e.g., driving an automobile, drinking out of cans, using nonbiodegradable wrappings such as plastic).  Consider substitute behaviors that would lower individual pollution.  Pay special attention to easy avenues to nonpolluting behaviors.

### 4.  "Radiation Phobia?"

The notion of "radiation phobia" raises some important issues.  So long as people lump all things nuclear together and find them all to be "bad," some benefits of nuclear physics will be retarded and progress toward eliminating the truly threatening applications will be slow.  There are positive outcomes of nuclear physics.  For example, Rosalyn S. Yalow won a Nobel Prize for the development of radioimmunoassay, a technique that involves treating biologic substances with radiation so that the presence of certain immunological entities can be detected.  It is estimated that this technique has saved many thousands of lives and that the numbers will eventually reach the millions.  Yalow can now be seen on TV in antismoking ads.  She is one of those who point out that cigarettes are much more dangerous than nuclear power plants.  (Incidentally, radon, as she has indicated, would not be such a significant threat if its effects did not combine with cigarette smoking: the great majority of radon-related deaths are among smokers.)  The use of radiation to preserve foods almost indefinitely is another example of potential positive uses of radiation.  Not only do people seem to think that all things nuclear are "bad," they seem to think that they are equally bad.

If students need to know that all things nuclear are not bad, they also need to know that some products of nuclear physics are worse than others.  Take nuclear power plants compared to nuclear weapons facilities as an example.  Nuclear power plants are relatively well regulated.  Prior to Chernobyl--and another Soviet nuclear plant disaster to which they later admitted--there have been few deaths worldwide directly attributable to power plant radiation exposure.  In the United States the number is very small.  By contrast, nuclear weapons facilities are relatively poorly regulated and have apparently been associated with numerous deaths (see the readings sections at the end of this chapter).  Yet the antinuke people have spent as much time protesting in front of power plants as they have in front of weapons facilities.  A thing to watch for in the future is continued lack of disasters associated with nuclear power plants and a possible trillion-dollar cleanup scandal associated with nuclear weapons facilities (the savings and loan fiasco may pale by comparison).

Armed with this information, you might start the discussion with "is there anything good about the application of nuclear physics?"  Then guide students to the idea tha some applications are more threatening than others and that some may be positive.  If students can appreciate that nuclear weapons are the real threat, they may be positive.  If students can appreciate that nuclear weapons are the real threat, they may act.  (As of this writing, the United States--Russian nuclear disarmament pact is signed but not implemented, because the former Soviet states have not all signed.)  Consider this discussion an exercise in critical thinking.

### 4.  The Greenhouse Effect

What can we do about the greenhouse effect?  First students need to understand what causes it. Start this discussion after students have read the book, or hope that some students will have the needed information beforehand. Or provide it yourself. Here is a short summary. $CO_2$ methane, chlorofluorocarbons (CFCs), nitrous oxides, and other gases form a blanket around the earth, letting light through but trapping heat much like a greenhouse. So far, $CO_2$ is the major contributor; methane and CFCs are increasing fast as are nitrous oxides. (As you recall, CFCs also deplete the ozone layer, thereby increasing ultraviolet-B with accompanying increases in the probability of skin cancer, cataracts, and the destruction of plankton--the beginning of the food chain in the world's oceans.) Excess $CO_2$ results primarily from the burning of fossil fuels such as oil, gasoline, and coal. Nitrous oxides also are emitted from the burning of fossil fuels and come from certain fertilizers. Excess methane comes from forest fires, landfills, rice paddies, and the digestive tracts of ruminant animals such as cattle. CFCs are found in aerosols that propel the contents of spray cans and in solvents that are used to clean computer components (microchips and circuit boards), as well as in refrigerants and foams.

Equipped with this information, students are ready to suggest ways they can contribute to reductions in greenhouse gases. Encouraging the planting of trees--and the preservation of existing trees--to help the uptake of $CO_2$ is a way to reduce $CO_2$. Also we can drive less--carpool and take public transportation--and demand that our politicians seek regulations that ensure cleaner burning of coal and oil. Nitrous oxides will also be reduced thereby. We can decrease methane by demanding tighter control of landfills and by eating less of the red meat that comes from cattle (then there will be less cattle). Aerosols have declined because of regulation. This observation suggests that we can do more to reduce CFCs. We can demand that other solvents be used to clean computer components (there are some available). We can also reduce CFCs by decreasing our dependency on air conditioners and refrigerators. Finally, we can demand the use of containers made of materials other than Styrofoam, perhaps of recycled paper. Here is a chance to empower students by helping them pinpoint actions they can take to save the environment.

---

## Learning Activities: Classroom Exercises/Demonstrations

---

### 14.1 "Dread Risks"

According to psychologist Paul Slovic (see *Science, 236,* April 17, 1987, pp. 280-285), a key to understanding risks and reacting appropriately to them is to assess them accurately. Unfortunately, certain risks, called dread risks, are quite resistant to accurate assessment: they are unfamiliar, involve fears of catastrophic future events and fatal consequences, and are perceived to be uncontrollable precursors of disaster. All of these characteristics of dread risks are reinforced by the media. In view of these characteristics, one can see why dread risks are inaccurately assessed: What is mysterious is especially frightening, and what is terribly fearful seems highly likely to occur. Thus, students can be expected to overestimate the incidence of dread risks relative to other risks.

Test this hypothesis, with regard to diseases, by asking students to guess the annual number of cases of each of several diseases, using the incidence of syphilis as a benchmark. AIDS fits the dread risk criteria and should be greatly overestimated, relative to other diseases. Students can provide their responses on a form found on the next page (and in the Study Guide). It is similar to Table 1 below, except that all statistics are missing except for syphilis. (Table based on information in *Morbidity and Mortality Weekly Report,* Vol. 39, May 18, 1990.)

---

### TABLE 1: Number of Cases of Various Diseases Accumulated during the First 19 Weeks of 1990

| | |
|---|---:|
| Measles | 7216 |
| Rabies (humans) | 0 |
| Gonorrhea | 239,884 |
| AIDS | 16,056 |
| Botulism (contamination of food) | 1 |
| Tetanus | 20 |
| Syphilis | 17,539 |
| Tuberculosis | 7,141 |
| Leprosy | 59 |
| Typhoid fever | 128 |

## HANDOUT FOR ACTIVITY # 14.1

## NUMBER OF CASES OF VARIOUS DISEASE ACCUMULATED
## DURING THE FIRST 19 WEEKS OF 1990

Measles

Rabies (humans)

Gonorrhea

AIDS

Botulism (contamination of food)

Tetanus

Syphilis                                    17,539

Tuberculosis

Leprosy

Typhoid fever

Copyright © 1997 by Allyn and Bacon

## 14.2  Social Readjustment Scale

What are the life events that generate the most stress?  As it turns out, most such events involve close relationships, an observation that may be news to many students.  To help them home in on events that may cause stress--the necessary first step in avoiding health-threatening stressors--have students examine the Holmes & Rahe Social Readjustment Scale (1967, *Journal of Psychosomatic Research, 11,* 213-218).

After they explore the scale thoroughly--it is included on the next page and in the Study Guide-- ask the students to find the top five most stressful events and rank them, giving a rank of 1 to the most stressful event.  Then instruct them to locate the bottom five, giving a rank of 43 to the least stressful, a rank of 42 to the next least stressful, and so on.  After the ranking is done, reveal the entire ranking by use of Table 2 below (from Allen [1990] *Personal Adjustment,* Brooks/Cole, used with permission). Have them comment on the degree to which their rankings have approximated the actual rankings based on a 100-point scale (marriage was the standard, set at 50).  Keep them going until it is clear to them that close personal relationships are the major source of the most stressful events.

### TABLE 2:  The Social Readjustment Scale

| Events | Score | Rank | Events | Score | Rank |
|---|---|---|---|---|---|
| Death of a spouse | 100 | 1 | Change in responsibilities at work | 29 | 23 |
| Divorce | 73 | 2 | Son or daughter leaving home | 29 | 23 |
| Marital separation | 65 | 3 | Trouble with in-laws | 29 | 23 |
| Jail term | 63 | 4.5 | Outstanding personal achievement | 28 | 25 |
| Death of close family member | 63 | 4.5 | Spouse begins or stops work | 28 | 25 |
| Personal injury or illness | 53 | 6 | Beginning or end of school | 26 | 26.5 |
| Marriage | 50 | 7 | Change in living conditions | 25 | 28 |
| Getting fired from job | 47 | 8 | Revision of personal habits | 24 | 29 |
| Marital reconciliation | 45 | 9.5 | Trouble with boss | 23 | 30 |
| Retirement | 45 | 9.5 | Change in work hours/conditions | 20 | 32 |
| Change in family member's health | 44 | 11 | Change in residence | 20 | 32 |
| Pregnancy | 40 | 12 | Change in schools | 20 | 32 |
| Sex difficulties | 39 | 14 | Change in recreation | 19 | 34.5 |
| Gain of new family member | 39 | 14 | Change in church activities | 39 | 14 |
| Business readjustment | 39 | 14 | Change in social activates | 18 | 36 |
| Change in financial state | 38 | 16 | Small mortgage or loan | 17 | 37 |
| Death of close friend | 37 | 17 | Change in sleeping habits | 16 | 38 |
| Change to different line of work | 36 | 18 | Change-# of family get-togethers | 15 | 39.5 |
| Change-# of spouse arguments | 35 | 19 | Change in eating habits | 15 | 39.5 |
| High mortgage | 31 | 19 | Christmas | 12 | 42 |
| Foreclosure of mortgage or loan | 30 | 21 | Minor violation of Law | 11 | 43 |

**HANDOUT FOR ACTIVITY # 14.2**

SOCIAL READJUSTMENT SCALE

| Events | Score | Rank | Events | Score | Rank |
|---|---|---|---|---|---|
| Death of a spouse | | | Change in responsibilities at work | | |
| Divorce | | | Son or daughter leaving home | | |
| Marital separation | | | Trouble with in-laws | | |
| Jail term | | | Outstanding personal achievement | | |
| Death of close family member | | | Spouse begins or stops work | | |
| Personal injury or illness | | | Beginning or end of school | | |
| Marriage | | | Change in living conditions | | |
| Getting fired from job | | | Revision of personal habits | | |
| Marital reconciliation | | | Trouble with boss | | |
| Retirement | | | Change in work hours/conditions | | |
| Change in family member's health | | | Change in residence | | |
| Pregnancy | | | Change in schools | | |
| Sex difficulties | | | Change in recreation | | |
| Gain of new family member | | | Change in church activities | | |
| Business readjustment | | | Change in social activities | | |
| Change in financial state | | | Small mortgage or loan | | |
| Death of close friend | | | Change in sleeping habits | | |
| Change to different line of work | | | Change-# of family get-togethers | | |
| Change-# of spouse arguments | | | Change in eating habits | | |
| High mortgage | | | Christmas | | |
| Foreclosure of mortgage or loan | | | Minor violation of Law | | |

Copyright © 1997 by Allyn and Bacon

### 14.3 Most Dangerous Physical Diseases

Students are likely to be plagued with misconception concerning which physical diseases are the most danger to them. There is much one can do about health hazards, but people often waste effort by focusing on the wrong dangers. For example, cardiovascular disease is by far the biggest killer of North Americans, and there if much one can do to avoid these disorders (e.g., exercise and diet control). Cancer, a much feared category of disorders, kills only about half as many as cardiovascular disease but may also be less controllable through behavioral intervention. If students see the two disease categories as equivalent in likelihood of cutting their lives short and equivalent in terms of possibilities for prevention, they may assume there is little they can do to save themselves. Have them consider the following list of disorders (Table 3) without numbers or ranks, found on the next page.

With accidents as the benchmark--its number alone is included on the following page and in the Study Guide--students could estimate the annual number of deaths attributed to each source and/or rank the top five killers, giving a rank of 1 to the most deadly. Then reveal to them what really are the big five killers. Finally, elicit comments until it is obvious that most of the top five are preventable with appropriate behavioral interventions. Time permitting, you may want to ask the students what social psychological methods might be used to get people moving in the direction of prevention. Methods for preventing smoking among youth and some ethnic groups are particularly relevant here.

### TABLE 3: Actual U.S. Fatalities and Ranks for Several Diseases and for Accidents

| Disease (or accidents) | Fatalities | Rank |
|---|---|---|
| Smallpox | 0 | |
| Tuberculosis | 3,690 | |
| Accidents | 93,990 | 4 |
| Stroke | 147,390 | 3 |
| Diabetes | 38,950 | |
| Cancer | 465,440 | 2 |
| Infectious hepatitis | 677 | |
| Heart disease | 763,380 | 1 |
| Syphilis | 410 | |
| Chronic lung disease | 75,220 | 5 |
| Measles | 5 | |

Based on data from Allen (1990), *Personal Adjustment*. Brooks/Cole.

**HANDOUT FOR ACTIVITY # 14.3**

ACTUAL U.S. FATALITIES AND RANKS FOR SEVERAL DISEASES AND FOR ACCIDENTS

| DISEASE (OR ACCIDENTS) | FATALITIES | RANK |
|---|---|---|
| smallpox | | |
| tuberculosis | | |
| accidents | 93,990 | |
| stroke | | |
| diabetes | | |
| cancer | | |
| infectious hepatitis | | |
| heart disease | | |
| syphilis | | |
| chronic lung disease | | |
| measles | | |

Based on data from Allen (1990), *Personal Adjustment*.  Brooks/Cole.

Copyright © 1997 by Allyn and Bacon

### 14.4  Weather Factors Affecting Social Behavior

"In every life, a little rain must fall."  Are temperature, ozone level, and ion content the only weather factors that affect social behavior?  How about precipitation or lack thereof (a sunny day)?  On a beautiful, sunny day have students generate five words to describe themselves.  Have them do the same on a rainy day as well as on two "average" (partly cloudy) days.  Students can "score" each other's words to show that a little sunshine can make a difference in how people describe themselves.  Simply have them exchange descriptions and place positive signs (+) by words that are favorable and negative signs(-) by unfavorable words.  (Don't score words that are neither favorable nor unfavorable.)  Consider a description favorable if it has more positive than negative signs.  Favorable descriptions should be more prominent on beautiful, sunny days, and unfavorable descriptions on day when it is raining or overcast.

In class, ask students why they described themselves in the way they did on assigned days.  Point out the precipitation factor in weather as a determinant of descriptions.  It should be the case that "beautiful days make for beautiful description:" we actually like ourselves better when our spirits are raised by a beautiful day.

### 14.5  Value Scale

The late Milton Rokeach's value conflict test might be altered to fit the case of pollution.  Give the students the value scale--found on the following page and in the Study Guide--and ask them to rank the items from 1 (most important to 18 (least important).  Then compare the mean ranks of items substituted for "equality" and "freedom" in positions 6 and 8 from the top.  Perhaps your students will find a clean environment for future generations more important than freedom to exploit the environment now.  Whether or not they do, it will be interesting to discover how environment issues stack up against the more personal issues found on the scale.  Ask them to volunteer which three items they ranked highest.  The information they provide may inspire some students to ask others why they ranked issues such as "an exciting life" or "a sense of accomplishment" above "a clean environment in the future."

**HANDOUT FOR ACTIVITY # 14.5**

VALUE SCALE

Rank

A comfortable life

An exciting life

A sense of accomplishment

A world at peace

A world of beauty

A clean environment in the future

Family security

Free use of the environment now

Happiness

Inner harmony

Mature love

National security

Pleasure

Salvation

Self-respect

Social recognition

True friendship

Wisdom

Copyright © 1997 by Allyn and Bacon

# Overhead Transparencies

These appear at the back of this manual.

**14.1** *Hardiness, Fitness, and Health*

**14.2** *Decisions and Choices to Make When the Symptoms of Illness Develop*

**14.3** *Concerns about Technological Hazards:  The Public versus the Experts*

**14.4** *High-Level versus Low-Level Goals in Life*

**14.5** *Environmental Behavior Can Be Changed by Legislation*

**14.6** *Three Gases Contributing to the Greenhouse Effect*

# Audiovisual Suggestions

### *Allyn and Bacon Video*

* *Health, Mind, and Behavior,* This Allyn and Bacon video discusses how research is forcing a profound rethinking of the relationship between the mind and the traditional model.  You can obtain a copy of this vidio by contacting your Allyn and Bacon representative.  (On Tape #12.)

### *Other Videos and Films*

*Environment,* NSC-1299, color, 16 mins.  Indiana University, Audiovisual Center, Bloomington, IN 47401.  This film outlines current environmental problems.

*People by the Billions,* GS-910, 28 mins.  Indiana University, Audiovisual Center, Bloomington, IN 47401.  Examines the current population explosion, considers past remedies for overpopulation, and suggests two methods to deal with the present problem.

*The Price of Pollution,* color video, 60 mins.  NETCHE Videotape Library, P.O. Box 833111, Nebraska 68501.  Famed environmentalist Barry Commoner discusses the wages of our sin, pollution.

*The City and the Self,* 50324, color, 53 mins.  Pennsylvania State University, Audiovisual Services, Special Services Building, University Park, PA 16802 (814-865-6314).  Study of human relations in the city based on psychological concepts formulated by Stanley Milgram.  Examines city dwellers' perceptions of their cities and their behavior in created situations.

*Noise:  The New Pollutant,* 31321, 30 mins.  Pennsylvania State University, Audiovisual Services, Special Services Building, University Park, PA 16802 (814-865-6314).  Illustrates the harmful effects of prolonged exposure to high levels of noise.

*Stress Reduction:  Strategies That Work,* PB124, video, 30 mins. Insight Media, 121 W. 85th Street, New York, NY 10024 (800-233-9910; 212-721-6316).  Presents the latest information on beating the stress that is associated with certain personalities.

*Health and Lifestyles:  Positive Approaches to Well-Being,* film, 28 mins.  Iowa Films, Media Library, University of Iowa, Iowa City, IA 52242.  This film is designed to motivate viewers to take responsibility for their own health by making informed decisions.

*Heart Attack:  Prevention,* film, 19 mins.  Iowa Films, Media Library, University of Iowa, Iowa City, IA 52242.  Presents a case study of the personality traits and lifestyle factors that make a person a prime candidate for coronary heart disease.

# Critical Thinking/Essay Questions

1. Cigarette companies are currently targeting African-Americans in ad campaigns to increase cigarette sales. What are the ethical issues involved here? What other promotion targets the same group?
2. Analyze yourself. What personal dispositions, behaviors, or concealments may affect your health?
3. Can you think of any personal dispositions, other than those covered in the text, that may affect the health of those who have them?
4. Explain the grand vizier's "geometric progression." Can you think of any reasons that it might not apply to population explosion in the future?
5. Indicate how some of the controversies in the United States concerning methods of birth control may spread to other countries.
6. List and discuss current environmental problems. What means would you suggest to mobilize people to do something about these problems?
7. Design a program to induce citizens to take action against litter. Trace the sequence of events that proceeds from legislation to behavior change to attitude change with regard to antilitter behavior.
8. Indicate how noise affects health, academic functioning, and social relations. What kind of noise is the most damaging?
9. Trace the psychological effects of air pollution, including that produced by smokers. What are the interpersonal problems involved with controlling "passive smoking?"

# Sources for Lecture

Abas, F. (1989, December). Rocky Flats: A big mistake from day one. *Bulletin of the Atomic Scientists*, pp. 19-24. Denver is downwind from the most infamous of several frightening nuclear weapons plants. The Rocky Flats story is a tale of things to come: we will have to face a multibillion-dollar cleanup during the later 1990s and early 2000s.

Carey, J., & Silberner, J. (1987, August, 17). Fending off the leading killers. *U.S. News and World Report*, pp. 56-65. A cogent summary of what one can do to save one's own life--a testimonial to the role of behavior in health. The end of the article is a "heart health" test.

Ehrlich, P., & Ehrlich, A. (1986, April). World population crisis. *Bulletin of the Atomic Scientists*, pp. 13-19. Two world-famous biologists present shocking statistics concerning the present and future population crises. They state that the birth of a baby in the United States is 200 times more disastrous than a birth in a third-world country, because an American baby will live to consume so much more.

Fackelmann, K. A. (1991, November 30). Many doctors would shun AIDS patients. *Science News, 140,* 356. Talk about doctor-patient communication problems...some physicians say they would not communicate with, or get near, AIDS patients.

Kunz, A. (1989, December). Highest disregard. *Mother Jones*, pp. 33-36, 44-48. Scientist Sherwood Rowland succeeded in convincing politicians and business figures that spray can propellants were destroying the ozone layer. Now he is battling the electronics industry over their use of solvents that destroy the ozone layer. So far he has made little headway.

*Morbidity and Mortality Weekly Report.* (1992, July 31). Trends in ischemic heart disease mortality. 41 (No. 30), 548-549 and 555. Heart disease due to reduction of the blood supply (therefore oxygen) to the heart muscle, leading to muscle destruction, is the leading cause of death in the United States. This article indicates that European-American men lead in death rate from this disease, followed by African-American men. Women, black and white, are far behind and show similar rates. All groups are displaying declines over time, but African-American women are leveling off, perhaps to increase in the future.

Revkin, A. C. (1988, October). Endless summer: Living with the greenhouse effect. *Discover,* pp. 50-61. this comprehensive and highly readable article maps out (literally) where and how the greenhouse gases will wreak their effects. Also contains information concerning sources of the effect and how it might be short-circuited.

Sagan, C., & Druyan, A. (1990, April 22). Is it possible to be pro-life and pro-choice? *Parade,* pp. 4-8. The answer is yes according to this famous scientist and wife Druyan, an activist who marshals the forces of science for the good of people.

Siegel, P. Z., et al. (1991, December). Behavioral risk factor surveillance, 1986-1990. *Morbidity and Mortality Weekly Report, 40.* This report looks at a number of behavioral factors in health: lack of leisure-time physical activity, sedentary lifestyle, smoking, being overweight, binge alcohol consumption, drinking and driving, and safety belt nonuse.

Slovic, P., Flynn, J. H. & Layman, M. (1991, December 13). Perceived risk, trust, and politics of nuclear waste. *Science, 254,* 1603-1607. Slovic and colleagues show how disposal of high-level radioactive waste has been impeded by "dread risk" fears of the public based on their perceptions of mishandling of nuclear weapons waste and lingering mistrust of everything nuclear. Turning around public perceptions will not be easy.

## Professional Update: Current Articles from Professional Sources

Baradell, J. G., & Klein, K. (1993). Relationship of life stress and body consciousness to hypervigilant decision making. *Journal of Personality and Social Psychology, 64,* 267-273. Private body consciousness (PBC) was related to decision making on an analogies task. There is little relationship between life stress and decision quality or strategies for low PBCs, but for high-PBC people increasing life stress was associated with poorer performance and the use of hypervigilant strategies.

Cohen, S., Tyrrell, D. A. J., & Smith, A. P. (1993). Negative life events, perceived stress, negative affect, and susceptibility to the common cold. *Journal of Personality and Social Psychology, 64,* 131-140. Subjects completed a questionnaire on stressful life events, perceived stress, and negative affects and then were exposed to a cold virus. High scores on each of the three scales were associated with higher risk of developing a cold. The relationship between events and illness, however, was mediated by a different biologic process than that between perceived stress and illness or negative affect and illness.

Freudenburg, W. R., & Pastor, S. K., (1992). NIMBYs and LULUs: Stalking the syndromes. *Journal of Social Issues, 48,* 39-61. Three main perceptions of the public's responses to technological risks are examined: views of the public as ignorant/irrational, selfish, and prudent. The first perception is deemed unsupported; analysis of the second two involves differences between citizens and specialists. The authors offer still another viewpoint.

Hallman, W. K., & Wandersman, A. (1992). Attribution of responsibility and individual and collective coping with environmental threats. *Journal of Social Issues, 48,* 101-118. Summarizes the many sources of stress that often accompany environmental threats, individual and collective strategies for coping with environmental threats, and the efficacy of these strategies. Some of the problems with measuring coping strategies and with gauging their success are discussed.

Liberman, A., & Chaiken, S. (1992). Defensive processing of personally relevant health messages. *Personality and Social Psychology Bulletin, 18,* 669-679. Following exposure to either a low- or a high-threat message, subjects for whom the message was high in relevance were less likely to believe in the threat. Processing measures suggested that high-relevance subjects processed threatening parts of both messages in a biased fashion.

Mendolia, M., & Kleck, R. E. (1993). Effects of talking about a stressful event on arousal: does what we talk about make a difference? *Journal of Personality and social Psychology, 64,* 283-292. Subjects talked about their emotional reactions to a stressful stimulus or about facts relating to it. Those in the emotional reaction condition showed stronger autonomic arousal during the talk phase, but a lesser reaction and more positive affect upon a second exposure to the stimulus.

Thompson, S. C., Sobolew-Shubin, a., Galbraith, M. E., Schwankovsky, L, & Cruzen, D. (1993). Maintaining perceptions of control: Finding perceived control in low-control circumstances. *Journal of Personality and Social Psychology, 64,* 293-304. Cancer patients' perceptions of personal control were related to coping with stress. Those with greater perceptions of control were less depressed. More important than control of the course of the disease was control of daily emotional reactions and physical symptoms.

Vaughan, E., & Seifert, M. (1992). Variability in the framing of risk issues. *Journal of Social Issues, 48,* 119-135. Variability in framing risk issues can exacerbate conflict, leading to differences among people as to which perspectives are judged legitimate or valid, what solutions are seen as reasonable, and what type of information is seen as useful or relevant.

*Related Readings:* The following selections from *Readings in Social Psychology: General, Classic, and Contemporary Selections,* 3rd Edition, by Wayne Lesko (Allyn and Bacon, 1997) accompany this chapter.

Krajick, K. (1988). "Private passions and public health." Users of AIDS testing centers and medical personnel react to AIDS testing. (Article 40).

Sommer, R., & Becker, F. D. (1969). "Territorial defense and the good neighbor." Use of markers to defend space in public areas varies as a function of area density. Neighbors are important for legitimizing space ownership. (Article 41).

Baron, R. A., & Bronfen, M. I. (1994). "A whiff of reality: Empirical evidence concerning the effects of pleasant fragrances on work-related behavior." The following questions are addressed in this article: "Do pleasant fragrances make us feel better? Do they have any impact on out behavior?" (Article 42).

# Table of Contents

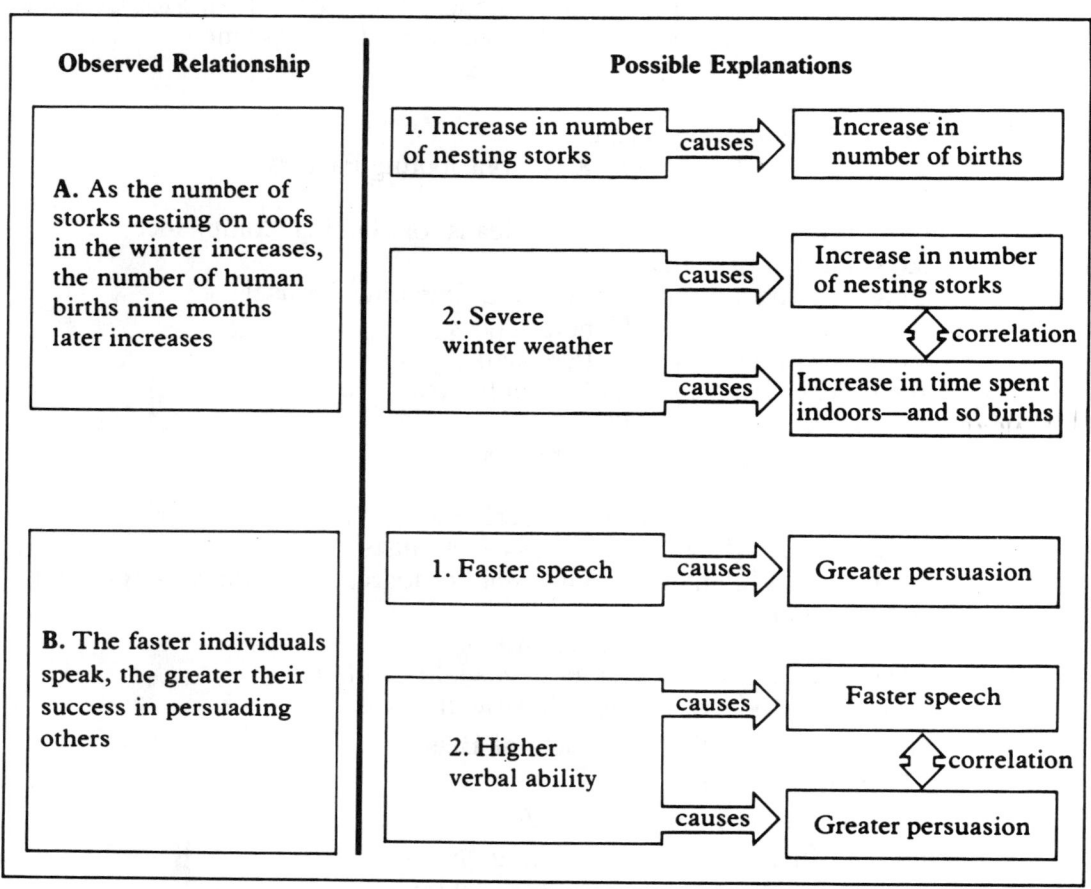

Copyright © 1997, 1994, 1991, 1987, 1984 by Allyn and Bacon

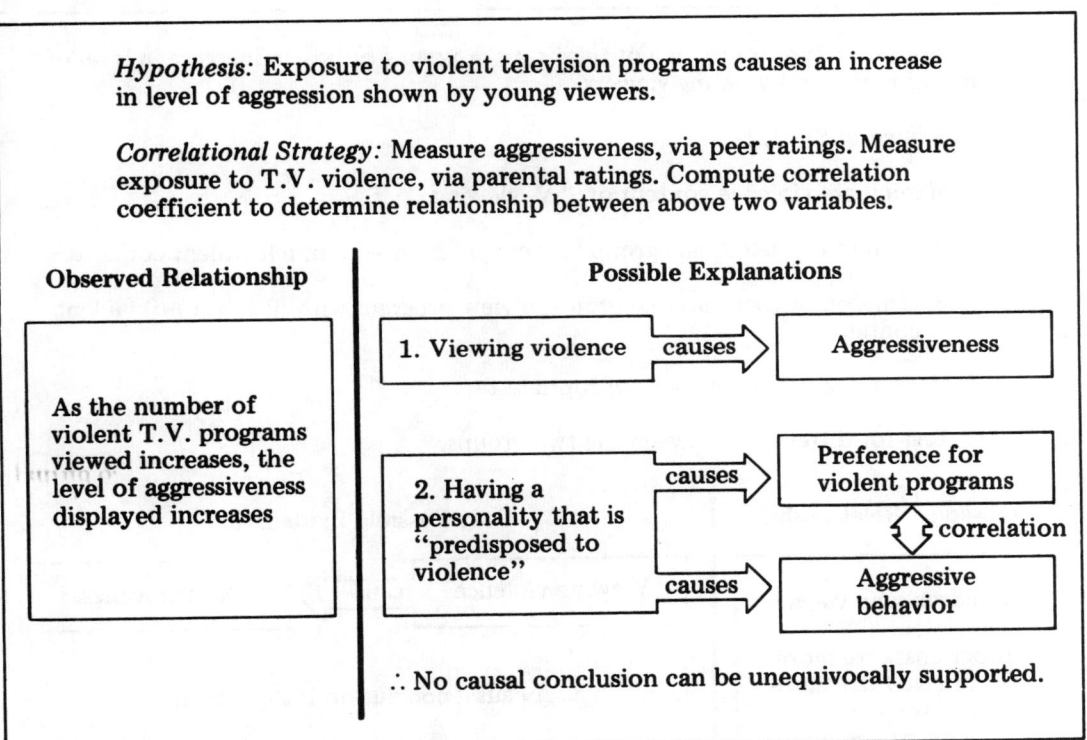

*Hypothesis:* Exposure to violent television programs causes an increase in level of aggression shown by young viewers.

*Correlational Strategy:* Measure aggressiveness, via peer ratings. Measure exposure to T.V. violence, via parental ratings. Compute correlation coefficient to determine relationship between above two variables.

**Observed Relationship**

**Possible Explanations**

As the number of violent T.V. programs viewed increases, the level of aggressiveness displayed increases

1. Viewing violence — causes → Aggressiveness

2. Having a personality that is "predisposed to violence" — causes → Preference for violent programs ⟷ correlation — causes → Aggressive behavior

∴ No causal conclusion can be unequivocally supported.

Copyright © 1997, 1994, 1991, 1987, 1984 by Allyn and Bacon

*Hypothesis:* Exposure to violent television programs causes an increase in level of aggression shown by young viewers.

*Experimental Strategy:*

  I. Manipulate violence content of T.V. viewing.

    A. Randomly assign one group to view program with much violent content.

    B. Randomly assign second group to view program with little (or no) violent content.

  II. Measure aggressiveness via appropriate test.

  III. Test for difference between the two groups.

**Observed Relationship**            **Only Possible Explanation**

| Children who viewed the violent T.V. programs were more aggressive than those who viewed the nonviolent program |
|---|

Viewing violence ⟶ **causes** ⟶ Aggressiveness

∴ A causal conclusion is supported

Copyright © 1997, 1994, 1991, 1987, 1984 by Allyn and Bacon

# Confounding of Variables: A Dangerous Trap for Unwary Experimenters

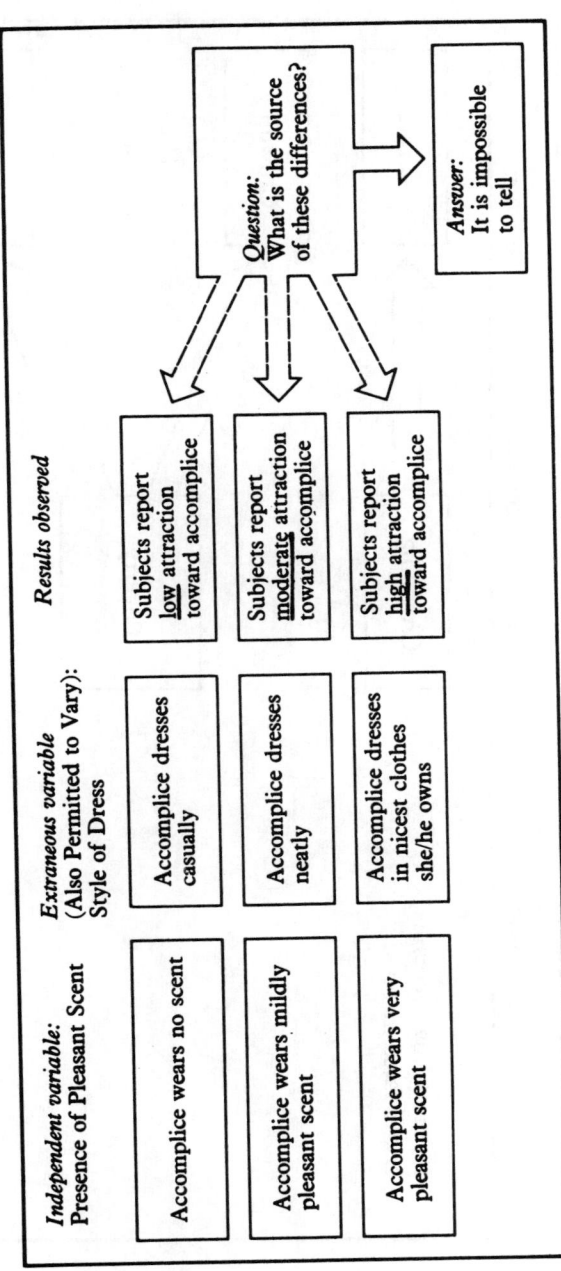

*Independent variable:*
Presence of Pleasant Scent

*Extraneous variable*
(Also Permitted to Vary):
Style of Dress

*Results observed*

Accomplice wears no scent

Accomplice wears mildly pleasant scent

Accomplice wears very pleasant scent

Accomplice dresses casually

Accomplice dresses neatly

Accomplice dresses in nicest clothes she/he owns

Subjects report low attraction toward accomplice

Subjects report moderate attraction toward accomplice

Subjects report high attraction toward accomplice

*Question:*
What is the source of these differences?

*Answer:*
It is impossible to tell

Copyright © 1997, 1994, 1991, 1987, 1984 by Allyn and Bacon

# Correlation versus Causation: A Subtle but Crucial Distinction

T–1.5

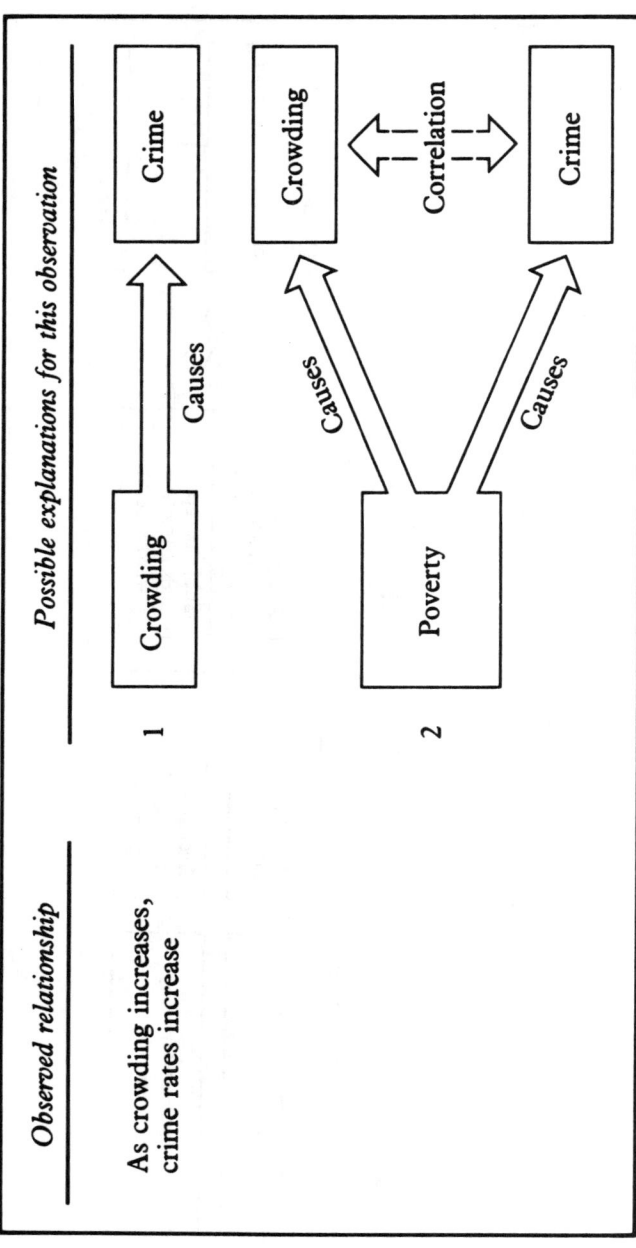

*Observed relationship*

As crowding increases, crime rates increase

*Possible explanations for this observation*

1   Crowding  → Causes →  Crime

2   Poverty  → Causes →  Crowding  ← Correlation →  Crime
            → Causes →

Copyright © 1997, 1994, 1991, 1987, 1984 by Allyn and Bacon

## Correspondent Inference: When Do We Infer the Traits of Others?

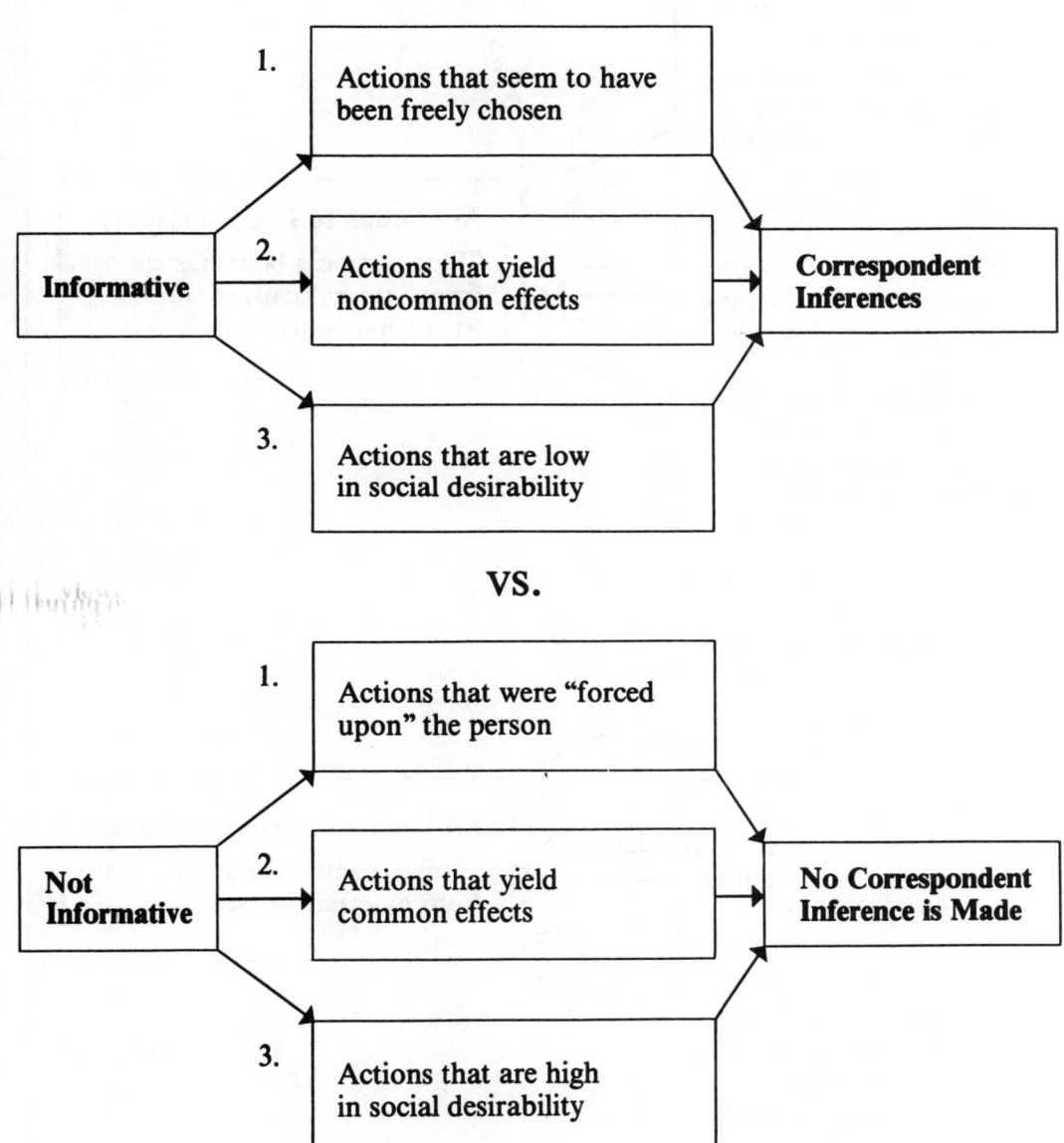

**Informative**

1. Actions that seem to have been freely chosen

2. Actions that yield noncommon effects

3. Actions that are low in social desirability

→ **Correspondent Inferences**

**VS.**

**Not Informative**

1. Actions that were "forced upon" the person

2. Actions that yield common effects

3. Actions that are high in social desirability

→ **No Correspondent Inference is Made**

Copyright © 1997, 1994, 1991, 1987, 1984 by Allyn and Bacon

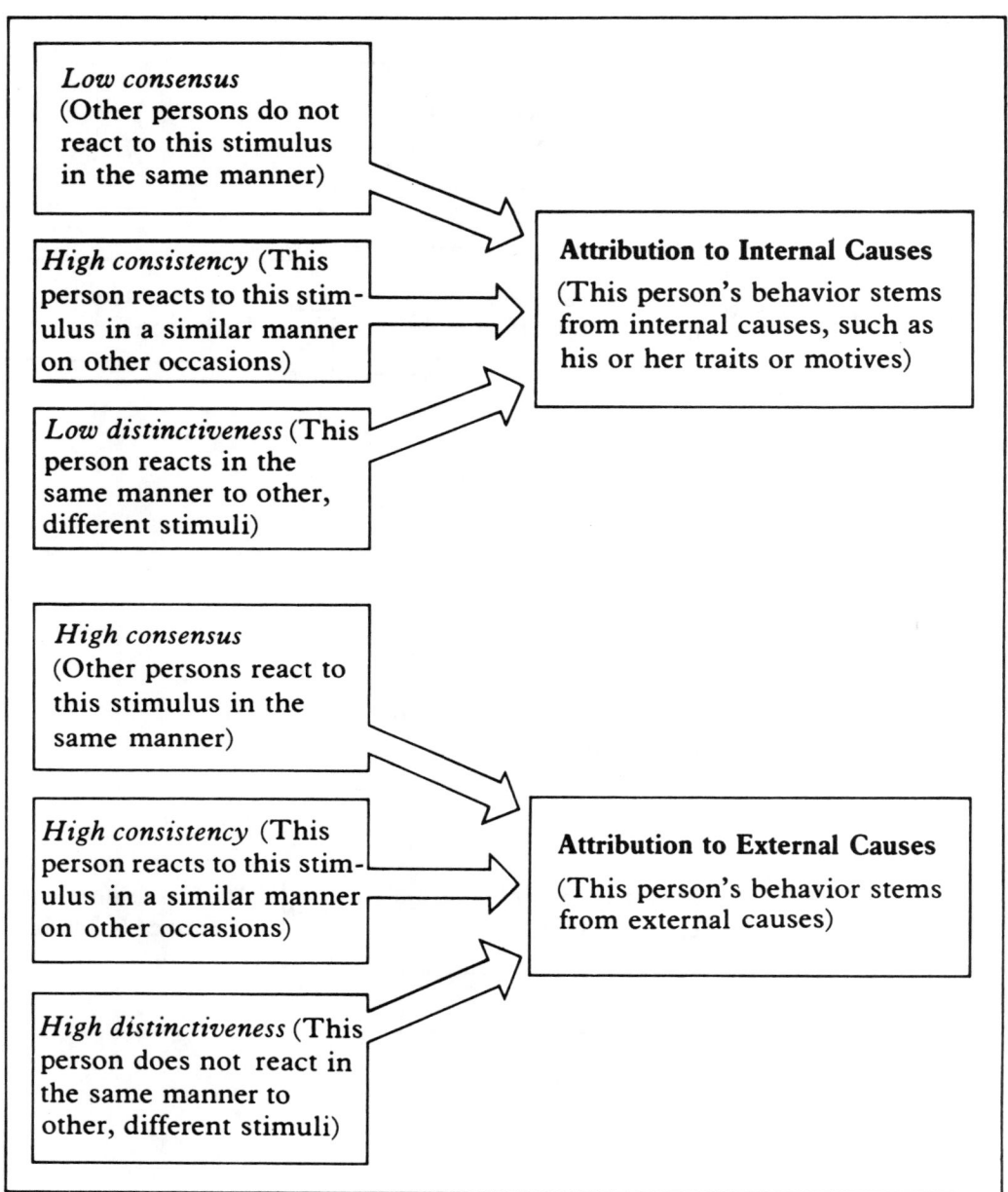

Copyright © 1997, 1994, 1991, 1987, 1984 by Allyn and Bacon

# Discounting and Augmenting: Two Basic Principles of Causal Attribution

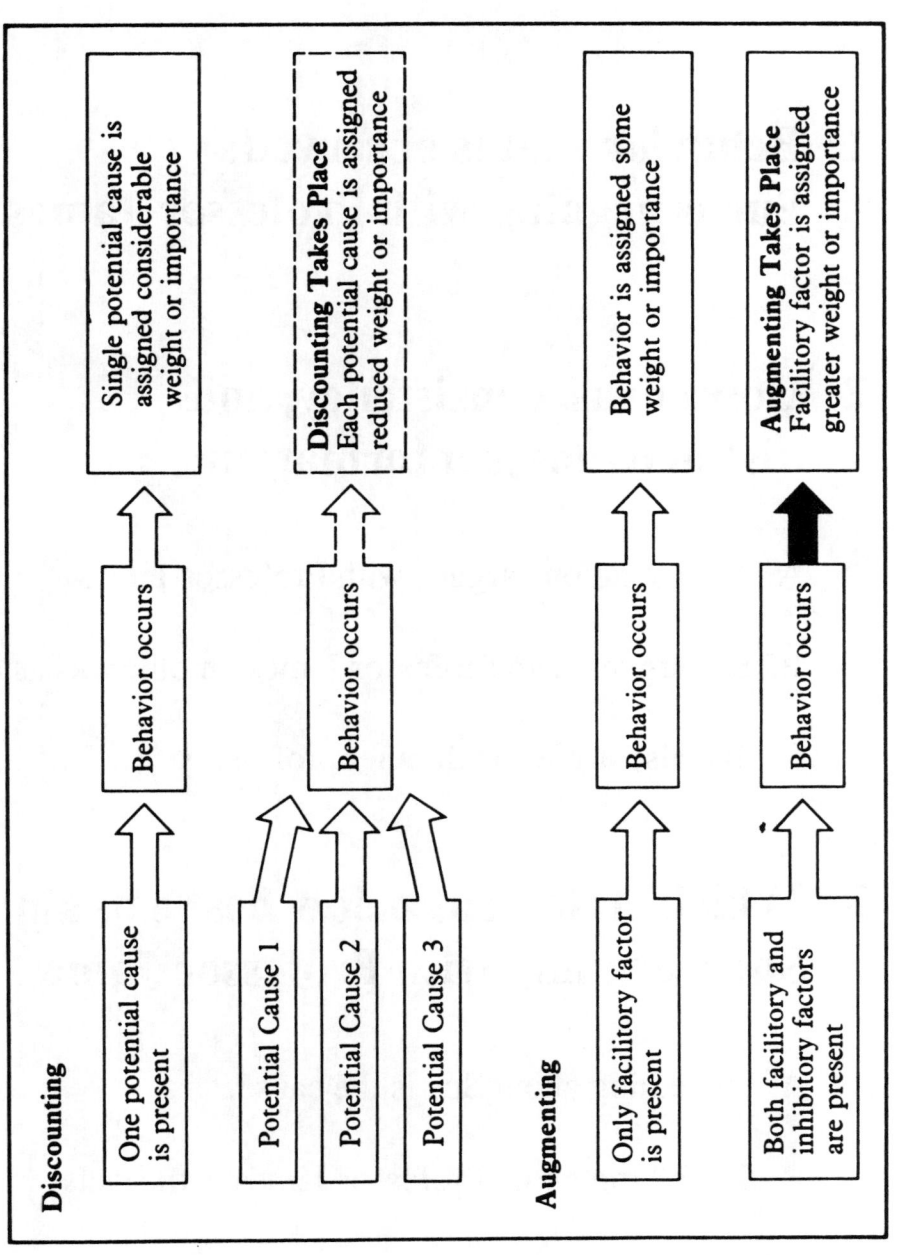

**Discounting**

One potential cause is present → Behavior occurs → Single potential cause is assigned considerable weight or importance

Potential Cause 1 / Potential Cause 2 / Potential Cause 3 → Behavior occurs → **Discounting Takes Place** Each potential cause is assigned reduced weight or importance

**Augmenting**

Only facilitory factor is present → Behavior occurs → Behavior is assigned some weight or importance

Both facilitory and inhibitory factors are present → Behavior occurs → **Augmenting Takes Place** Facilitory factor is assigned greater weight or importance

Copyright © 1997, 1994, 1991, 1987, 1984 by Allyn and Bacon

1. **Behavior that is observed: Sue is arguing with Professor James**

2. **Consensus, consistency, and distinctiveness information:**

   A. Almost no one argues with Professor James.

   B. Sue argues with Professor James on other occasions

   C. Sue also argues with other professors.

3. **Which statement below best explains Sue's arguing with Professor James?**

   A. Something about Sue is the cause.

   B. Something about Professor James is the cause

Copyright © 1997, 1994, 1991, 1987, 1984 by Allyn and Bacon

## 1. Behavior that is observed: Lori is arguing with Professor Ward

## 2. Consensus, consistency, and distinctiveness information

A. Many people argue with Professor Ward.

B. Lori argues with Professor Ward on other occasions.

C. Lori does not argue with other professors.

## 3. Which statement below best explains Lori's arguing with Professor Ward?

A. Something about Lori is the cause.

B. Something about Professor Ward is the cause

Copyright © 1997, 1994, 1991, 1987, 1984 by Allyn and Bacon

# 1. Behavior that is observed: Ann is arguing with Professor Sanders

# 2. Consensus, consistency, and distinctiveness information:

A. Almost no one argues with Professor Sanders.

B. Ann argues with Professor Sanders on other occasions.

C. Ann does not argue with other professors.

# 3. Which statement below best explains Ann's arguing with Professor Sanders?

A. Something about Ann is the cause.

B. Something about Professor Sanders is the cause.

(No simple attribution seems logical; instead, we may require some type of person/situation interaction explanation.)

Copyright © 1997, 1994, 1991, 1987, 1984 by Allyn and Bacon

# Self-Schemata and Memory

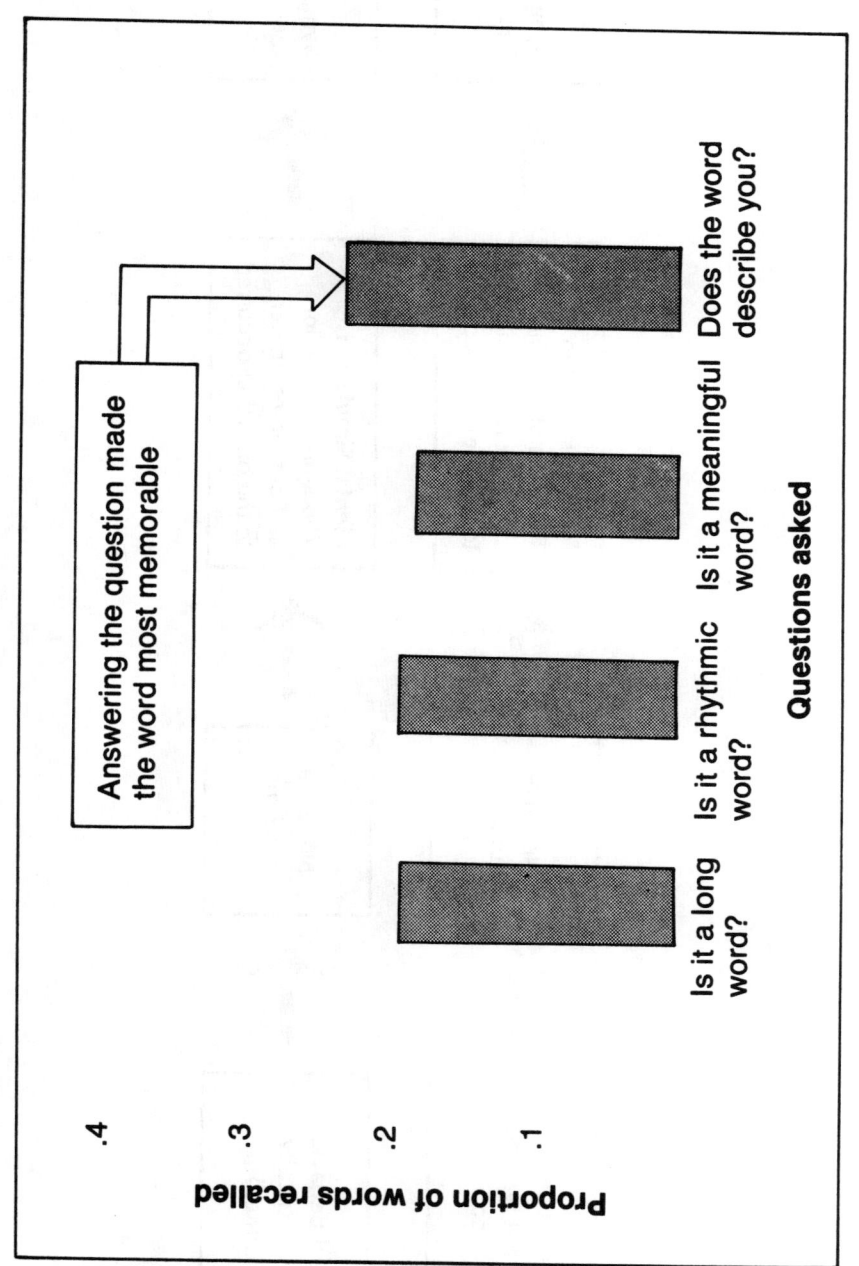

Questions asked

Proportion of words recalled

Is it a long word?

Is it a rhythmic word?

Is it a meaningful word?

Does the word describe you?

Answering the question made the word most memorable

.4

.3

.2

.1

Copyright © 1997, 1994, 1991, 1987, 1984 by Allyn and Bacon

# Mental Simulations and Sympathy for Victims

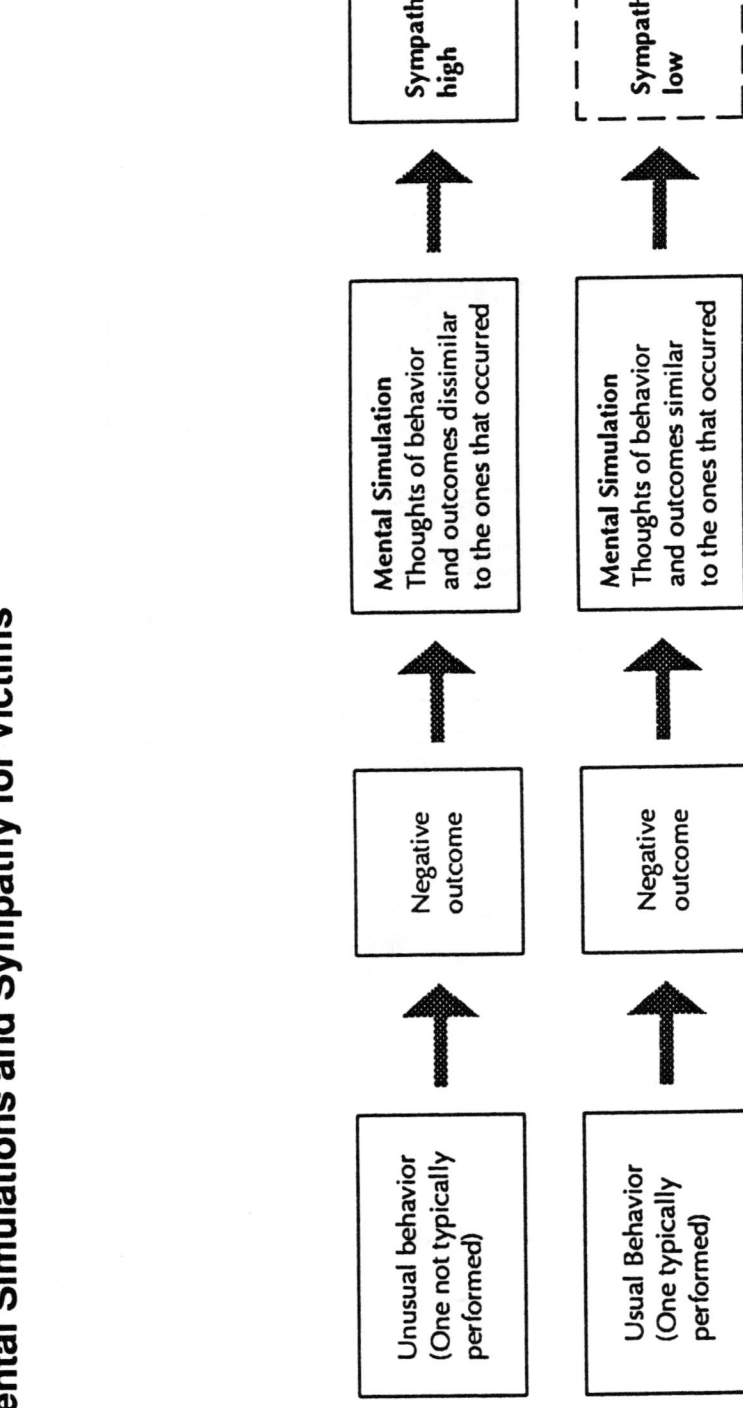

Copyright © 1997, 1994, 1991, 1987, 1984 by Allyn and Bacon

**Mood and Social Judgements: A Field Study**

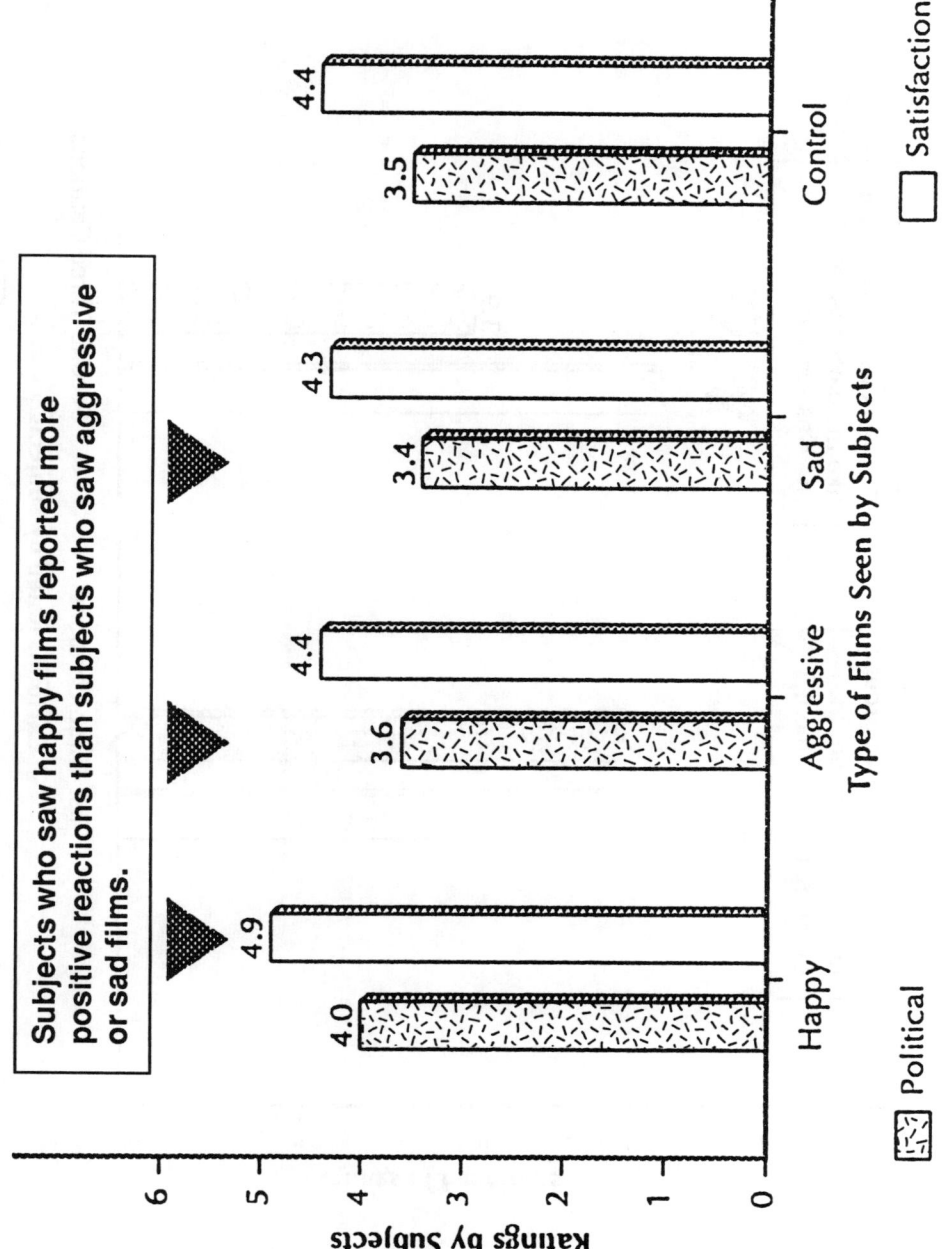

Subjects who saw happy films reported more positive reactions than subjects who saw aggressive or sad films.

Ratings by Subjects

6
5
4
3
2
1
0

Happy          Aggressive          Sad          Control

Type of Films Seen by Subjects

4.0  4.9
3.6  4.4
3.4  4.3
3.5  4.4

Political

Satisfaction

Copyright © 1997, 1994, 1991, 1987, 1984 by Allyn and Bacon

# How Cognition Sometimes Shapes Affect

T–3.4

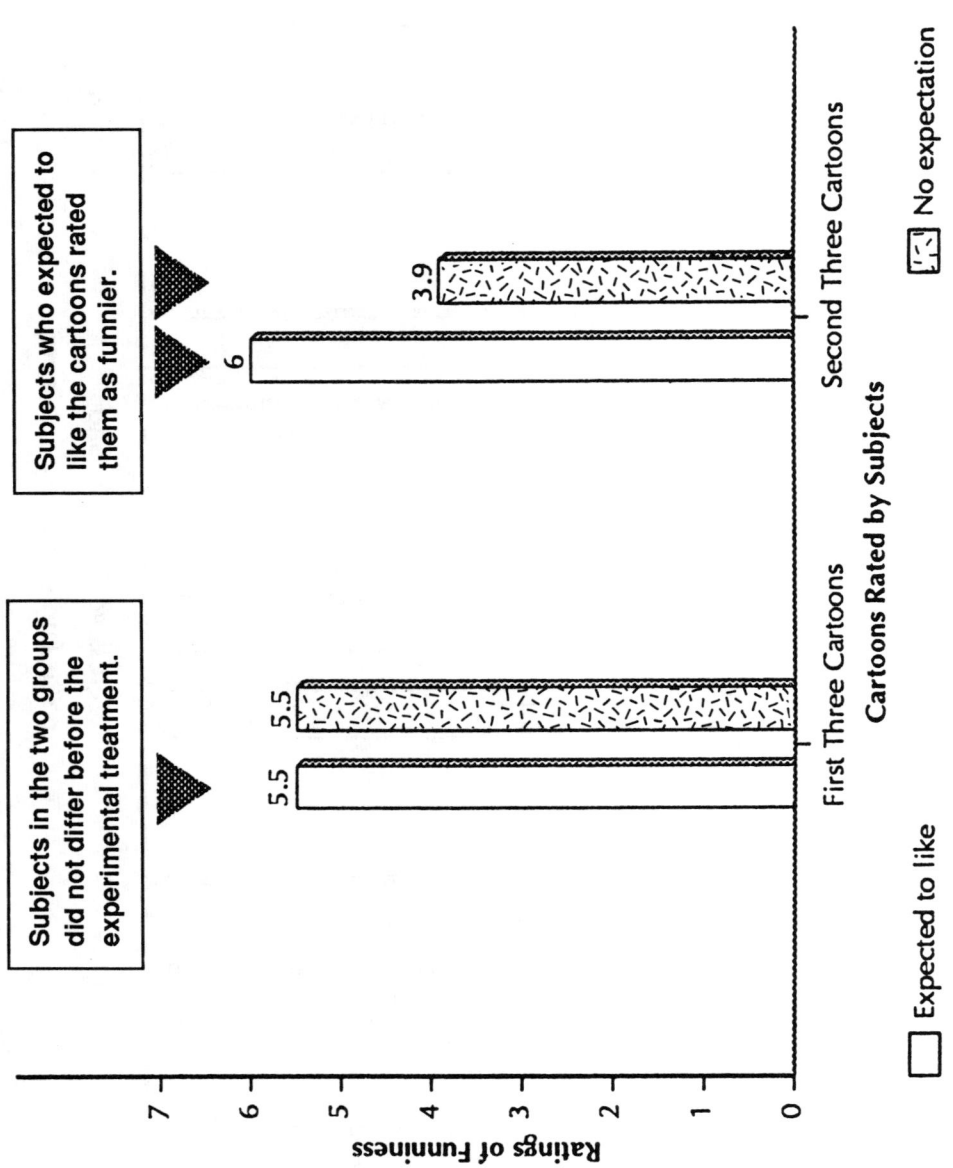

Subjects in the two groups did not differ before the experimental treatment.

Subjects who expected to like the cartoons rated them as funnier.

Ratings of Funniness

7 6 5 4 3 2 1 0

First Three Cartoons

Second Three Cartoons

Cartoons Rated by Subjects

5.5 5.5 6 3.9

☐ Expected to like ▨ No expectation

Copyright © 1997, 1994, 1991, 1987, 1984 by Allyn and Bacon

# Cognitive Dissonance Theory in a Nutshell

*What is cognitive dissonance?*
Feeling of *inconsistency* produced when two pieces of information held "in a person's head" are in conflict.

*What is the source of this cognitive dissonance?*
Usually caused by a conflict between our *belief* about something and the *knowledge* that we have performed a behavior contradictory to that belief.

*How do people usually get rid of dissonance?*
Since we don't like dissonance, we change our belief to make it consistent with our action.

Copyright © 1997, 1994, 1991, 1987, 1984 by Allyn and Bacon

# The Forced Compliance Paradigm for Studying the Effects of Engaging in Attitude—Discrepant Behavior

*Stage One:* Obtain a sample of subjects who have a uniform attitude on some issue.

A. One way is to use a "real world" issue where there is general agreement (example: a tuition increase uniformly opposed by students).

B. Another strategy is to induce a "laboratory" attitude (example: have subjects perform a task that uniformly is perceived to be dull and boring).

*Stage Two:* Have subjects perform an attitude—discrepant action.

A. Have them give a talk *favoring* tuition increase.

B. Have them convince the "next subject" that the task is *fun and interesting.*

*Crucial Variable in Stage Two*
The amount of justification or reward provided for subject to perform attitude-discrepant action.

*Stage Three:* Measure the subject's attitude about the tuition increase or the task.

Copyright © 1997, 1994, 1991, 1987, 1984 by Allyn and Bacon

# Dissonance: The Price of Inconsistency

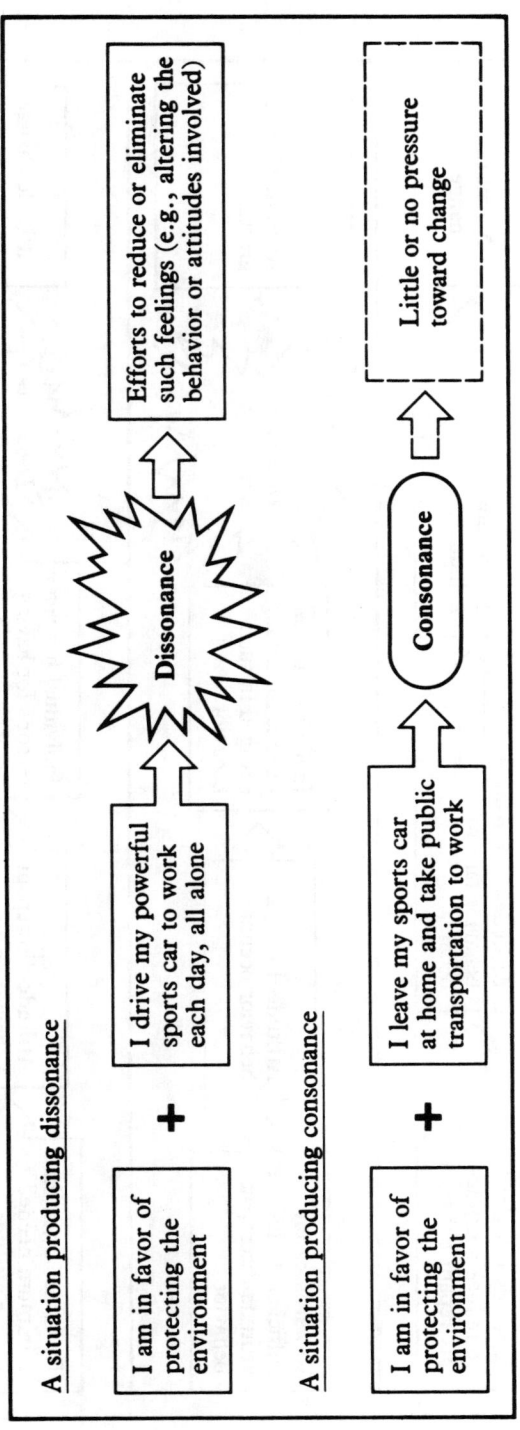

A situation producing dissonance

I am in favor of protecting the environment

+

I drive my powerful sports car to work each day, all alone

Dissonance

Efforts to reduce or eliminate such feelings (e.g., altering the behavior or attitudes involved)

A situation producing consonance

I am in favor of protecting the environment

+

I leave my sports car at home and take public transportation to work

Consonance

Little or no pressure toward change

Copyright © 1997, 1994, 1991, 1987, 1984 by Allyn and Bacon

# Rewards and Forced-Compliance: Why "Less" Sometimes Leads to "More"

| Rewards too small to induce attitude-discrepant behavior | → | Attitude-discrepant behavior fails to occur | → | No dissonance is induced | → | No attitude change |

| Rewards barely sufficient to induce attitude-discrepant behavior | → | Attitude-discrepant behavior occurs | → | Individual has *few* reasons for having engaged in such behavior | → | Dissonance *large* | → | Attitude change great |

| Rewards larger than minimum needed to induce attitude-discrepant behavior | → | Attitude-discrepant behavior occurs | → | Individual has *many* reasons for having engaged in such behavior | → | Dissonance *small* | → | Attitude change small |

Copyright © 1997, 1994, 1991, 1987, 1984 by Allyn and Bacon

# Income
# Religion
# Age
# Race
# Employment
# Education
# Social contact
# Low neuroticism
# Optimism
# Health

Copyright © 1997, 1994, 1991, 1987, 1984 by Allyn and Bacon

# Evolution of Beliefs in Traits

### Up to the 1950's

Trait measures are "x-ray" to the mind

### 1960's through 1970's

Underlying assumption of traits,
behavioral consistency, undermined

### 1980's

Traits can predict when defined narrowly,
when individual differences in consistency considered
and when traits-situations jointly considered

Copyright © 1997, 1994, 1991, 1987, 1984 by Allyn and Bacon

# Personality Development

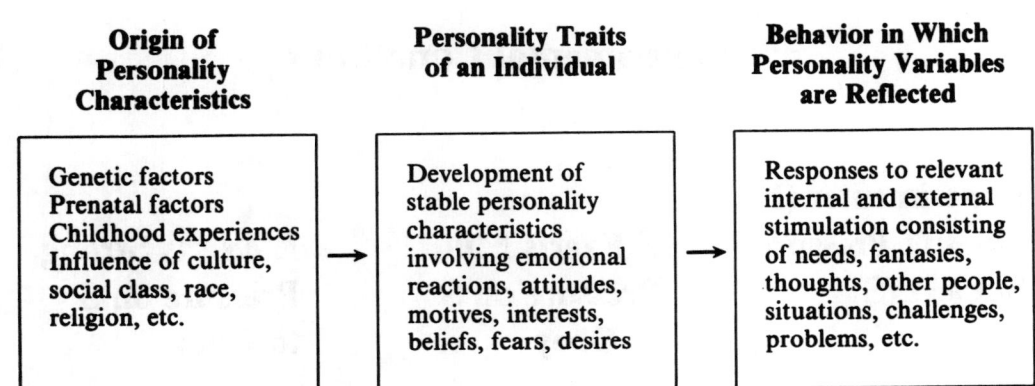

| Origin of Personality Characteristics | Personality Traits of an Individual | Behavior in Which Personality Variables are Reflected |
|---|---|---|
| Genetic factors Prenatal factors Childhood experiences Influence of culture, social class, race, religion, etc. | Development of stable personality characteristics involving emotional reactions, attitudes, motives, interests, beliefs, fears, desires | Responses to relevant internal and external stimulation consisting of needs, fantasies, thoughts, other people, situations, challenges, problems, etc. |

# Personality Measurement

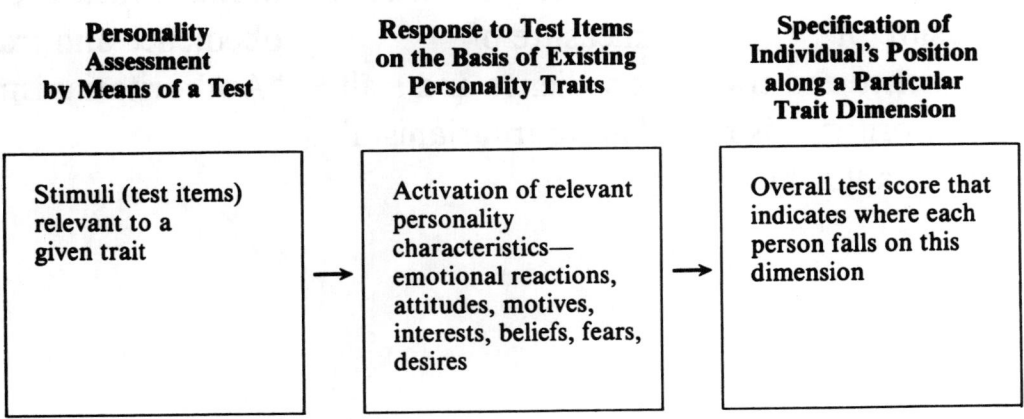

| Personality Assessment by Means of a Test | Response to Test Items on the Basis of Existing Personality Traits | Specification of Individual's Position along a Particular Trait Dimension |
|---|---|---|
| Stimuli (test items) relevant to a given trait | Activation of relevant personality characteristics— emotional reactions, attitudes, motives, interests, beliefs, fears, desires | Overall test score that indicates where each person falls on this dimension |

Copyright © 1997, 1994, 1991, 1987, 1984 by Allyn and Bacon

## Experimental Conditions

| Experimenter (E) Doesn't Pressure Subject (S) to Obey | E Exerts Mild Pressure on S to Obey | E Exerts Strong Pressure on S to Obey |
|---|---|---|
| Weak tendency to obey; strong correlation between measure of obedience and trait "Authoritarianism" (see Chapter 5) | Moderate tendency to obey; weak correlation between measure of obedience and trait "Authoritarianism" | Strong tendency to obey; no correlation between measure of obedience and trait "Authoritarianism" |

Copyright © 1997, 1994, 1991, 1987, 1984 by Allyn and Bacon

**Integrative Research using both Social and Personality Variables**

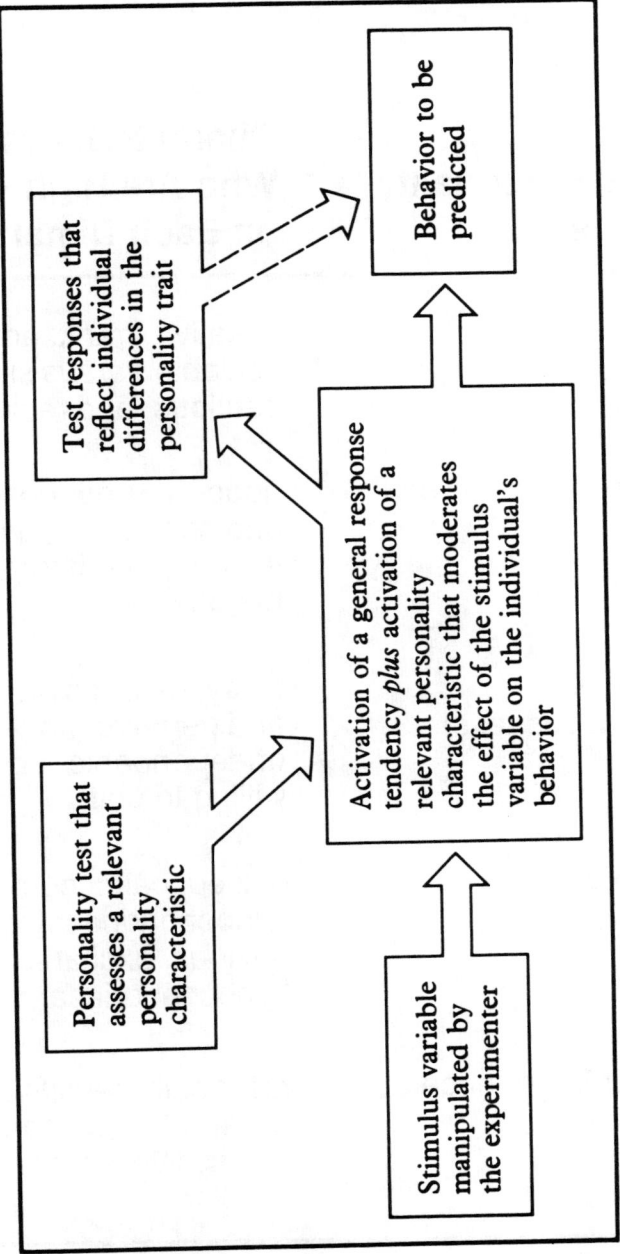

Copyright © 1997, 1994, 1991, 1987, 1984 by Allyn and Bacon

| Five Basic Personality Dimensions | Characteristics of Those Who Are High versus Low on Each Dimension |
|---|---|
| Extraversion | talkative, frank, adventurous, and sociable *versus* silent, secretive, cautious, and reclusive |
| Agreeableness | good-natured, not jealous, gentle, and cooperative *versus* irritable, jealous, headstrong, and negativistic |
| Will to Achieve (or Conscientiousness) | fussy, responsible, scrupulous, and persevering *versus* careless, undependable, unscrupulous, and willing to quit |
| Emotional Stability (or Neuroticism) | poised, calm, composed, and not hypochondriacal *versus* nervous, anxious, excitable, and hypochondriacal |
| Openness to Experience (or Culture) | artistically sensitive, intellectual, polished, and imaginative *versus* insensitive, narrow, crude, and simple |

Copyright © 1997, 1994, 1991, 1987, 1984 by Allyn and Bacon

| Characteristics of Authoritarian Personality | Test Items Constructed to Measure Characteristic |
|---|---|
| Conventionalism | A person who has bad manners, habits, and breeding can hardly expect to get along with decent people. |
| Submission to a strong leader | Obedience and respect for authority are the most important virtues children should learn. |
| Aggression | Homosexuals are hardly better than criminals and ought to be severely punished. |
| Destruction and cynicism | The true American way of life is disappearing so fast that force may be necessary to preserve it. |
| Power and toughness | People can be divided into two distinct classes: the weak and the strong. |
| Anti-intraception | The businessman and the manufacturer are much more important to society than the artist and the professor. |

Copyright © 1997, 1994, 1991, 1987, 1984 by Allyn and Bacon

# A Theory of the Relationship between Racism and Prejudice

T-6.1

The relationship between racism and prejudice. Top curve shows the degree to which racism is incorporated along with other aspects of the culture. Bottom curve shows the degree to which racism shows up in social reactions.

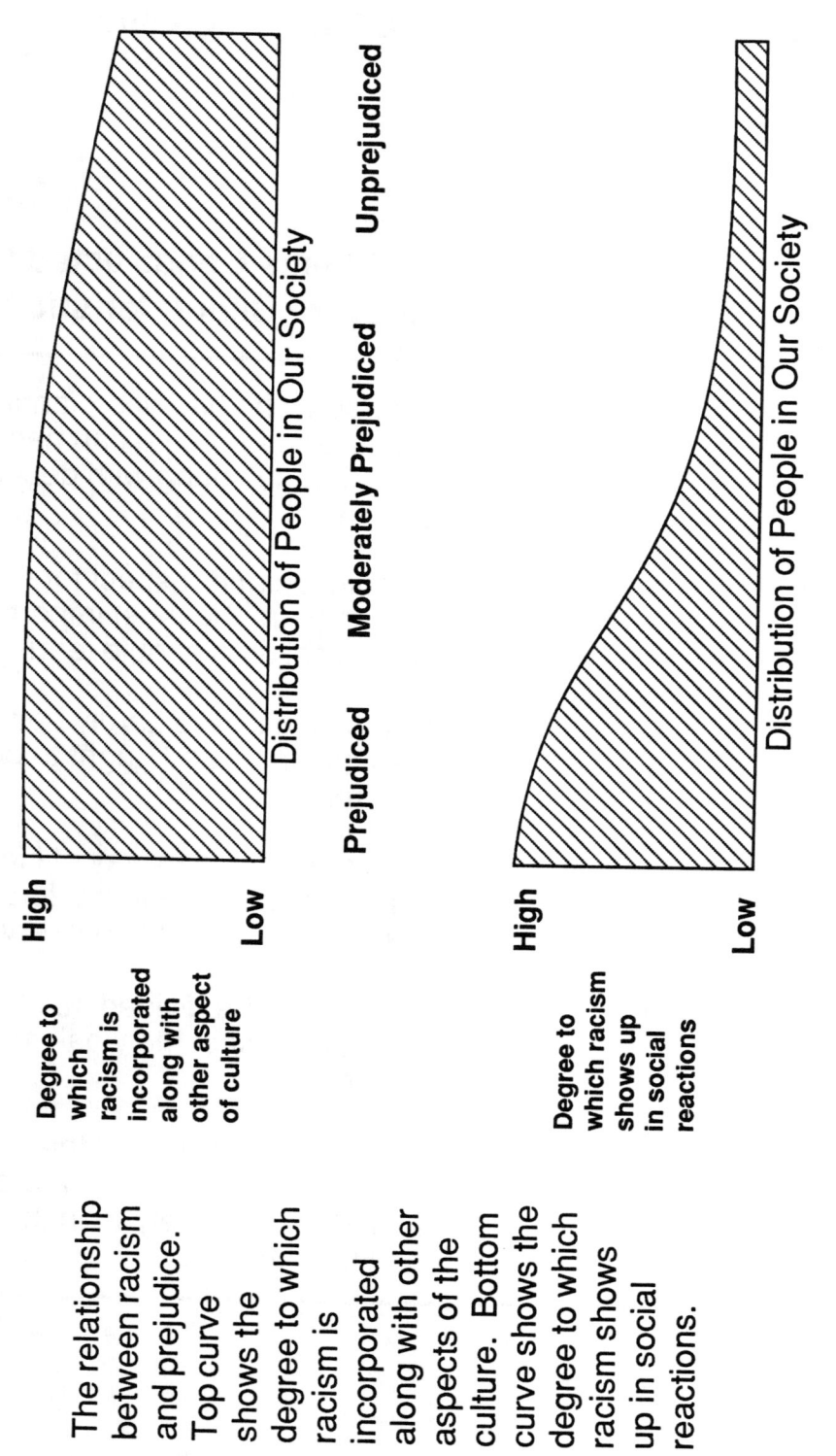

Degree to which racism is incorporated along with other aspect of culture

High

Low

Prejudiced    Moderately Prejudiced    Unprejudiced

Distribution of People in Our Society

Degree to which racism shows up in social reactions

High

Low

Prejudiced    Moderately Prejudiced    Unprejudiced

Distribution of People in Our Society

Copyright © 1997, 1994, 1991, 1987, 1984 by Allyn and Bacon

**Projective** (e.g., "evil figures" in TAT pictures are perceived to be minority persons)

**Semantic Differential**

"An American Indian"

good____:____:____:____:____:____:____:____:____:____bad

**Anchored Scales**

"Foreigners are generally less intelligent than Americans"

agree ____ ____ ____ ____ ____ ____ ____ ____ ____ ____ disagree

**Behavioral** (e.g., when several chairs are present and a minority person is seated next to a wall, how closely to the minority person will a given person place her/his self, relative to when a nonminority person is seated next to the wall)

**Check List** (instruction: check all the groups listed below with whom you enjoy having close relations)

**Stereotype Endorsement** (instruction: check all of those statements that you would endorse)

**Adjective Generation Technique** (see prosocial chapter of this manual) (instruction: Write down five adjectives to describe a _____ person; e.g., female, Chinese, black, etc.)

**Bogus Pipeline** (explained on next transparency)

Copyright © 1997, 1994, 1991, 1987, 1984 by Allyn and Bacon

**"Direct Intergroup Conflict":**   White Californians turning
                                    Japanese-American business
                                    competitors in to authorities
                                    for incarceration during
                                    World War II.

**"Social Categorization":**        "Us" (the "Good Guys")
                                    versus "Them" (the
                                    "Bad Guys").

**"Personality":**                  Authoritarians submit to a
                                    "leader" (e.g., Hitler) who will
                                    "save" them from the objects
                                    of their fear and loathing.

**"Early Experience":**             Media and parental reactions
                                    paint a picture of minorities
                                    as inferior.

Copyright © 1997, 1994, 1991, 1987, 1984 by Allyn and Bacon

# The Tendency to View Outgroups as More Homogeneous than Ingroups: Empirical Evidence

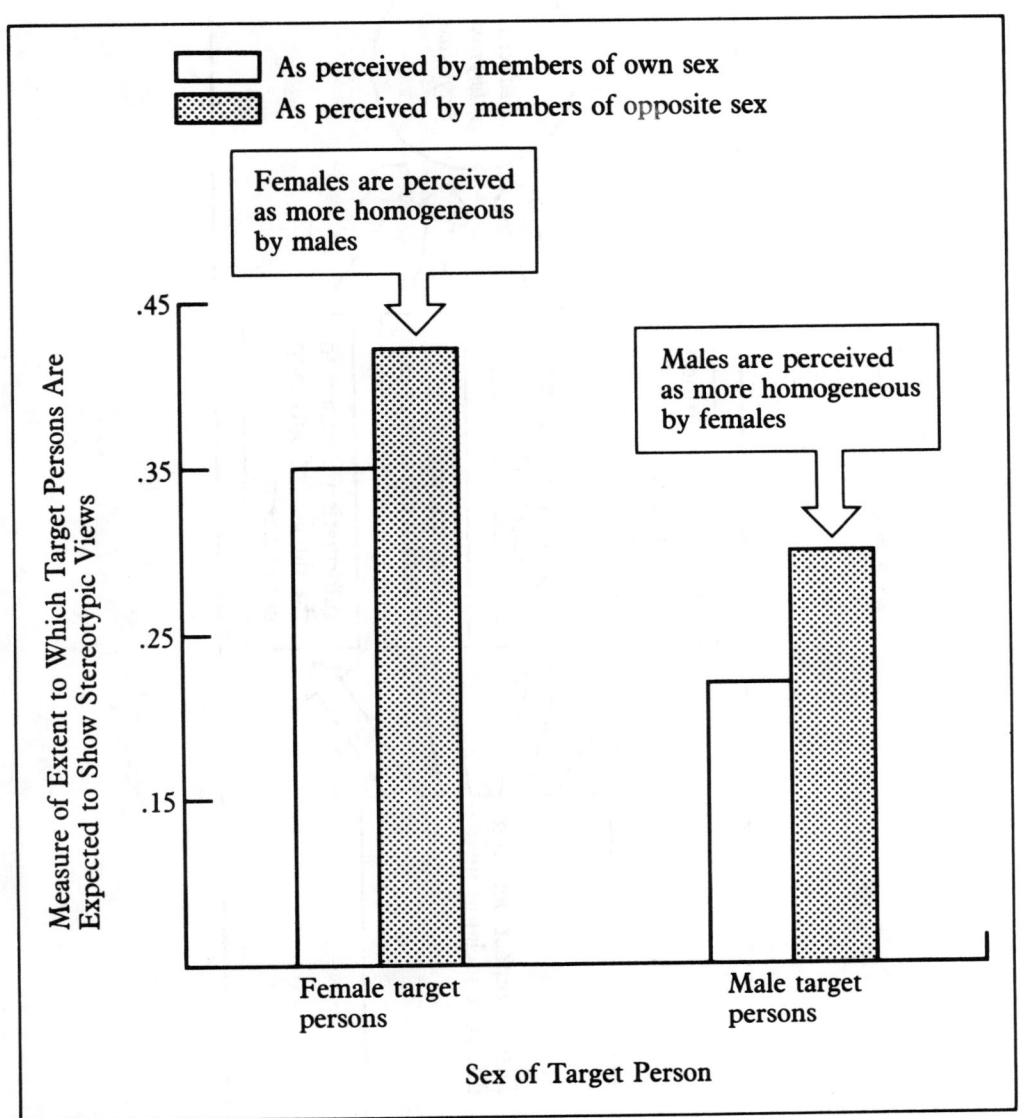

Copyright © 1997, 1994, 1991, 1987, 1984 by Allyn and Bacon

# Intergroup Contact: How It Exerts Its Effects

Direct contact between different social groups

- Increased recognition of similarity
- Increased attraction produced by the "mere exposure" effect
- Disconfirmation of negative stereotypes
- Information contrary to the illusion of outgroup homogeneity

*Reduced intergroup prejudice*

Copyright © 1997, 1994, 1991, 1987, 1984 by Allyn and Bacon

# Male and Female Executives: The Stereotype that Failed

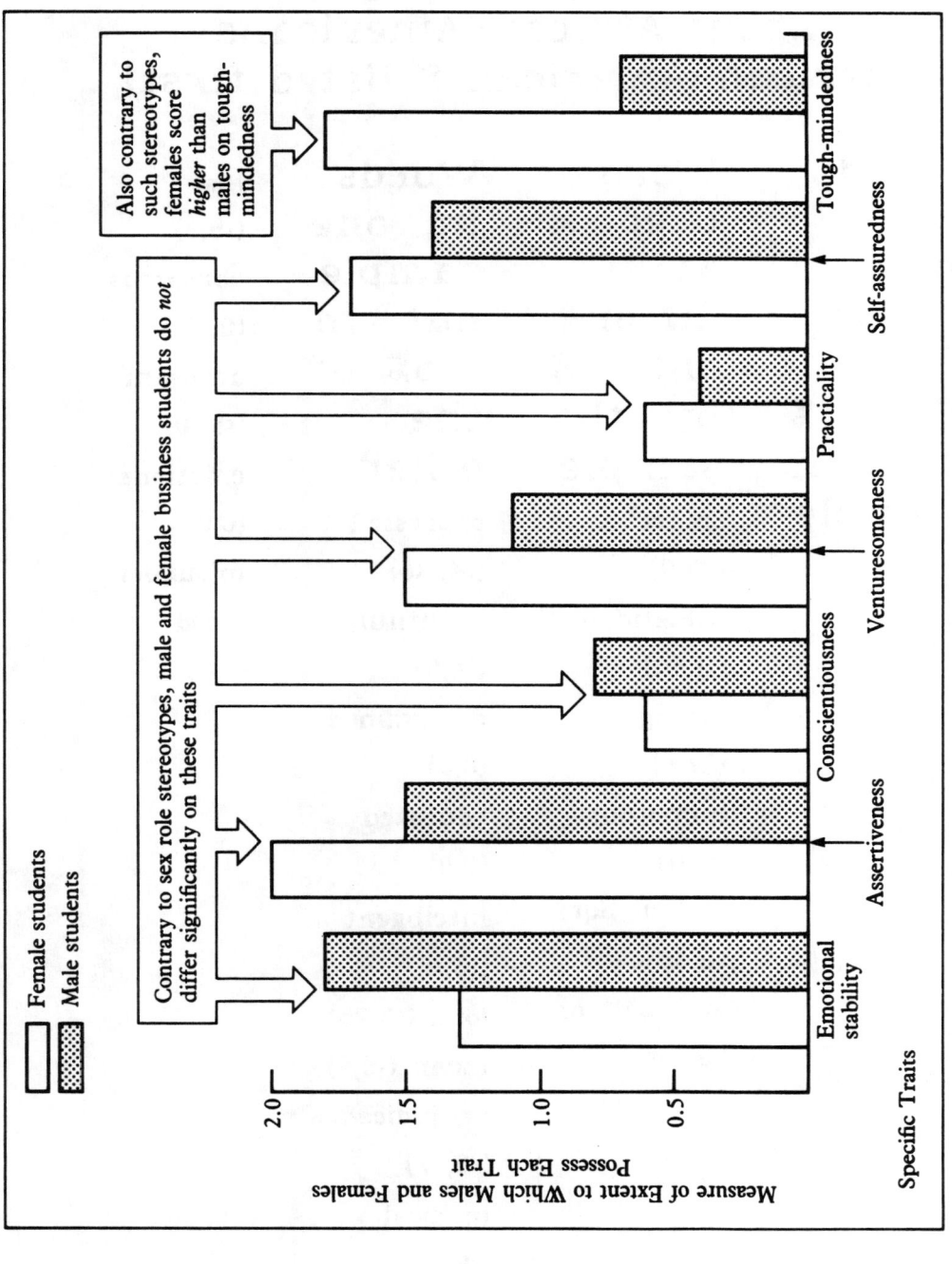

Copyright © 1997, 1994, 1991, 1987, 1984 by Allyn and Bacon

# Agreements and Disagreements about African-Americans
## (African-American % listed first)

| Words used by about the Same % of each Sample* | Words used at differ-ent % by the sample | Words in one sample but in < 5% of the other | fast (<5,6) |
|---|---|---|---|
| corrupt (8,11) | smart# (27,9) | oppressed (14, <5) | obnoxious (0,7) |
| independent (10,10) | athletic (11,40) | beautiful (14,0) | arrogant (<5,10) |
| funny (6,10) | strong (27,6) | determined (8,0) | emotional (6,0) |
| friendly (10,11) | humorous (6,21) | educated (8,0) | misunder-stood (6,0) |
| poor (6,6) | # Chi Sqrs significant at .03 or better | intelligent (13,<5) | |
| *Chi Sqrs not significance | | loud (<5,25) | |
| | | mean (<5,9) | |
| | | prejudiced (<5, 7) | |
| | | musical (<5,7) | |
| | | moody (0,6) | |

Copyright © 1994 by Allyn and Bacon

Copyright © 1997, 1994, 1991, 1987, 1984 by Allyn and Bacon

# Agreements and Disagreements about European-Americans
## (European-American % listed first)

| Words used by About the Same % by each Sample | Words used at Different % by the two Samples | Words in one Sample, but in < 5% of the Other |
|---|---|---|
| inventive (12,6)* | competitive (19,6) | egotistical (7,<5) |
| smart (32,19) | prejudiced (10,22)* | free (6,0) |
| greedy (19,11) | corrupt (6,41) | happy (6,0) |
| educated (7,8) | *Chi Sqr. signifi- | kind (6,0) |
| rich (10,13) | cant at least at | mean (<5,16) |
| *Chi Sqr not | the .04 level | humorous (12,<5) |
| significant | | lazy (12,<5) |
| | | intelligent (10,<5) |
| | | racist (0,10) |
| | | selfish (0,11) |
| | | independent (12,<5) |
| | | arrogant (15,<5) |
| | | conceited (7<5) |
| | | friendly (15,<5) |

Copyright © 1997, 1994, 1991, 1987, 1984 by Allyn and Bacon

# The Reinforcement-Affect Model of Attraction

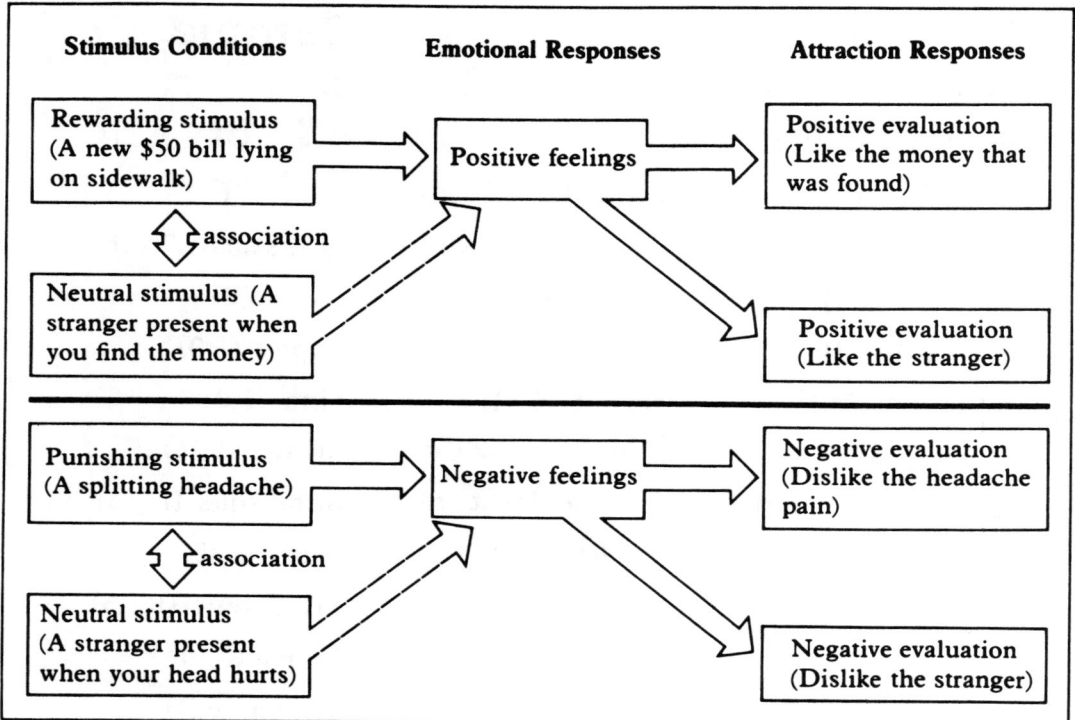

Copyright © 1997, 1994, 1991, 1987, 1984 by Allyn and Bacon

# The Three-Factor Theory of Passionate Love

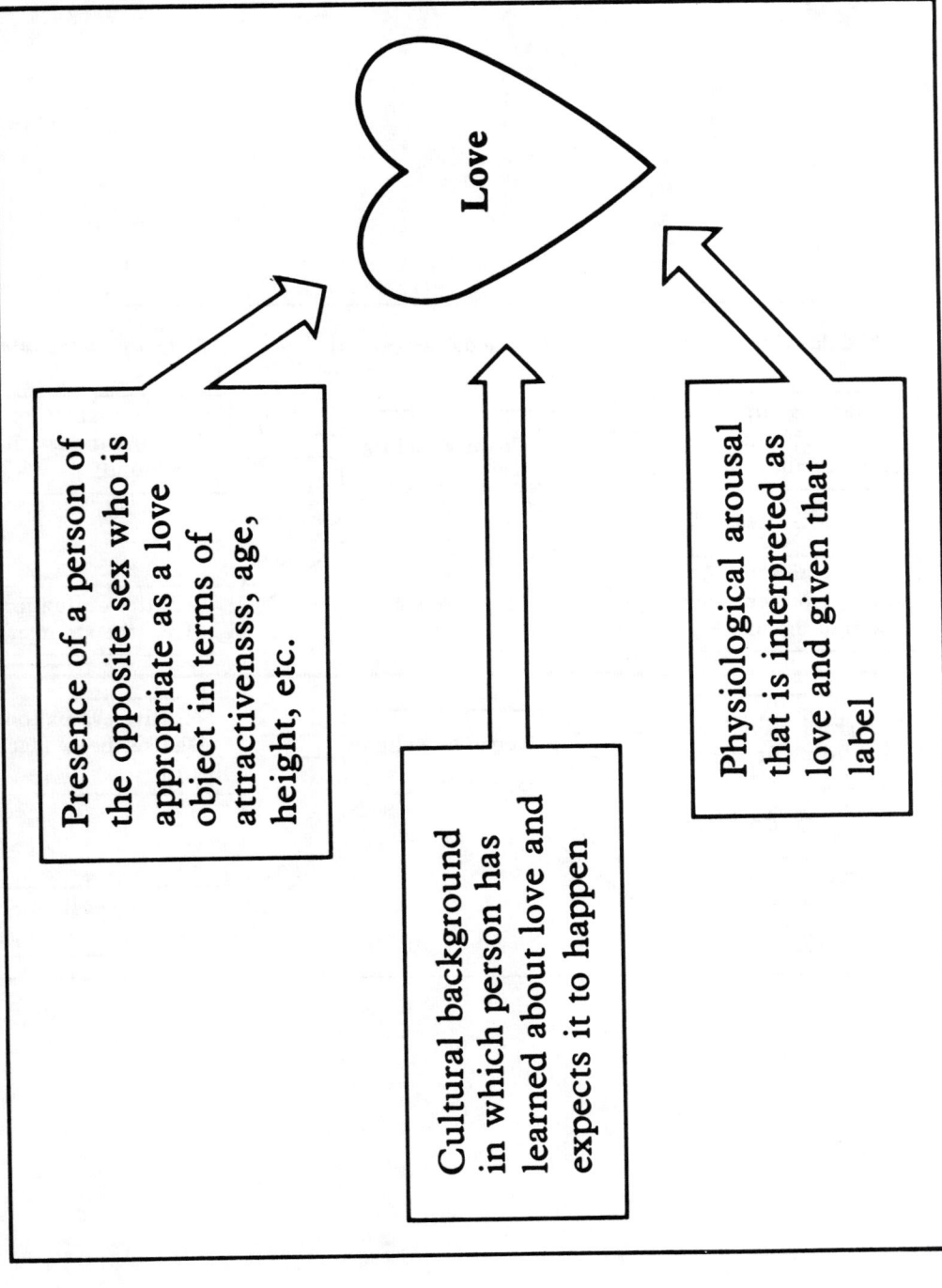

Presence of a person of the opposite sex who is appropriate as a love object in terms of attractivensss, age, height, etc.

Cultural background in which person has learned about love and expects it to happen

Physiological arousal that is interpreted as love and given that label

Love

Copyright © 1997, 1994, 1991, 1987, 1984 by Allyn and Bacon

# The Reinforcement-Affect Theory: How Some Relationships May Start

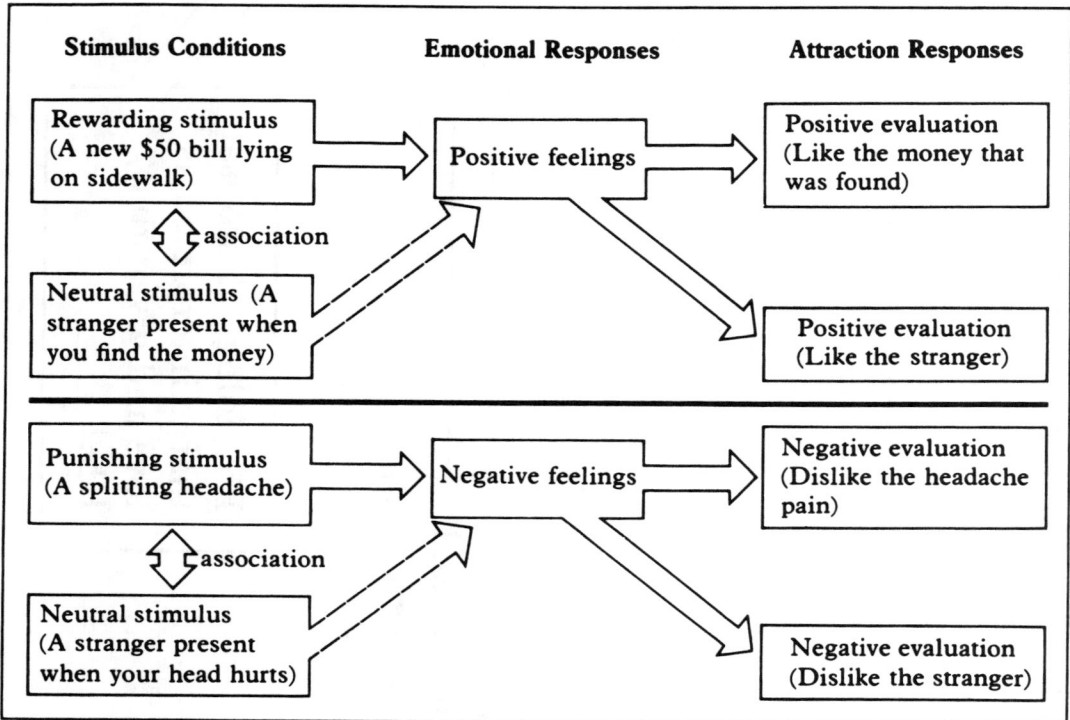

Copyright © 1997, 1994, 1991, 1987, 1984 by Allyn and Bacon

# An Unromantic Explanation of Passionate Love

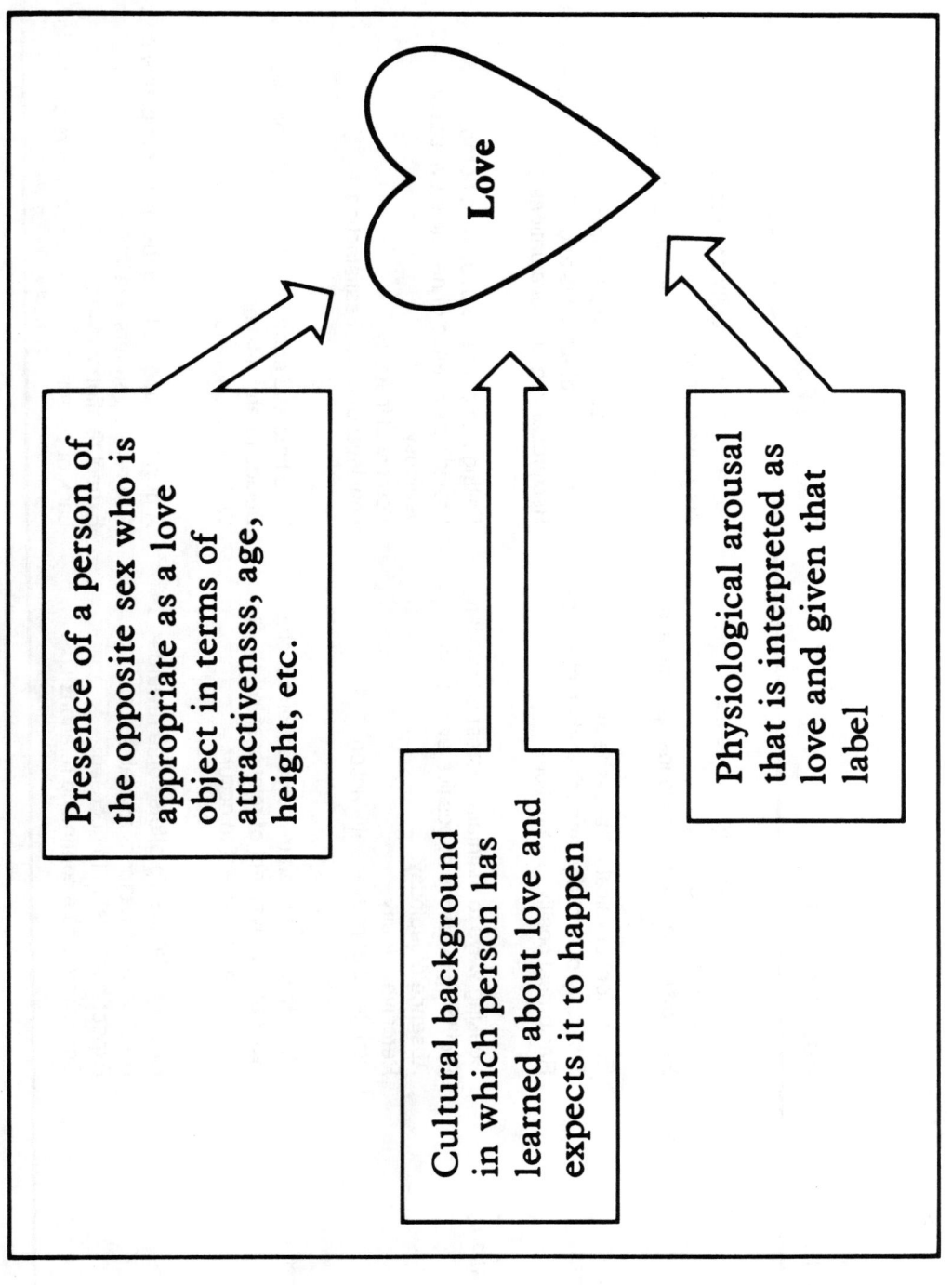

Presence of a person of the opposite sex who is appropriate as a love object in terms of attractivensss, age, height, etc.

Cultural background in which person has learned about love and expects it to happen

Physiological arousal that is interpreted as love and given that label

Love

Copyright © 1997, 1994, 1991, 1987, 1984 by Allyn and Bacon

# Levinger's Theory that Relationships Pass through Five Stages from Beginning to End

| Stage of Relationship | Positive Factors | Negative Factors |
|---|---|---|
| *Initial Attraction* | Propinquity and repeated exposure<br>Positive emotions<br>High affiliative need and friendship motivation | Absence of propinquity and repeated exposure<br>Negative emotions<br>Low affiliative need and friendship motivation |
| *Building a Relationship* | Equivalent physical attractiveness<br>Similarity of attitudes and other characteristics<br>Reciprocal positive evaluations | Nonequivalent physical attractiveness<br>Dissimilarity of attitudes and other characteristics<br>Reciprocal negative evaluations |
| *Continuation* | Seeking ways to maintain interest and variety<br>Providing evidence of positive evaluation<br>Absence of jealousy<br>Perceived equity<br>High level of mutual satisfaction | Falling into a rut and becoming bored<br>Providing evidence of negative evaluation<br>Jealousy<br>Perceived inequity<br>Low level of mutual satisfaction |
| *Deterioration* | Much time and effort invested in relationship<br>Work at improvement of relationship<br>Wait for improvement to occur | Little time and effort invested in relationship<br>Decide to end relationship<br>Wait for deterioration to continue |
| *Ending* | Existing relationship offers some rewards<br>No alternative partners available<br>Expect relationship to succeed<br>Commitment to a continuing relationship | A new life appears to be the only acceptable solution<br>Alternative partners available<br>Expect relationship to fail<br>Lack of commitment to a continuing relationship |

Copyright © 1997, 1994, 1991, 1987, 1984 by Allyn and Bacon

# Sternberg's "Triangular Model of Love"

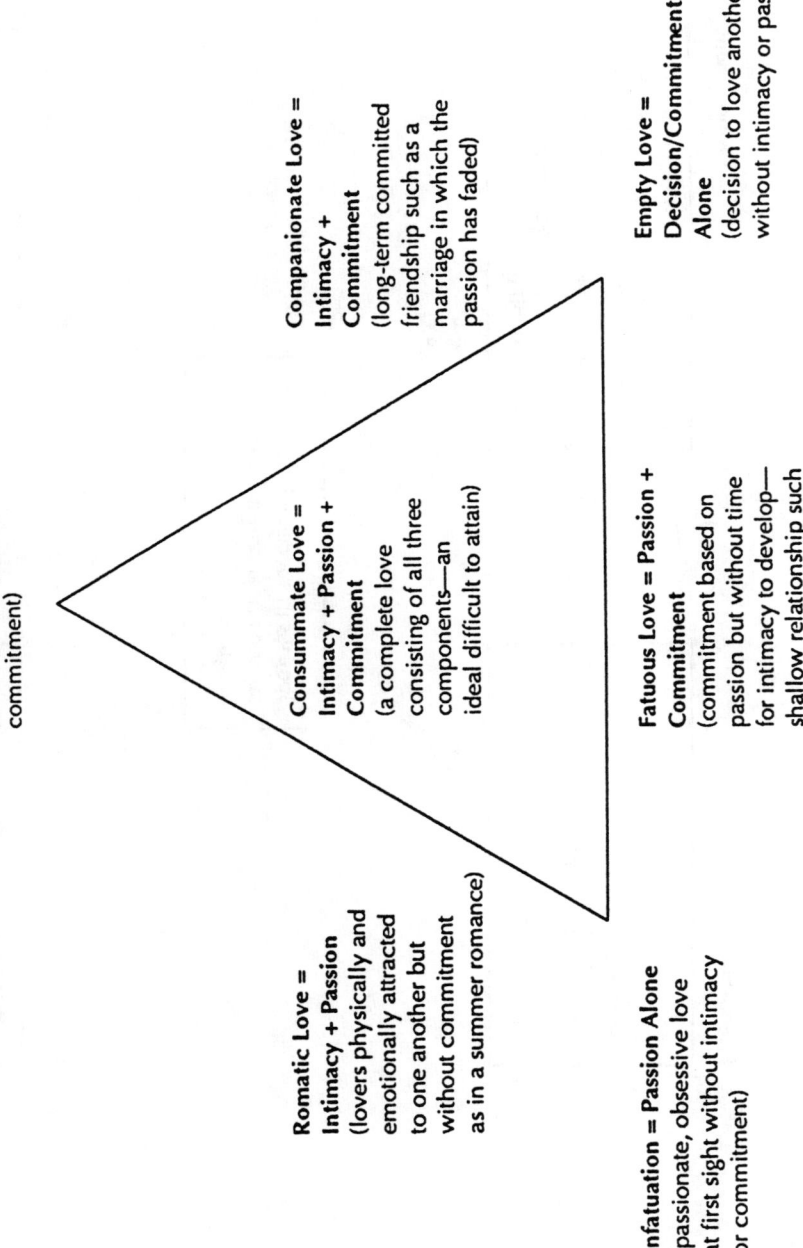

**Liking = Intimacy Alone**
(true friendships without passion or long-term commitment)

**Companionate Love = Intimacy + Commitment**
(long-term committed friendship such as a marriage in which the passion has faded)

**Empty Love = Decision/Commitment Alone**
(decision to love another without intimacy or passion)

**Romatic Love = Intimacy + Passion**
(lovers physically and emotionally attracted to one another but without commitment as in a summer romance)

**Consummate Love = Intimacy + Passion + Commitment**
(a complete love consisting of all three components—an ideal difficult to attain)

**Fatuous Love = Passion + Commitment**
(commitment based on passion but without time for intimacy to develop—shallow relationship such as a whirlwind courtship)

**Infatuation = Passion Alone**
(passionate, obsessive love at first sight without intimacy or commitment)

Copyright © 1997, 1994, 1991, 1987, 1984 by Allyn and Bacon

# Relationships among Findings in the Lauer's Study of 351 Married Couples

**Friendship**

My spouse is my best friend

I like my spouse as a person

**Commitment**

Marriage is a long-term commitment.

Marriage is sacred.

I want the relationship to succeed.

An enduring marriage is important to social stability

Spouses in successful marriages say their relationship lasted because....

**Similarity**

We agree on aims and goals.

We agree on a philosophy of life.

We agree on how and how often to show affection.

We agree about our sex life.

**Positive Affect**

My spouse has grown more interesting

We laugh together

I am proud of may spouse's achievements

Copyright © 1997, 1994, 1991, 1987, 1984 by Allyn and Bacon

# Behaviors That Upset Both Males and Females

In a relationship, partners who are unfaithful or abusive upset both males and females. In addition, several sex-specific behaviors are also upsetting. Explanations for these differences include a sociobiological emphasis on different reproductive strategies for the two sexes and a socialization emphasis on differences in what males and females learn about appropriate sex roles.

*Behaviors That Upset Both Males and Females*
Unfaithfulness
Physical abuse
Verbal abuse

*Male Behaviors That Upset Females*
Trying to demand or force sex
Ignoring a female's opinions and treating her as inferior or stupid
Hiding his emotions, acting tough, drinking or smoking excessively
Neglecting her, ignoring her, failing to say he loves her
Being thoughtless or rude, teasing her

*Female Behaviors That Upset Males*
Sexual rejection, being unresponsive
Moodiness, acting bitchy
Self-absorbed with her appearance and clothing

Source: Based on data in Buss, 1989.

Copyright © 1997, 1994, 1991, 1987, 1984 by Allyn and Bacon

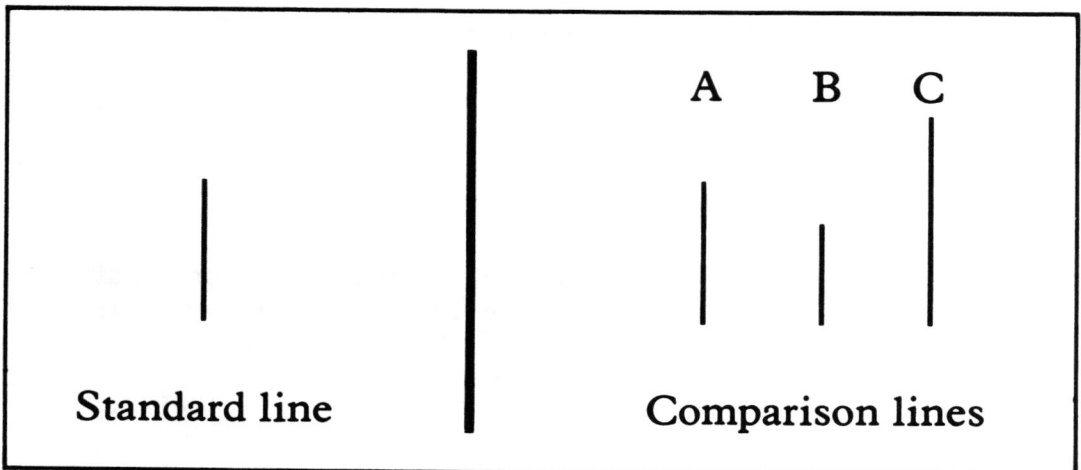

Standard line        A   B   C       Comparison lines

Copyright © 1997, 1994, 1991, 1987, 1984 by Allyn and Bacon

| When the Sexes Might Differ in Conformity | When the Sexes Don't Differ in Conformity |
|---|---|
| when the issues on which pressure is applied more relevant to one sex | when the issues on which pressure is applied not more relevant to one sex |
| when the experimenter is male | when the experimenter is female |
| when objects of conformity pressure are under direct surveillance | when objects of conformity pressure are not under direct surveillance |

Copyright © 1997, 1994, 1991, 1987, 1984 by Allyn and Bacon

| "foot-in-the-door" | "door-in-the-face" | "low balling" |
|---|---|---|
| **Self-perception:** after first complying, sees self as "one who does that sort of thing" | **Self-presentation:** after first refusing, one looks bad by refusing again | **Commitment:** after agreeing, one becomes committed to agreement |
| **View of helping:** after first complying, sees helping in a more positive light | **Reciprocal concession:** after requester has "backed down," one feels need to reciprocate | **Unfulfilled obligation:** after agreeing one feels obligated to requester |

Copyright © 1997, 1994, 1991, 1987, 1984 by Allyn and Bacon

# The Tendency to Obey: Some Key Contributing Factors

High status of the authority figure

Belief among subordinates that the source of authority—not they—will be responsible for their actions

Absence of a clear-cut point for switching to disobedience

The gradual nature of many obedience situations (at first, following orders has only mild consequences; only later are more harmful effects produced)

A strong tendency to obey direct commands

Copyright © 1997, 1994, 1991, 1987, 1984 by Allyn and Bacon

# The Social Influence Model (SIM)

T-9.5

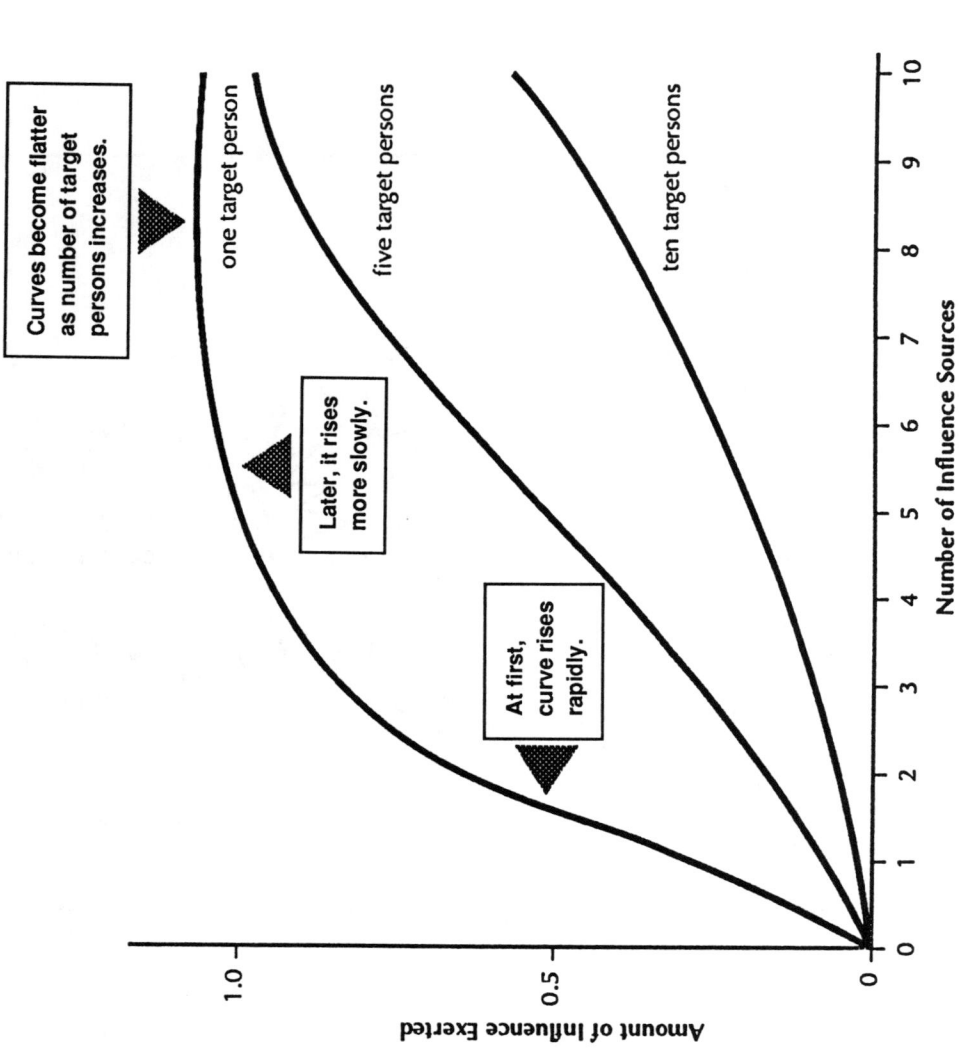

Amount of Influence Exerted

Number of Influence Sources

Curves become flatter as number of target persons increases.

one target person

Later, it rises more slowly.

At first, curve rises rapidly.

five target persons

ten target persons

Copyright © 1997, 1994, 1991, 1987, 1984 by Allyn and Bacon

# Bisanz and Rule's Complete List of Means of Gaining Compliance

| Name of Technique | Description |
| --- | --- |
| Ask | Simply present request |
| Present information | Offer facts or evidence to persuade target person |
| Mention personal benefits | Indicate how target will benefit from complying |
| Mention relationship | Mention existing relationship between requester and target |
| Bargain | Requester offers to do something in return |
| Invoke norm | Indicate that others would comply |
| Make moral appeal | Make appeal to a moral value (e.g., it's the right thing to do) |
| Butter up | Make target feel good in some manner (e.g., flattery) |
| Emotional appeal | Beg, plead, throw a tantrum, sulk |
| Criticize | Attack target for not complying |
| Deceive | Mislead target to gain compliance |
| Threaten | Threaten target to gain compliance |
| Force | Use force to gain compliance |

Copyright © 1997, 1994, 1991, 1987, 1984 by Allyn and Bacon

# Good Samaritan Roadmap

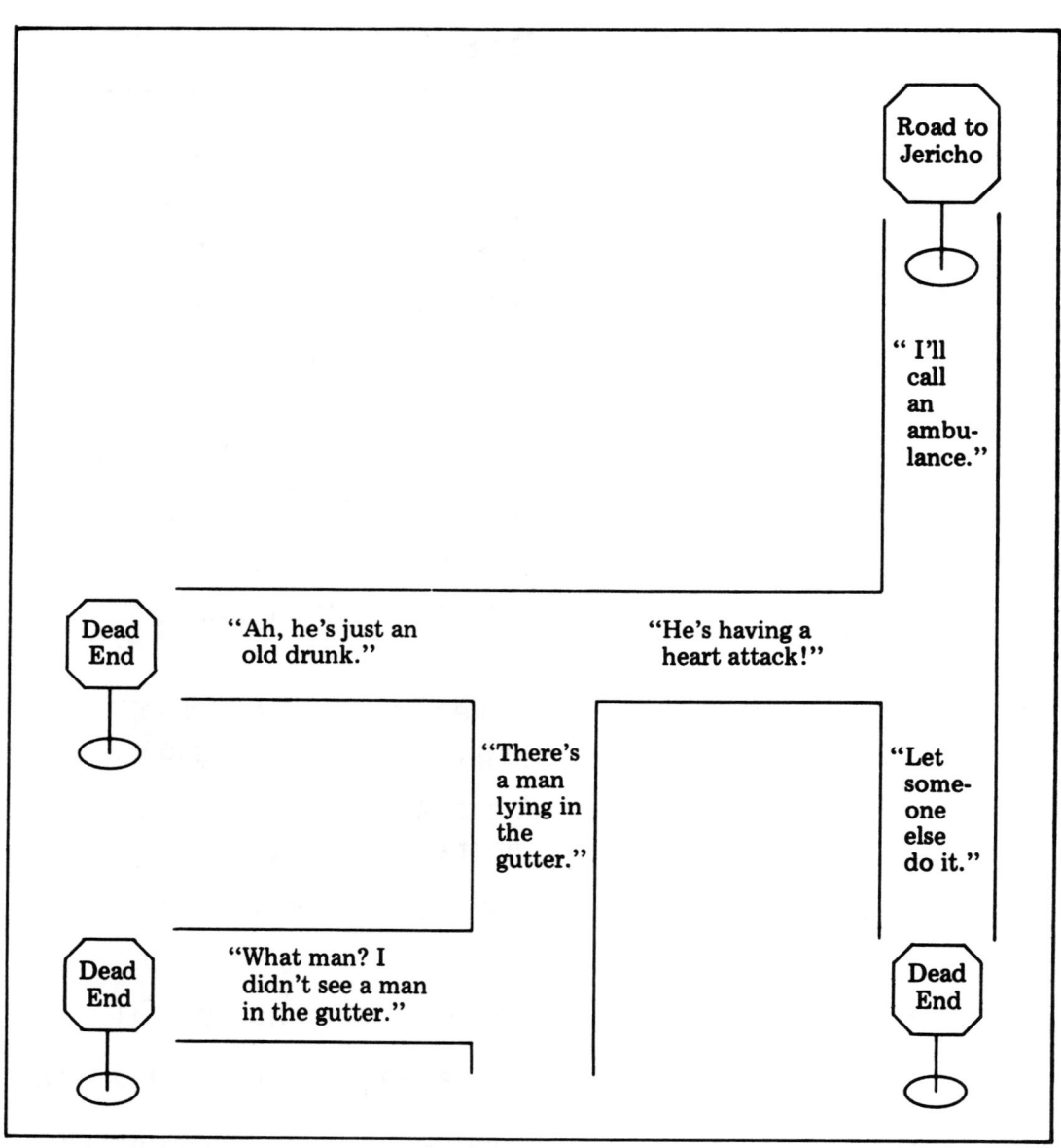

Copyright © 1997, 1994, 1991, 1987, 1984 by Allyn and Bacon

# Helping as a Function of Empathy and Empathetic Arousal

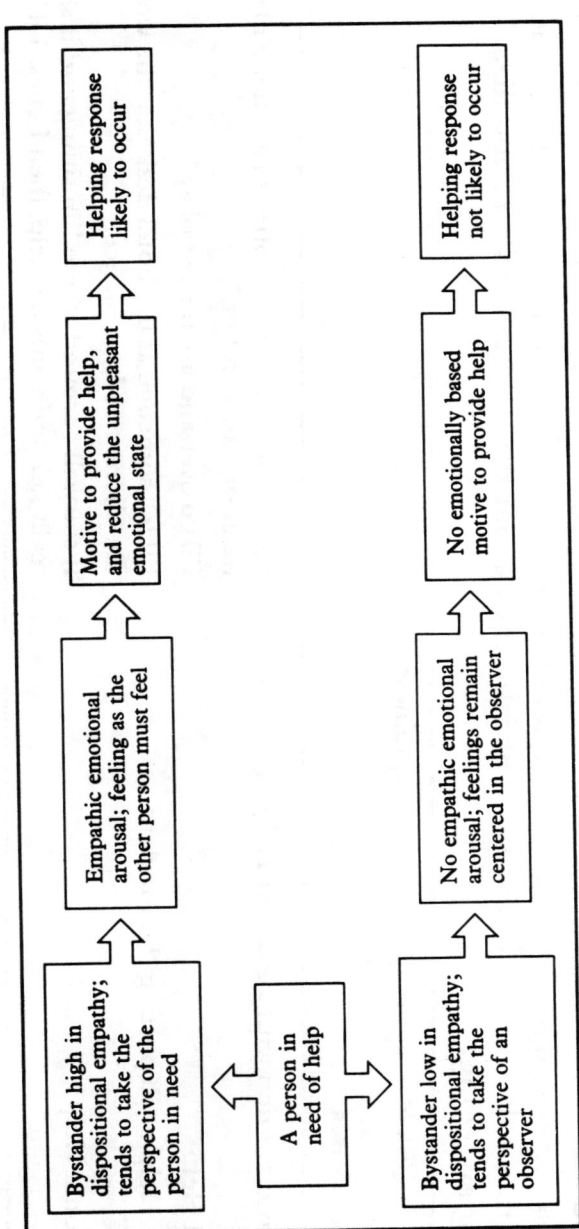

Copyright © 1997, 1994, 1991, 1987, 1984 by Allyn and Bacon

# Six Levels of Helpfulness-Unhelpfulness

Analysis of responses to specific emergency situations suggests that the extent to which bystanders help or fail to help can be categorized as falling at six levels. In the example here, subjects were asked to imagine themselves overhearing a woman saying that she is feeling ill, dizzy, and anxious. The subjects were asked what, if anything, they would do in this situation. Their responses ranged from a direct intervention with a plan about what to do on one extreme to a refusal to help based on attributions about the woman and a rationalization for not doing anything.

Six levels of helpfulness–unhelpfulness

**Helpful Responses**

1. Direct Intervention with a Plan for Helping

   "I'll give her my seat, and offer to get her a glass of water or wait with her."

2. General Help

   "I'll go over and ask if she's okay."

3. Indirect Help or Reporting the Incident

   "I'll tell someone at the hotel desk that the woman on the phone needs assistance."

4. Conditional Help

   "If she walks around where I'm sitting and if she looks really sick and wants my help, then I guess I'll help her."

**Unhelpful Responses**

5. No Help or Interaction

   "I think I'll read this magazine."

6. Refusal to Help Along with an Attribution or Rationalization

   "I'm not going to help her. The information probably isn't important anyway."

*Source:* Based on data in Lang, 1987.

Copyright © 1997, 1994, 1991, 1987, 1984 by Allyn and Bacon

# Components of Altruistic Personality

In an attempt to identify the factors that make up the altruistic personality, investigators compared citizens who witnessed a traffic accident and provided first aid to the victim with citizens who witnessed such an accident and did not provide first aid. As indicated here, five personality characteristics were found to differentiate the two groups. Together these characteristics identify altruistic individuals.

## Components of the altruistic personality

| Individuals Who Administered First Aid after a Traffic Accident | Individuals Who Failed to Administer First Aid |
|---|---|
| Were higher in internal locus of control | Were lower in internal locus of control |
| Believed more strongly in a just world | Believed less strongly in a just world |
| Felt more socially responsible (were interested in public matters and involved in the community; felt a sense of duty) | Felt less socially responsible |
| Had higher empathy component in self-concept. | Had lower empathy component in self-concept |
| Were less egocentric | Were more egocentric |

*Source:* Based on data in Bierhoff, Klein, & Kramp, 1991.

Copyright © 1997, 1994, 1991, 1987, 1984 by Allyn and Bacon

# Motivations Underlying AIDS Volunteerism

Those who volunteer to help in the AIDS epidemic do so on the basis of five different motivations. Thus, the same overt behavior can satisfy quite different needs. Those who recruit volunteers do best to aim different kinds of recruiting messages to those whose motives differ. Interestingly, recruits who continue such work over time are more likely than those who quit to be motivated by the "self-centered" motives—enhancement of self-esteem or desire for personal development.

Motivations underlying AIDS volunteerism

**Motivation for Volunteering to Help in the AIDS Epidemic**

| | |
|---|---|
| 1. Personal Values | "Because of my humanitarian obligation to help others" |
| 2. Desire to Increase Understanding | "Because I want to learn how people cope with AIDS" |
| 3. Community Concern | "Because of my concern and worry about the gay community" |
| 4. Personal Development | "I want to challenge myself and test my skills" |
| 5. Enhancement of Self-Esteem | "I want to feel better about myself" |

Source: Based on data in Snyder & Omoto, 1992.)

Copyright © 1997, 1994, 1991, 1987, 1984 by Allyn and Bacon

1. Uninvited pressure for sexual favors
2. Uninvited and deliberate touching
3. Uninvited letters, phone calls, or materials of a sexual nature
4. Uninvited sexually suggestive looks or gestures
5. Uninvited pressure for dates
6. Uninvited sexual teasing, jokes, remarks, or questions

Copyright © 1997, 1994, 1991, 1987, 1984 by Allyn and Bacon

## Aggression as Innate

Freud — "death instinct" redirected toward others

Lorenz — "fighting instinct" disperses populations over wide areas maximizing use of available resources

Sociobiology — aggression a part of the evolutionary process because it was adaptive

## Drive Theories

External conditions such as frustration give rise to motive to hurt

## Social Learning Theories

Aggression is viewed as a learned social behavior that can be altered

Copyright © 1997, 1994, 1991, 1987, 1984 by Allyn and Bacon

# Aggression: Causes and Cures

| Possible Causes | Possible Cures |
|---|---|
| Frustration | Disapproving commentary about T.V. violence |
| Verbal attack | Nonaggressive models |
| Physical attack | Punishment |
| Models of aggression | Catharsis |
| Heightened arousal | Mild sexual arousal |
| Strong sexual arousal | Nonhostile humor |
| Alcohol | Generating empathy |
| Aggressive cues | Marijuana |
| Audiences | |
| Crowding | |
| Heat | |
| Personality | |
| Genes | |
| Gender | |
| Hostile humor | |

Copyright © 1997, 1994, 1991, 1987, 1984 by Allyn and Bacon

**Media Violence: Mechanisms Underlying the Effects**

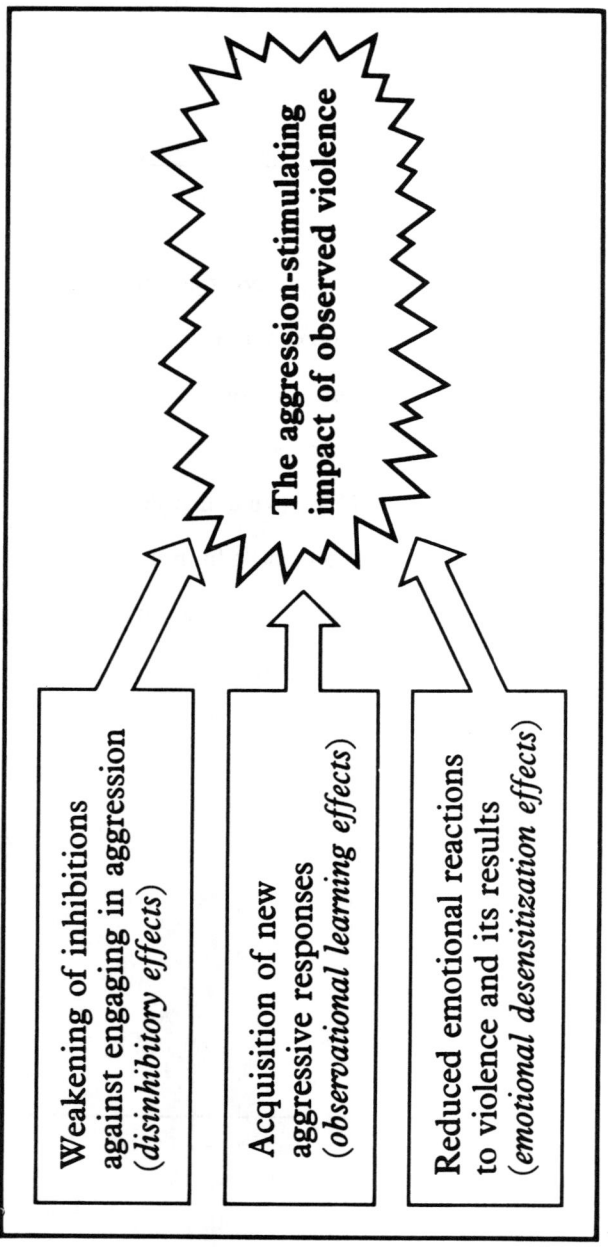

Weakening of inhibitions against engaging in aggression (*disinhibitory effects*)

Acquisition of new aggressive responses (*observational learning effects*)

Reduced emotional reactions to violence and its results (*emotional desensitization effects*)

**The aggression-stimulating impact of observed violence**

Copyright © 1997, 1994, 1991, 1987, 1984 by Allyn and Bacon

# Aggression according to the Neoassociationists

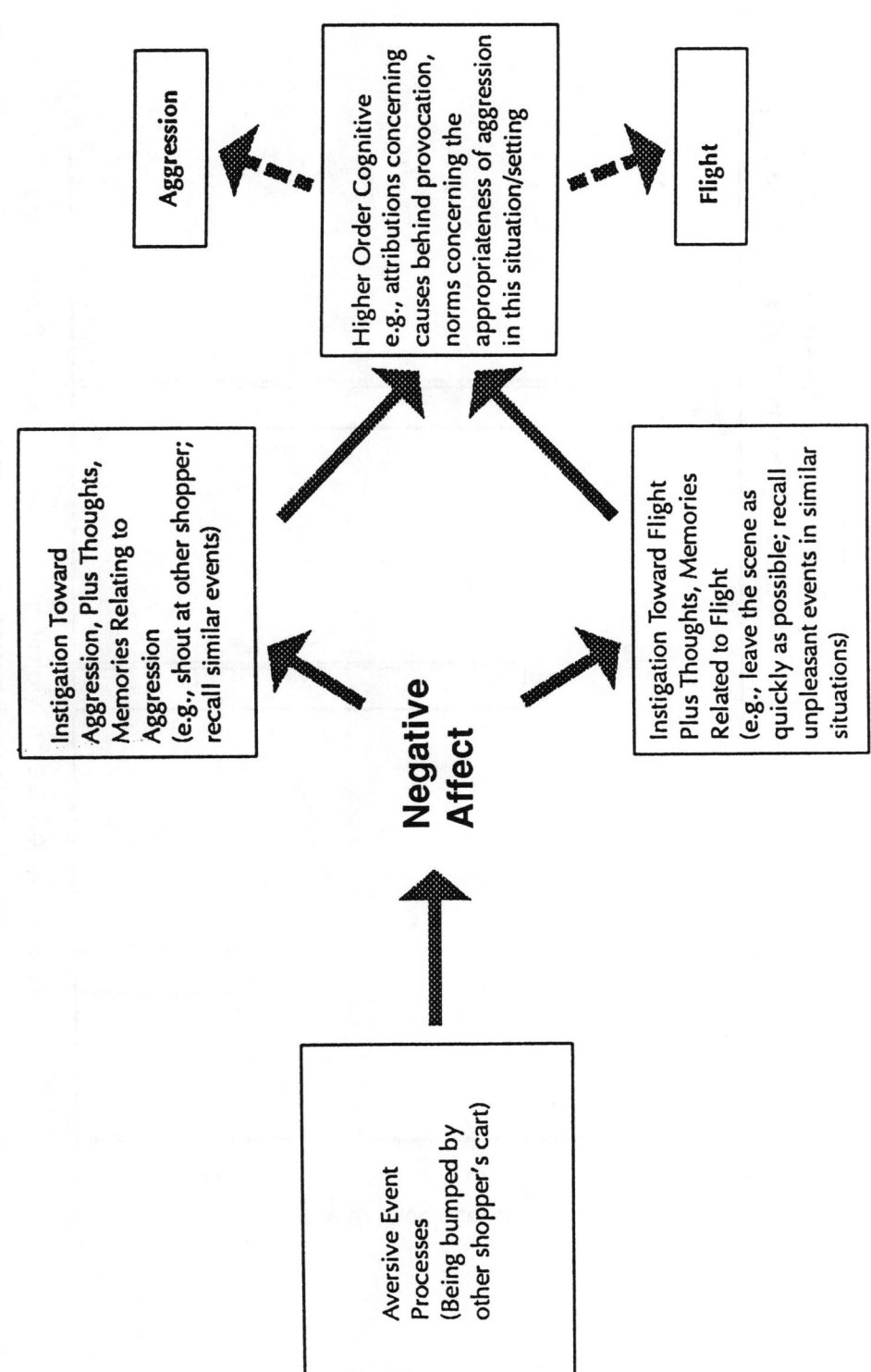

**Aversive Event Processes**
(Being bumped by other shopper's cart)

↓

**Negative Affect**

**Instigation Toward Aggression, Plus Thoughts, Memories Relating to Aggression**
(e.g., shout at other shopper; recall similar events)

**Instigation Toward Flight Plus Thoughts, Memories Related to Flight**
(e.g., leave the scene as quickly as possible; recall unpleasant events in similar situations)

**Higher Order Cognitive**
e.g., attributions concerning causes behind provocation, norms concerning the appropriateness of aggression in this situation/setting

**Aggression**

**Flight**

Copyright © 1997, 1994, 1991, 1987, 1984 by Allyn and Bacon

# The Effects of Violent and Nonviolent Pornography on Males' Aggression toward Females

T-11.6

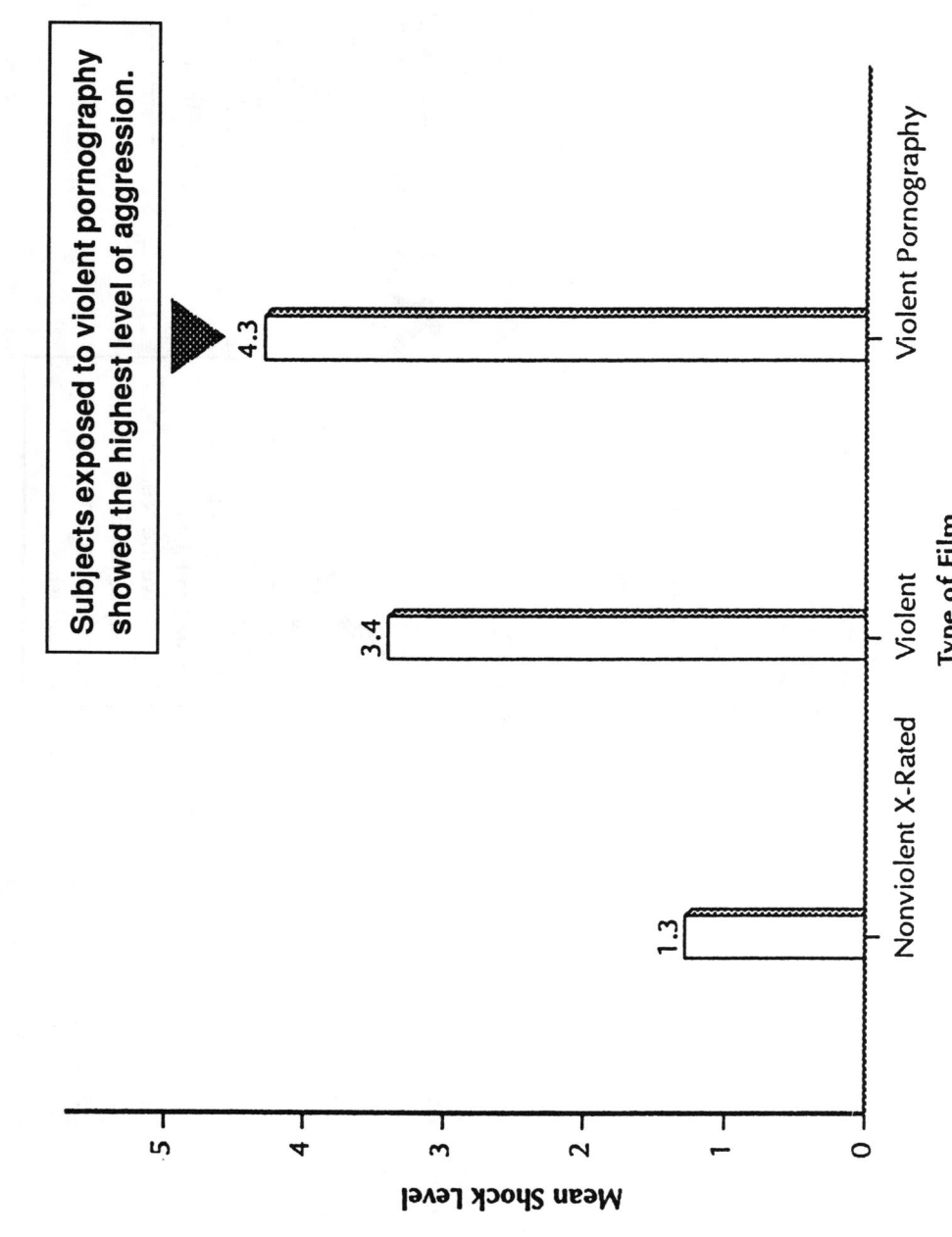

Subjects exposed to violent pornography showed the highest level of aggression.

Copyright © 1997, 1994, 1991, 1987, 1984 by Allyn and Bacon

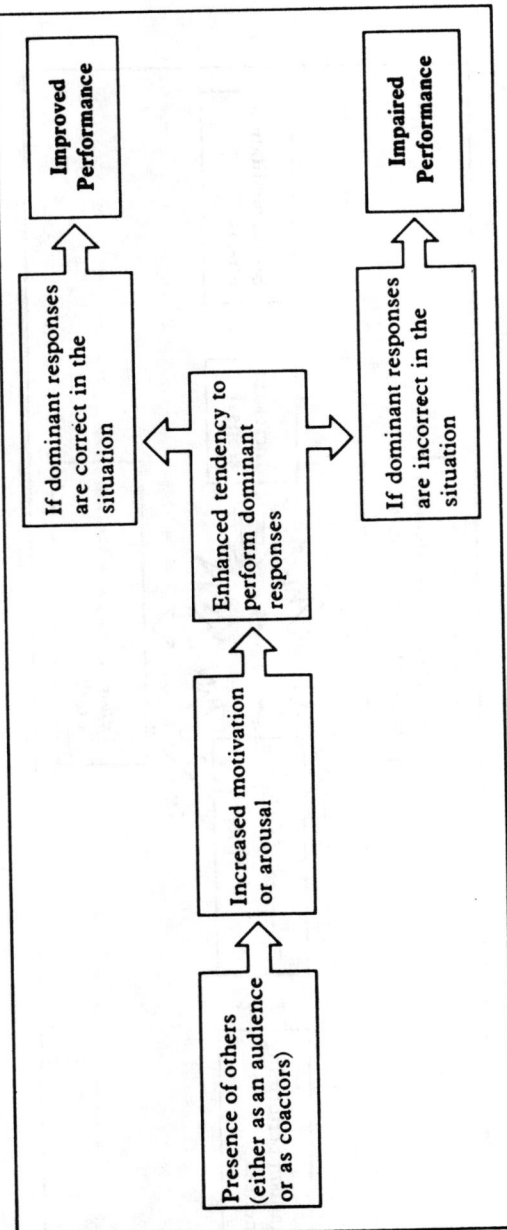

# The Drive Theory of Social Facilitation

Presence of others (either as an audience or as coactors)

Increased motivation or arousal

Enhanced tendency to perform dominant responses

If dominant responses are correct in the situation

Improved Performance

If dominant responses are incorrect in the situation

Impaired Performance

Copyright © 1997, 1994, 1991, 1987, 1984 by Allyn and Bacon

# The Distraction—Conflict Theory of Social Facilitation

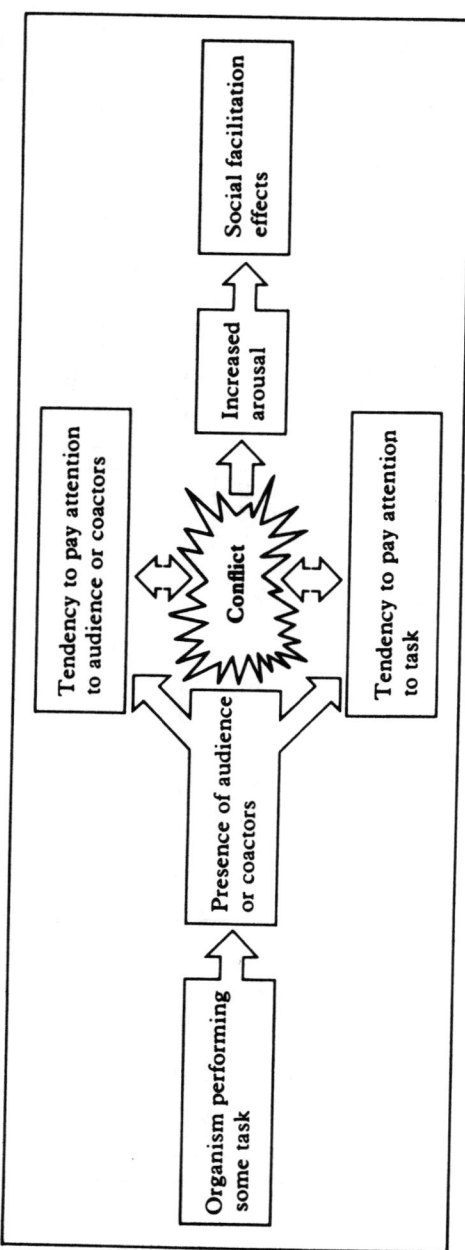

Copyright © 1997, 1994, 1991, 1987, 1984 by Allyn and Bacon

# The Contingency Model of Leadership Effectiveness     T-12.3

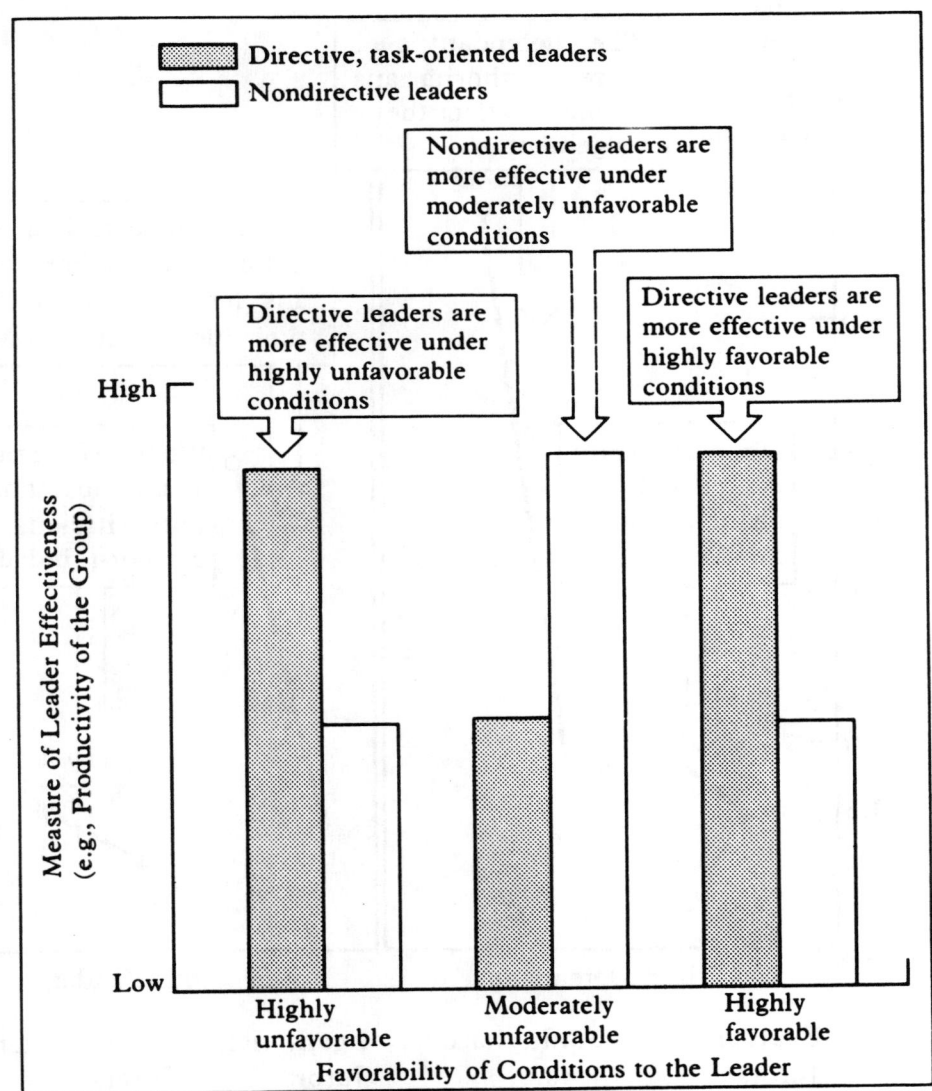

Copyright © 1997, 1994, 1991, 1987, 1984 by Allyn and Bacon

# Unfair Punishment: Different Sets of Biases T - 13.1

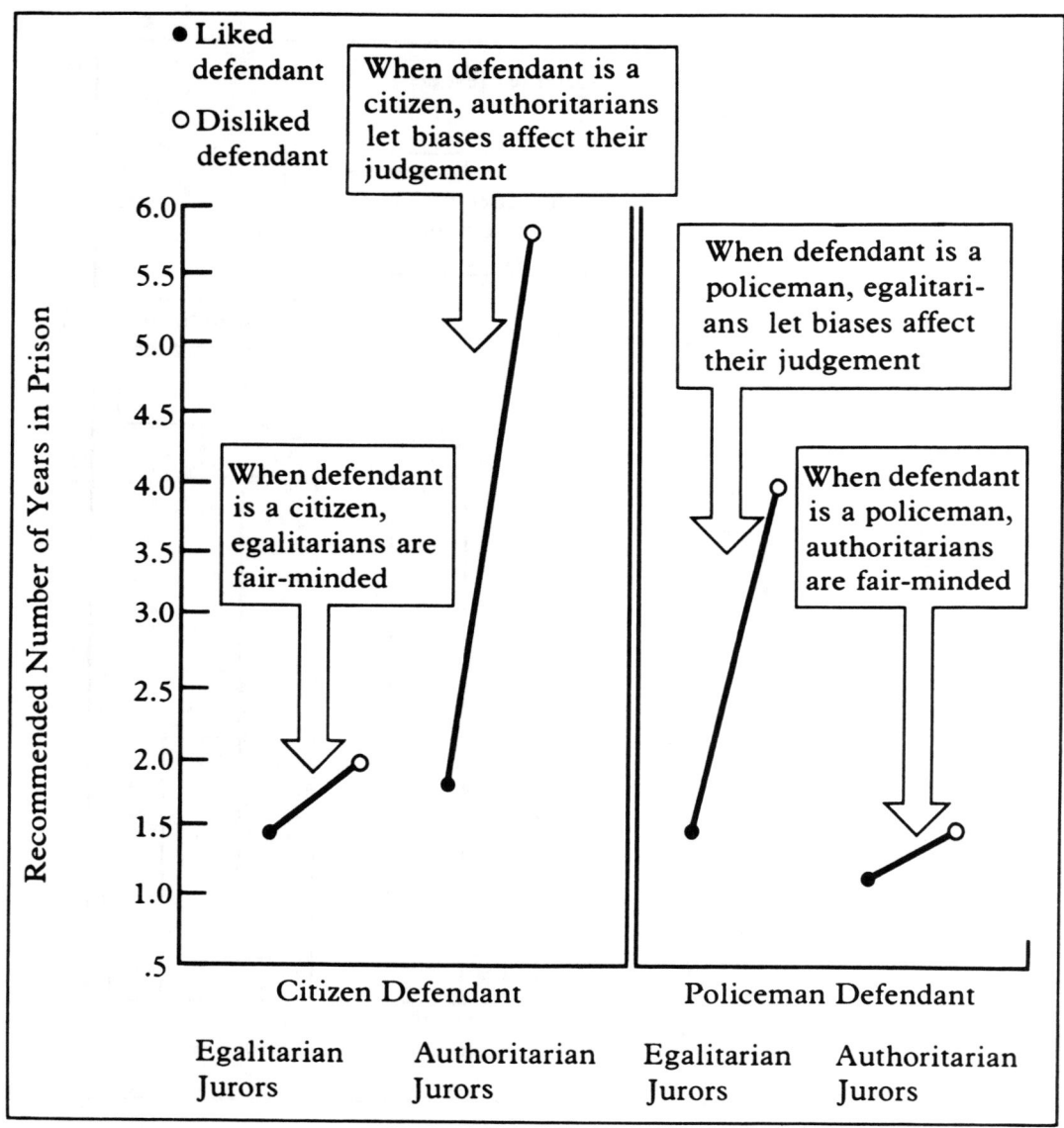

**● Liked defendant**

**○ Disliked defendant**

When defendant is a citizen, authoritarians let biases affect their judgement

When defendant is a policeman, egalitarians let biases affect their judgement

When defendant is a citizen, egalitarians are fair-minded

When defendant is a policeman, authoritarians are fair-minded

Recommended Number of Years in Prison

6.0
5.5
5.0
4.5
4.0
3.5
3.0
2.5
2.0
1.5
1.0
.5

Citizen Defendant

Policeman Defendant

Egalitarian Jurors

Authoritarian Jurors

Egalitarian Jurors

Authoritarian Jurors

Copyright © 1997, 1994, 1991, 1987, 1984 by Allyn and Bacon

# The Bennington Experience

Research at Bennington College that began in the 1930s indicated that the political attitudes of students shifted in a liberal direction during their four years at this institution. Follow-up studies discovered that these liberal attitudes were maintained in the decades after graduation. As shown here, Bennington graduates consistently preferred the more liberal candidate in U.S. presidential elections over the years, while other women (matched in educational attainment and age) consistently preferred the more conservative candidate.

The Bennington experience: Liberals for a lifetime

**Voting Patterns (Percentages): Bennington Women versus Comparable Women**

| 1952 | | *Eisenhower* | *Stevenson* |
|---|---|---|---|
| | Bennington Women | 42.6 | 57.4 |
| | Comparable Women | 64.3 | 35.7 |
| 1960 | | *Nixon* | *Kennedy* |
| | Bennington Women | 26.0 | 74.0 |
| | Comparable Women | 75.0 | 25.0 |
| 1968 | | *Nixon* | *Humphrey* |
| | Bennington Women | 32.9 | 66.5 |
| | Comparable Women | 79.1 | 18.6 |
| 1976 | | *Ford* | *Carter* |
| | Bennington Women | 31.2 | 68.8 |
| | Comparable Women | 54.9 | 45.1 |
| 1984 | | *Reagan* | *Mondale* |
| | Bennington Women | 26.4 | 73.3 |
| | Comparable Women | 73.0 | 25.7 |

*Source:* Based on data from the Institute for Social Research, *National Election Studies, 1952–1984.*

Copyright © 1997, 1994, 1991, 1987, 1984 by Allyn and Bacon

# What is Important in Selecting a Jury

Before a trial begins, attorneys take part in a jury selection process in which they look for certain positive and negative characteristics and ask various questions in an effort to decide which prospective jurors should be retained and which should be excused. When attorneys were asked to indicate the most important characteristics and the voir dire (to speak truthfully) questions they most often ask, these were the results.

## What do attorneys seek in selecting a jury?

| Characteristics Attorneys Say Are Important in Jury Selection | Voir Dire Questions Attorneys Say They Ask Most Often |
|---|---|
| Intelligence | What is your attitude about this kind of crime? |
| Age | What is your general reaction to police officers? |
| Appearance | How much have you heard about this case in the media? |
| Occupation | Were you ever the victim of this kind of crime? |
| Open-mindedness | How do you feel about someone who has been arrested? |
| Gender | Do you have any racial bias? |
| Attentiveness | Have any of your acquaintances ever been arrested or convicted |
| Impressibility | Do you have any relationship with any of the individuals connected with |
| Race | this case? |

*Source:* Based on data from Olczak, Kaplan, & Penrod, 1991.

Copyright © 1997, 1994, 1991, 1987, 1984 by Allyn and Bacon

# Equity and Inequity in Social Exchange

**Equity is perceived to exist**

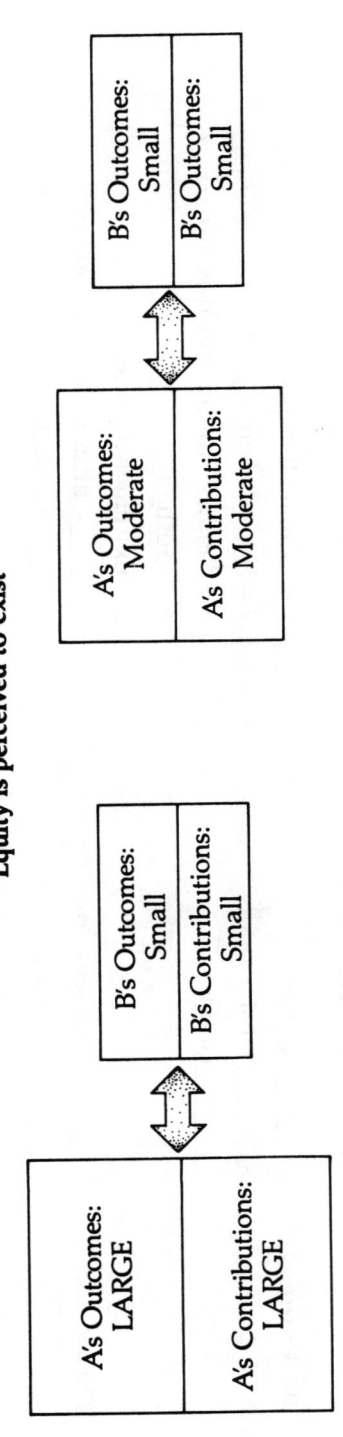

**Inequity is perceived to exist**

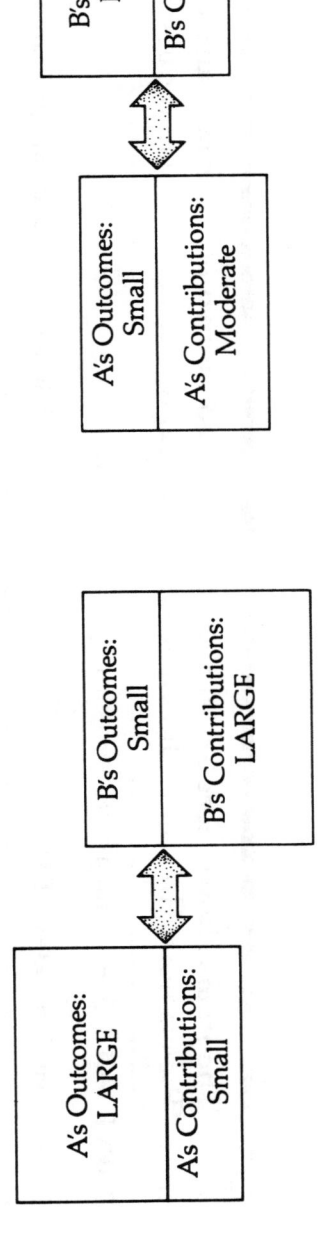

Copyright © 1997, 1994, 1991, 1987, 1984 by Allyn and Bacon

# Questionnaire Measure Job Satisfaction

The items shown here are similar to those used on two popular measures of job satisfaction. (Please note: the items shown are not identical to ones on the actual questionnaires.)

**TABLE 14.4** Questionnaires for measuring job satisfaction

## Job Description Index (JDI)

Enter "Yes," "No," or "?" for each description or word below:

*Work itself:*

_____ Routine

_____ Satisfactory

_____ Good

*Promotions:*

_____ Dead-end job

_____ Few promotions

_____ Good opportunity for promotion

## Minnesota Satisfaction Questionnaire (MSQ)

Indicate the extent to which you are satisfied with each aspect of your present job. Enter one number next to each aspect.

1 = Not at all satisfied

2 = Not satisfied

3 = Neither satisfied nor dissatisfied

4 = Satisfied

5 = Extremely satisfied

_____ Utilization of your abilities

_____ Authority

_____ Company policies and practices

_____ Independence

_____ Supervision, human relations

Copyright © 1997, 1994, 1991, 1987, 1984 by Allyn and Bacon

| **Common Stressful Events among College Students** | **Common Stressful Events among Others** |
|---|---|

*High Levels of Stress (71 to 100 points)*

| | |
|---|---|
| unwed pregnancy | death of spouse |
| father in unwed pregnancy | death of parent |
| | divorce |

*Moderate Levels of Stress (31 to 70 points)*

| | |
|---|---|
| parents divorce | death of close relative |
| flunking out | death of close friend |
| loss of financial aid | jail term |
| failing important course | major injury or illness |
| sexual difficulties | marriage |
| argument with romantic partner | loss of job |
| on academic probation | increased workload on job |
| change of major | |
| finding a new love interest | |

*Low Levels of Stress (1 to 30 points)*

| | |
|---|---|
| outstanding achievement | minor violations of the law |
| enrolled for first semester | |
| conflict with instructor | |
| lower grades than expected | |
| transfer to a different college | |
| change in social activities | |
| change in sleeping habits | |
| change in eating habits | |

Copyright © 1997, 1994, 1991, 1987, 1984 by Allyn and Bacon

# Decisions and Choices to Make when the Symptoms of Illness Develop

T - 14.2

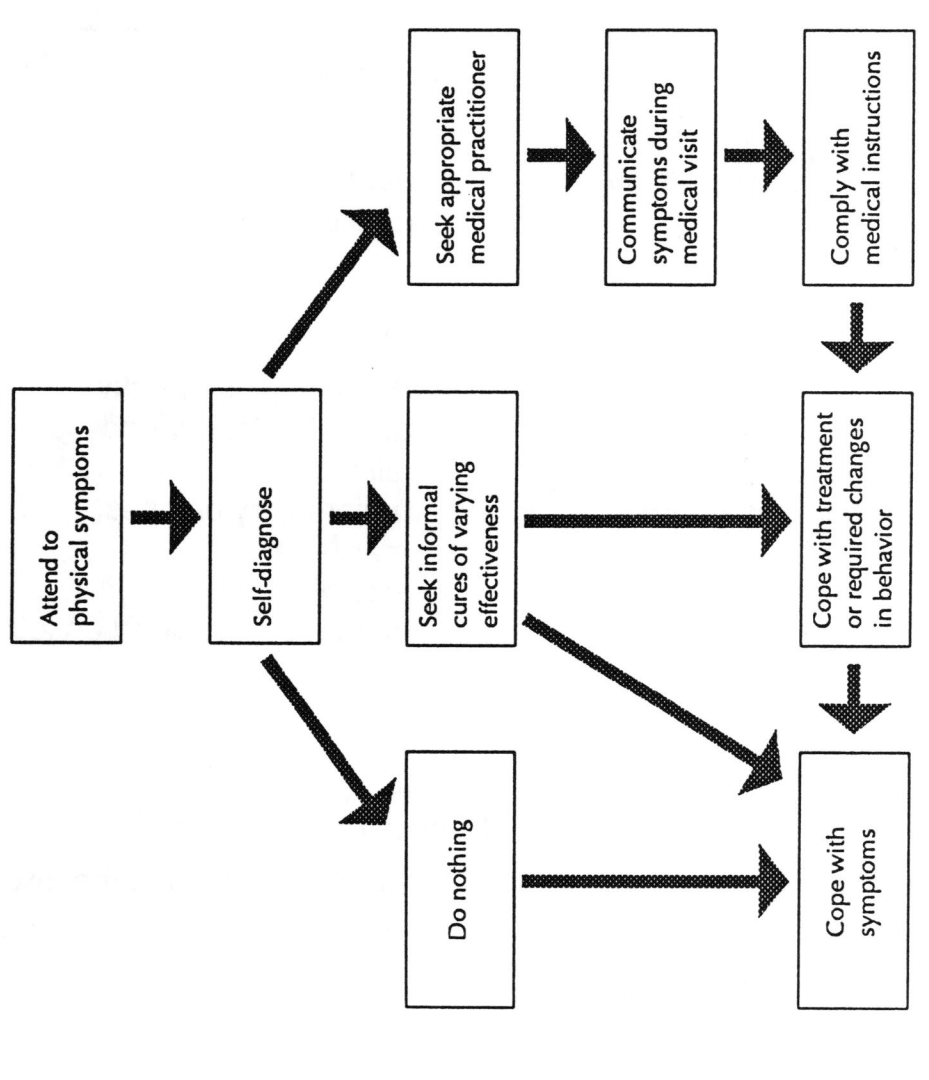

Attend to physical symptoms → Self-diagnose

Self-diagnose →
- Seek appropriate medical practitioner → Communicate symptoms during medical visit → Comply with medical instructions
- Seek informal cures of varying effectiveness
- Do nothing

Comply with medical instructions → Cope with treatment or required changes in behavior

Seek informal cures of varying effectiveness → Cope with treatment or required changes in behavior

Cope with treatment or required changes in behavior → Cope with symptoms

Do nothing → Cope with symptoms

Copyright © 1997, 1994, 1991, 1987, 1984 by Allyn and Bacon

# Concerns About Technological Hazards

Surveys indicate that people are concerned about the dangerous effects of technology on our health and safety. Scientific experts at the Environmental Protection Agency agree that hazards exist, but their assessments tend not to match those of the general public. People in general seem to worry most about immediate, short-term problems, while the scientists are more concerned about future, long-term problems.

Concerns about technological hazards: The public versus the experts

| | Perceptions of the General Public | Perceptions of Experts |
|---|---|---|
| *Highest Concerns* | Contaminated drinking water<br>Storage of toxic chemicals<br>Cancer-causing chemicals | Global climate change<br>Species extinction and loss of biological diversity<br>Soil erosion and deforestation |
| *Moderate Concerns* | Pesticide residue in food<br>Air pollution<br>Nuclear power plant accidents | Herbicides and pesticides<br>Pollution of surface water<br>Acid rain |
| *Low Concerns* | Car accidents<br>Transport of explosives<br>Food preservatives | Oil spills<br>Groundwater pollution<br>Escape of radioactive materials |

*Source:* Based on data in Pilisuk & Acredolo, 1988, and Stevens, 1991a.

Copyright © 1997, 1994, 1991, 1987, 1984 by Allyn and Bacon

# High Level Versus Low Level Goals in Life

Personal strivings are the characteristic recurring goals that a person is trying to accomplish in his or her life. People differ in whether they strive for relatively difficult, abstract goals or relatively easy, concrete ones. Those who emphasize high-level strivings experience more psychological stress (because they can't meet their goals) but less physical illness (because their commitment increases hardiness). Those who emphasize low-level strivings experience less emotional discomfort (because they can reach their goals) but more illness (because of a lack of commitment).

**TABLE 13.2**  High-level versus low-level goals in life

**Low-Level, Concrete Strivings**

I want to deepen my relationship with God.
I want to be totally honest.
I want to be a fun person to be around.
I want to compete against myself rather than against others.
I want to increase my knowledge of the world.

I want to look well-groomed and clean-cut.
I want to be funny and make others laugh.
I want to look attentive and not bored in class.
I want to be organized and neat—clean my room and make my bed.
I want to work hard or at least look like I'm working hard.

*Source:* Based on data in Emmons, 1992.

Copyright © 1997, 1994, 1991, 1987, 1984 by Allyn and Bacon

legislation regulating one aspect of environmental behavior: the bottle bill

compliance with the law based on monetary rewards and acceptance of social norms

new behavior becomes habitual

attitudes about the bottle bill become more favorable, a shift based on the desire for consistency

attitudes generalize, resulting in positive views about other environmental issues

Copyright © 1997, 1994, 1991, 1987, 1984 by Allyn and Bacon

# Three Gases Contributing to the Greenhouse Effect

| Type of Gas | Amount of Contribution to Greenhouse Effect | What Must Be Done to Stabilize Amount of the Gas in the Atmosphere |
| --- | --- | --- |
| carbon dioxide | 50% | reduce emissions by 50 to 80 percent through changes in behavior and in technology |
| methane | 25% | reduce emissions by ruminants (cattle, sheep, etc.) through changes in their diets |
| chlorofluorocarbons | 25% | use of this gas must be totally banned |

Copyright © 1997, 1994, 1991, 1987, 1984 by Allyn and Bacon